MULTIMEDIA MAGIC

(REVISED AND UPDATED SECOND EDITION)

MULTIMEDIA MAGIC

(REVISED AND UPDATED SECOND EDITION)

By

S. GOKUL

BPB PUBLICATIONS
B-14, CONNAUGHT PLACE, NEW DELHI-110001

REPRINT 2025

First Edition 2005

ISBN: 978-81-8333-069-5

LIMITS OF LIABILITY AND DISCLAIMER OF WARRANTY

Distributors:

BPB PUBLICATIONS
20, Ansari Road, Darya Ganj
New Delhi-110002
Ph: 23254990/23254991

DECCAN AGENCIES
4-3-329, Bank Street,
Hyderabad-500195
Ph: 24756967/24756400

MICRO MEDIA
Shop No. 5, Mahendra Chambers,
150 DN Rd. Next to Capital Cinema,
V.T. (C.S.T.) Station, MUMBAI-400 001
Ph: 22078296/22078297

BPB BOOK CENTRE
376 Old Lajpat Rai Market,
Delhi-110006
Ph: 23861747

Published by Manish Jain for BPB Publications, 20 Ansari Road, Darya Ganj, New Delhi-110002
and Printed at Manipal Technologies Limited, Manipal

www.bpbonline.com

Dedicated to
Krishnaswamy Balaji
and
Syed Ibrahim Ahmad

Trademark Acknowledgements

Windows 3.1, Windows 95, Windows NT, Windows 2000, Windows XP and Windows Media Player are registered trademarks of Microsoft Inc, USA

3D Studio, 3D Studio Max and Animator Studio are registered trademarks of Kinetix Inc. USA

Alias Wavefront and Maya are registered trademarks of Alias Systems Corporation USA

AWE32, Sound Blaster, Wave Blaster and Video Blaster are registered trademarks of Creative Labs, Singapore

Paintshop Pro is a registered trademark of Jasc Inc USA

QuickTime is a registered trademark of Apple Computers USA

All other trademarks are owned and registered by respective organisations.

Acknowledgements

I fall short of words to pen down anything for the co-operation and encouragement extended by my wife throughout the making of the second edition of this book. But for her support, this book might not have taken shape. My parents extended their warmth, support and co-operation as the book was taking shape.

But for the efforts of Mr.R.Venkatachari, this book would not have come out at all. My sincere thanks go with him.

People at 'The DQ Week - Chennai' a Cyber media (I) Ltd. publication stood by my side, as this project took shape. I'd particularly like to thank the then editor – Mr. Syed Ibrahim Ahmed – for providing room for writing articles on the same subject.

My deepest gratitude goes with Mr.Krishnaswami Balaji of Singapore who was always encouraging me to bring out a second edition of this book.

I sincerely thank my publishers, BPB Publications, for taking up the second edition of this book.

Foreword to Second Edition

As I sat one fine day and started thinking about bringing out a second edition for my book Multimedia Magic, I realised that significant volume of material had to be re-written revised and rephrased. Technology had grown significantly over the years, requirements of students had changed and Tools had become dramatically simple or complex.

Multimedia has been introduced as one of the subjects in most universities and colleges. This book takes into account the syllabus laid out by some of these universities and tries to cover most – if not all – topics in a simple and lucid language.

I always believed that students as well as professionals should use this book. Though the majority of the material is meant for a novice, professionals with reasonable experience in one media or other will find useful tips and hints that were gained by experience on real world projects.

While maintaining the overall layout of first edition and even the chapter titles to some extent, the inner material has been extensively revised to reflect the latest trends in technology and concepts. Windows 2000 has been taken as the baseline Operating system throughout the book. So most of the examples and illustrations were developed on a Windows 2000 system – unless explicitly stated. Useful tables have been added at appropriate places to give an overview of different things that are being discussed.

Many examples have been added from Multimedia projects in which I was directly involved. Hence the advice and notes I have provided on those examples are not merely theoretical.

Multimedia – like any other information technology stream - is a fast moving world. But I strongly believe that there are fundamental concepts and methodologies that stay for a longer period of time than the tools themselves. Hence I urge the readers to pay attention to the overall understanding of concept rather than how to do this techniques for a specific tool. In this respect, the treatment of this book is significantly different from many other books on Multimedia tools and technologies.

I'd like to encourage the readers to write what they feel about the book – things that can be added, revised or updated. They will help me to shape the future editions of this book.

I thank the publishers for giving me an opportunity to share my ideas, thoughts and experiences in the world of multimedia – it has been a greatly rewarding experience from my side.

S.GOKUL

e-mail: seshadrigokul@yahoo.com

Contents in Detail

PART I

INTRODUCING MULTIMEDIA

PART OVERVIEW

Welcome to the wonderful and fascinating world of multimedia! With its numerous possibilities and applications literally carving out a new era in communications and the media world, multimedia has already made rapid strides in the recent past taken the information technology super highway by storm!

Part I, which contains only one chapter, introduces multimedia technology to a beginner and aims to develop a clear-cut and conceptual understanding of the same, by way of definitions and classifications.

Chapter 1

Components of Multimedia

CHAPTER OVERVIEW

This chapter begins with an introduction to the digital age in which we find ourselves today, followed by discussions on what is multimedia and what makes up multimedia. Next, we look at the mediums that are used to deliver multimedia contents and how they influence the nature of contents.

We also take a brief look at the exciting range of applications that have been made possible due to rapid advances in multimedia technology. In short, this chapter lays down the conceptual foundation for what we will be doing, throughout the rest of the book.

1.1 Dawn of the Digital Age

We are right in the midst of a digital age - heavily influenced by media.

Media bombards us from every conceivable arena - right from cinema theatres, televisions and various other audio equipments to computers and all the new generation electronic gadgets. We use media to communicate, collaborate and why, even co-exist!

Information has become much more powerful in the present century than ever before. The Internet has revolutionized the way the information was shared and accessed across the globe. Today, we literally - if not politically - stand as a single global entity, linked by a huge global network called World Wide Web.

Media is employed to delivering requisite information to the users, in required formats. Understood. So, what is multimedia?

The possibilities seem to be endless. Creatures of Jurassic age, even the time frame of which is unimaginable, come alive in the silver screen with their huge roars and fusses... military copters and jet fighters seem to fly right above our heads in the new CD games... professional quality music is stemming out of a serious business PC...

Now it's possible for the little tom to bring out some real jazz chillness in his own composition using computers - without even moving out of his drawing room! And 3D Software advertisements call to awaken the Spielberg in you...

Imagine the possibility of producing a movie - as good as Toy Story right from your PC! Amazing, isn't it?

Multimedia is no more a fantasy technology, exclusively meant for entertainment business - it has become a reality, a necessity and even mandatory under various contexts. It is the next generation blending of conventional media elements - to take advantage vice versa and deliver information in an emphatic and compelling manner.

While thinking about multimedia, it is virtually impossible to overlook the advancements in digital technology - that have made real life Multimedia applications, possible.

So, let us enter this wonderful and fascinating world of digital entertainment - not just as consumers, but also as potential producers!

1.2 What is Multimedia?

The term multimedia means many things to many people. To some, it is entertainment and educational CD-ROMs - like Microsoft Encarta and National geographic compendium. To others, it might be the latest 3D effect they see in a Hollywood movie or some fancy flash website they came across recently.

In reality, multimedia technology does include all of the above applications and many more.

So, what is multimedia? How can it be defined?

Multimedia can be defined as that technologywhich engages a variety of media - including text, audio, video, graphics and animation - either separately or in combination, using Computers, to communicate ideas or to disseminate information in a compelling manner.

If that is not enough, have a look at how the Interactive Multimedia Association of USA, defines Multimedia:

Multimedia is compelling communication, Education, Entertainment and Reference that appeals to all senses.

Perfect – Isn't it?

1.3 Scope of Multimedia – in this book

From the general definitions, it is clearly evident that multimedia encompasses a wide spectrum of applications and technology. However, in this book, we will limit ourselves to multimedia contents produced with the help of a computer.

This immediately implies that we will be dealing only with *digital media* – as only digital media is accessible via Computers. But this is not a serious restriction, as we will find that we can, after all, employ multiple mediums to deliver our media contents – like VCD / DVD Players, Electronic Audio Gadgets, Mobile Phones and TV / Cinema Films. In short, while we only use Computers to *produce* Multimedia – we may choose to *distribute* the contents thus produced via various other devices.

In a little while from now, we will clearly discuss the approach we will be taking – to master Multimedia technology.

1.4 Digital medias that make up Multimedia

Any one or more of the following media and / or a combination of these, are generally employed in all Multimedia projects:

1. Digital Audio
2. Digital Text
3. Digital Graphics
4. Digital Animation
5. Digital Video

The extent, to which a particular kind of media is employed, is mainly determined by the nature and scope of the project.

For example, a Multimedia CD-ROM title on the great English music composer, Beethoven, may naturally feature a number of sound samples from his famous symphonies; whereas an Internet website on – say a 3D Special effects production house – will naturally feature rich graphics and many 3-Dimensional animation clips from various films it has handled in the past.

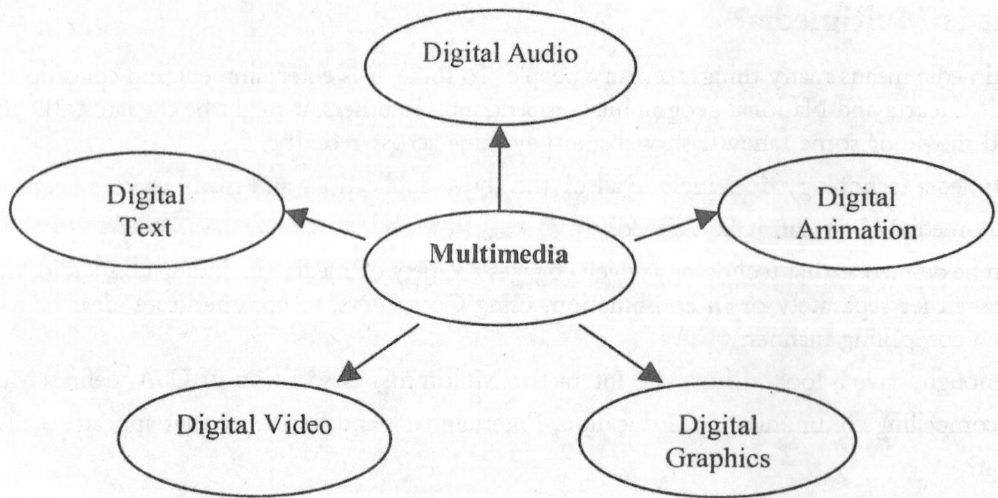

Figure 1: Multiple media elements that make up Multimedia

Let us take a high level look at what these different media elements are – as understood and implied in the Book.

- **Digital Audio**: Under this category, we can include digital music, recordings, speeches, natural sounds etc. Our aim and scope, in dealing with this medium, is two fold:

  First, we will try to set-up our Multimedia audio system properly – so as to derive the best possible digital audio experience out of our computer.

  Second, (which is likely to annoy our family members – if they are around) is to engage in various digital audio experiments, so that we can create some wonderful digital sounds and music for our own personal projects.

  Part three of this book deals with almost all aspects of multimedia audio in great detail.

- **Digital Text:** The usual text – as seen in Websites and Multimedia CD-ROMs falls under this category of media. We will be discussing different aspects of presenting texts for various applications and mediums, with some focus on Website building – since Multimedia texts are most effective in media rich websites.

  We will also be dealing with various animation effects that can be applied to Multimedia texts – so in certain sense, we also cover some ground on 2D and 3D animations.

  All these discussions constitute part four titled 'Multimedia Texts'.

- **Digital Graphics:** Herein, we include all kinds of digital pictures - like photographic images, drawings and all other forms of art works. It's this media that makes up a visually engaging title or an attractive website; hence the extensive graphics that's bundled with almost all of the Multimedia CD-ROMs .The old adage " *A picture is worth, a thousand words*", still seems to hold good in the digital age.

  Our focus will be to produce digital graphics for various applications and projects. Since digital graphics is a very exhaustive subject by itself, we will have to restrict ourselves to some of the preliminary concepts and techniques.

  Part five of this book is dedicated to multimedia graphics.

- **Digital Animation:** Digital animation is the art of producing movements to static objects. The artificial movements of texts or characters, created in virtual environments using specialised software packages – fall under this category.

  To me, animations are the most interesting part of Multimedia computing ...but it comes with a hitch: It's extensively time consuming and demands tremendous artistic vision and capabilities on the part of the developer. There are two-dimensional and three-dimensional animations.

In part six of the book, we discuss multimedia technologies that enable us to create animations for various purposes.

- **Digital Video:** Digitised video contents like VCDs, DVDs and mpegs fall under this grouping.

  Our scope is to learn how to digitise and edit basic videos and how to create VCDs and DVDs – so that they can be played on various players that are compatible.

  Part seven is dedicated to multimedia video technology.

Perhaps, the most difficult part of multimedia computing is that all these independent media elements have to be organised as single sequential stream of information and delivered. This may not only necessitate an in-depth understanding of the nature of every media and different ways of manipulating the same for a particular project, but also a capability to make use of the appropriate kind of media, in the appropriate place, at the appropriate time.

1.5 Our approach to understanding Multimedia

Since we have quite a large ground to uncover, it is safe to layout an approach to adopt – before we embark on our learning journey. Have a look at the figure.

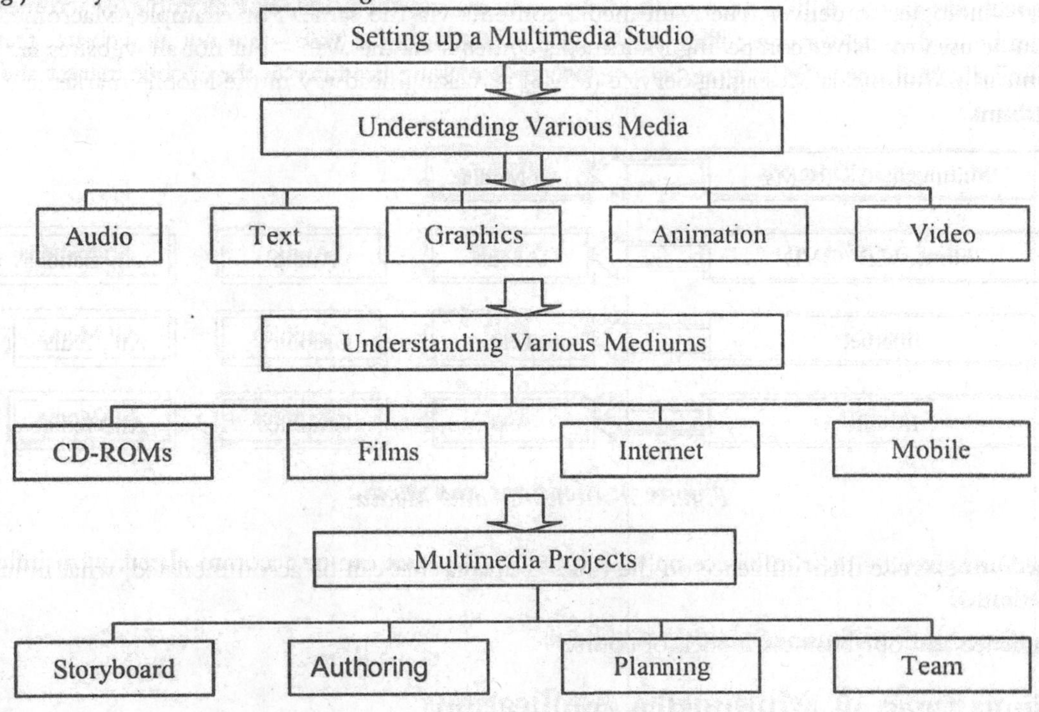

Figure 2: Our approach to understanding Multimedia

The figure should be self-explanatory.

We begin with setting up and tuning our Multimedia Hardware, so that we have a 'Multimedia Studio' – in which we can conduct our learning experiments. We then proceed with leaning each type of media – one by one, followed by various kinds of mediums available for delivering our Multimedia Contents.

In the end, we try to integrate various media elements using authoring tools to deliver some "compelling" contents. We also look at some of the project management concepts and teams that come to effect – in reasonably complex projects.

1.6 Mediums for Delivery

As indicated earlier, though our production station is going to be a Multimedia Computer, our delivery mediums can be different.

Let us try to list out some of the mediums available for us:

1. Multimedia CD-ROMs
2. Films, VCD / DVDs / other Digital Video Formats
3. Internet
4. Mobile
5. Other miscellaneous mediums

It will be interesting to analyse what kind of media can be delivered via these mediums – as it is obvious that not all kinds of media can be delivered via all of them.

You will be wondering why I've distinguished all media in Internet and Mobile mediums.

The reason is that while Text and Graphics mainly dominate the present day Internet and Mobile mediums, we already have technologies to deliver true multimedia contents via the same. For example, Macromedia's Flash technology can be used to deliver compelling Multimedia contents via the Web – but not all websites feature Flash, as on date. Similarly, Multimedia Messaging Service (MMS) is making headway in the Mobile market and will soon hit the mainstream.

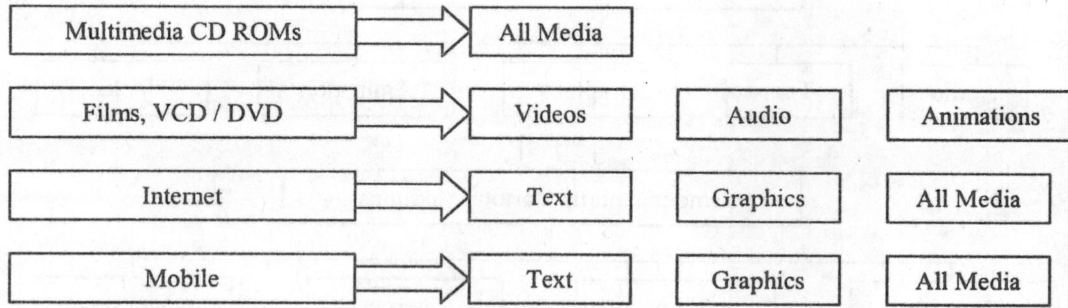

Figure 3: Mediums and Media

While the mediums exercise their influence on the types of media that can be accommodated, what influences our choice of mediums?

The target audience and our business model, of course!

1.7 Various types of Multimedia Applications

Our discussions will not be complete, without listing various applications that make use of Multimedia technologies today. While doing this exercise, we will also try to include what sorts of mediums are used to deliver the same.

1.7.1 Interactive Applications

1. Multimedia Games (CD-ROM & Internet)
2. Computer based training and tutorials (CD-ROM & Internet)
3. Edutainment Titles (CD-ROM)
4. Encyclopaedias / Knowledge Banks (CD-ROM & Internet)
5. Multimedia Websites (Internet)
6. Mobile Games (Mobile Phones)

1.7.2 Non-Interactive Applications

1. Corporate Presentations (CD-ROM & Internet)
2. 2D / 3D Animations (Films, VCD/DVD and CD-ROMs)
3. Digital Videos (VCD/DVD and CD-ROMs)

As you can see, this listing is just indicative and by no means, comprehensive.

Having classified the applications as interactive and non-interactive, it becomes essential to discuss what we mean by interactivity.

1.8 Interactive multimedia and non-interactive multimedia

Most CD-ROM titles and games are of interactive nature - i.e. the user participates in every stage of the proceedings, as the title advances... and that's what makes the Multimedia titles all the more interesting!

Of course, the extent of interactivity may vary depending upon the titles, but the general tendency is to keep the same as high as possible, so that the user enjoys greater participation in the show.

But in a corporate presentation or a multimedia demo, the audience just watch the show as it proceeds from the beginning to the end in a sequential manner. These are examples for non-interactive multimedia.

1.9 Summary

Multimedia is an amalgamation of various conventional and non-conventional media put together. Digital multimedia is the order of the day, employing various kinds of mediums and devices for its all-pervasive usage.

Depending upon the nature of application and target audience, appropriate media is chosen. The type of delivery medium selected, influences the nature of multimedia contents.

Multimedia is being used for a variety of applications. They can be broadly classified as interactive and non-interactive multimedia.

1.10 Keywords

- ❑ **Multimedia:** A technology that employs different kinds of media like text, audio, video, graphics and animation, either separately or in combination - using computers, to communicate ideas or to disseminate information.
- ❑ **Interactive Multimedia:** A multimedia application, which allows the user to interact with the ongoing proceedings, in some way or other.
- ❑ **Edutainment:** A methodology of teaching academic curriculum, in an interesting and entertaining manner.

The CD drive, used for reading CD-ROMs, can be external or internal drive, and can have either an IDE or SCSI interface. The two main parameters that ultimately govern the performance of CD drives are data transfer rate and seek time.

PART II

SETTING UP A MULTIMEDIA STUDIO

PART OVERVIEW

Before we start doing any serious work on multimedia, we need to set up a multimedia workstation – with all the necessary hardware, software and drivers and configure it to achieve the best possible performance.

Multimedia technology is characterised by it's own set of hardware and software peripherals, which a normal computer may not consist of; and those that are equipped with such peripherals are generally called as 'multimedia computers'. Literally every media demands it's own exclusive set of peripherals, which make a multimedia computer a complex and expensive goodie!

The part starts with two introductory chapters on multimedia hardware and software essentials and concludes with the third, uncovering the fundamentals of digital media.

Chapter 2

Multimedia: The Hardware Essentials

CHAPTER OVERVIEW

Chapter two starts with an introduction to what makes up the multimedia hardware, followed by discussions on various hardware peripherals - most of them in the form of add-on cards.

The accessories and peripherals made use of by end consumers are usually lesser than that of the professionals who are directly involved in producing multimedia contents. We discuss these differences and look at some of the system configurations recommended for both classes of people.

Our discussions on multimedia hardware would be incomplete without those catchy 'multimedia upgrade kits' and the often-misleading 'plug and play' concepts...

It should be emphasised here that this chapter is meant to provide only an overview to all the peripherals that make up the ultimate multimedia system. Individual peripherals have bean dealt with - in much greater detail, in the later chapters.

2.1 Introduction

Today, most computers come equipped with multimedia capabilities – and this is particularly true, if you are buying things off the shelf. You can include all branded laptops, desktops and business and home computers in this category. But, if you are building a PC all by yourself or upgrading one of your old PCs to multimedia PCs, then you will have a broad spectrum of choice in choosing your multimedia peripherals.

The purpose of this chapter is to highlight some of the basic hardware peripherals and cards that are doing media content handling for you.

For example, when you were watching a DVD movie on your laptop, you probably didn't bother to see what peripherals were doing what kind of work. Now it is time to lift the hood and take a quick look at the various peripherals that work in harmony to deliver such wonderful multimedia contents.

Let us begin with the two distinct types of multimedia hardware that have emerged – followed by discussions on what peripheral equipment handles what kind of media and so on.

2.2 Multimedia hardware evolution

Traditionally, Computers were built by those who never imagined, even in their wildest dreams, that one day, computers will be comprehending with alien signals like Music and Video! Hence, the basic architecture of the Computer was not designed to support them directly.

The PC speaker, which was then added only to give warnings signals to the user, is perhaps, the forefather of all multimedia hardware today, and was misused beyond limits by the old DOS games. Some kind hearted folks took pity on it and developed something called a sound card or an audio board ...But, audio was only the *second* media to get the privilege of being handled computers - graphics had already entered the scenario by then, though not with millions of colours, as it is today.

From then onwards, many specialised equipments were slowly developed to make computers understand and play almost all other kinds of media...and this creative process continues even today.

Since every other kind of media demanded *its own set of hardware / software interfaces* to get along with the computer, peripherals were mercilessly added to the otherwise innocent PC, until the entire space inside the cabinet was occupied by countless PCB Boards!

But, things have changed much over these years and today, we see multimedia capabilities being built right into the heart of PC's motherboard architecture, so that you are left with some more space in the cabinet and a little piece of mind!

2.3 Basic types of multimedia hardware

Today – we have two distinct kinds of multimedia hardware available in the market:

1. Those with multimedia enabled motherboards – requiring little or no additional multimedia peripherals.
2. Those build with additional multimedia peripherals.

For example, you may choose to buy a motherboard with audio input and output capabilities and thus save some cost on buying an external sound card. Or you may choose to buy a basic motherboard without multimedia capabilities and later on, add your favourite sound card to it.

Now, the obvious question is: Which is the way to go forward?

Well, it depends on your usage. It depends on what you want to do with your sound card. It depends on how much audio capabilities you need for your multimedia project at hand.

For example, if you simply want to build up a professional multimedia system and use it for exploring various multimedia applications – then probably a Motherboard integrated multimedia is enough. But, if you are an audio professional – who wants to create next generation audio effects for your latest album, then you probably need a dedicated Sound card with advanced capabilities.

One good news, is that you can first buy a multimedia-integrated motherboard – if you are not sure how you will use it and later on *choose* to buy a Sound card and make use of the same. We will see how this can be done, as we go along.

2.4 Multimedia add-on peripherals

For a moment, let us forget motherboard-integrated multimedia and concentrate on external multimedia peripherals. As noted earlier, we need dedicated interfaces to handle different kinds of media.

Most of the multimedia Hardware Interfaces, take the form of ***Add - On cards** or **Peripheral Cards*** (which are basically printed circuit boards with the relevant chips / integrated circuits and input or output sockets built in) that fit into the 16/32 bit slots inside the computer. The necessary connection jacks alone protrude at the rear end of the system cabinet, so that you can connect them to the relevant external cables.

These cards basically provide an *analog to digital interface* between the external media handling devices, like the Tape or Video recorder and the Computer, so that data can be transferred between the two.

Let us see what are all the various types of cards available for us. Have a look at Figure 2.1.

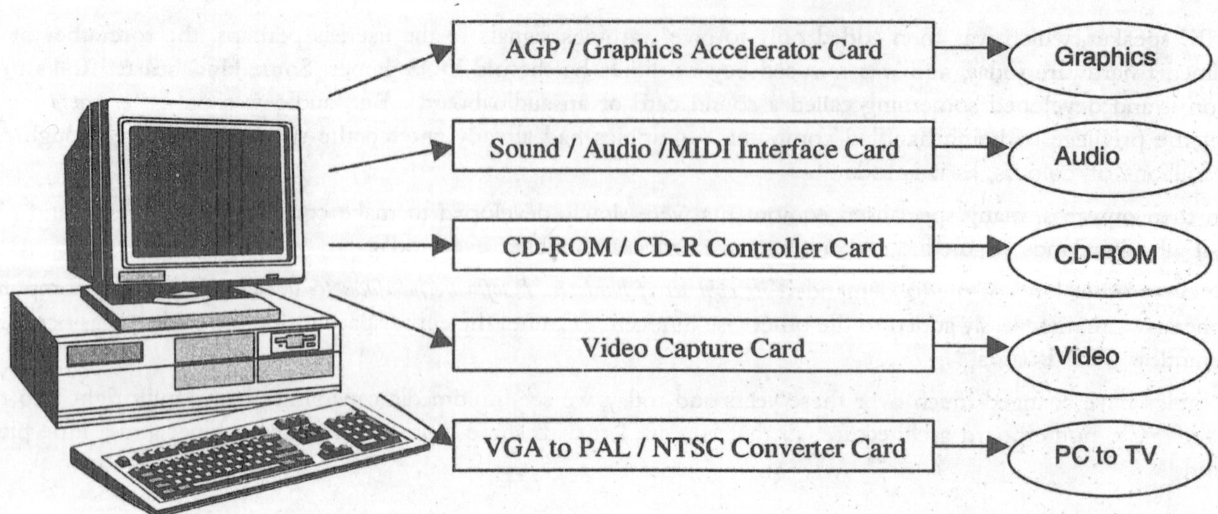

Figure 4: Various types of multimedia add-on cards that handle various types of media

Brief descriptions of what these cards are all about should be suffice for now. Later on, when we are to address each Media type in detail, we can learn more about them.

- AGP / Graphics accelerator cards interface between the computer and the monitor. While AGP cards merely handle the colour display and resolution, graphics accelerators do sophisticated 3D graphics acceleration and rendering for better visuals and performances in multimedia games.
- The sound cards or the audio cards manage almost all possible kinds of audio – including digital audio, MIDI (Musical instruments digital interface), mp3 etc. Remember! You need a pair of speakers or headphones and of course, two good ears to actually hear the sounds as they come out of a sound card.
- The CD Controller Cards handle CD-ROM/CD-R Drives and are usually supplied along with the Drives. These cards are applicable only for Internal CD-ROM and CD-R Drives.
- Video Capture Boards – as the name implies – capture Analog video contents from VCRs and Handy cams into the computer, in digital video format.
- VGA to PAL/NTSC Converters are meant for viewing PC Contents via a Television. PAL is an Asian TV standard and NTSC is an American standard.

Table 1: Multimedia add-on cards and their usage

Card	Who will need them?
Basic AGP Card.	All (Users / Professionals)
3D / Graphics Accelerator Cards	3D Animation Professionals / Gaming Maniacs
Basic Sound Cards	All (Users / Professionals)
Advanced Audio Cards with various additional capabilities	Music / Audio Professionals
CD-ROM Controllers	All those who use Internal CD Drives
Video Capture Card	Digital Video Professionals / Those who want to 'create' their own VCD / DVDs
VGA to TV Converter	3D Animation / Video Professionals

Fortunately, not all of these cards are needed for *playing back* the multimedia contents inside the Computer. But professionals, who may want to *create and edit* various types of multimedia contents, end up with a variety of these cards.

For a better understanding, let us try to format a matrix – with multimedia peripheral cards on one side and those who will be using them on the other side.

2.5 External multimedia equipments

Apart form all those add-on cards that we listed in the above section; we may need some external multimedia equipments – to carry out our tasks.

Some of them are:

1. Scanners
2. Digital Cameras
3. Digital Handy cams / Camcorders
4. Colour Inkjet Printers
5. Microphones
6. Multimedia Speakers

Similar to multimedia peripherals, not all of us will require all of the above listed equipments. It all depends on the nature of multimedia projects and activities that are at our hand, how we want to do etc.

2.6 How to choose the right multimedia peripherals and equipments?

Given the myriad of brands and products available in the multimedia peripherals category, it is but a complex exercise to choose the best products among the lot and to identify those that provide professional services and offer good value for money.

A good starting point, before buying any piece of multimedia hardware – is to check up IT magazines and websites and catch hold of any reviews/comparisons about the product. There are many magazines that provide periodic test results each year and offer awards for the best of the breed in all category.

Unfortunately, I am not able to recommend you any brands straight away - though I can share some of the products / brands I have personally tried and found satisfaction.

Table 2: Multimedia peripherals and brands I have tried

Hardware	My Suggestions and Comments
Mother Boards	Any decent brand with Intel/AMD Chipsets
Processor	Intel, AMD
3D / Graphics Accelerator Cards	NVIDIA GeForce Fx series of cards – could be expensive but offer good results. There are many other less expensive brands that offer good value for money.
Sound Cards	Creative has been a market leader in this segment for a long time.
CD-RW	Many brands – HP, Samsung, Yamaha etc
Scanners	HP. I have not tried any other brand.
Digital cameras	Many brands. Nikon is my choice.

I repeat that the above list is rather suggestive and certainly not conclusive and it certainly does not imply that other brands not specified here are less superior in performance. Things do not remain stagnant in the world of IT and brand superiority is always subject to changes over a period of time.

There are quite a bit of things to watch out and specifications to be noted, before buying a particular piece of multimedia hardware. For example, while buying a Video capture card, you should notice the size of the captured video as well as the frame rate at which the capture occurs. We will reserve these discussions for the later chapters – wherein we focus on each media in detail. Thus, the discussions on video capture cards will fall under those topics that cover digital video.

2.7 Installation Tips

It is nearly impossible for us to discuss how each and every multimedia hardware device has to be installed on a Computer. Literally, every piece of Hardware we purchase should come bundled with installation manual and device driver software – if not ask for the same.

However, we can list out a few generic guidelines here, which should be relevant – irrespective of the type of hardware you buy.

- Windows 2000 editions and above, come bundled with scores of device drivers and chances are that it might recognise your multimedia hardware automatically and install the default drivers on its own. However, for best performances, it is best to make use of device drivers and application software that comes bundled with the equipment. We will see how to change the default device drivers – in our discussions on device drivers in the next chapter.
- Ensure that the new hardware is compatible with the motherboard and other peripherals you have already got. If one slot is not working for a particular piece of hardware, try another.
- Ensure that the operating system is, indeed, making use of the hardware it is supposed to use. For example, assume that your motherboard is having an integrated audio device. Now, if you are to purchase a Sound Card for advanced features, you should ensure that the Operating System is making use of the new hardware bit instead of the old one, which is still installed and available for Windows. How to ensure this? The next section explains.

2.8 Finding the multimedia peripherals installed on your computer

Microsoft Windows OS has inbuilt capabilities to work with many of the multimedia peripherals and equipments that we discussed so far. How to recognize what are all the different kinds of multimedia software installed on your computer and identified by Windows?

Follow the procedure below, which has been illustrated on a Windows 2000 Professional edition.

1. Go to Start → Settings → Control Panel → Sounds and Multimedia. Double click on the icon.
2. The Multimedia Options panel opens up. This is probably the main place you need to refer, to know what are all the multimedia hardware devices installed in the system. As shown in the figure below, there are separate tabs for audio and other multimedia installed.
3. Click on the Audio tab and you will see the list of Hardware devices used for Sound Playback / Recording and MIDI Playback. The preferred device is the one that is currently being used by the Operating system. You may want to ensure that your new audio board is listed and used as the preferred device. If you check use only preferred devices, Windows will not consider alternative devices at all.
4. You can actually click on the 'Advanced' button- just out of curiosity and see what pops up. But I'll reserve my discussions on them for later chapters!

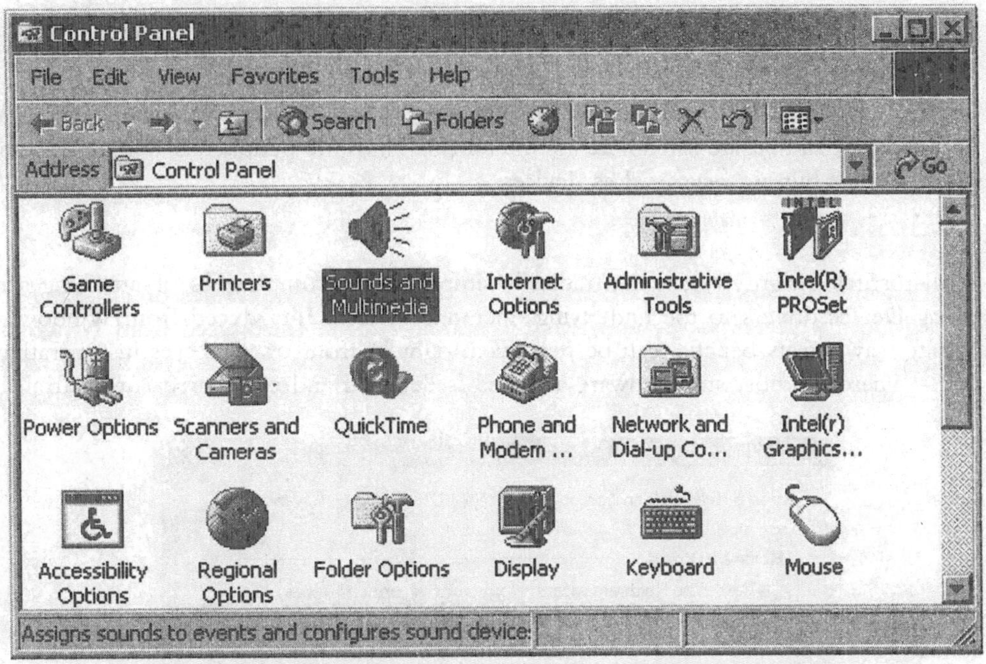

Figure 5: Reaching Sounds and Multimedia Panel from Control Panel

There is yet another place wherein you can see all the multimedia hardware installed in the system. This is however, recommended only for advanced users. Follow the procedure detailed below, if you are interested.

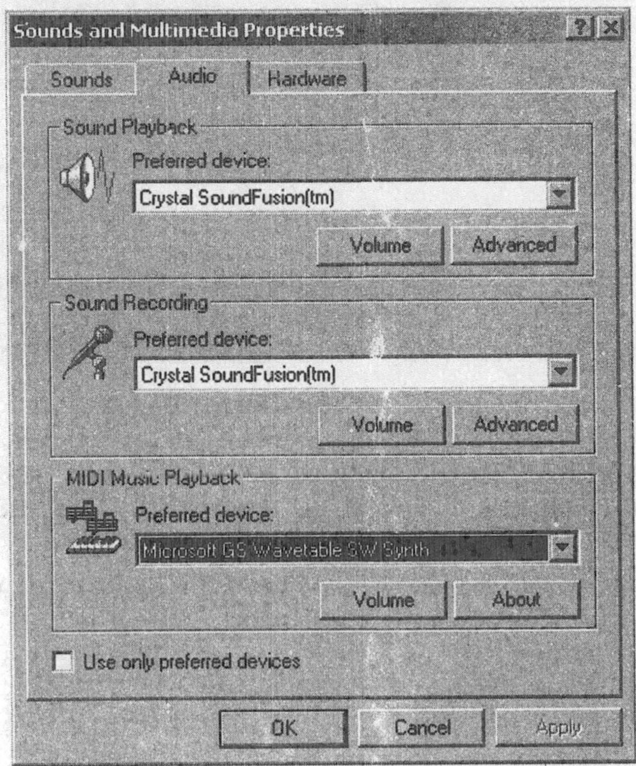

Figure 6: Sounds and Multimedia Panel in Windows 2000

1. Go to My Computer (Right Click) à Properties à Hardware tab. Choose the Device manager button.
2. The Device manager panel opens up.
3. Double click on Sound, video and game controllers. You will see a list of devices installed on your system.
4. Please note that not all that are listed here are multimedia hardware peripherals. Some of them - like codecs - represent software but are registered as devices.

2.9 Plug and play

Plug and play is Microsoft's design concept that radically simplified the complexities of attaching a new hardware device and installing Device drivers to the underlying operating system. Introduced from Windows 95, Plug and play has come a long way and its benefits can be perceived, right in front of your eyes in Operating systems like Win 2000 and XP – wherein almost any hardware attached is detected and configured automatically!

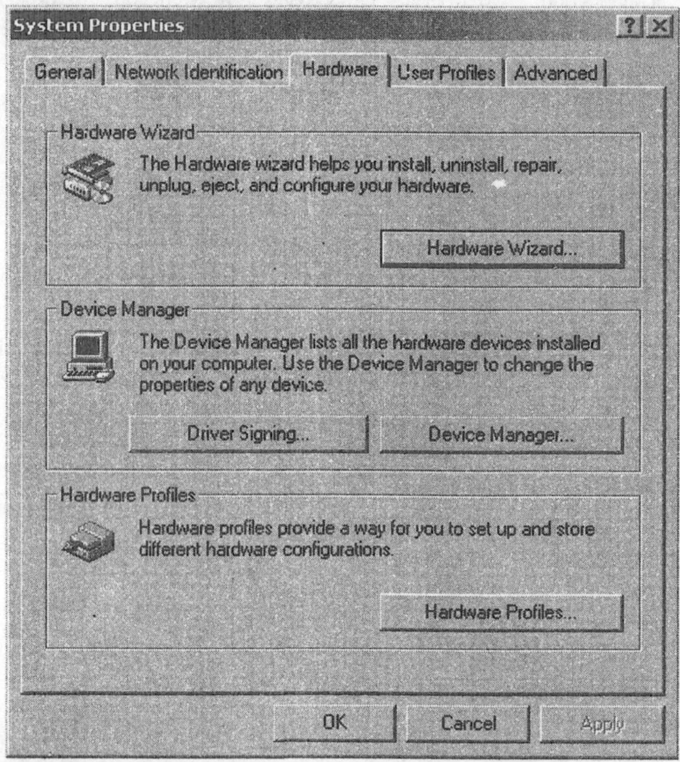

Figure 7: Reaching Device Manager

Plug and play specifications affect both hardware and software. The interactions pervade end to end and require the combined participation of the underlying PC's BIOS, the Hardware peripheral, Device driver and the Operating system.

We will not go into the details of plug and play beyond this, as it is out of scope of this work.

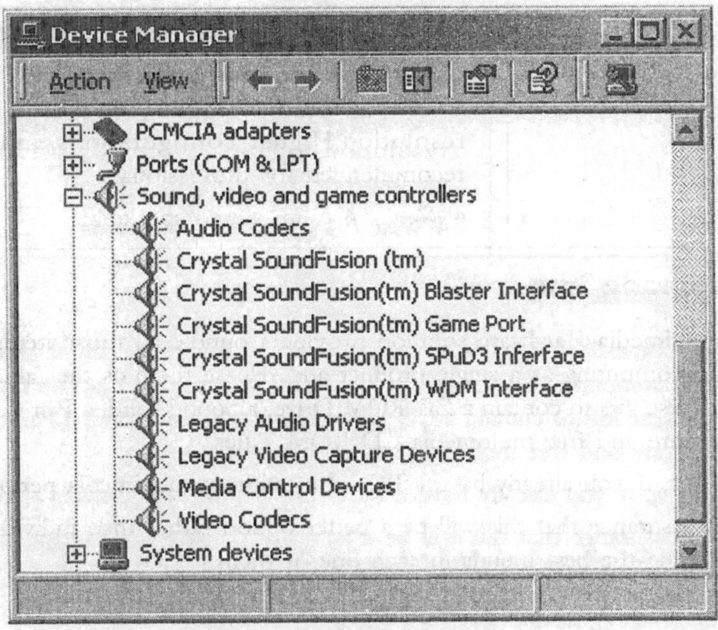

Figure 8: Device Manager Panel

2.10 A typical multimedia system configuration

Let me see if I could provide you with the configuration information of a typical multimedia system – that can be put to use for all of our projects coming up in the following chapters. I know my recommendation will be obsolete pretty soon, as more powerful processors keep hitting the market every six months – so, validate these details with your hardware dealer before making the purchase!

Also, this list *does not mean* that if your hardware is of lesser capacity than what is recommended, you should upgrade! If you are slightly lagging behind – here and there, you can still cope up. However, if you are managing a 4 to 5 year old Computer and want to do sophisticated work detailed in the coming chapters, then you may hit some bottlenecks.

Table 3: A typical multimedia system configuration

Hardware	Minimum required / Recommended spec
Processor	Intel Pentium 4 Processor with 2+ GHz or its equivalent. Anything higher is most welcome.
RAM	128 to 256 MB DDR SDRAM 1 GB recommended for 3D Animation & Video Professionals
Hard Disk	20 GB or more.80 GB recommended for 3D Animation, Audio & Video Professionals
CD ROM	24X read speed.52X recommended.
CD-R and CD-RW Drive	Highly recommended for all multimedia Professionals. Minimum 10X writing speed.
AGP / Graphics Accelerator	32 MB Dynamic Video Memory.Professional 3D Graphics accelerator with 64 MB DDR Video memory recommended for 3D / Video professionals.

Sound Card	Creative series of sound cards or their equivalent.Anything higher would be for professionals.
Monitor	17" and above with 24 Bit colour and 1024*768 resolution.Higher configurations and LCD Monitor recommended for professionals.
Speakers	4 Watt / 4 Ohm stereo speakers

2.11 Multimedia upgrade kits

Quite a good number of multimedia Hardware solution providers bundle all those items, other than the system itself, needed for multimedia computing as a single product and release them as the famous 'Multimedia upgrade kits'. You can usually expect these kits to contain a CD ROM Drive, a Sound Card, a Pair of Speakers, a Microphone and a set of associated Software and free multimedia CD ROM Titles.

You may want to consider this, if you already have a PC – but without multimedia peripherals.

I cannot really give you any assurance that this will be a better option rather than individual buys - because you'll miss the opportunity of selecting the best brands in each one of them.

But the obvious advantages are:

1. Lower Cost (in many of the cases)
2. Assured compatibility between the Devices and of course,
3. The free multimedia CD Titles.

If you are buying a PC afresh, do not consider this option; buy a multimedia enabled Computer off the shelf or assemble it with the brands you like most.

2.12 Summary

Two kinds of multimedia hardware are available in the market: Those with multimedia capabilities built into the motherboard and those that are available by means of add-on peripherals. Add on peripherals offer more choices and flexibility.

Apart from peripherals that fit into the motherboard, multimedia production also requires external equipments like scanners, digital cameras etc. The requirements may vary depending upon the project under development. A computer's operating system allows us to see what sort of multimedia peripherals have been installed on a system.

Microsoft Windows plug and play concept makes installation and configuration of device drivers easy.

Conventional computers can be upgraded to multimedia computers with the help of multimedia upgrade kits.

2.13 Keywords

- **Device drivers:** Software that provides the necessary interface required for interactions, between the Operating System and the multimedia hardware peripherals attached to the system.
- **Plug and play:** A set of design specifications incorporated with Microsoft's Windows OS, for most hardware and the software peripherals, that enables easy recognition and installation of device in Microsoft Windows platform.

Chapter 3

Multimedia: Setting up the Software

CHAPTER OVERVIEW

Having seen the multimedia hardware details in the previous chapter, it is time to look at some of the multimedia software rudiments.

Multimedia software is a very generic term encompassing a wide variety of tools and applications. Herein, we will be covering device drivers, multimedia player software that recognize and play different kinds of media, multimedia creation software – which are required to create and edit digital multimedia contents and finally, multimedia application software – which are end products enriched with multimedia contents.

The whole chapter has to be perceived as a curtain raiser to many of the forthcoming chapters, wherein, we will be discussing the multimedia creation tools and applications we can develop with them, in great detail.

3.1 Introduction

The term 'multimedia software' is very generic and conceptual in nature. Theoretically, any type of software performing some multimedia function or other can be termed 'multimedia software'. When detailed, it encompasses a wide variety of tools, applications, packages, device drivers and utilities – all related to multimedia, in one way or other.

Looking at the tools that are commercially available, the trouble only deepens. For example, how do you distinguish Microsoft Media Player and encoder? What sets Adobe Photoshop different from Acrobat? And where do multimedia CD-ROMs like Microsoft Encarta fit in?

Our first task is to categorize them into various groupings, so that it will be clear about what multimedia software we will be learning about, in this book and why.

3.2 Multimedia software categories

For the sake of our discussions, we will divide multimedia software into four broad categories.

1. **Device driver software** - meant for installing and configuring multimedia peripherals
2. **Media players** meant for handling multimedia file formats
3. **Media conversion tools** meant for encoding / decoding multimedia contents and for converting one file format to another.
4. **Media editing tools** meant for creating / editing digital multimedia data
5. **Multimedia authoring tools** meant for combining different kinds of media formats and deliver them as multimedia contents and
6. **Multimedia applications** created with the help of above-mentioned tools & packages.

At this stage, it is imperative to have a bird's eye view of all these different categories of software and understand how they are differing from one another. Later on, during our exclusive discussions on every media type, we will be getting back to them with a sharper focus.

3.3 Device drivers

Every other hardware peripheral to be installed on a computer needs a device driver – that interfaces between the peripheral and the operation system. It is through the device driver software that the operating system instructs the peripheral device to carry on the instruction provided by the user.

For example, when you increase or decrease the volume of sound in windows operating system – the calls are issued out of OS and converted to specific instructions understandable by the audio card through the device drivers - and the speaker volume is subsequently increased or decreased.

In most of the cases, the Device driver software comes bundled with the peripheral equipment you buy. Even if it is not so, chances are high that a compatible driver is already available in your Operating system – particularly so, if it is Windows 2000 and above.

In order to derive maximum performance from the multimedia peripheral, it is best to make use of the Driver supplied by the manufacturer. Hence, it is important to ensure that the Driver software has been included with the equipment – before you pay the vendor.

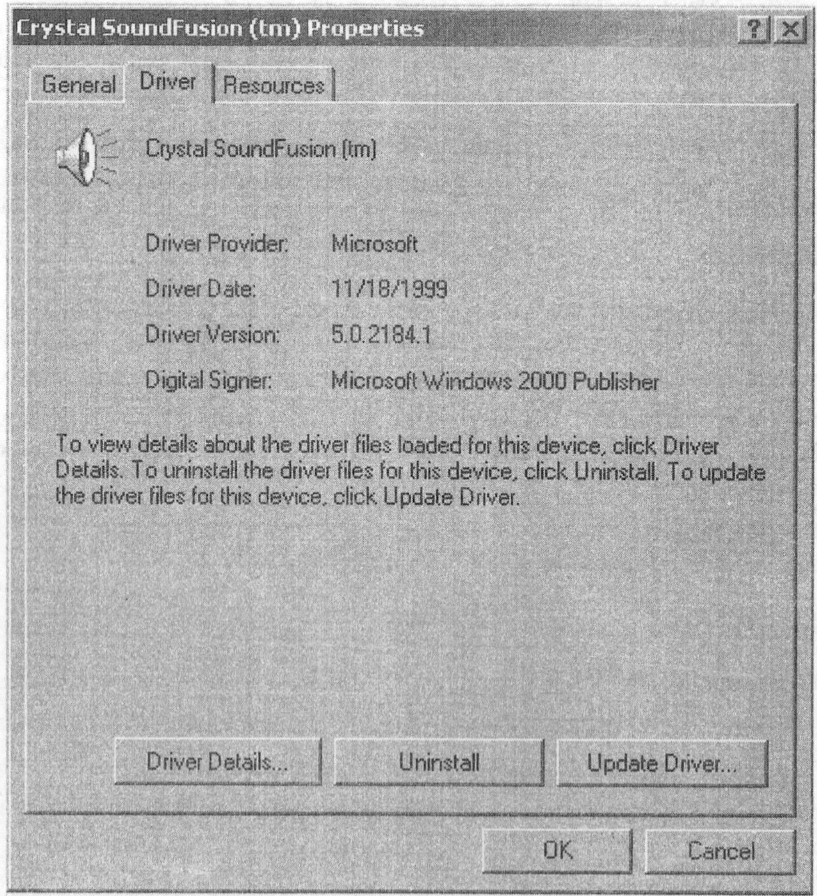

Figure 9: Device driver details for a given multimedia peripheral

During installation, Windows will prompt you with a dialog box – asking you to supply the necessary Device drivers. If not, then it means that Windows has already identified a proper driver for the hardware.

To know whether the device has been properly installed – with all the required drivers, the best place to consult is the Device manager. If you see a yellow question mark near any of the devices, then it means that the hardware has not been installed properly or the Driver is not available.

To see what Driver a particular device is using, right click over the device icon in the Device manager, choose properties and look at the panel that pops up.

If your device is installed and running properly, there is no need to change the drivers etc. Of course, if your vendor recommends an update to the driver, then you may consider downloading the relevant driver patch from the Internet and applying the same by means of 'update driver'.

It is best to undertake this exercise, if you are sufficiently informed about the peripheral and its drivers or can avail the services of a support engineer, nearby!

3.4 Media players

Media players are applications that can play one or more kinds of multimedia file formats. Most of them are available free of cost and can be downloaded directly from the Internet.

Let us see some of the most famous Media players that are used by consumers and professionals alike.

1. **Microsoft Windows media player** – Probably the most famous in the lot, Windows media player plays a wide variety of media file formats like Wav, mp3, mpgs, mov, avi… and what not? It is usually bundled with the Windows Operating system and can be reached at Start à Programs → Accessories → Entertainment → Windows Media Player.

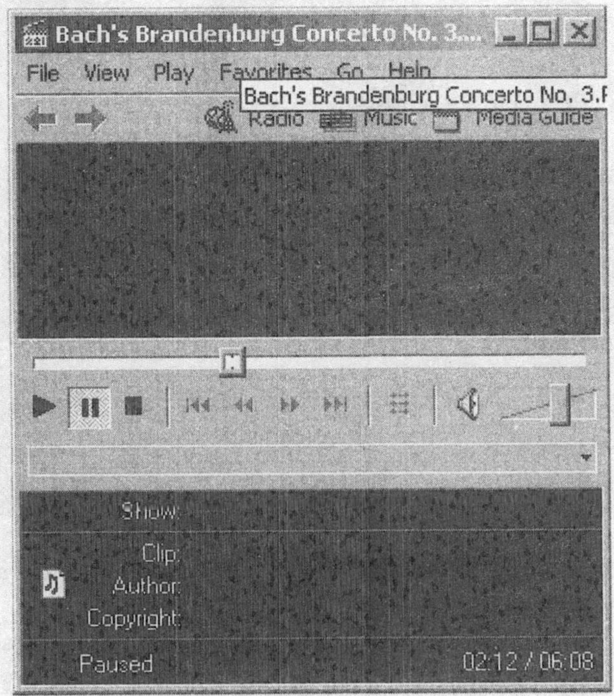

Figure 10: Windows Media Player – playing a MIDI File

However, if you want to download the latest Media player which is above the one that comes with your OS, checkout the following website:

http://www.microsoft.com/windows/windowsmedia/default.asp

2. Apple's QuickTime player is also an equally popular player in the market. It has attractive options for adding some cool sound effects like boss, treble etc. Also, you can download some of the latest movie trailers in QuickTime format from Apple's website.

   To download the latest Quick Time player, check out the following URL:

   http://www.apple.com/quicktime/

   There is an advanced version of QuickTime Player called the QuickTime pro – but this is not free.

3. After Windows media player and QuickTime, it is the Real One player that has captured the hearts of users around the world. The attraction of this player is that it can play streaming real audio and real video files at decent speeds.

   To download the latest player, check out the following URL:

   http://www.realaudio.com

Figure 11: Apple's Quick Time Player – playing a .mov File

4. The next important media player that comes in our list is Macromedia's Flash Player. Macromedia flash is perhaps the most famous technology for delivering multimedia contents over the Internet and we will be spending a good deal of time to understand the same – later in these chapters. Unlike other media players, Flash player will be installed as a Web browser plug-in component.

   To download the latest flash player, check out:

   http://www.macromedia.com/software/flashplayer/

3.5 Media conversion tools

When you undertake multimedia projects, you constantly feel the need to change the media file formats from one to another. A true multimedia professional should be well aware of the wide range of choices he has got – in this direction and take advantage of specific file formats.

The need for conversion arises mainly because of the fact that multimedia professionals have to put up with uncompressed media file formats – whereas the multimedia consumers can only be provided with compressed file formats.

Professionals work with uncompressed files – because, they do not want to lose the quality of contents, as the media contents undergo editing. But once all the editing is done and the required contents available for delivery, then the file size needs to be reduced by means of compression. This will enable easy distribution to end consumers.

For example, Audio professionals always prefer to work with uncompressed file formats like .Wav files – but during distribution, this may be converted to .mp3 or any other suitable file format that serves the purpose best, without losing much quality.

There are other needs for multimedia files format conversions – as well. For example, you might want to convert one of your favourite VCDs to DVDs! This necessarily involves file format conversions and you may need suitable tools to do that.

Media conversion tools are meant for this purpose. There are scores of free / cheap tools available in the Internet - for converting file formats and to do encoding / decoding. The following table lists some of the file format conversations, frequently undertaken by professionals.

Table 4: Multimedia file format conversions

Media	File format conversions frequently done
Audio	Wav to mp3 and vice versa
	Aifff to Wav / mp3 and vice versa
	Midi to mp3, Wav etc.
	Wav to WMA (streaming audio)
	CD Audio to Wav and vice versa
Video	AVI to Mpeg file formats and vice versa
	VCD to DVD file formats
	Avi to animated GIF
	AVI to WMV (streaming video)
Graphics	Many file format conversions involved.
3D Animation	Models / Wire frames file format conversions

There are scores of other media file formats and conversions involved in real life – so the above table is just a sample and not an exhaustive listing.

Also, the process of multimedia file format conversion is not as simple as it sounds and there are a number of things to be taken care of. We will focus upon this – as we proceed to delve deep into each media, in detail.

3.6 Media editing tools

Multimedia editing tools are meant for editing various types of digital media contents. Raw media files are hardly useful; they need to be edited, massaged and converted to required file formats – to satisfy the requirements of a given project.

Learning these different tools and making an effective / combined use of all of them – is what constitutes the core of multimedia learning. In the chapters that follow, we will be focussing mostly on many of these tools and utilities. For each media, there are different sets of tools available from different vendors.

But, the unfortunate part is that there is **no single tool** that can be purchased for editing all kinds of media...! Which means that you end up buying one good tool for editing every other media!

For example, if your project involves audio, video and some graphics – then you are most likely to end up with at least two to three tools, if not more! The reason is that the nature of these media are so different from one another, that it is virtually impossible to provide editing tools for all of them – in a single application.

Let me try to list out some of the famous professional editing tools, available for each media.

Table 5: Multimedia Editing Tools

Media	Tool	Company
Audio	Cool Edit Pro	Syntrilliyum Software(http://www.syntrilliyum.com)
	Sound Forge	Sonic Foundry(http://www.sonicfoundry.com)
	Sonar	Twelve tone systems(http://www.cakewalk.com)
	Wave lab	Steinberg(http://www.steinberg.com)
Video	Adobe Premiere	Adobe systems(http://www.adobe.com)
	Video Studio	Ulead(http://www.ulead.com)
	Windows Movie Maker (XP Only)	Microsoft(http://www.microsoft. com)
Graphics (Image editing)	Adobe Photoshop	Adobesystems(http://www.adobe.com)
	Corel Photo paint	Corel
	Photo Impact	Ulead(http://www.ulead.com)
Graphics (Vector illustrations)	Adobe Illustrator	Adobe systems(http://www.adobe.com)
	Corel DRAW	
	Freehand	Macromedia(http://www.macromedia.com)
3D Animation	3D Studio Max	Discreet
	Maya	Alias Wave front(http://www.alias.com)
	SoftImage	Avid Technology(http://www.softimage.com)
	Light wave 3D	Newtek(http://www.newtek.com)

Professionals and industry folks use the above listed tools.

I have not included the free tools and shareware utilities – since the listing may grow too long.

The options and capabilities available with these different kinds of tools may vary, depending upon the quality of the product. Hardcore multimedia Professionals make use of advanced packages and others stick to lower end products. Interestingly, some very good tools are available in the freeware / shareware category as well – and we will be taking a look at some of them, later in the chapters.

3.7 Multimedia Authoring Tools

Authoring tools enable creation of true multimedia contents. By providing abilities to handle and amalgamate multiple media, authoring tools open out the doors of unlimited imagination - to a creative professional.

We will briefly list out some of the leading authoring tools here and reserve our detailed discussions for later chapters.

Table 6: Multimedia Authoring Tools

Product	Company
Director	Macromedia(http://www.macromedia.com)
Author ware	Macromedia(http://www.macromedia.com)
Flash	Macromedia(http://www.macromedia.com)
Tool book Instructor	Click2learn(http://www.click2learn.com)

3.8 Multimedia Applications

Today, multimedia applications are made use of in many spheres of life – from educational institutions to enterprises and entertainment, its usage is wide and complex.

We will try to classify these wide varieties of applications into specific categories – hopefully for a better understanding and appreciation.

- ❑ Knowledge books / reference applications: These applications, mostly issued as multimedia CD- ROMs, serve as encyclopaedias or references - on a variety of topics.

  Many titles are currently available in the market, in this category. Since multimedia can handle many types of Media interfaces, the information available in various media forms, pertaining to a particular topic are effectively integrated and stored.

  Examples of these applications are Microsoft Encarta and Manorama's Knowledge adventure CD-ROMs

- ❑ Training and classroom applications (CBT): More popularly known as the CBTs (Computer Based Training/ Tutorials), these applications make use of multimedia technology to teach some academic curriculum or technical topic. We will meet one very interesting CD ROM in the following section, wherein the very multimedia Technology has been ingeniously used to teach... Well, multimedia technology!

- ❑ Gaming and entertainment applications: This category includes all Computer games, adventures and other related stuff that make use of multimedia technology. It should be admitted that games remain as one of the most popular applications of multimedia – with thousands of titles being available in the market and thousands more under production!

- ❑ 3D/ Graphics applications: 3D Animation and graphics technologies used for Movies and Television dramas have evolved into a separate stream of businesses. This multi-billion dollar industry is growing at a tremendous pace – throughout the world.

- ❑ Presentation applications: These applications are mainly used in corporate boardrooms. Though simple PowerPoint applications still remain as the most popular choice, there are many occasions to call for specialized multimedia presentations for clients and business partners.

- ❑ Public utility kiosks / Touch screen applications: These applications are exclusively developed for public access - in places like Hotels, Airports etc.- for delivering the required information in an interactive and lively manner. They necessarily make use of one or more Public Information Display Systems (PIDS).

- Miscellaneous applications: We can include all other miscellaneous multimedia applications that fail to fit into any of the above categories – here.

3.9 CD Premiere: A Meeting with the Professor

Welcome to **'Professor Multimedia'** - an edutainment (or CBT) CD ROM for learning multimedia Technology in an interactive manner, published by Individual Software Inc., USA.

This title is introduced here, for two reasons:

1. With this, we get to know how a typical multimedia CD-ROM works and how each media is employed to deliver an engaging title. This knowledge will be useful for us, because it will help us to understand the power and specialities of each media, in a better way.
2. In a way, this CD Title is slightly different from all others. There is certainly some degree of innovation in utilizing the very technology, which it is supposed to teach us: In other words, it's *multimedia, learning through multimedia!*

3.10 The Journey

Most of the multimedia CD-ROM titles install few executable files (applications), DLLs (Window Dynamic link libraries) and other files required for their operations. These are usually installed in a directory of user's choice, on the Hard disk.

Professor Multimedia CD-ROM installs around 6 MB of such files and creates its own Icon under the Program manager in Windows.

Figure 12: Professor Multimedia CD-ROM

When we click on the icon…presto!

We enter the professor's personal premises - a 3D room with a multimedia PC, with a voice greeting us to the world of multimedia; and a menu is thrown open to us immediately.

This again, is typical for many multimedia CD-ROMs, particularly the edutainment ones, which are organised into various topics through which the user can navigate freely. This Main menu, in turn, splits up to various submenus that take us directly to any part of the title we want to access.

This is another advantage of Interactive media: At any stage, we can come back to this menu and go directly to another topic of our choice...!

Professor Multimedia has the following topics in the Main menu: Pizzazz, Elements of Multimedia, The Multimedia Presentation, Multimedia Applications, Glossary and Tips and Multimedia Quiz.

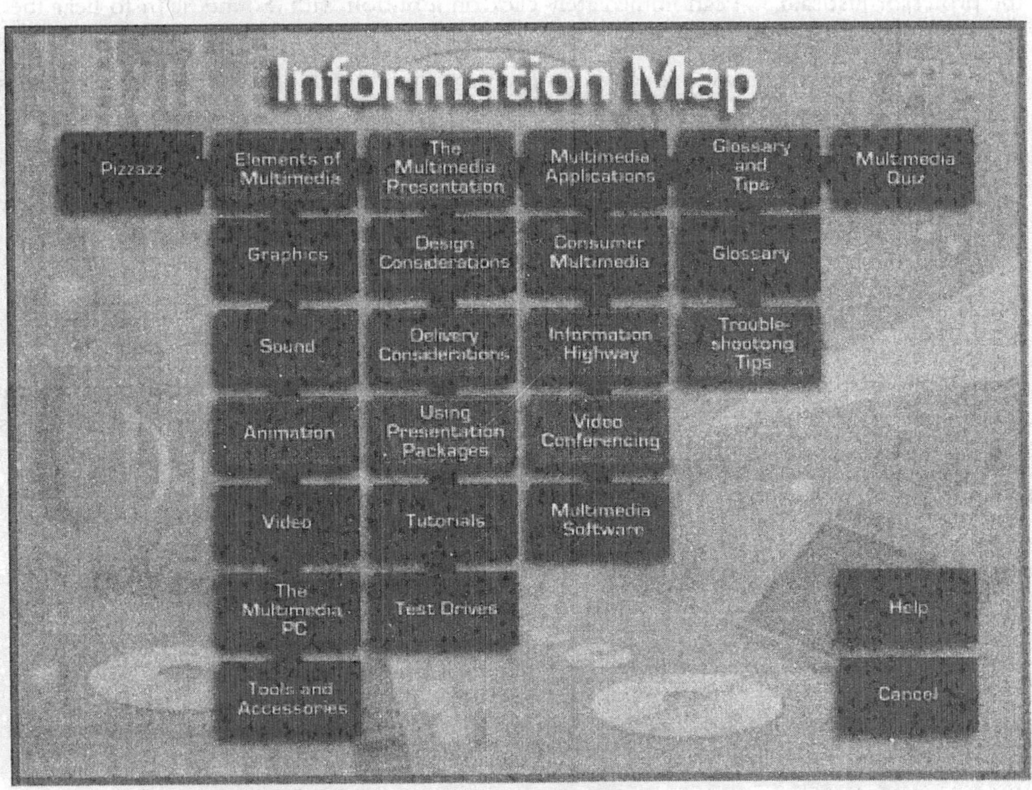

Figure 13: Professor Multimedia Menus and Sub-menus

Additionally, there is a Guided Map that lists all the Submenu items apart from the Main menu, in the form of a Map, which, in turn, facilitates greater navigation control and independence - as we skim through the title.

3.10.1 Eat the pizzazz

The Pizzazz section gives a sneak preview of what multimedia is all about: Some fine sound clips… accompanied by animation and video, introduce us to the world of multimedia wonders. The capabilities and powers of the technology also get some illustration. Now, are we all set to bottle the genie?

3.10.2 Elements of multimedia

The second part, which is the very heart of the title, has the following as the sub menu items: Graphics, Sound, Animation, Video, The multimedia PC and tools and Tools and accessories.

When we click on, say, the animation button, we directly enter the world of mind boggling 2D and 3D computer animations; and as we begin to understand and appreciate what's meant by a "Text Animation", we are suddenly pointed out that throughout our proceedings, till this current screen, how many text animations have passed by!

Oops! We try to sit erect - and begin to watch the title with an entirely different perspective!

This is yet another strength of multimedia: Explaining things with extensive graphics and animations, which can easily make one, understand the concepts clearly. Remember... a picture is worth a thousand words!

The title proceeds to explain all other medias in a similar manner...Immediately providing us with direct examples of the subject and without mincing up with words! Imagine hearing a real sixteen-bit .Wav audio file, immediately after reading what a sixteen-bit sound is all about! Well, you may say it is a direct hit!

As we go along, we perceive yet another advantage of multimedia learning: Supposing we didn't hear what the tutor...sorry, the professor just said, we can immediately click on a button with 'Sound' icon to hear the lesson once again!

This is the power of multimedia over conventional Video Training sessions without the irritation of countless rewinding and fast forward sessions with your dear old VCR!

As our aim is just getting to know how a typical multimedia CD-ROM feels like, and certainly not reviewing Professor Multimedia in its totality, let's give a bidding farewell to our dear professor!

3.11 Summary

The term 'multimedia software' can mean many things: device drivers, media players, media conversion tools, editing tools, multimedia authoring tools and end applications - all come under this broad umbrella.

Device drivers allow the base operating system to execute various tasks on the hardware peripherals. Media players enable playing the contents of a particular media type - say an audio file or a video file. Media conversion utilities convert multimedia contents from one file format to another relevant file format.

Editing tools help us to edit and even create multimedia contents. Authoring enables cocktailing multimedia contents in different proportions and the end result is multimedia applications.

Multimedia applications can be loosely classified as reference multimedia, training and classroom multimedia, gaming and entertainment multimedia, presentation multimedia, kiosk multimedia and others.

3.12 Keywords

- ❑ **Device drivers:** Software that provides the necessary interface required for interactions between the operating system and the multimedia hardware peripherals attached to the system.

Chapter 4
Understanding Digital Data

CHAPTER OVERVIEW

This small chapter is devoted to digital data. Remember that all multimedia contents are nothing but digital data.

The chapter begins with an overview of what an analog signal is and why it cannot be used in computers, followed by discussions on digital signals and the process of converting analog signals to digital data (often called as the digitising process).

Two important parameters connected with digitising process viz. the sampling rate and the sampling size - have also been dealt with, in detail.

4.1 Introduction

Various kinds of media, as we perceive them in our daily life with the help of electronic equipments - say, the music that's coming out of a tape recorder or the movie clip that's being broadcast in television - all of these are basically *Analog signals*, in nature.

But in the world of multimedia computing, all data are digital data.

Before we start exploring the media, let us understand what are all the different fundamental forms of data. We will begin with analog signals, as they were the first to arrive.

4.2 Meeting the analog signal . . .

The word *analog* means *'continuously varying'* - and in fact, the whole world is 'analog' by nature.

For example, let us consider sounds.

We produce sounds by fluctuating a medium. And this medium is the air that surrounds the sound source. When a music note is coming out of the speakers, the surrounding atmospheric air is actually compressed and decompressed at various rates - depending upon the source signal, and this process ultimately carries the media from the source to the destination - in our case, our ears.

Consequently, what it means is that there is no sound, without a medium! We may not be able to hear anything if the music is being played in vacuum.

When these variations are recorded electronically as some form of signals, say, over a magnetic media, then they become reproducible - as the signals can be understood and played back at a later point of time. This is the fundamental principle behind all electronic media handling devices and transmissions.

The signals thus recorded, are called ***analog signals***.

If we were to follow a single analog wave very closely, we will end up with something as shown in the figure. This curve, which is the most common representation of an analog signal wave, is mathematically called a ***'sine curve'***. This curve is formed by a series of crests (upward movements) and troughs (downward movements) occurring at specific intervals of time. The height of a signal wave at any point of time is its *Amplitude* and the specific time intervals, at which it occurs is called its *Frequency*.

4.3 The world of digits

Fortunately or unfortunately, the world of Computers is full of digits - zeros and ones, at the micro level. That means, at any point of time, only two states can be represented by Computers and these signals are called *Digital Signals*.

Thus, it becomes impossible to handle Analog signals using Computers, as the latter necessarily varies in magnitude, with time - continuously. So, How are we to represent sounds, movies and all other interesting media signals which are basically in Analog format, in a way computers can understand and handle?

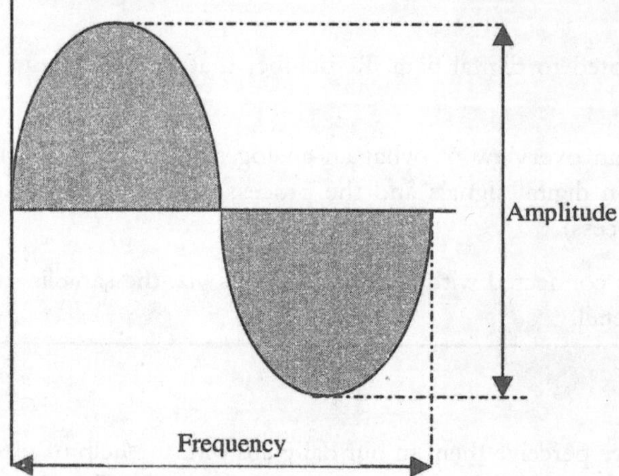

Figure 14: A typical analog signal

The technique is to create an approximately similar Digital signal, as that of the original Analog signal - using very large quantities of zeros and ones. This conversion process will be applied to multimedia data – before it is fed into the computers.

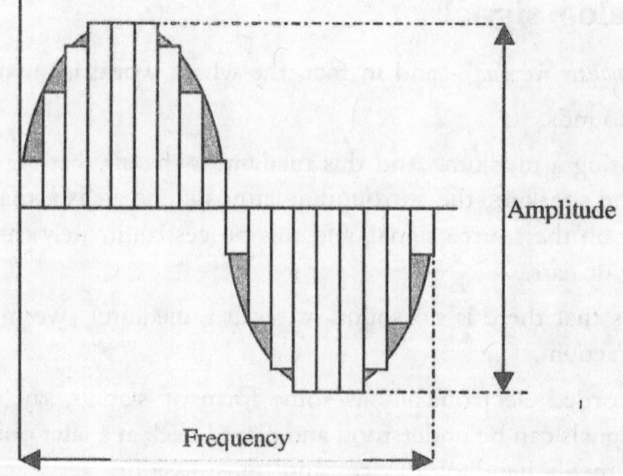

Figure 15: Analog to digital conversion process

The following figure, illustrates this process of converting Analog signals to equivalent Digital signals.

In a way, it is nothing but fooling around the innocent computers, to manage aliens signals - by representing them in a form that's familiar to them.

But, this technique demands its own price to pay: Usage of binary digits in very large quantities results in voluminous data! And that's why necessarily all multimedia programs and data file sizes are incomparably huge!

This principle of *'Digitising'* the Analog source signals, is the very heart of all multimedia Computing. Almost all multimedia handling peripherals and devices, which we met earlier in the earlier chapters, basically try to accomplish, only this.

For example, a Sound card converts the Analog sound signals to Digital signals and feed them into the Computer during recording. It also converts all digital data, after all editing and manipulations, back to their earlier form, during playback.

4.4 Secrets of digital recording

Let us take a good look at a typical Digitised wave signal, which is shown in the figure below:

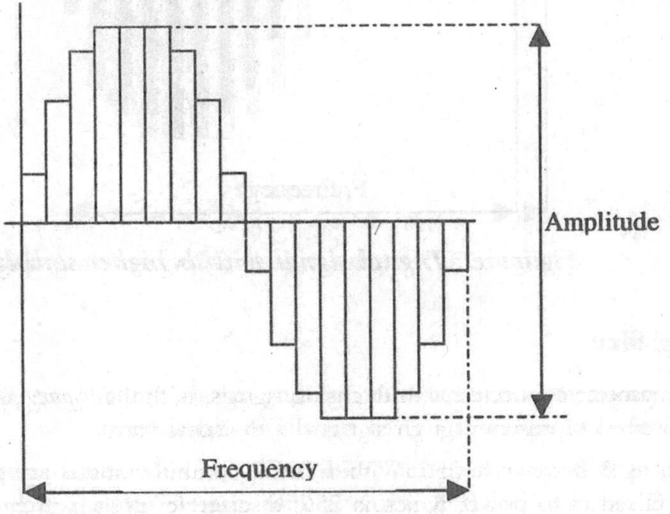

Figure 16: A typical Digital signal

It's more or less like a staircase steps that ascend and descend perpetually. You can see how a sample of the original Waveform has been recorded, over precise increments of time- by repeating which - the original signal has been reconstructed intelligently.

4.4.1 Sampling Rate

How often these samples are taken during digitising, is called the *'Sampling Rate'* and is a very important parameter in reconstructing the original signal. Because, closer these samples are (i.e. at lesser time intervals), better is the similarity between the source and the digitised signal.

In other words, a higher sampling rate implies that more samples are taken during the given time interval and ultimately, the quality of reconstruction is better.

To illustrate this, I've included another digitised sample of the same source signal we saw earlier. This time, it has a higher sampling rate than it's predecessor. You will notice that this wave is closer in its construction to the original source signal, than its predecessor.

The Sampling rate is measured in terms of ***Hertz***, Hz in short, which is the term for Cycles per second. A Sampling

Rate of 6000 Hz (or 6 kHz, which is a more common usage) implies that the samples are taken - 6000 times in one second: and this signal will be better than one with a 4000 Hz Sampling Rate.

However, there is a cache here: Higher Sampling rates *also* imply, whether you like it or not, increased file sizes! So, a compromise must be stuck between the quality of the Signal and Size of the resulting file.

Usually, a sampling rate that is twice as that of the highest frequency expected from the source, is made use of. For example, if you're recording a Sound signal which reaches, say, around 2000 Hz at its maximum level (Which is typical for a human voice), then you can comfortably use a sampling rate of 4000 Hz - for decent reproduction.

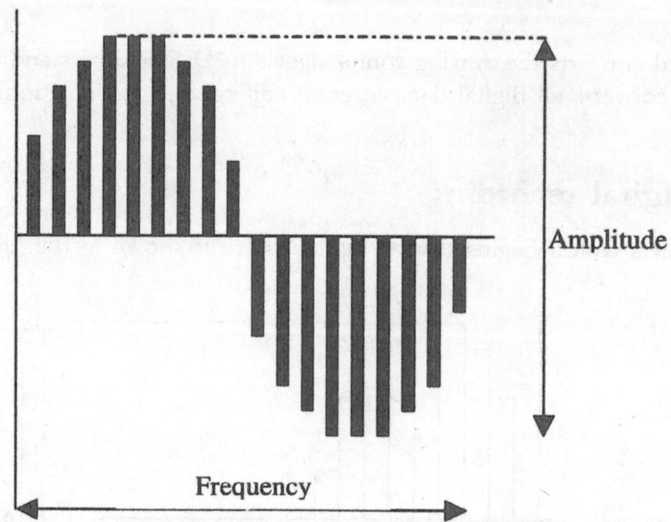

Figure 17: Digital signal with higher sampling rate

4.4.2 Sampling Size

Another important parameter connected with digitising signals, is the '*Sampling Size*' - which is the number of zeros and ones (Bits), required to represent a given signal - in digital form.

For example, by using 8 Bits, we have 256 (With 1 Bit, 2 combinations are possible; so, with 8 Bits, the possible combinations are -2 raised to power 8, which is 256) discrete levels, which can be used to construct an Analog signal.

Again, the higher the sampling size, the better is the reproduction, as the reconstruction of the signal will be closer to the original.

Thus, a digitised signal with 16 Bit Sampling size, which implies a whooping 65,536 discrete levels, is much more indistinguishable from the original signal, than its 8 Bit partner; Similarly, a 32 Bit recordings sound a lot better than 16 Bit.... and, Hold your breath! Some professional recordings even employ 64 bits of sampling size! And, of course the menace is sill out there: As you increase the sampling size, the file sizes become astonishingly huge!

So here is the lesson to remember:

In digitising any source signal, engage higher sampling rates and sampling sizes - after taking care of the expected file sizes and the storage space available for recording multimedia data.

Multimedia computing did not evoke good response in its infancy, as a good digital video clip file with sound lasting for just one minute sat on a mind boggling 45 to 50 MB of hard disk space...and when a few animations and graphics were added...Good heavens! The hard disk was full!

So, the need for a huge, powerful and yet, commercially viable storage medium was strongly felt and it was only after the introduction of the reliable CD-ROM storages, which could store more than 600 MB of data effortlessly at bare minimal costs, that multimedia rose to its full bloom.

4.5 Summary

Almost all kinds of media that we perceive in our daily life are basically analog signals - or continuously varying signals. But computers can handle only digital data. Hence, all of these analog signals must be converted to digital signals, before they can be processed using computers.

This conversion process is called digitising and almost all multimedia peripherals perform this process.

Two important parameters that govern the ultimate quality of digitising are: sampling rate and sampling size.

4.6 Keywords

- **Analog signals:** Continuously varying signals, used to record media wave patterns.
- **Digital signals:** Signals constructed solely using zeros and ones, which the computers can understand and handle.
- **Digitising:** The process of converting analog signals to equivalent digital signals, by way of taking discrete samples.
- **Sampling rate:** The time interval taken between two samples of the original analog data, during digitising process.
- **Sampling size:** The number of zeros and ones (bits) required to represent a given analog signal, in digital form.

PART III

MULTIMEDIA AUDIO

PART OVERVIEW

Multimedia digital audio gets the privilege of being the first media to be explored in detail, in our ongoing discussions on various aspects of multimedia technology.

Detailed chapters on various design / production and programming aspects of digital audio take you to the very depth of core multimedia professionalism.

The first chapter introduces the underlying principles of digital audio. Second and third chapters deal with the celebrated sound cards or audio cards in great detail. The last two chapters mercilessly crack down the myths surrounding MIDI (Musical instrument digital interface) technology and let you explore the joy of creating your own synthesized music.

Chapter 5

Digital Audio

CHAPTER OVERVIEW

This chapter is a curtain raiser for our detailed discussions on digital audio technology.

Some of these discussions may sound a lot similar to our earlier discussions on digital data – but please note that digital audio is characterised by its own dimensions and attributes that distinguish them from general digitising process characteristics.

5.1 Introduction

Computers were making sounds (noises?) even before the advent of multimedia and digital audio technology.

Small beep sounds meant that the user was trying in vain, to accomplish a task that the computer has failed to recognize - a missing comma... perhaps, and when he pressed the 'Enter' key again and again in irritation, the computer beep was actually a warning to notify that the user was actively engaging himself in the process of impairing the innocent keyboard.

And sounds louder than a polite beep meant something much worse - may be, the paper deck had slipped out of the printer carriage again or your five year old was finally successful in pulling the draw containing all those backup floppies and files, out of the computer table!

Sigh!

Things are much better now and multimedia technology has taken us far away - You can listen to your favourite CD Music album, even during the office hours...if the earphone is small enough to skip the attention of your fellow employees and more so, your boss.

So, Welcome to the world of multimedia digital audio technology!

I can understand your urge to meet those sound blasters and the notorious MIDIs... But, wait!

The digital audio theory first, please.

5.2 Digital audio definition

Digital audio is the technology, by which sound signals are represented as a series of binary digital data - necessarily zeros and ones - which the computers can understand and comprehend.

Once digitised, the sounds can be processed like any other binary file, using the relevant audio editing and playback software. It is the responsibility of the audio software, to understand and interpret the sounds properly.

5.3 Why going digital?

Though the primary purpose of digitising sound is to make the multimedia computer understand and comprehend audio signals, we do get some additional benefits in this exercise.

There are certain unique features, which Digital audio enjoys over its predecessor – Analog audio. Let us see what they are and how they are beneficial to us.

- Digital audio is less susceptible to degradation or distortion, as it gets edited and processed. Or, we can also say that we have better control over the degree of quality degradation and distortion that is permissible.
- Editing audio with computers makes cutting, pasting and manipulating the parent signals, very easy. Also, lots of special effects like 'echo' or 'reverberation' can be artificially added, thus giving us more room for creativity.
- It is possible to record, edit and mix digital audio, without the need for expensive equipments. In a while from now, we will see how to set up an inexpensive multi track recorder and mixer – right inside your drawing room! On the other hand, Analog audio demands very expensive Hardware and a host of equipments to accomplish the same.
- Digital audio can be stored as digital data, in reliable mediums like the CD-ROMs - thus extending their shelf life to more than fifty years on an average without losses! Compare it with magnetic media like tapes – which are very difficult to maintain, over the years.

All these benefits are, however, subjected to the fact that the original data should have been digitised in high quality. It is rather difficult to improve the quality of a bad digital recording.

Today, digital audio has almost become the 'de-facto' standard for all professional recording / playback and distribution purposes.

5.4 Audio sampling

As with other forms of digitizing, Digital audio files are constructed by receiving Analog signals, taking out samples of the same at certain intervals and reconstructing the pattern using zeros and ones. This conversion process is often known ; audio sampling.

Special processing chips and electronic circuits, technically called Analog to digital converters (ADC), are used to accomplish this.

Refer the following figure, for a schematic representation of this process.

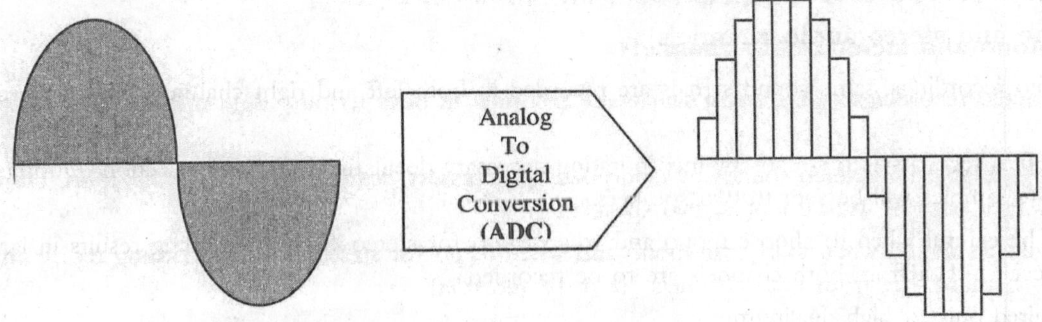

Figure 18: ADC and DAC Processes

5.5 Audio sampling parameters

As with any other digitizing process, digital audio data quality is controlled by two main attributes: Audio sampling rate and Audio sampling size. Apart from these two, mono and stereo channels – which characterise all audio signals, also come into play.

5.5.1 Audio Sampling Rate

Audio sampling rate refers to the rate, at which sound samples are recorded, from the incoming Analog audio source. Sampling rates are measured per channel, along the X-axis - in terms of Hertz (Hz), which is the unit for cycles per second.

If your Audio card's manual says that the operating frequency is 11 kHz (Kilo Hertz - equal to one thousand Cycles per second), then, it means that around 11,000 audio samples are taken - in one second!

The higher the frequency, the better -because, if more number of samples are taken during a given time interval, then the wave reconstruction is relatively smooth and resembles the original signal – better.

The four sampling rates or sampling frequencies that are often used are: 11.025 kHz, 22.05 kHz, 44.1 kHz and 48 kHz. In order to appreciate the varying quality of audio these different sampling rates can produce, let us construct a table.

Table 7: Sampling rates and quality

Sampling rate (in kHz)	Quality
8	Telephone voice
18.9	CD-ROM/ XA standard
32	Digital radio / Televisions
44.1	CD Audio
48	DAT (Digital Audio Tape) recording – used in recording studios.

I mostly use **44.1 kHz** for all my music recordings.

5.5.2 Audio sampling size

Audio sampling size refers to the number of zeros and ones used to record the incoming signal. It is recorded along the Y-axis. This size depends upon the bits of data your digital sound systems can handle. Typically, an eight-bit sound system can record signals at around 256 quantum steps.

Larger audio sampling sizes can produce better quality sounds. A sixteen-bit recording is adequate for all normal usage, though professional recordings demand thirty-two bits or more.

5.5.3 Mono and stereo audio channels

In Mono audio recordings, same sound signals are recorded in both left and right channels. But in stereo, they're different.

Digital audio files record stereo sounds by incorporating necessary details in their header section. During playback, alternating byte samples will be sent to two speakers.

Once should be careful when to choose mono and when to go for stereo. Stereo recording results in larger audio file sizes – because data from both channels are to be recorded.

Stereo is required only *for* high quality music.

For other sounds and speeches, go in for mono recording without second thoughts.

5.6 Digital audio recording pitfalls

Normally, two types of problems can be anticipated in digital audio recording processes:

- ❑ **Quantization:** The value of each sound sample, during ADC process, is rounded off to the nearest integer value and it sometimes results in unwanted background noise.

- ❑ **Clipping:** During ADC, if the amplitude of the samples is greater than the intervals available, the wave is clipped in the top and the bottom and it sometimes results in severe distortions of fine music.

The sampling parameters have to be carefully assigned, in order to avoid quantization and clipping.

5.7 Digital audio file sizes

Uncompressed digital audio files consume huge disk space. An approximate idea of the disk space requirements - for a specific digital audio recording, can be calculated using the following formula:

Disk space required per second of recording (in Bits) = Sampling size (in Hz) × Sampling rate (in Bits) × Channel Multiplication Factor.

Note: Channel Multiplication factor is 1 for Mono recordings; 2 for stereo.

For example, a 16 bit Sound System, recording signals at 44 kHz in stereo will take up 16 × 44000 × 2 = 176000 bytes or roughly 172 KB per second!

5.8 Digital audio playback

During playback, the digital audio files are converted back to their parent form viz. analog signals and are fed into the speakers .The process involved is necessarily a reversal of A D C i.e. Digital to Analog conversion (DAC). Refer the following figure for a schematic representation of the same.

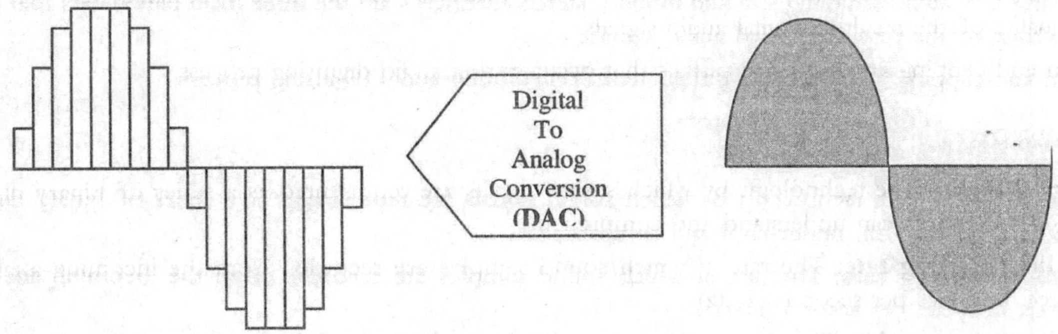

Figure 19: DAC Processes

The basic digital sound manipulation systems in almost all of the current multimedia computers are usually built up with their own amplifier circuits and can handle around 4 W at 4 Ohms on each channels; but, if you want to have a really 'surround' stereo effects-drop it at the earliest opportunity and go in for better amplifications using external amplification circuits, accompanied by higher capacity speakers.

It is not necessary that the digital sound should always be converted to analog signals for output. Some of the latest digital audio devices and digital speaker systems can accept digital signals directly from the sound card.

In fact, many professional multimedia audio cards today, come with dedicated jacks for analog output and digital output!

5.9 Digital audio file formats

The table lists down all the popular digital audio file formats in use:

Table 8: Popular audio file formats

File format	Remarks
Wav	Microsoft's wave file format. Most famous in windows. Uncompressed.
Aiff	Apple's Audio interchange file format. Used in Silicon graphics machines as well.
Mp3	MPEG Audio – Layer 3. Most famous in the Internet. Compressed.
Ra	Real audio. Well known for streaming audio with no footprints on the local computer. Compressed.
Voc	Creative's sound blaster format
au	Sun's audio format.

5.10 Summary

Digitising is the processes of representing audio signals as a series of zeros and ones.

Apart from being comprehensible to computers, digital audio has several advantages over analog signals.

Audio sampling rate, audio sampling size and mono / stereo channels - are the three main parameters that ultimately decide the quality of the resulting digital audio signals.

Quantization and clipping are two usual pitfalls that occur during audio digitising process.

5.11 Keywords

- **Digital audio**: The technology, by which sound signals are represented as a series of binary digital data, which computers can understand and comprehend.
- **Audio sampling rate**: The rate at which sound samples are recorded from the incoming analog audio source, in cycles per second (Hertz)
- **Audio sampling size**: The number of zeros and ones used to record the incoming analog signal, in bits of data.

Chapter 6

The Sound Cards

CHAPTER OVERVIEW

This chapter features in depth discussions on multimedia sound cards –the physical hardware devices that enable computers to make noise...sorry, music.

It starts with the basic composition of a sound card, followed by various analog devices that can connect to the sound card using various jacks. This is followed by procedures on how to rightly configure the sound card in a windows 2000 environment. The chapter concludes with discussions on audio compression-decompression schemes and other miscellaneous topics.

Schematic and diagrammatic representations of the concepts explained have been presented throughout the chapter.

6.1 Introduction

We saw, in the previous chapter, that the digital recording and playback is achieved by means of ADC and DAC Converters. All these conversion circuitry and a host of other electronic circuits that perform various other audio manipulation functions are bundled into the multimedia computers, in the form of electronic Printed circuit Boards. These boards are usually known as the *sound cards* or *audio cards.*

Though the basic function of sound cards is simple digital audio recording and playback, over a period of time, they have grown to encompass complex functionality like MIDI recording / playback, Wavetable synthesis, Environmental audio etc.

6.2 Basic composition of a sound card

Almost all sound cards available in the market today, consist of the following devices:

- An ADC Converter for capturing the incoming analog audio signals
- A DAC Converter for converting digital audio back to analog signals
- A Digital signal processor (DSP) for doing various audio computations
- Direct memory access (DMA) Channels for reading and writing audio data.
- A RAM memory chip for dedicated audio memory
- MIDI Interface for connecting MIDI compatible music instruments like Keyboards
- IN and OUT Jacks for connecting microphones, headphones, speakers and many other devices
- A Gaming port for joystick
- A CD ROM Interface

Most of the new generation cards fit into what is called a PCI (Peripheral Component Interconnect) Slot.

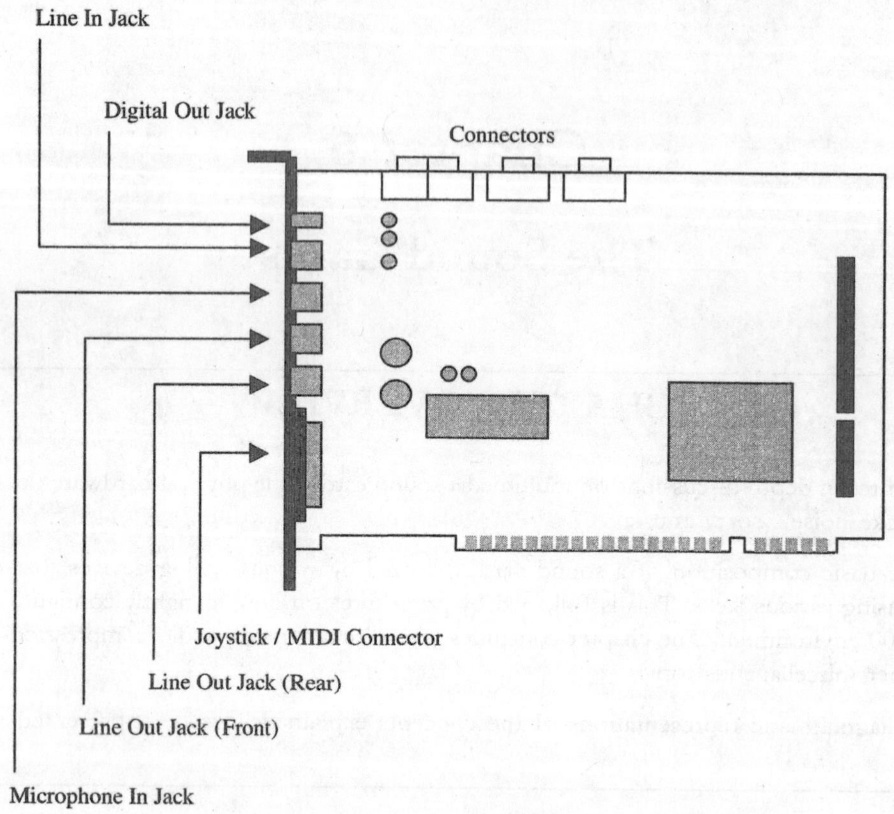

Figure 20: Basic composition of a sound card

Please do not buy the relatively older ISA Slot cards – even though they may seem to be somewhat cheaper than PCI! Because ISA audio cards are things of a bygone era and you will soon find that you have to replace it with a PCI.

6.3 Sound card connectivity

A sound card may be connected to many input sources and output devices - through relevant external jacks. The following table attempts to provide an overview of these connectivity options available:

Table 9: Sound card connectivity options

Source	Input / Output device	Jack /Connector
Analog input sources	Microphone	Mic In
	Radio / Tape recorder	Line In
	CD Player	CD Audio Connector
Digital input sources	DAT (Digital Audio Tape) advanced models only)	RCA SPDIF In(Available in
	CD-ROM Drive	

Analog output devices	Headphones / small speakers	Line Out
	External amplifiers and surround sound speakers	Line Out (Front / Rear)
Digital output device	DAT (Digital Audio Tape) advanced models only)	RCA SPDIF Out(Available in
	CD-Recordable	
	Digital speaker systems	Digital out
Others	Joystick / Gaming devices	Joystick / MIDI Port
	MIDI compatible music keyboard	Joystick / MIDI Port

Kindly note that all these different devices require appropriate cables and wires, to get connected to the jacks meant for them. For example, a tape recorder needs a male-to-male stereo pin – to hook on to the sound card.

These cables / pins and wires adopt different sets of international standards. You should choose the devices and sound card in such a way that you could ultimately hook on the devices without much trouble.

The diagram illustrates some of the input / output devices connecting to the sound card.

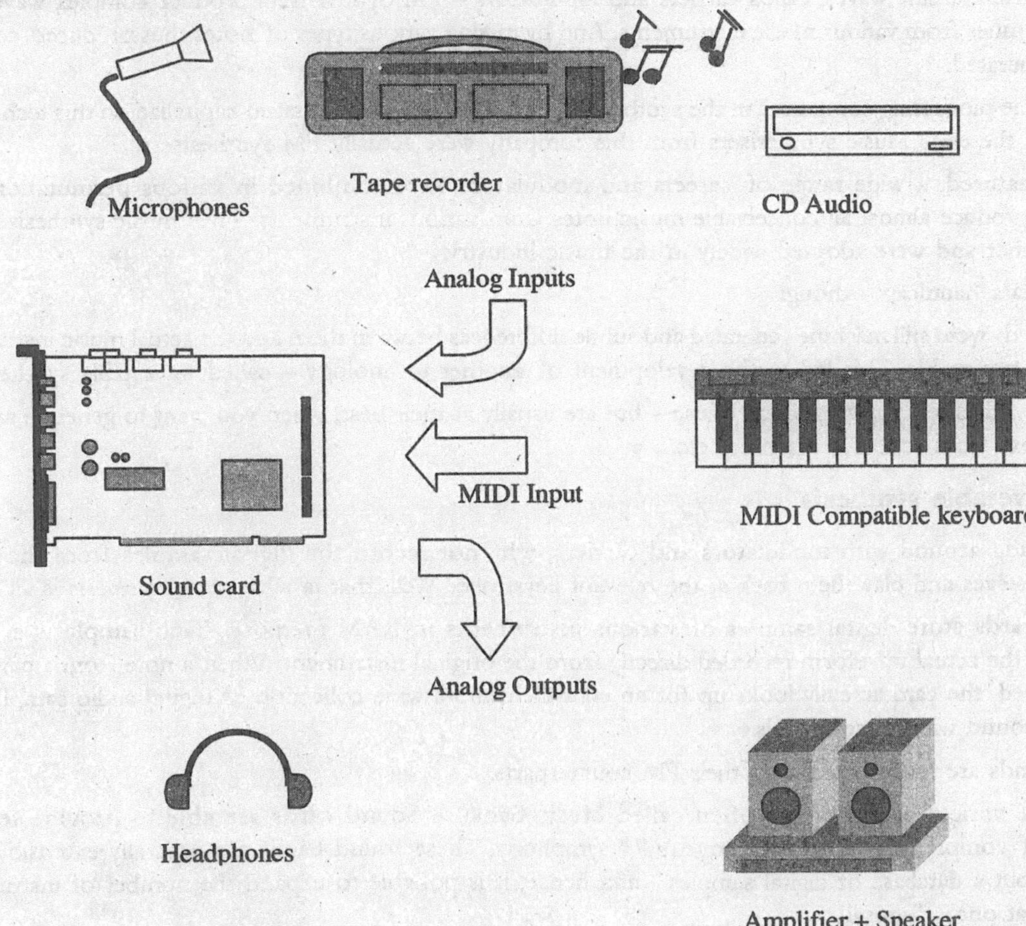

Figure 21: Sound card connectivity

6.4 Sound cards as CD drive interfaces

CD ROM drives with IDE interface need an IDE card for working with the motherboard. Almost all Sound cards today come bundled with this IDE interface for CD ROM Drives. Hence, if you are buying a Sound card, you may as well save a slot in your Motherboard by not fixing an IDE interface card.

A small cable links this Sound card IDE interface with CD ROM Drive. Your sound card kit should come bundled with this cable.

6.5 Music synthesis

The process by which a sound card "creates" Music is called *the Sound synthesis or the Audio synthesis technology*. In fact, many of the music keyboards we know - like Casio and Yamaha, make use of similar technology to reproduce the notes of various tunes and percussion instruments.

There are two fundamental types of Audio synthesis: *The FM Synthesis* and *The Wavetable Synthesis.*

6.5.1 The FM synthesis

FM synthesis is a relatively older technology.

By mixing two different sine waves, called carriers and modulators – FM Synthesisers produce complex waveforms that resemble the tunes from various music instruments. And by mixing various types of notes thus produced, complex music can be generated.

Yamaha, one of the pioneering companies in the synthesised music today, was the first to capitalize on this technology and almost all of the early Music synthesisers from this company were actually FM synthesisers.

As technology matured, a wide range of careers and modulators were combined in various permutations and combinations to produce almost all conceivable music notes from various instruments. Thus music synthesisers and keyboards got richer and were adopted widely in the music industry.

But one thing was a handicap – though.

FM synthesis sounds were still machine generated and subtle differences between them and the actual music instruments were, very much, noticeable. This led to the development of another technology – called wave table synthesis.

As on date, FM synthesisers are very much in use – but are usually at their best, when you want to generate artificial sounds – like those from robots / machines etc.

6.5.2 The wavetable synthesis

Instead of blending around with modulators and carriers, why not record the digital samples from the actual instruments themselves and play them back at the relevant keystroke? Well, that is what wave synthesis is all about!

Wave synthesis cards store digital samples of various instruments in RAM memory. Each sample is a digital representation of the actual waveform recorded directly from the original instrument. When a note from a particular instrument is played, the card actually looks up for an equivalent in its wide collection of digital audio samples and reconstructs the sound with those models.

The resulting sounds are much better than their FM counterparts.

By having a wide variety of samples – often called Music banks – Sound cards are able to provide realistic representations of complex notes like Beethoven's 7th symphony. These sound banks are naturally extensible – as they are nothing but a database of digital samples - and hence, it is possible to expand the number of instruments that are available at one's disposal.

How real, can Wavetable synthesis, bring Computer generated music close to the original ones? Well, it depends on the following factors:

- ❑ The overall quality of the sample recordings. Better the quality closer will be the reproduction.

- The frequency used for recording samples. Suitable frequencies should be adopted for playing back various ranges of notes.
- The number of samples recorded per instruments. Wider variety of samples ensures better range of notes. But more samples obviously result in more memory.
- The audio compression algorithms used to store and retrieve samples. Compressions that do not deter the quality of original recordings will result in high quality reproductions.

6.6 Motherboard integrated audio peripherals

Instead of having the pain of installing a new additional peripheral for handling audio, many motherboard manufacturers, these days – bundle sound card capabilities right into the motherboard itself, in the form of a dedicated audio chipset.

While this option certainly saves some bucks from leaving your purse, it is generally noticed that the audio capabilities they offer are very minimal and are unlikely to satisfy a multimedia professional.

Hence we will not be discussing much about them.

6.7 Configuring sound cards under Windows 2000

When a new Sound card is inserted into the PCI Slot and the computer is rebooted, it is highly likely that Windows 2000 will find a suitable driver for the card from its database and may install the same, if you give the go ahead. It may ask for the Win 2000 CDs, if the driver is not available in the hard disk.

However, as we had observed in one of the earlier chapters, it is always better to make use of the manufacturer's device driver, in order to obtain better performances and have greater control over the hardware.

The lesson is: *Never ever forget the device driver CD ROM – when you purchase a sound card!*

This should particularly be kept in mind, when you are making OEM purchases – without nicely packaged boxes and installation tool books.

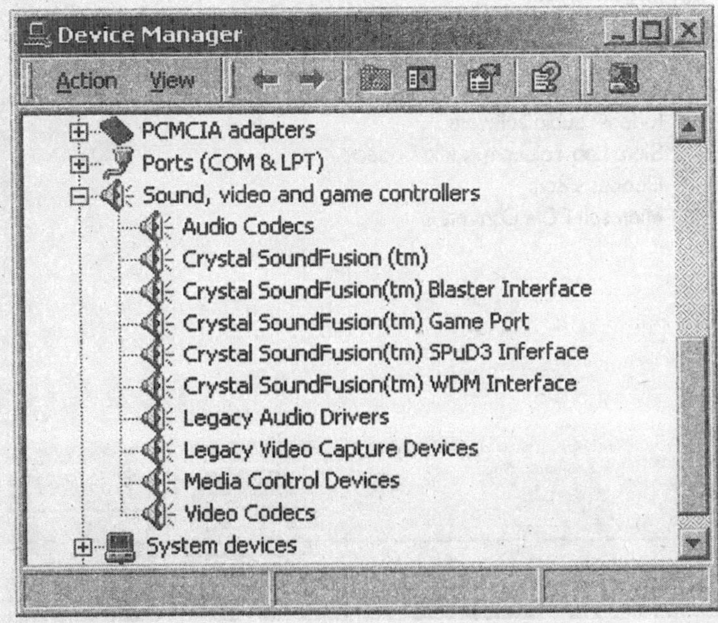

Figure 22: Device manager panel, showing all the audio devices installed.

Once a sound card is properly installed on the system, the device manager should list out all the corresponding audio devices – as shown below:

6.8 Audio codecs

Apart from device drivers, Windows need one more set of software for playing back a wide variety of sound formats. These are called audio codecs (acronym for compression – decompression algorithms).

Figure 23: Reaching audio codecs properties

You can take a quick look at the various audio codecs installed on your system, by right clicking the audio codecs icon under device manager and choosing properties.

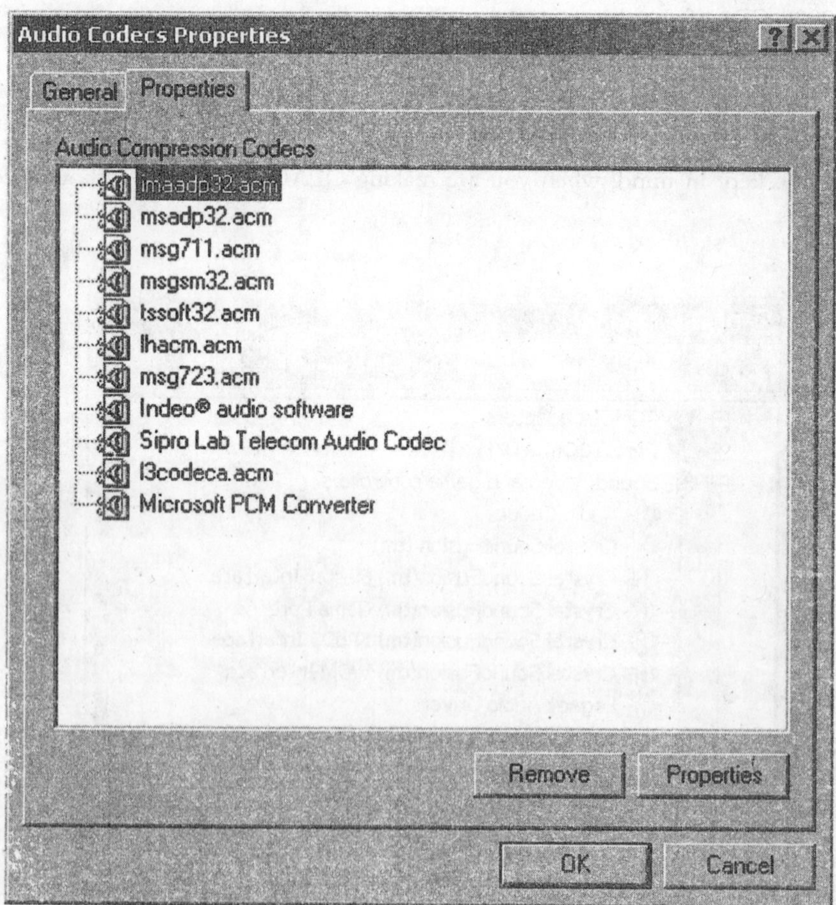

Figure 24: Audio codecs installed

Windows does not store audio in its natural form – because of stupendous memory requirements. It makes use of some compression algorithm while storing audio data and applies the decompression algorithms during playback. Mp3 technology – which has revolutionised online music distribution via the Internet – is nothing but an advanced audio compression- decompression algorithm!

Windows 2000 comes bundled with a host of audio codecs, and Windows media player is capable of downloading the relevant codecs via the Internet, on demand.

6.9 Capabilities of sound card

Almost all sound cards available in the market today, are capable of performing many functions, as detailed in the table below.

Table 10: Functionalities of a Sound card

Core function	Remarks
Digital audio playback	Play back various kinds of digital audio files
CD Playback	Play Audio CDs from CD-ROM
Digital audio recording	Record music from microphone and various other analog sound sources.
Digital audio editing	Manipulate the audio signals recorded as digital data
MIDI Playback / Recording	Synthesized music recording / creation and playback
Joystick	Providing an interface for Joystick / Gaming devices.

We will be looking at many of these functions in great detail, in the chapters that follow.

6.10 Summary

Audio cards are electronic PCB boards that basically perform analog to digital conversions and digital to analog conversions, apart from a host of other functions. Three main types of audio cards are the sound cards, the midi interface cards and the wave blaster cards. The process by which a sound card creates music is called the sound synthesis. Currently wave synthesis technology is widely in use.

Sound cards perform a variety of complex audio handling functions including digital audio playback and recording, CD audio playback, and MIDI audio playback and recording.

The sound cards have to be properly configured under the host operating system, in order to perform to its fullest potential.

6.11 Keywords

- **FM synthesis:** The technique of blending around with a range of frequency modulations to produce audio that resembles the original analog sound data.
- **Wavetable synthesis:** The technique of bundling a wide variety of built in sound samples (i.e. actual recordings) of various music instruments and reconstructing the sounds by looking up for samples.

Chapter 7

Audio Recording and Editing Techniques

CHAPTER OVERVIEW

Having seen so many concepts and theories related to digital audio, are you in a dire urge to "do something"? This chapter shows you the way…

First learn how to play different audio files using different multimedia content players. Understand what is the difference between different kinds of players and wonder why there are so many varieties of players in the market.

A more exciting exercise would be to do a piece of digital recording on your own! You may want to dust out some of your old Hindi song collections in cassettes and convert them as mp3s or sing a karaoke number and distribute it to friends.

Interesting discussions on one of the famous audio editing tools available in the market – Syntrillium's Cool Edit 2000 – makes this chapter even more compelling.

7.1 Introduction

Having seen the configuration and installation of a sound card, it is time to make use of them to jazz up our drawing rooms or create some captivating karaoke numbers from the oldies!

In this chapter, we will be learning all the tips and tricks to do professional playback and recordings.

7.2 Capabilities of a sound card

Table 11: Functionalities of a Sound card

Core function	Remarks
Digital audio playback	Play back various kinds of digital audio files
CD Playback	Play Audio CDs from CD-ROM
Digital audio recording	Record music from microphone and various other analog sound sources.
Digital audio editing	Manipulate the audio signals recorded as digital data
Audio file manipulation	Audio file format compression / transformations
MIDI Playback / Recording	Synthesized music recording / creation and playback
Joystick	Providing an interface for Joystick / Gaming devices.

Almost all sound cards available in the market today, are capable of performing many kinds of audio editing, recording and manipulation functions. The following table details some of the functions that can be expected in most cards. The rest of our chapter is devoted to mastering each of these functionalities.

7.3 Digital audio playback

Today, quite a number of free and shareware software are available in the Internet, for playing a very wide variety of digital audio file formats. The file formats that are frequently used, include .wav, .mp3, .aif, .aiff, .mid, .snd, .au,.mpa, .wma etc.

Let us first list out some of the most famous digital audio playback software available today. It should be noted that many of the players mentioned below, are not just restricted to digital audio alone; they handle a wide variety of other multimedia file formats as well.

Table 12: Some of the famous digital audio playback software

Software	Remarks
Windows media player	Play back various kinds of digital audio files
Apple's QuickTime media player	Play Audio CDs from CD-ROM
Media one	Play back various kinds of digital audio files
Creative media player	Play back various kinds of digital audio files

7.4 Windows media player

Windows media player, from Microsoft – is perhaps, the de facto multimedia player, on the Windows platform. Since its inception in Windows 95 days, this software has been growing from strength to strength. Today, it is a very powerful application that supports many advanced features in digital media playback and recording.

Windows media player is much more than a multimedia player – it is a Jukebox, CD Recorder and surround sound creator – all combined into one. The only hitch is its massive size: the latest version is around 13 MB!

First, let us see the different versions of Windows media player and the Operating systems they support.

Table 13: Different versions of windows media player

Windows Media Player version	Supported platforms
9 series	Best with Windows XP – but is also available for Win 98 SE, Millennium Edition (ME) and Win 2000.
7.1	Win 98, Win 2000 and Millennium Edition (ME), Mac OS 8.1 and above
6.4	Windows 95, Win NT 4

The 9 series is understandably a very complex beast with multitudes of functions and capabilities.

In this book, we will limit our discussions to Version 9 under windows 2000; and in the present chapter, our concentration is on the audio capabilities of the same.

7.4.1 Downloading and installing media player

The home of Windows media player is located at the following URL:

http://www.microsoft.com/windows/windowsmedia/players.aspx

This page should give you a glimpse of all the latest versions of Media players, available online. Almost all of them should be free for usage. At the time of writing this, Version 9 series was the latest.

Links for appropriate downloads should be available from the above URL – on the left-hand side navigation bar. I downloaded MPSetup.exe and installed the same without a hitch – on my Windows 2000 PC. At the end of installation, you should be careful while associating media player with all the multimedia file formats. Because, Windows media player will then become a default player for the entire range of selected file formats; and you will not be able to invoke any of your favourite players by double clicking on the file names.

Once installed, the default screen pops up and you will be able to access the program from

Start → Programs → Accessories → Entertainment → Windows media player

7.4.2 Using media player for digital audio

Media player program has the following menu items: File, View, Play, Tools and Help.

It also has the following button controls: Play, Stop, Fast-forward, Rewind, Previous and Next.

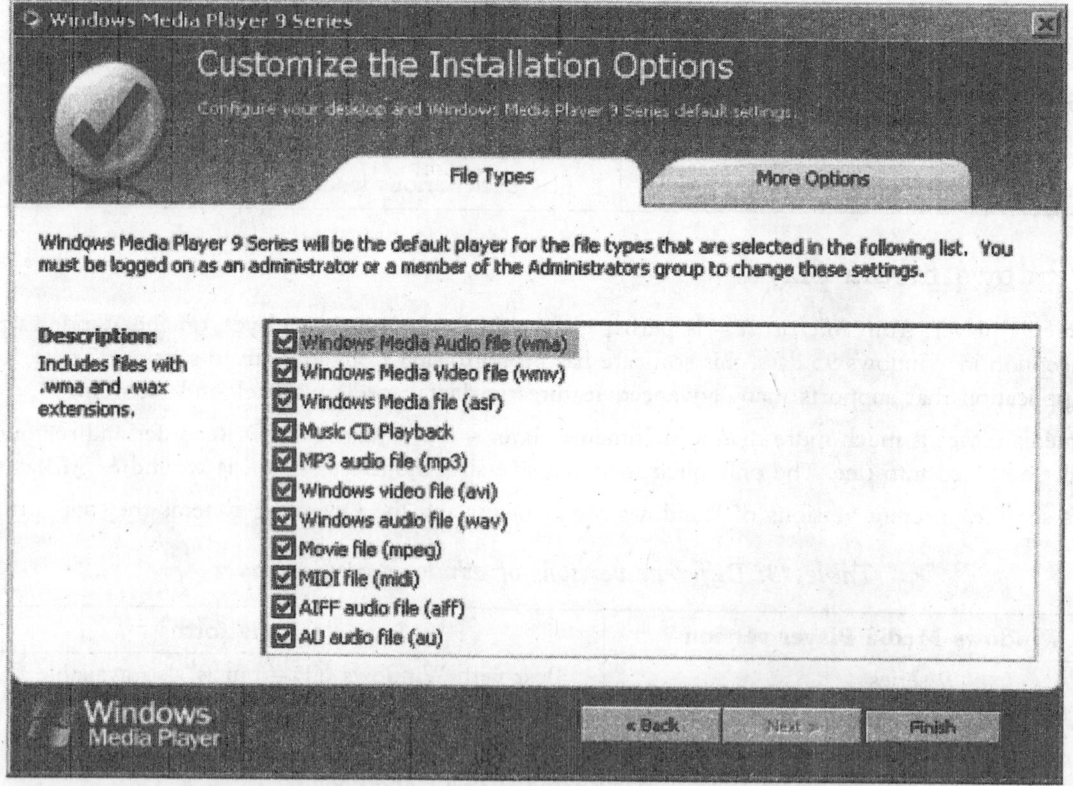

Figure 25: File format association with media player

File menu items allow you to open and close all multimedia files - including digital audio files like *.wav, *.snd, *.au, *.aif and *. aiff, MIDI audio files like *.mid, *.midi and *.rmi, Windows media audio file (*.wma.) and MPEG Audio files (.mp3)

Once a valid multimedia file is opened, all the buttons of the media player get activated. To play the file, Click on the triangular 'Play' Button. Those who don't have any other audio files to try can browse the Windows media directory for a sample. For example, if you have installed Windows under C:\Windows, then the media directory is at C:\Windows\Media.

Figure 26: Media player playing a MIDI file

7.5 Apple's QuickTime

Apple computer's QuickTime is another popular multimedia player software for Mac and Windows. The latest version can be downloaded at the following URL:

http://www.apple.com/quicktime/download/standalone/

Figure 27: QuickTime media player

Like Windows media player, you need to set up the file associations during installation. Once installed, the program can be invoked from desktop icon or from program manager group.

QuickTime plays all the digital audio file formats of the Macintosh platform like .aiff and .au. One hitch, however, is that it needs to convert some of the Windows file formats to .mov before playing... for example, if you try to open a simple MIDI file, QuickTime will say that it needs to convert this to a .mov file before playing – which is really an unwanted trouble. In such cases, you may as well play the file straight away from Windows media player!

7.6 Media One+ player

Media One is a popular shareware for playing a very wide variety of multimedia file formats.

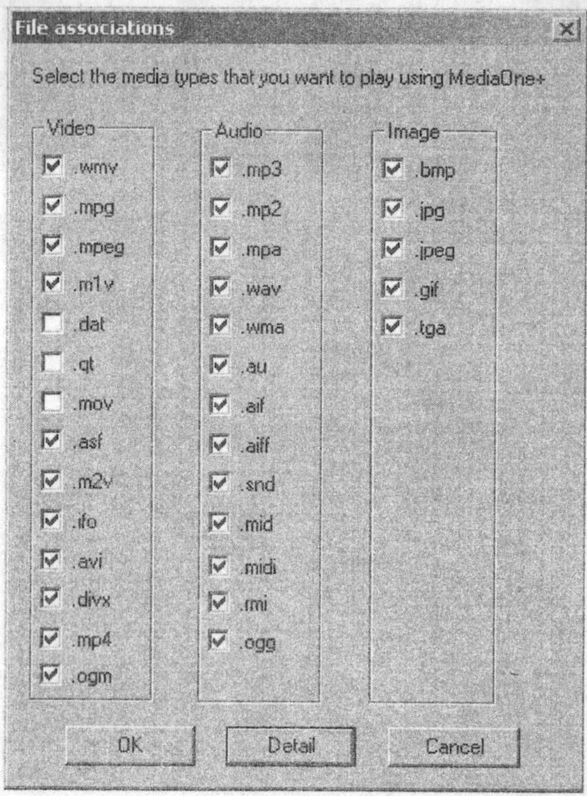

Figure 28: Media One supported file formats

It is perhaps the only player with very small memory footprint and size (around 500 KB!) and handles most of the digital audio file formats with great efficiency. Though the sophistication of windows media player cannot be expected in this cute little program, it is well worth a try!

Figure 29: Media One+ Player

The program can be downloaded from http://www.media1moon.com

7.7 Digital audio recording techniques

Sound cards can be used to record audio signals from various sources like tape recorders, microphones, CD players etc. The recorded signals will be stored in the hard disk (or any other storage mediums), in one of the preferred file formats – usually .wav in Windows.

Why do we want to record digital signals at all? Here are some of the reasons:

- ❑ You may want to convert some of your old favourites from audiotapes to mp3 or Audio CDs.
- ❑ You may want to convert your Audio CDs to mp3 collections
- ❑ You may want to sing and record your own voice or music for your personal project or simply for fun!
- ❑ You may want to do professional recordings for your multimedia project or animation video

Many of the strategies and techniques we discuss here, are meant for personal recording environments at small office / home office only. However, before concluding the topic, we will briefly discuss how professional recordings are done in recording studios and how they can be made use of – in our multimedia projects.

7.8 Audio recording software

We first need to download and install an audio capture or recording software – before even we can begin the audio recording process.

Microsoft windows operating system comes with a cute little recorder program, suitable for simple and short recordings. It is available under start à Programs à Accessories à Windows recorder. It even has some nice editing options! But, since it cannot record anything beyond a minute, it is not suitable for long recordings. At the best, you can use it to test the quality of microphones etc.

If you have purchased a sound card along with the CD-ROM that comes bundled with it, then it usually has a sophisticated recording program and it is best to make use of the same for all recordings. For example, all Creative's audio cards come bundled with their own audio recording software – with extensive options for doing various kinds of recordings.

If – by some reason or other – you do not have any recording software at hand, then you can download one of the shareware programs from the Internet. I use audio grabber software available from http://www.audiograbber.com-us.net, to do my recordings.

You can also check http://www.download.com - with the search string "sound recorder". Quite a number of shareware and freeware popped up, when I checked.

The recording software usually does not matter much – as long as it has some of the basic capabilities and is able to provide interface to line inputs and microphone inputs. But what does matter – is the recording options you set, as they have a profound impact on the ultimate quality of your recordings.

7.9 Recording options

Before we even start the recording process, we need to set-up our environment and decide upon some environment options, like whether to record the signals in mono or stereo mode, at what frequency and sampling rate to record etc.

7.9.1 Mono vs. stereo recording

Mono recording usually gives decent results with microphone based voice recordings – without any music. It can also be used for solo instrument performances or for music with minimal set of instruments. However, if you are capturing songs or music from a tape recorder or a CD audio player, better use stereo options.

Stereo recordings usually require much more space than mono recordings – since two different sound signals have to be captured and stored.

7.9.2 Sampling size

We have already discussed in one of the earlier chapters, what sampling size was and how it affected the quality of recordings. Here, we will just discuss various sampling size options available and when to use what etc.

The sampling size options, usually available are 8 Bits/sec, 16 Bits/sec, and 32 Bits/sec. The increment in the resulting file size – from 8 bits to 16 bits can be astonishing and hence should be taken note of, before hand. Otherwise, halfway through your recording – you may get disk full error from the operating system.

It is usually better to go for 16 bps recordings – unless you want to compress the ultimate file size very substantially. Even then, you can actually do the recording in 16 bps and then convert the file to 8 bps – using one of the audio editing software.

32 bits are advisable – only for very professional recordings with a wide range of notes.

7.9.3 Sampling rate

The usual sampling rates are 11.025 kHz, 22.05 kHz, 44.1 kHz and 48 kHz.

Use anything less than 22 kHz for personal recordings and 44 or 48 for professional recordings. I normally use 44.1 kHz for most of my recordings.

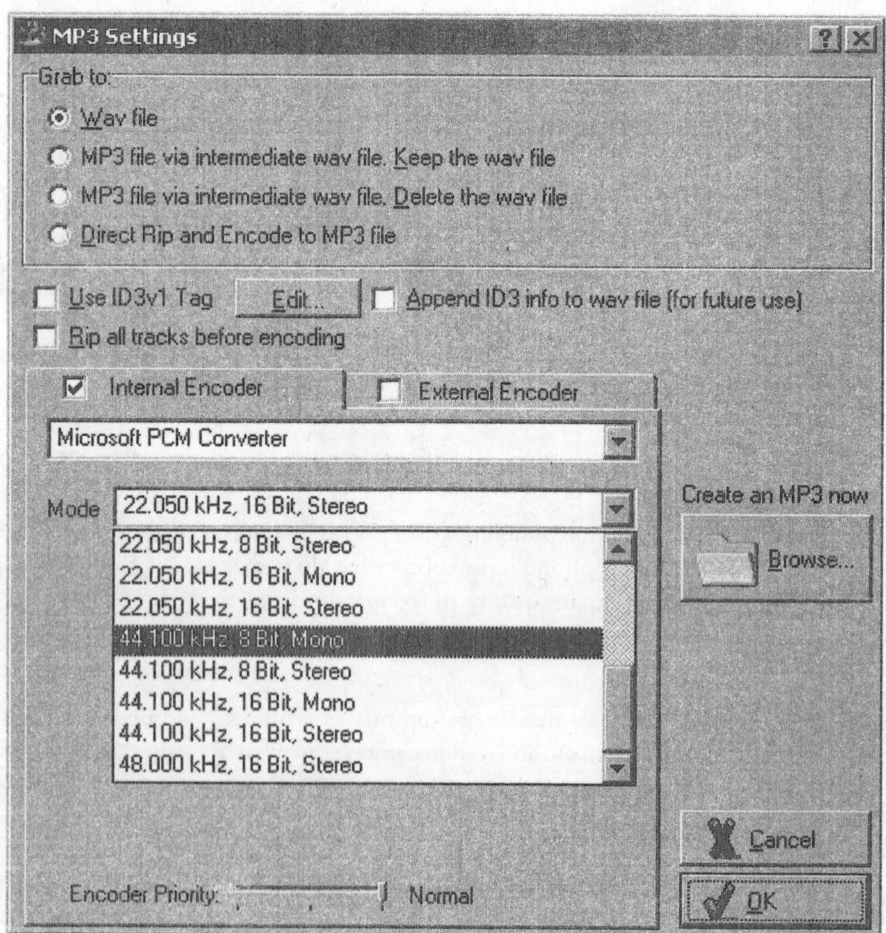

Figure 30: Setting the recording options in audio grabber software

Once you have decided upon the recording options, set those options in the recording software you are using. I've provided the illustration – with audio grabber.

7.9.4 File size requirements

The following table gives an approximate idea of the file size requirements for a one-minute recording, under various sampling rates and sizes.

Table 14: Different recording options and corresponding file sizes

Channels – Sampling size – Sampling rate	Approx. file size requirements for one-minute recording (uncompressed)
Mono – 8 bps – 11 kHz	5.03 MB
Stereo – 16 bps – 22 kHz	40.28 MB
Stereo – 16 bps – 44 kHz	80.56 MB
Stereo – 32 bps – 22 kHz	80.56 MB
Stereo – 32 bps – 44 kHz	161.13 MB

Do not worry about storing such huge files in your hard disk!

Usually, once the recording is done, we will be able to edit and compress the file using one of the codecs available and the size will become manageable, by then.

7.10 Setting up the recording environment

Doing a microphone based recording is much more difficult than a tape or CD recording – in a SOHO atmosphere.

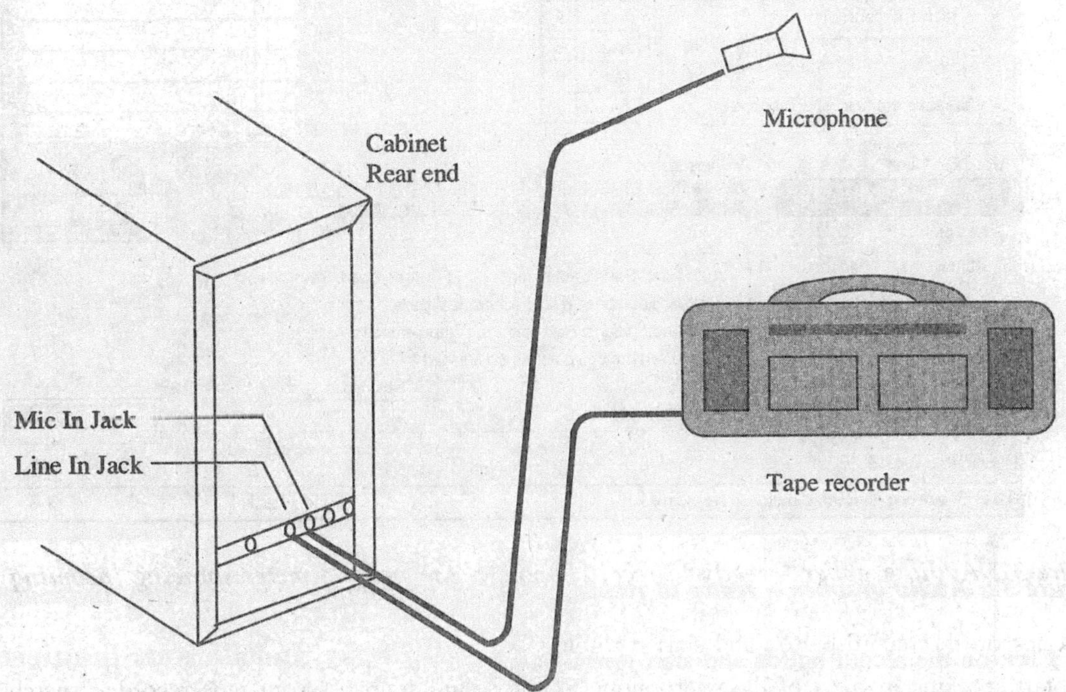

Figure 31: Setting up the audio recording equipments

If you are planning a microphone-based recording – select a place with least external noise and disturbances and move your computer there. Connect the microphone wire to the mic-in jack of the sound card, on the rear end of the cabinet – as shown in the figure.

Close all the doors and if possible, have sound absorbing materials like coir board or thermo coal around – so that the echo within the room is minimised. Set up the audio recording software with desired settings and go ahead with the recording as desired.

If you are recording something from Tape or a CD Player, then it becomes a pin-to-pin transmission of audio signal, and best results can be expected – without disturbances. All you need to do is to buy an appropriate cable with male-to-male stereo pins on either end. Then you can insert one end of the cable into sound card's line-in jack and the other into headphone jack and go ahead with the recording.

7.11 Various steps in audio recording process

1. Keep the microphone / line-in socket plugged into the sound card. If the audio source is a tape recorder, hook up the 'headphone out' or 'speaker out' jack to 'line-in ' jack of the sound card.
2. Activate the sound recorder or any other recording software from the accessories program group.
3. Verify that the volume control is adjusted properly and that the program properly receives the incoming signals.

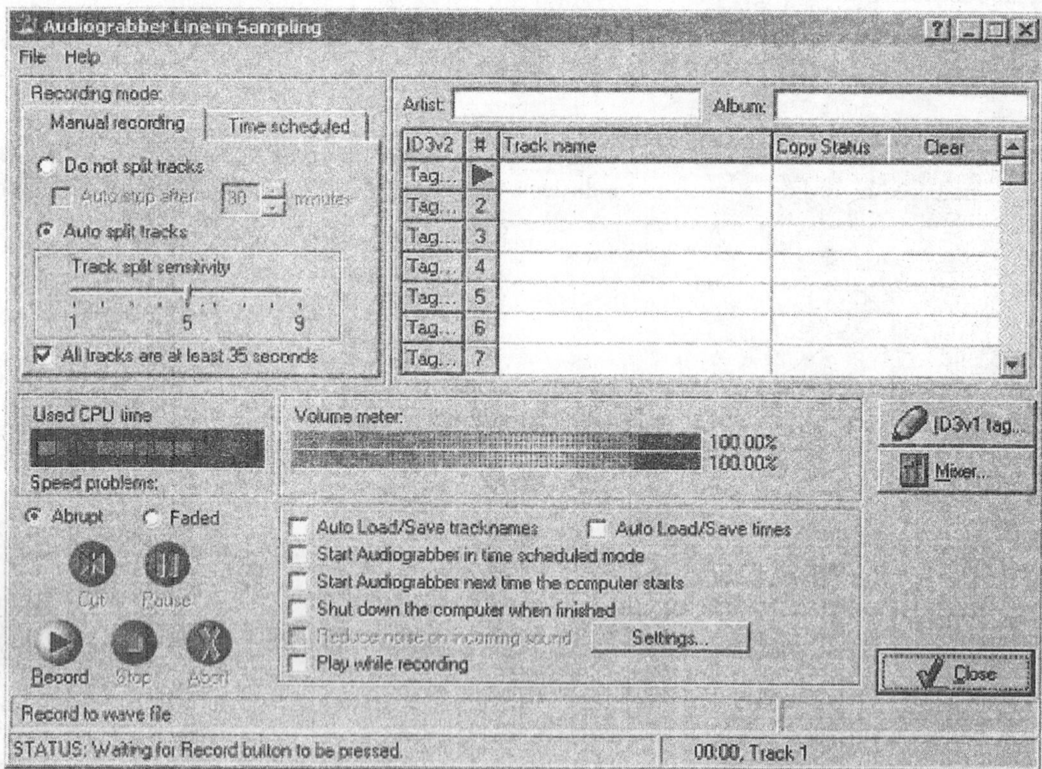

Figure 32: Audio grabber – ready to record. Look at the volume meter showing incoming signals.

4. Click on the record button and start recording.
5. Start speaking in front of the microphone. If the sound source is your tape recorder, switch on the play button.

6. If proper recording is happening, then you should see some movements in the volume meter. You may want to do a test piece and playback the same – before doing the actual recording.
7. To stop the recording process, click on the stop button.
8. Save the file and play back, using one of the media player programs.

7.12 Recording sounds with windows sound recorder

As mentioned earlier, windows operating system comes up with a neat utility program for recording sounds via a microphone – called the sound recorder. Apart from recording sounds, this utility can also open, edit and playback any .wav file.

To view the variety of recording options that are available, click on the audio properties in the sound recorder's edit menu. The audio properties window that pops up, shows both recording as well as playback environment settings.

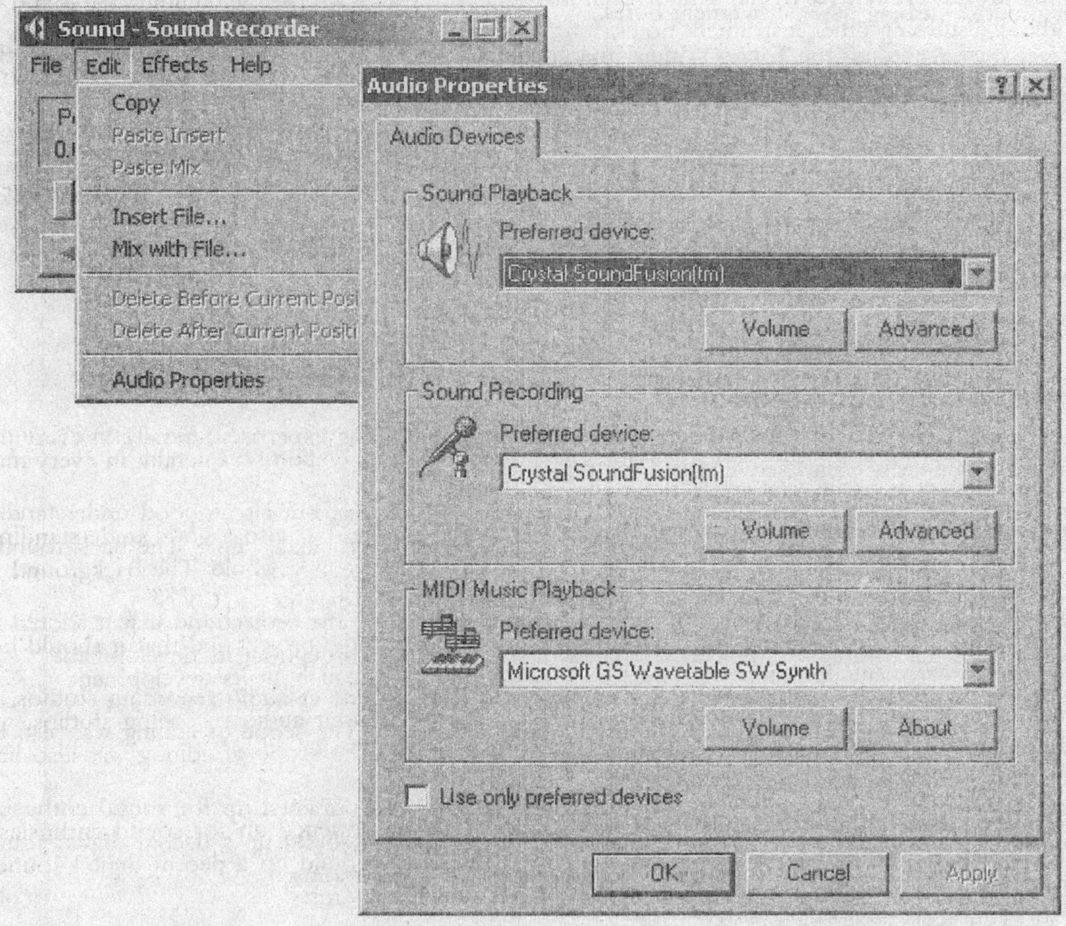

Figure 33: Audio properties in windows sound recorder

Once the options are selected, one can begin the recording process.

7.13 Professional multi-track recording

What we have been talking about – all along – is a simple home recording process with Mono and Stereo channels. But for slightly more serious business and professional purposes, we need more sopnisticated recording applications.

For example, you may want to record Human voice in one track and mix it with some other pre-recorded music in another track. Or, while recording a music performance – you may want to record different instruments in different tracks and control them at the instrument level.

All these things and more - are possible, with professional recording software and studio-based recording.

If you are doing a one-time recording, then it is best to approach professional recording studios. These studios charge their clients on per-hour basis and the charges are nominal. Many Television and radio advertisements are recorded here – You will be able to find one in all cities of India wherein there is some base for entertainment industry.

Recording studios usually make use of DAT tape (Digital Audio Tape) for recording. Of late, CD Audio based recording is becoming more popular and the studio you approach is most likely to have this option.

When recordings are done in studios, highest quality of audio can be expected – with very little or no disturbances. You can also control the volume & treble/bass of each instrument to the best possible combination – and even edit the same, without disturbing other instrument notes.

I did the voice-over recording for Tourist's India multimedia CD-ROM (whose demo is included with this book), in a chennai based audio recording studio. The quality speaks for itself.

If you are to do audio recording quite frequently and if you want to set-up a mini studio in your home or office itself, then consider buying a professional audio recording software. Cakewalk series of software from Twelve Tone systems have been enjoying quite a big popularity among the audio professionals across the world. Check out their latest home recording solutions at

http://www.cakewalk.com/Products/HomeRecording.asp.

Cakewalk studio – in particular is an amazing piece of software and is well worth a try.

7.14 Digital audio editing process

Sound editing constitutes an important part of multimedia audio computing expertise. Literally, in every multimedia project, a sound engineer is exclusively engaged for this purpose.

Effective sound editing not only demands a sense of creativity and timing, but also a good understanding of the audio theme under production and a perspective projection of the project - as a whole. The background audio or music, play a very crucial part in elevating the '*combined multimedia experience*'.

In fact, some feel that it's even wrong to treat audio as a separate part of the project and that it should be treated as the central thread that maintains ambience and aura of the project – throughout its development.

Till the advent of multimedia technology, sound editing was mainly done at audio recording studios, with very expensive equipment that almost occupied a hundred square feet room. The scope of editing was also limited, as digital handling of audio data was not possible by then.

After the arrival of digital audio storage, a whole new world of colours opened up for sound enthusiasts - and soon, computers also started making noises. Now, anybody can hope to build up a decent digital sound effects studio at affordable costs – without moving out of his or her drawing rooms.

All thanks to multimedia audio technology!

A question that comes naturally raises at this point is:

Why do we need to edit sounds at all?

7.15 Need for audio editing

The dire need for editing audio, arises out of one or more of the following reasons, listed below:

1. We need to cut out unwanted bits and pieces of audio, from the original recording. Disturbances almost certainly creep-in, during the beginning and at the end of recording sessions.

2. We may want to reduce the length of the audio recording, to suit the required time gap. Controlling the audio time duration is extremely difficult with the original sound sources. Often, the recording is either a bit short or a bit long! Seldom do we find a sound piece that perfectly matches the required timings. This factor becomes particularly important in presentation shows and animated movies.
3. We may have to enhance audio quality / volume or chillness in certain places.
4. We may have to take care of mistakes and errors that have been committed and not noticed during the original recording session.
5. We may wish to add some special sound effects, which could not be added during recording.

All these are, but a tip of the iceberg...a lot more problems surface during the actual recording process - making audio editing, almost an inevitable exercise.

7.16 Audio editing terminology

In a typical Audio Editing environment, the following operations are frequently performed:

- **Trimming:** Every recording is usually associated with a blank space for a few seconds before and / or after the required sound. The process of removing these blank spaces is called trimming. Removal of blank spaces, apart from reducing the audio file size considerably, enable perfect time matching and further editing operations easy. Trimming is usually done, by cutting out the recorded piece - using the 'Cut-File' feature in audio editing programs.
- **Splicing:** Splicing process refers to removal of unwanted sounds that have crept in, during the recordings. This is also accomplished by means of 'Cut-file' feature in editing programs.
- **Reassembling:** One may want to assemble several stray pieces of audio together, to make up a single file. This process, accomplished by 'cutting', 'copying', and 'pasting' multiple sound clips, is called reassembling.
- **Volume control:** Increasing or decreasing the volume, of either portions, or the whole of recorded audio clippings, is called volume control. This becomes particularly important during reassembling operation; as different sounds pieces may have been recorded at different volume levels, they all have to be neutralised, to the same level of volume - so that the resulting file sounds as an integral audio piece.
- **Time stretching:** We have already seen the importance of matching audio with time slice available. All good editing programs give us an option to either stretch or contract the audio clipping, to suit the particular time slot. This feature can be expected in some of the digital video editing software as well, wherein, a selected sound sample can be matched over a selected sequence of video or animation.
- **Fade ins and fade-outs:** This special feature has been so extensively bundled with almost all sound editing software, that it's no longer considered in the 'special audio effects' category! This is the process of smoothing out the beginning and the end of audio files, for gradual transition effects.
- **Re-sampling:** This is the process of reducing the sound quality from 32 bit recordings to 16 bit or from 16 bit to 8 bit - thus reducing the quality of the recorded audio – slightly and eventually reducing the ultimate file size - substantially.

The need for re-sampling usually arises, when the expected file sizes are much larger than that was originally expected. Re-sampling, in general, does not result in severe degradation of audio quality; in most cases, the changes are so thin that they are hardly noticeable. All speech recordings or voice over - can be conveniently re-sampled to 8 Bits, without sacrificing quality.

7.17 Basic audio editing with windows sound recorder

The windows sound recorder program introduced earlier can be used to perform some preliminary audio editing functions. All the functions are available under the effects menu.

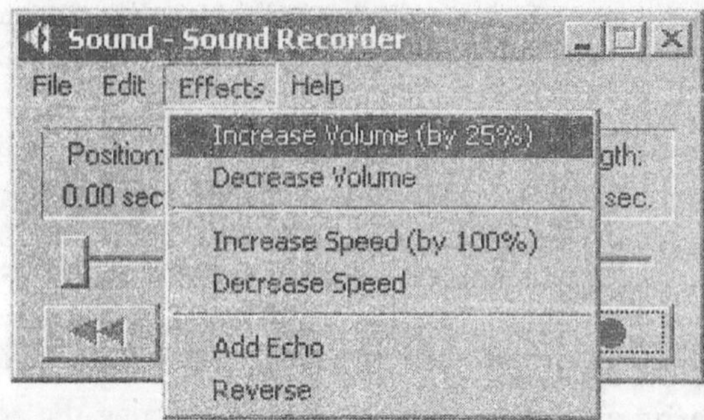

Figure 34: Basic audio editing with windows sound recorder

- **Volume control:** Increase / decrease volume - Makes the volume of the source file, to increase or decrease.
- **Playback speed:** Increase / decrease speed - Makes the playback speed of the source file, to increase or decrease. (If you have recorded some voice other than your own, just apply this effect and have some real fun!)
- **Special effects:** Add echo - Adds a mild echo effect to the audio signals. Reverse - Reverses the playback of the source file. Mix - Mix two sound files, one over the other.

You can play around with windows sound recorder's editing options to wet your hands with basic audio editing – before delving deep into more serious editing programs. And I can promise you that this experience can be quite a bit of fun!

7.18 Advanced audio editing with cool edit

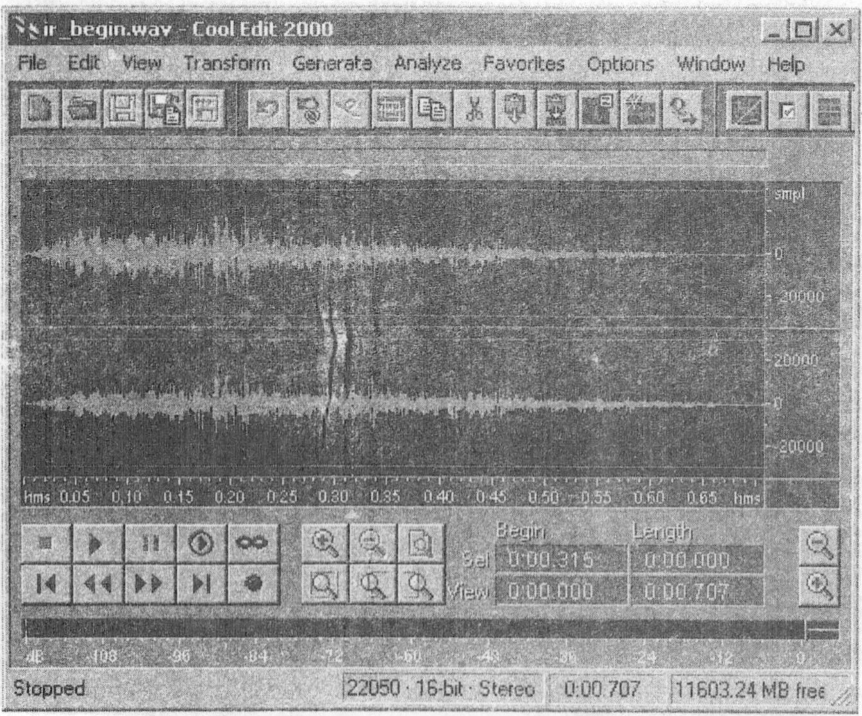

Figure 35: A simple audio file waveform – as displayed in cool edit

'CoolEdit' from Syntrillium Software Corporation (http://www.cooledit.com) is one of the most advanced audio editing software you can find in the market. By exploring Cool edit, we will get an exposure to the world of audio editing and recording professionals, techniques and tactics they use and possibly we may also apply some of these capabilities in our own projects.

I have tried to present the topic in such a way that we are not dealing with features that are very specific to this software. Most of the capabilities we will be discussing here should be available in most – if not all – professional audio editing software in the market today.

7.19 Cool edit - core features

Cool edit's audio features can be grouped under the following categories:

1. Audio playback – playback digital audio files of various file formats
2. Audio recording – record various types of audio.
3. Audio analysis – perform various kinds of analysis over the recorded audio
4. Audio editing – cut, paste, delete audio data
5. Audio transformation – add special effects to audio files
6. Audio file formats conversion – convert wav to mp3 etc.

Let us take a brief preview of each of this functionality.

7.20 Audio playback

Though cool edit can play a very wide range of file formats like .wav, .au, .mp3. .aif, .pcm, .snd etc., it is best not to make use of this software for playback.

Because, when you try to open an audio file with cool edit, it first tries to draw up the waveform of the audio file – which can take up a very long time. This is absolutely unnecessary for simple audio playback – which can be done without much delay by windows media player or quick time player.

Hence, it is best to use cool edit – only for professional recording and editing and not for simple tasks like playback. You should keep this in mind – while installing cool edit, because there will be a dialog box to associate all the audio file formats with cool edit program. If you do not want to use cool editing for audio playback, remember to uncheck all common file formats like .wav and .mp3 from associating themselves with the program.

7.21 Audio recording

Audio recording is simple and straightforward.

Just play the desired audio file or bring in audio from external sound sources using line-in jack. Simply press the record button to begin the recording process.

7.22 Audio analysis

There is a menu item called analysis – within the cool edit main panel, under which the frequency analysis tool is located. When you click on the option, cool edit does a clean scan of the entire audio file, does a complex Fourier transformation calculations – and draws up a frequency analysis graph of the left and right channels that make up the audio file.

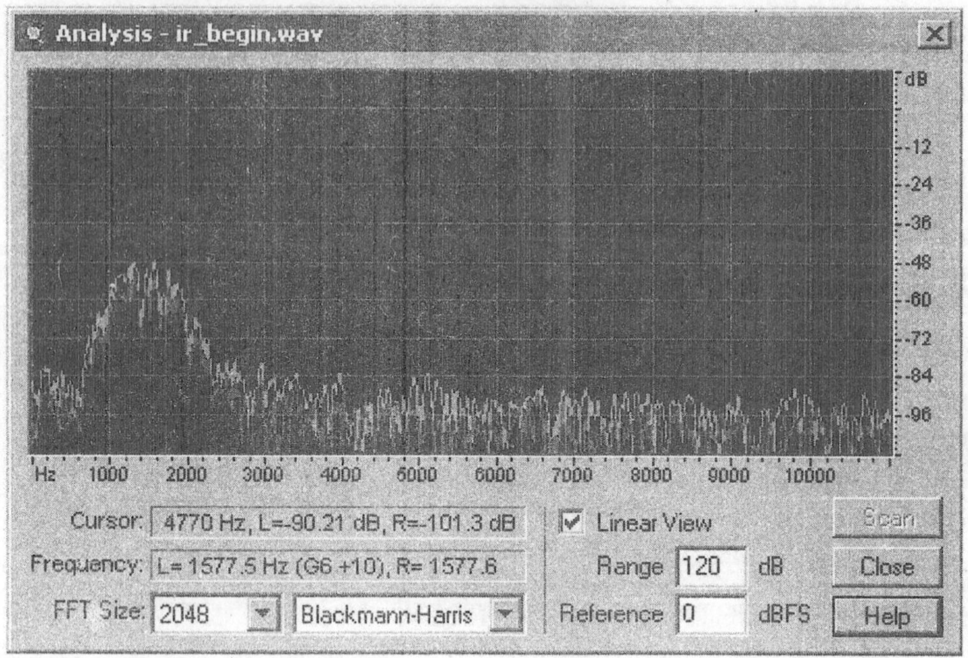

Figure 36: Audio frequency analysis – as done by cool edit

This graph is useful for audio professionals – to analyse the overall frequency modulations and decibel changes in the audio file and do the necessary transformations.

7.23 Audio editing

Audio editing capabilities constitute the core feature of cool edit.

With cool edit we can delete, cut, copy and paste audio files at our own will and wish – just like editing text in MS Word!

More than that, by assembling various audio clippings from different audio file sources, we can actually create entirely new audio files of our own (*hopefully without violating copyrights*)!

All the editing options are available under cool edit's Edit menu.

Let us see how to do some basic editing operations. The process goes like this:

1. Open the audio file you want to edit. The file opens up with a graphic display of the underlying wave pattern.
2. Playback the audio clips several times and decide the portions to be edited. It is better to note down the time period of the clips, which you want to cut or copy - like, from 11th second to 21st Second.
3. Select the portions you want to edit, with the mouse. The time period note helps you to select the exact portions you want to edit.
4. 'Cut' or 'Copy' the selected portions, with the 'Edit' menu options. The portions of the selected audio file are copied to the windows clipboard.
5. 'Paste' the audio clips in the right place in the right file.

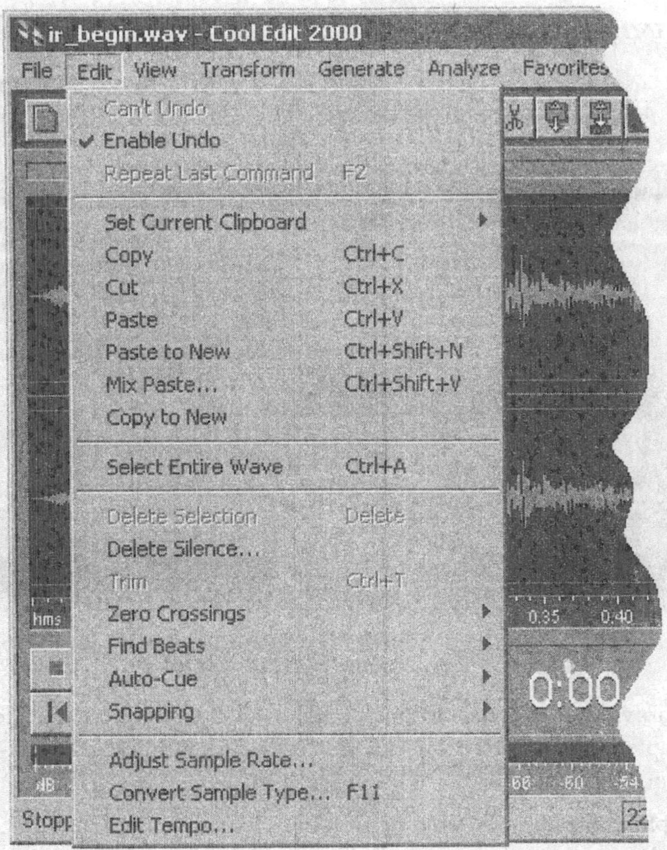

Figure 37: Audio editing features available with cool edit

6. There is an option called Mix paste. This is interesting – it helps us to blend 2 different wave files into one! For example, if you want to add light background music to your human voice over, you can copy the music clip and then mix paste the stuff over voice over. This mix paste options are illustrated in the figure. You can have complete control over the volume of the clipping that is mixed into the original audio; this is particularly useful for providing background music.

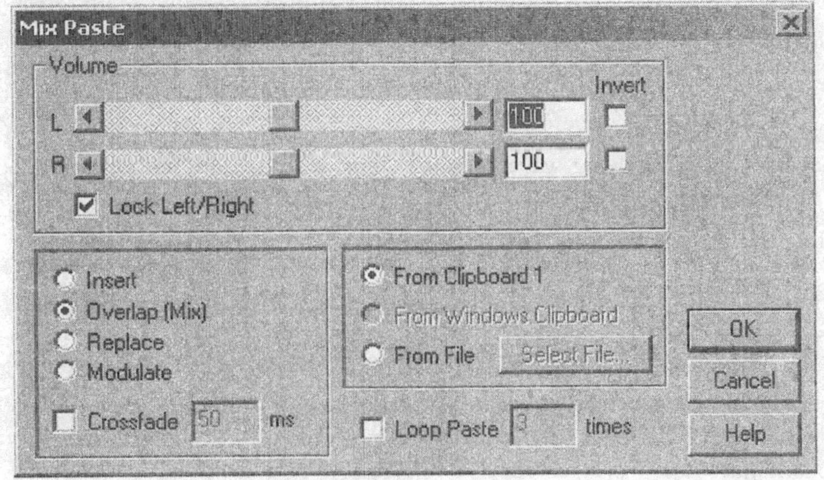

Figure 38: Mix paste dialog box

7.24 Audio transformation

Apart from editing, we can also *transform* the basic audio file – with a number of special effect options that are available with cool edit. All these different options are located under the transform menu.

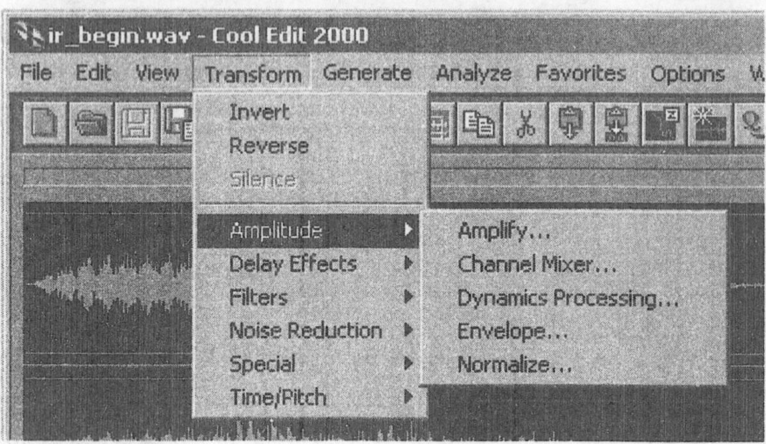

Figure 39: Different types of audio transformation options are available with cool edit.

It may not be possible to provide an exhaustive treatment of all these effects and how to make the best use of them – within this small chapter. However, we will discuss few of these effects below – for wetting our hands with audio transformation techniques.

- **Amplitude → Amplify:** Amplify the volume of both channels. Using amplify, we can also provide fade in and fade out effects i.e. increase or decrease the amplitude of the sound gradually. Time of fading in or out becomes important and it's better to apply this effect after making the selections and not to the entire file.
- **Amplitude → Channel mixer:** Control the volume of left and right channels.
- **Delay effects → Delay:** Introduce a small delay between the channels. Should be used with care
- **Delay → echo:** Adds an echo effect to the file. The results can be perceived only after applying the filter and cannot be imagined in advance. Depending upon the underlying wave pattern, this effect can be very interesting or even be disappointing, at times.
- Noise reduction → Remove the background noises and tape hissing sound. Sometimes it does have an unwanted effect on the original audio – may not be very successful, all the time. Should be used after trials on the original audio
- Stretch → A very useful effect to slightly "stretch" the duration of the audio file. Excessive stretching will, however, distort the original waveform!
- **Reverse:** Reverses the underlying wave pattern. Unusual and funny patterns can be obtained, particularly with respect to human speech.
- **Invert:** Inverts the underlying wave pattern...Crests become troughs and vice versa.
- **Silence:** Inserts a silent pause within the clip. i.e. it makes the selected region, silent

7.25 Audio file format conversions

Most of the audio editing and transformation work is done on uncompressed or least compressed audio file formats like wav. But, before being distributed to the consumers via web or CD-ROMs, they have to be compressed – because of space constraints.

After the advent of mp3 and its dramatic size reduction - for the given audio quality, conversion from various conventional file formats (like wav) to mp3 has become very common. Mp3 comes in several flavours and can be tuned for better quality or better size.

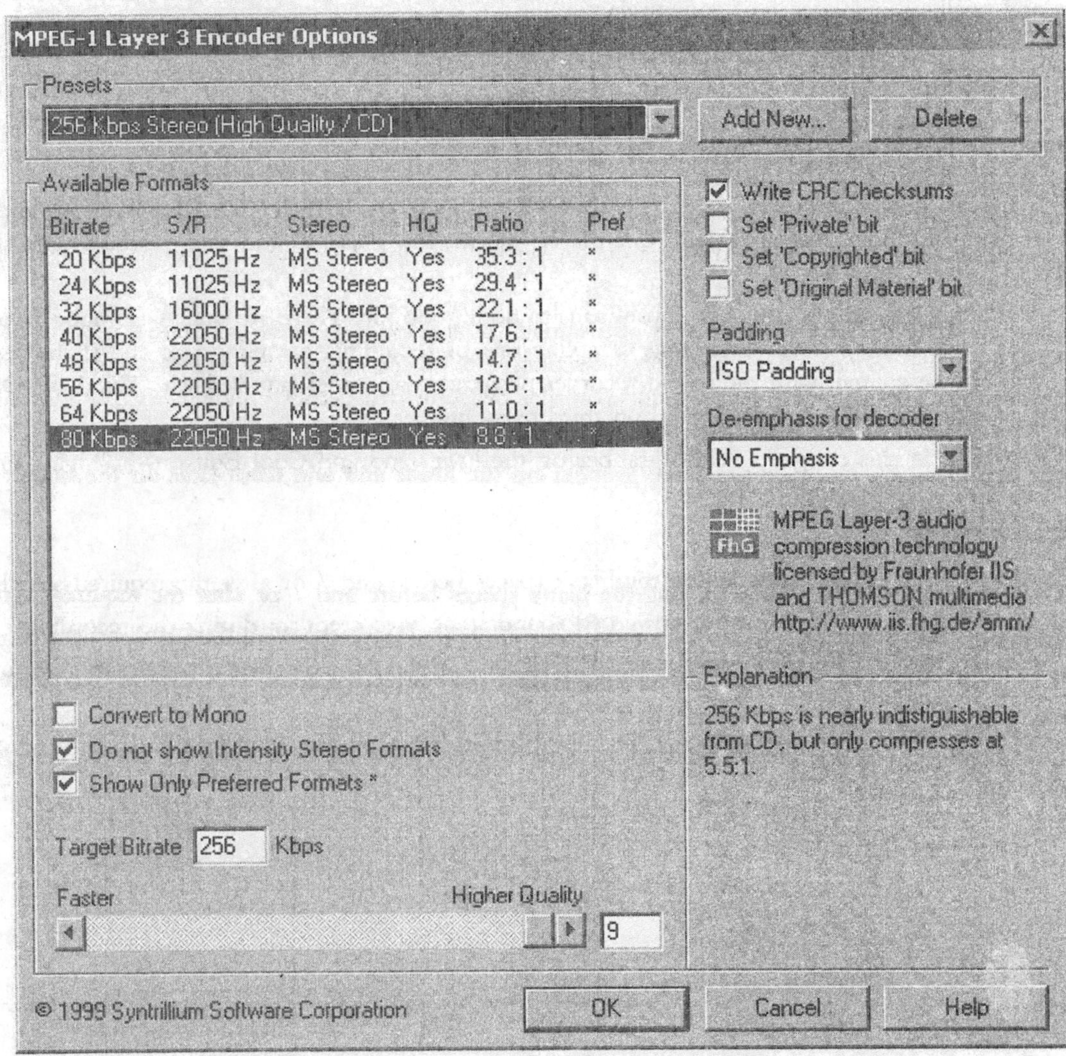

Figure 40: mp3 encoding options with cool edit

Cool edit provides options to convert between various file formats – including wav, au, aif, mp3, pcm, snd and what not?

Here, we will just focus on the mp3 file format conversion options of cool edit.

The format conversion to mp3 is sometimes called mp3 encoding – since it is not a simple file format conversion, but actually a complex compression and encoding process. There are quite a number of encoders available in the market today – and their quality also varies.

The mp3 encoding offered by cool edit is one of the best I have seen in the industry: it adopts the compression algorithm patented by Fraunhofer IIS and Thomson Multimedia (http://www.iis.fhg.de/amm/). But the hitch is that this is not bundled with cool edit core application – it has to be purchased separately.

Once you try to save a file as mp3, you will get various conversion options in the dialog box that pops up. You can choose from a wide range of pre-sets available. By pre-set, we mean a specific combination of bit rate – sample rate –channels – and quality of the resulting audio file.

Higher bit rates result in bigger file size and better quality. The pre-set you choose should be determined by the specific size and quality requirements of your project.

7.26 Summary

Capabilities of a multimedia sound card are many: audio file playback, CD audio playback, audio recording, MIDI recording etc. In order to get the best out of sound cards, we need appropriate software tools.

Digital audio playback is easy and there are excellent tools available in the market - for free! Windows media player from Microsoft, Apple's QuickTime and Media one player lead the lot. These utilities can handle almost all varieties of audio files like .wav,.aiff, .mp3, midi etc.

Digital audio recording is a serious business if you want to do a good job. There are quite a number of parameters to watch out for - like mono/ stereo recording, sampling rate of recording, sampling size etc. If the recording is a short test, you can be content with the sound recorder program that comes bundled with Windows OS, but for meaningful recordings you may have to depend on third party utilities.

We covered two tools in this category: Audio grabber on the lower end and Cool Edit on the higher end.

7.27 Keywords

- **Trimming:** The process of removing the blank spaces before and / or after the required signals.
- **Splicing:** The process of removing unwanted sounds that have crept in, during the recordings.
- **Re-assembling:** The process of assembling several stray pieces of audio files together, to make up a single file.
- **Re-sampling:** The process of reducing the sound quality from 32 Bit recordings to 16 Bit or from 16 Bit to 8 Bit.

Chapter 8

The MP3 Revolution

CHAPTER OVERVIEW

This small chapter is exclusively meant to discuss MPEG Audio layer III technology – more popularly known as mp3.

We will be looking at the core concepts behind mp3 – how it achieves such a stupendous rate of compression, what is the sacrifice in quality we make, how mp3 will shape up in the future and so on.

One of the fundamental concepts behind mp3 is the acoustic capability and limitations of a human ear. The chapter also introduces, rather briefly, this field of study called psychoacoustics.

8.1 Introduction

In the previous chapter, we saw how sounds can be recorded as digital audio files using a sound card and relevant software. We also saw that audio files have to be compressed using some audio compression algorithms before being stored into the computer – because of massive memory requirements.

MPEG Audio layer III or simply mp3 is perhaps the most notable technology that has changed the landscape of digital music and the Internet music forever. The impact of mp3 is so significant that its influence is felt above and beyond the world of computers: In digital audio players, disc formats, recorders and a whole range of other electronic equipments.

This chapter covers some grounds related to mp3. We will begin with the invention of mp3 and its popularity with the growth of Internet.

8.2 The Birth of mp3

The Fraunhofer Institute, Denmark (http://www.iis.fraunhofer.de) invented mp3. A fruit of nearly twenty years of research work by Dr.Karlheinz Brandenburg and his associates, mp3 has grown steadily from being a research thesis to becoming almost a standard in the world of digital music.

Though the initial work had started in early 80s, mp3 started to look serious only in 1986 and efforts to make it an audio compression standard started in 1988. In 1994, the first mp3 decoder for windows had appeared. But mp3 had to wait for bit more time – almost till 1998-99, before becoming a global phenomenon.

The growth of Internet and the need for distributing songs and digital music over the web had a lot to do with the popularity of mp3. In April 1999, the string "mp3" became the string most widely searched for – in all search engines. From researcher's white papers, it had become an industry standard!

8.3 Need for audio encoding

Uncompressed audio files are very huge in size and are not easy to handle.

A three-minute song, recorded at a sampling rate of 44.1kHz and a sampling size of 16 bits with two stereo channels will consume around 30 MB of storage space. If we were to download this file from the Internet - at a comfortable access speed of around 64 kbps, it would still take nearly an hour to download! Even if the audio file were compressed using one of the conventional audio compression algorithms, its size would still be substantially large, making it impractical to distribute over the net.

Enter mp3!

Using mp3 compression algorithms, the same audio file at 44.1kHz, 16 bits and 2 channels can be compressed to roughly 3 MB! Or roughly one tenth of its original size... with little or no loss of quality!

A 3 MB file is not very difficult to download even if the speed of net access is pretty low.

So, how mp3 achieves such a high degree of compression rate with relatively no noticeable loss of quality? The secret lies somewhat in the acoustic capabilities of a human ear and its limitations. This specialised field of study is called psychoacoustics.

Mp3 achieves its very impressive audio compression by making the best use of results available from psycho acoustic study. The key concept is in finding out what are all the sounds that are audible to human ears at any point of time, in a given song. If a particular instrument sound is barely audible or not audible at all, why storing it in the file?

8.4 Psychoacoustics

The term psychoacoustics stands for the study on the characteristics of the human auditory system. Two concepts of psychoacoustics are particularly important in our context.

They are:

- Hearing perception
- Masking

How sensitive our ears are, to a particular range of frequency - is what is called the hearing perception. The sensitivity of the human auditory system is very good for frequencies between 2.5 kHz and 5 kHz. Our ears are less sensitive to anything above or below these frequencies. The threshold in quiet represents the audio sensitivity. Any tone, above or below this threshold will not be perceived.

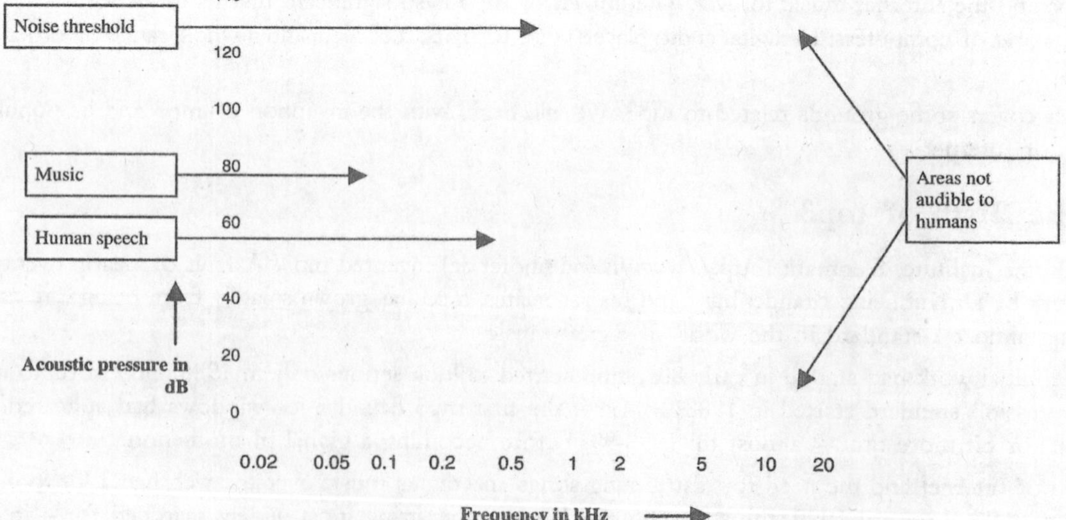

Figure 41: Hearing perception of a human ear

From the perspective of audio encoding, signals that are not audible to the human ears can be removed. This reduces the overall size of the file.

The second concept is masking. Masking is the phenomenon by which a short, loud sound covers or masks the quieter, longer sound of the strings for a moment. For every tone in the audio signal, a masking threshold can be calculated. If another tone lies below this masking threshold, it will be masked by the louder tone. Thus, it remains inaudible to the listener.

Again from the perspective of audio encoding, these inaudible signals can be removed.

There is another phenomenon associated with masking. It is called pre-masking and post-masking.

Human brain needs certain fraction of time to differentiate between two different sounds of varying loudness. For example, if a loud sound follows a quiet sound – it takes 20 milliseconds for the brain to perceive the loud sound. This is what is called pre-masking. Similarly, it takes nearly 200 milliseconds for the brain to identify a quiet sound that follows a loud sound!

During these very short periods, we may as well continue with the earlier sound or have no sound signal at all! The user will not perceive it.

The quality of mp3 encoding will very much depend upon the fineness with which it takes care of all these psychoacoustics models and phenomena. Not all mp3 encoders take care of all these factors and hence the difference in quality between two commercial mp3 encoders.

8.5 Mp3 encoders

An mp3 encoder is a piece of software that can convert digital audio files in other formats to mp3 files. Encoders make use of psychoacoustics phenomena to find our what are all the unnecessary portions that can be removed from the original file, without being noticed by the user – thus trimming down the overall size of the file. It then uses Huffmann encoding algorithm to further compress this data – cleansed from unwanted frequencies.

Not all encoders take care of all the different factors associated with psychoacoustics; hence the quality of mp3 encoding vastly differs from one encoder to another. This can be easily tested by encoding the same song with two different encoders – while maintaining the process parameters like bit rate, compression ratio and channels. Try to use a digital music file with human voice in it – to perceive the differences very clearly.

Mp3 encoders are available in two flavours: They can either be purchased as a stand-alone program or as a plug-in to one of the commercial audio editing programs available in the market. Go to http://www.download.com and search for 'mp3 encoders' – to see a whole list of free and shareware software available for download. Click on the 'use rating' hyperlink to see all the software that received the best user rating. Choose the one that appeals to you most!

One of the best encoders I have tried is from Fraunhofer Institute –the inventors of mp3. To have a look at their audio-video solutions, go to http://www.iis.fraunhofer.de/amm/app/index.html.

8.6 The mp3 encoding cycle

It will be interesting to see the process cycle through which a digital audio file such as .wav goes through, from its nascent form to encoded mp3. This cycle is detailed below.

The first step is the creation of signal spectrum – which consists of 576 sub-bands – by passing the audio signal through a filter bank. This process requires complex filters and makes use of an algorithm called discrete cosine transformation. In real time, it calculates all the unnecessary frequencies and eliminates them iteratively.

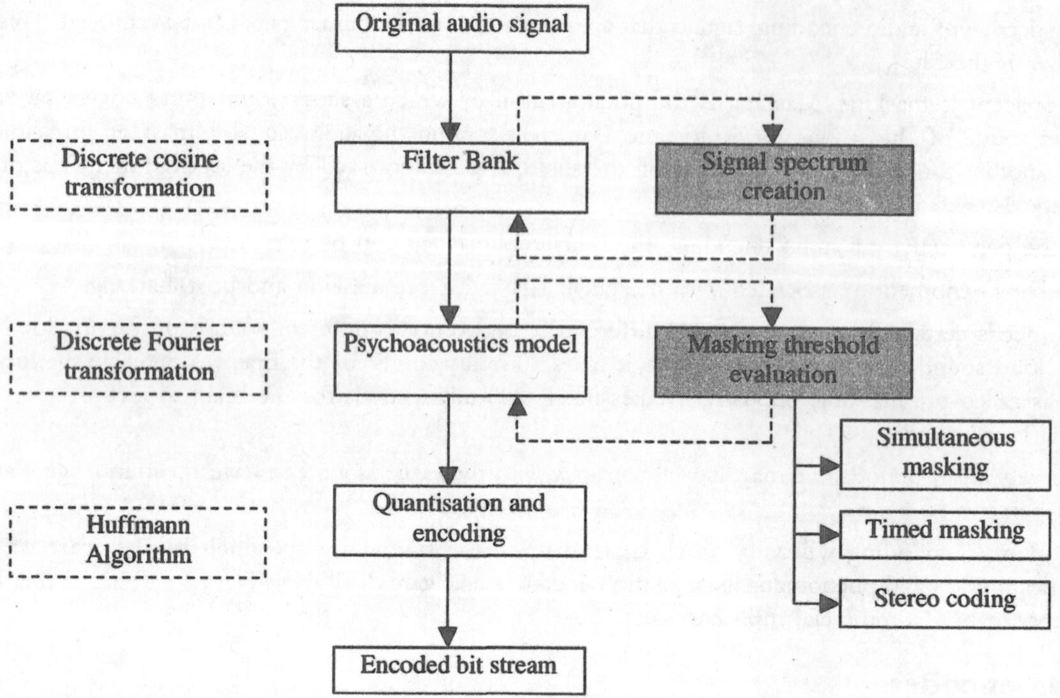

Figure 42: Hearing perception of a human ear

The second step is to pass the filtered signal spectrum through the psychoacoustics model built within the encoder. Here, the model calculates the masking threshold for each of the sub-bands in the entire spectrum and decides what are all the frequencies which are to be masked. The process involves another algorithm called discrete Fourier transformation. The stereo effects are also transformed by means of a process called joint stereo coding.

Quantization process results in further data reduction, followed by Huffmann encoding for compressing the resulting file. The latter can reduce the file size up to twenty percent or more without losses.

The last step is the formation of bit stream, which is recorded as an mp3 file.

8.7 Encoding parameters

There are three important parameters that you can control, during the mp3 encoding process. They are:

- ❑ Bit rate
- ❑ Sampling rate
- ❑ Compression ratio
- ❑ No of channels

Bit rate denotes the average number of bits that one second of audio data will consume. The usually units here are kbps, which is kilobits per second, or 1000 bits/s. Kbps is also useful to match the encoding quality with the downloading speed of the Internet. For example, if you want one-second duration of the song to be downloaded per second at the rate of 64 kbps Internet access – then you should use 64 kbps as your bit rate.

The following table provides you with an indicator to the combinations you could use and the resulting quality:

Table 15: Different combination of parameters in mp3 encoding

Bit rate (kbps)	Bandwidth (kHz)	Channels	Reduction ratio	Quality
8	2.5	Mono	96:1	Telephone quality
16	4.5	Mono	48:1 Short wave or better	Radio quality –
32	7.5	Mono	24:1	Radio quality – AM or better
56 to 64	11	Stereo	26:1 or 24:1	Radio quality – FM or better
96	15	Stereo	16:1	Near CD quality
112 to 128	>15	Stereo	14:1 or 12:1	CD Quality

The settings I mostly use for my recordings are 128 kbps bit rate at best quality (which means compression ratio is less), stereo and 22.05 kHz. This is denoted as the CD quality music in the above table.

8.8 Summary

Mp3 stands for MPEG Audio layer III. It is an advanced compression algorithm for compressing digital audio files. A compression ratio of 1:10 or even more can be achieved with mp3.

Psychoacoustics or the study of acoustic capabilities of human ear forms the basis for mp3 compression. Signals that cannot be heard or are suppressed by louder signals are identified and eliminated in mp3. Mp3 encoders are commercial software tools or libraries that perform mp3 compression over audio files. The mp3 encoding cycle is a complex process involving advanced mathematical algorithms.

Parameters involved with mp3 compression are bit rate, compression ratio, signalling frequency and channel information.

8.9 Keywords

- ❑ **Psychoacoustics:** Study on the characteristics of the human auditory system.
- ❑ **Mp3 encoding:** The process of compressing digital audio data using mpeg audio layer III algorithms.
- ❑ **Bit rate:** The average number of bits that one second of audio data will consume.

Chapter 9

MIDI Fundamemtals

CHAPTER OVERVIEW

MIDI or Musical instrument digital interface is conceptually different from digital audio. It is a refined form of music storage and reproduction.

This chapter takes you through the world of MIDI, covering how MIDI stores music information and what differentiates MIDI from other forms of digital audio. The chapter then explores Microsoft's general MIDI standards, the de-facto standard for MIDI technology. It also touches the device capabilities of MIDI in a windows environment.

9.1 Introduction

Digital audio files, though are being extensively used in many multimedia audio applications, have their own limitations - the major one being their exorbitant file sizes.

A small dash sound that lasts for less than a second takes up around 25 KB and a sound file that runs just for around 12 seconds comfortably occupies more than 2.5 MB of precious hard disk space! For example, the audio file 'chord.wav' - located under windows media directory (usually c:\windows\media) lasts for one second or so, but its size is 95 KB!

Such massive file sizes pose serious issues, when music has to be played on for hours together, in a typical project. This necessitated the need for inventing alternative forms of music storage and distribution and audio research labs across the globe were investing their time and energy for a breakthrough.

In the meantime, the electronic musical keyboard giants like Casio and Yamaha were trying to evolve some standards for communicating the keyboard and synthesize signals electronically, across several disparate platforms.

The end result was the concept of MIDI.

Multimedia audio pioneers like the creative labs and Ad Lib wasted no time in managing to adopt these standards intelligently into their audio cards.

Today, computers can straight away talk to any MIDI compatible electronic keyboards – without a hitch!

Over the period of time, MIDI technology has never looked back and managed to carve out it's own enclave in the multimedia market segment. MIDI has the ability to reproduce fine / noise-free electronic music and enjoys astonishingly smaller file sizes.

9.2 The concept of MIDI

The concept of MIDI goes like this:

Instead of storing the actual sound samples in the form of analog signals, a typical MIDI file just records the description of the ongoing music. This description includes the start of a note, its pitch, length, volume and other musical attributes such as vibrato.

Details like the different musical notes that are being played at any point of time – by a particular instrument, their sequence, their time duration etc. are noted down in the form of numeric data. Capturing this information for all instruments that are being played at any point of time is nothing but digitally creating the comprehensive music notes of the composer.

During playback, these notations are read and understood by MIDI compatible devices such as sound cards and electronic keyboards, which then refer to a database of pre-recorded sound samples of various instruments and play the appropriate note.

These notations follow international standards, so that the music information can be exchanged between computers and other musical instruments such as synthesizers! The encoded instructions transmitted between such MIDI devices are called MIDI messages.

Depending upon the quality and range of presets available, this synthesized music can get very close to the original ones. For example, try to play Beethoven's 5th Symphony MIDI file that is installed under windows media directory – and you will be amazed at the level of precision and quality.

MIDI is capable of recording more than 16 tracks of different notes from various instruments, simultaneously. It is also possible to edit a particular track's volume, tempo, notes etc. without affecting the rest. This gives unprecedented flexibility in editing the recorded music.

MIDI data can also be understood by a host of several other electronic instruments and keyboards – apart from computers. This results in seamless flow of audio data across a wide variety of synthesizers, keyboards and multimedia devices, facilitating integration and synchronization.

In olden days, a concept called FM synthesis was used to generate the music notes from various instruments. But, of late, a better technology called Wavetable synthesis has replaced FM synthesis in almost all devices.

The biggest limitation of MIDI is that it can record only music data and not just any form of audio signals!

9.3 Comparing MIDI with digital audio

It could be recalled that digital audio files store all kinds of audio data in the form of numerical samples that are converted back to audio waves during playback. A whole lot of ADC and DAC conversions are involved in this transformation cycles.

On the other hand, MIDI stores just music data and records data as musical notes and instruments.

Both techniques are widely used in multimedia audio applications and both have their own inherent blessings and limitations.

Table 16: Differentiating MIDI from digital audio

Factor	Digital audio	MIDI
File size	Huge	Very less
Quality of music and disturbances	Varies. Susceptible to noises noises or disturbances	Mostly stable. No
Editing and manipulation	Inflexible	Highly flexible
RAM and processing power	More	Less required
Playback	Highly consistent	Inconsistent
Audio	All kinds of sounds	Only music
Knowledge of music	Required, but not compulsory	Compulsory

Let us do a comparative analysis of these two forms of audio data storage, in the light of various factors like file size, processing power require etc. This will help you to choose the right form of audio, for a given purpose at hand.

9.3.1 File Sizes

The main attraction of MIDI is it's amazingly low file size. The difference is so significant that it is even unfair to compare it with digital audio.

In some cases, the compression ratio is as high as 1: 1000! This is obviously due to the basic difference in capturing audio data, which was explained earlier.

For example, with a 100 KB digital audio file, you cannot hold more than a few seconds of audio data whereas a MIDI file of the same size may run well over 6 to 10 minutes!

Windows users can check out all the MIDI files located under the windows media directory and make a comparison of various file sizes and their duration.

More often than not, file size becomes a very important factor in most multimedia projects. The limitation is set by the storage capacity of the CD-ROM media, which is around 640 to 700 MB today.

Thus, it is important to remain conscious about the size of various media files involved in the project. It is best to make use of MIDI for all background music, which may have to last for long duration and depend on digital audio for the rest.

Also, for applications involving Internet multimedia, file size becomes a critical constraint because of the downloading time associated - and MIDI offers a reliable solace.

9.3.2 Quality of music

Unlike digital audio, MIDI recordings are not susceptible to external disturbances or additional 'hisses' or 'noises'. This is because, all recordings are done electronically and there is absolutely no intervention of external mediums like air - which degrade the quality of the resulting audio files.

Thus, in most of the cases, MIDI music is usually far more superior than it's counterpart.

However, for decent MIDI playback, at least a 16-bit soundboard with wave table synthesis technology is the minimum requirement.

9.3.3 Editing and manipulation options

As far as editing operations are concerned, MIDI is far more flexible than digital audio files.

Literally, each and every note of the instruments that are being played back can be controlled. The very pitch of individual instruments- or the music piece as a whole - can be manipulated. The tempo of playback can be altered to suit the required time frame. The volume of every individual instrument can also be altered to one's will and wish.

All these fancy capabilities are not available in digital audio, wherein various music notes often blend and mix with each other as a single stream – unless recorded on separate tracks.

Cutting, copying and pasting the notes of individual instrument notes is also very much possible!

Thus, it is possible to mix up three different instruments and notes from three different recordings, and reconstruct a fourth music file with them! I have done it several times in my projects, with reasonable success rate!

The time length of the recording can be stretched or contracted without much sacrifice in quality.

9.3.4 RAM / Processing power required

MIDI file playbacks demand much lesser RAM and processing power, than digital audio files.

This becomes a constraint to be considered in multimedia projects, wherein several things have to be handled simultaneously. For example, you may have to throw the appropriate piece of information, fetch the relevant background music and play it in the background and in the meanwhile - keep yourself ready for any mouse clicks or other interactions from the user.

If relevant RAM or processing power is not available at any point of time, the time taken to respond for an action might be delayed and there is always the fear of machine suspending – which is the last thing you want to happen on a client's machine!

With all these positive aspects in its defence, MIDI does have its own share of limitations too.

The following paragraphs detail the same.

9.3.5 MIDI Playback

The main disadvantage of MIDI, which amounts to lot of negative credit - is the high degree of inconsistency associated with its playback.

During playback on a client's machine, the operating system tries to look out for the appropriate instruments or their equivalents and tries to load them on demand. It then reconstructs the MIDI music and plays back. Thus, the quality of MIDI music directly depends upon the underlying sound cards and sound samples available in them.

Unless the user's playback audio platform is similar to or at least comparable to that of the developer's card, the results shall be quite ambiguous.

This problem degenerates further, because of the variations in the 'Instrument tables' across different audio boards that supply the required sample notes to MIDI, during playback.

The end result is that MIDI files do not sound the same across different audio cards.

In case of digital audio, the story is quite different.

As these audio files are simply large chunks of numbers and do not depend upon any Instruments library during playback, the playbacks under a variety of audio platforms are quite consistent.

Even under totally different hardware environments and between audio boards from different manufacturers, digital playback manages to remain the same. Because of this fact, many multimedia CD-ROM producers prefer to use digital audio files instead of MIDI.

In cases where the playback environment is known beforehand, MIDI will obviously stand out as a better choice. Also, with simpler and limited usage of popular Instruments - like piano - during recording, MIDI playbacks maintain tolerable consistency.

9.3.6 An experiment to try

Try to play a good MIDI music file in a 64-bit audio card.

Then, try to play the same file using a 32-bit card or even less.

The difference could be minor or very significant – depending upon the number and range of instruments used.

9.3.7 Limitations of MIDI audio

Throughout our discussions on MIDI, I've only used the phrase 'MIDI Music' and not MIDI audio.

Because, unlike digital audio files, MIDI can hold only music and instrument data and not all kinds of sounds!

In particular, MIDI is incapable of recording human voice - an element usually associated with most of the multimedia projects. This is because of the fact that human voice is basically transmitted over air and can only be recorded as digital data.

Also, one cannot hope to develop a library of human sound samples and create all possible combinations of voices that can be made use of by MIDI! Only some expensive MIDI boards meant for high-end applications are capable of 'emulating' human voice and many times, the results are far from satisfactory.

9.3.8 Handling MIDI

Last but not the least, intelligent MIDI manipulations demand some decent understanding of the western or eastern music theory. There are software which even print out MIDI files as pure western music notes...such is the integrity of MIDI files!

The best option available for those who don't have proper music knowledge is to lookout for royalty-free MIDI music banks available in the Internet.

The best practise is to make use of both digital audio as well as MIDI files, in a given project and try to strike a balance between the two.

9.4 The general MIDI standards

Microsoft introduced a set of MIDI standards with its windows 3.1 operating system that have ultimately become the industry norms and are now known as 'The General MIDI Standards'. Almost all MIDI hardware and software developers now confine to this, or make their systems compatible with these standards.

MIDI files that confine to Microsoft's standards are called device independent MIDI files i.e. these files have best chances of producing the same kind of music, even under a varying hardware and software configurations that are compatible with general MIDI standards.

Microsoft divides all MIDI compatible devices into two streams:

- Base level MIDI devices
- Extended level MIDI devices

Let us explore these two categories, further.

9.4.1 Base level MIDI devices

Base level MIDI devices are those that are capable of playing back at least three melodic instrument tracks - with at least six notes being played simultaneously and a percussion track - with at least three notes being played simultaneously.

Melodic instrument tracks are those that contain musical notes - like the piano sounds and the percussion tracks are those that carry the accompanying rhythms, like the drumbeats.

The earliest family of sound cards - particularly those using FM synthesis technology, confined to base level MIDI devices. The ultimate music resulting from these devices were preliminary in nature and are not comparable to that from extended level MIDI devices

9.4.2 Extended level MIDI devices

Extended level MIDI devices are those that are capable of playing back at least nine melodic instrument tracks - with at least sixteen notes being played simultaneously, along with a percussion track - with at least sixteen notes being played simultaneously.

Almost all-decent sound cards, these days, can be called as extended level MIDI devices.

9.5 Polyphony

Before focussing our attention on the actual channel assignments in general MIDI standards, it's important to understand a concept called polyphony.

Polyphony is the technique of accompanying more than one musical note to be played simultaneously, during recording. For example, the piano alone may produce more than three different notes, simultaneously. In western music school, this is what is called a chord.

So, based on our earlier notations, we can conclude that base level MIDI devices allow 6-note polyphony for melodic instruments and that the extended level MIDI devices allow a lot more – 16 to be precise.

9.6 General MIDI channel assignments

We saw earlier that those MIDI files that confine to Microsoft's general MIDI standards are called device independent MIDI files.

These files store two different streams of instruments, for each music piece that's recorded - one for base level MIDI and another for extended level MIDI.

Out of the 16 MIDI channels available, the general MIDI mapping assignments are as follows:

Table 17: General MIDI mapping assignments

Channels	Purpose
1 to 9	Extended level melodic instruments with 16 note polyphony
10	Extended level percussion instruments with 16 note polyphony
13 to 15	Base level melodic instruments with 3 note polyphony
16	Base level percussion instruments with 3 note polyphony

When a new piece of MIDI hardware is installed, all these mappings are automatically taken care of.

If the additional hardware is an extended level MIDI device, the base level channels are ignored and if the hardware is base level device, the extended channels are ignored. Usually, pre-developed MIDI maps are supplied along with the installation driver, which informs the operating system regarding the mapping preferences to be looked after, during MIDI playback.

9.7 General MIDI instrument assignments

The General MIDI standards also dictate a standardized program change mapping system and a standardized set of Instrument samples.

For example, all general MIDI compatible devices have acoustic grand piano instrument sample matched to number 0, violin matched to number 40 and so on. This also means that the same instrument sample issues out of every other MIDI compatible device, when a call to specific Instrument is made.

The general MIDI Instrument assignments define 128 such Instruments, covering all types of melodic and percussion instruments imaginable.

In order not to make things more complicated, most of the MIDI device vendors adopt the same set of 128 instrument samples and sound effects with their product.

With so much pre arrangement, you should be wondering why we observed earlier that MIDI playback is ambiguous. Remember! The MIDI music is reconstructed from the back of sound samples held by the device. These sound samples will certainly vary from one manufacturer to the other and hence the difference in the ultimate MIDI music.

9.8 The preferred MIDI device on your system

To see what is the preferred MIDI device that plays the MIDI music on your system, you can refer to the same sounds and multimedia window in the control panel.

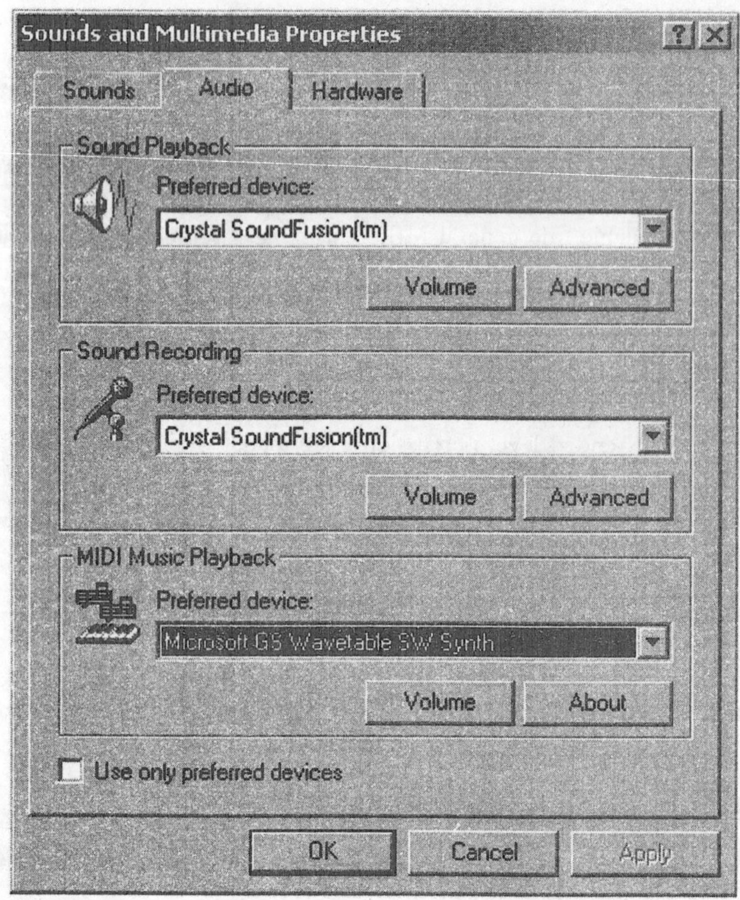

Figure 43: Preferred MIDI device on your system

9.9 Summary

MIDI files store audio data as environment variables - and not as audio signals issued out of the source.

MIDI and digital audio are characterised by inherent advantages as well as limitations. Both types of audio are generally employed in multimedia projects – MIDI is best suited for background music while digital audio is for voice over and other miscellaneous sounds.

Microsoft's general MIDI standards, defining all instruments, mapping and channels associated with MIDI devices have become industry standards. MIDI files that adhere to these standards are conceptually known as device independent MIDI files.

9.10 Keywords

- **Base level MIDI devices:** MIDI devices capable of playing back at least three melodic instrument tracks - with at least six note polyphony and a percussion track - with at least three note polyphony.
- **Extended level MIDI devices:** MIDI devices capable of playing back at least nine melodic instrument tracks - with at least sixteen-note polyphony and a percussion track with at least sixteen-note polyphony.

Chapter 10

Working with MIDI

CHAPTER OVERVIEW

This second chapter on MIDI as well as the last chapter on multimedia audio details how to set up a professional MIDI music studio at home and start recording your own MIDI hit numbers.

MIDI recording demands equipment and expertise. Hence, it makes sense to check out the royalty free MIDI music banks available in the market before getting your hands busy with the MIDI keyboard.

This chapter also covers MIDI editing techniques, using a piece of software utility called the MIDI sequencer.

10.1 Introduction

In the previous chapter, we had developed a conceptual understanding about MIDI and saw how MIDI files are different from nsormal digital audio files. In this chapter, we will focus our views on setting up a MIDI recording environment and editing the same using sequencer software.

While playing back MIDI files can be easily achieved with the help of windows media player or any other multimedia player program, recording a MIDI piece is reasonably complex. You need to buy a MIDI compatible music keyboard, cables and sequencer software.

That is why it makes sense to make use of ready-made MIDI music against creating one on our own.

10.2 MIDI recording vs. MIDI gallery files

Before you get down to record a specific piece of MIDI music for your project, it is worthwhile to check up the royalty free MIDI music libraries that are available in the market and on the Internet. These libraries contain hundreds and thousands of pre recorded MIDI music files, for various themes and occasions. Chances are high that you may find a specific piece that will actually suit your requirements. This will save you lot of time and effort and in most of the cases, the price you pay will be worth it.

Check out the following websites for such free and paid MIDI music banks:

http://www.musicrobot.com

http://www.mididb.com

http://msod.formata.org/topdowns.html

http://www.ifni.com

10.3 Setting up a MIDI music studio

We shall now discuss how to set up a personal MIDI music studio environment for our own use.

We need to have the following hardware, peripherals and software:

- ❑ A MIDI compatible synthesizer electronic keyboard
- ❑ MIDI plug in cables
- ❑ MIDI sequencer software

The following paragraphs depict what they are and why we need them.

10.3.1 A MIDI compatible synthesizer electronic keyboard

Synthesized music is something that's not natural, but emulated. But when you hear a piece from one of the latest models, you feel as though their notes are more natural than the original instruments themselves.

Such is the level of fineness and sophistication modern music keyboards are endowed with.

To record your MIDI music, you need to purchase a MIDI compatible music keyboard. Yamaha, Casio and Roland are some of the names well known in this arena.

Please note that most of the low-end keyboard models may not have MIDI compatibility. Only those at the higher end – which may cost a fortune – are blessed with such advanced capabilities.

One quick check to find out whether a keyboard is compatible with MIDI or not – is to lookout for MIDI output sockets. If there is one, then it is most likely that the keyboard is MIDI compatible. Also, look out for the 'General MIDI compatible' wordings in the information booklet or product brochure.

If you are not a full time musician or if it is a one-off exercise, then it is better to hire a MIDI compatible keyboard from relevant sources like the light music troupes.

High-end keyboards are capable of supporting hundreds of instrument banks – apart from a host of other interesting features.

There are few audio cards that can send MIDI data from sources other than synthesizer keyboards – like the electric guitars. However, this may not be necessary in most of the cases, as you have various lead and base guitar options in the synthesizer keyboard itself.

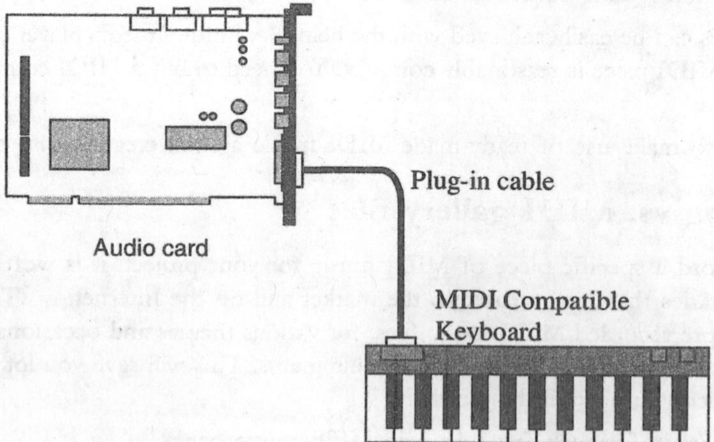

Figure 44: Connecting a MIDI keyboard to sound card.

10.3.2 MIDI plug- in cables

These cables establish the actual electronic connection between the sound card and the MIDI compatible keyboard. In general, these are not readily bundled with sound card or multimedia kit and have to be purchased separately.

Keyboard's MIDI-OUT port must be connected to sound card's MIDI-IN socket.

When you restart the computer, windows must be able to identify this new MIDI device and configure the same for recording.

10.3.3 MIDI sequencer software

MIDI sequencer is a piece of software that allows you to open the various instrument tracks in the MIDI file and edit them to the finest detail possible.

Various tracks available with the MIDI file are usually displayed in graphics form and you have the option of editing every single track without disturbing the other!

Some sequencing software even displays the music notes in western notation form. This facility is a very useful feature for professional composers, who can then compose notes for various instruments and tracks, print them out and issue them to instrumentalists directly.

One such MIDI sequencing software that is quite popular is the 'Music sculptor' from Aleph omega software. We will discuss this utility later, in an exclusive section.

10.4 Recording MIDI music

- Keep the electronic keyboard at a convenient place near the computer.
- Connect the 'MIDI Out' jack of the keyboard to the 'MIDI / JOYSTICK In' connector jack of your sound card.
- Open the MIDI sequencer software and start with a 'New File' option in the File menu.
- Pre-set the synthesizer keyboard with the appropriate instrument selections and rhythm backgrounds.
- When you are ready for the recording, push the 'Record' button in the sequencer software.
- Start playing the notes you want to record.
- When you are done, click the 'Stop' button and stop the recording process.

If you are not fluent enough to play the music keyboard with ease, you may find it very difficult to maintain the right keystrokes, while keeping up the time and rhythm.

If you are a new bee to the world of music, be prepared to do some hectic editing!

All your keystrokes are recorded on the MIDI Music file. Some advanced sequencing software even allow you to record as many as sixteen different channels of data, each containing different instruments!

If you want to undertake such complicated recordings – involving multiple tracks and instruments, you may have to select the channels one after another and play the relevant notes. Alternatively, you can also connect several keyboards simultaneously and place one musician at every board and start recording all the keystrokes simultaneously.

Once the recording is over, the resulting file can be saved with the 'Save as' Option in the sequencing software. The files are usually stored with a .mid extension.

10.5 Editing MIDI music files

This is perhaps the most difficult part of the exercise!

Once the MIDI recording is over, we need to edit the resulting MIDI Data. Apart from simple editing operations like removing the silence before and after the notes, there are many other operations that can be applied upon the recorder file.

For example, the time duration required for a specific MIDI piece may be a bit lesser or greater than that of the actual recording. In such cases, the files may have to be edited to suit the required time intervals.

MIDI sequencer software allows us to cut, copy and paste relevant pieces of instrument notes – just like Microsoft Word for text! Since different instrument streams and notes can be cut and manipulated within the same MIDI file, the sequencer software gives full power and freedom to a creative music composer, to experiment with incredible ease and innovation.

Quite a number of MIDI sequencer software is currently available in the market today.

Some are bundled along with the sound cards and the rest are available as separate packages.

Fortunately, a good many number of simple sequencer software are available as shareware and freeware, across the Internet. For understanding the fundamental MIDI editing operations, we will take up one such shareware called "Music Sculptor ".

10.6 Music sculptor

Music sculptor has a very simple and easy to use interface.

You can open any valid file with a .mid extension. As the file opens out, a graphical representation of all the tracks available within the file are displayed.

Music sculptor can show the MIDI music files in two modes - Keyboard mode and Track mode. Track mode is usually preferable for all editing operations.

The opened file can be played back with the 'Play' button that protrudes out from the tools box.

As the file is being played from the beginning, a rectangular pointer moves along the time track, which has been divided into equal number of intervals. This pointer is very useful for pin pointing and selecting the required track / sequence along the right time interval, during the editing operation.

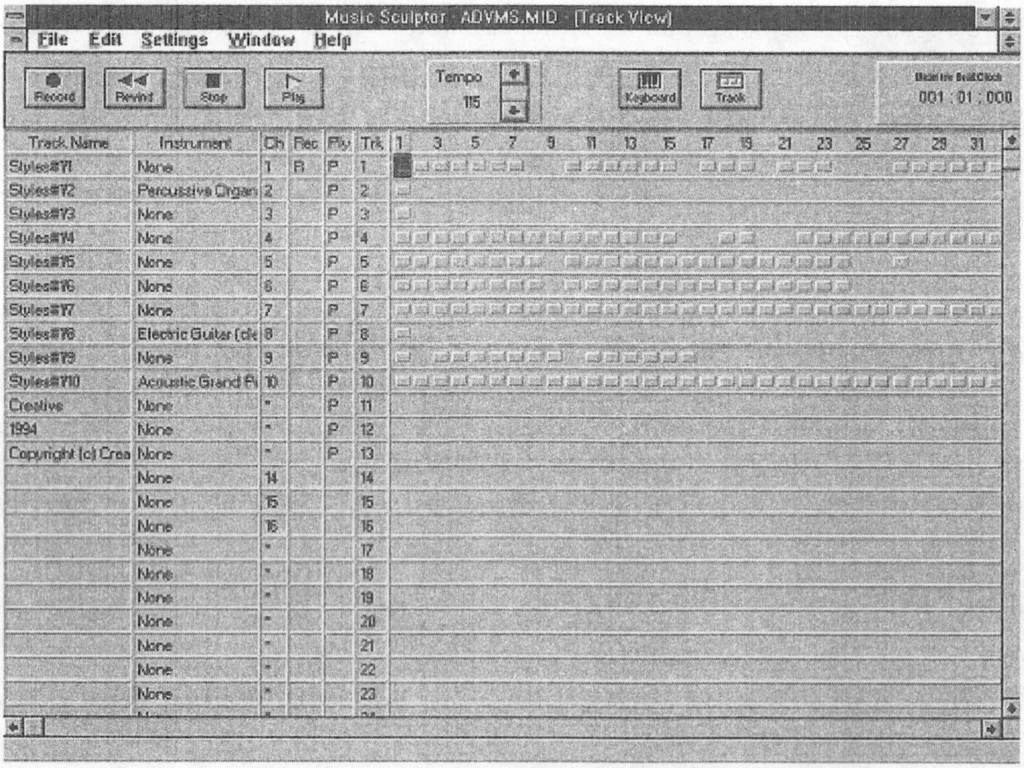

Figure 45: Music sculptor interface

After playing back the file several times, you can decide upon the tracks and notes to be edited. If need be, an individual track alone can be selected and played back, to hear the notes of that particular instrument. (In the figure that follows, I have selected three such tracks for editing).

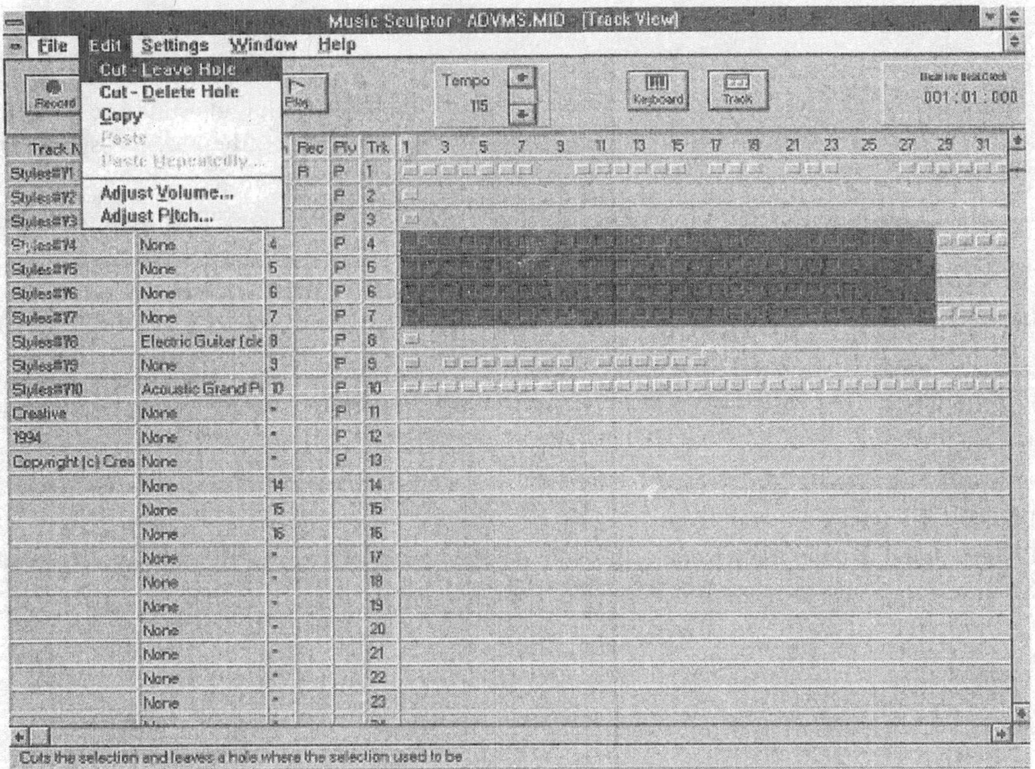

Figure 46: Editing tracks with music sculptor

Once the portions to be edited are decided accurately without ambiguity, the actual editing operation starts.

Unwanted portions can be selected and deleted, using the 'Cut' menu option.

In cut, there are two options available: To cut without leaving hole and to cut and leave the holes. Selecting the first option deletes the entire segment, leaving no time gap. The second option deletes the specific notes from the file, but leaves the time gap, as it is. The first choice is suitable, when all the tracks along a particular time interval are selected and removed and the second is meant for selecting and removing notes of specific instruments.

Selecting a portion of the file segment and copying it repeatedly can extend a small MIDI piece to a prolonged duration of time. This feature is particularly useful for creating background music, wherein, some specific notes are to be repeated over a period of time.

MIDI integrity is so powerful, that the edited pieces seamlessly blend with the parent piece and are hardly noticeable. Thus, even professional music performances can be created with the help of MIDI and with little effort.

10.7 Pitch correction

Apart from all the operations discussed above, Music sculptor also allows us to edit the pitch of a specific instrument - a feature that is very useful while different pieces of instrumental notes are cut and pasted - to evolve a new MIDI file.

When a Music score is conducted with several Instruments, the pitch or scale of each instrument is adjusted to be similar, to produce the synchronisation we enjoy with the blending of various kinds of music notes. Similarly, even with MIDI files, every instrument participating in a particular file is set to the same frequency, to produce a melodious synchronisation.

Now, when different Instrumental notes from different files are integrated with the editing options available, chances are that they may not maintain the same pitch, resulting in an asynchronous music.

It's exactly here, that the pitch correction feature comes to the rescue.

By selecting those notes which are asynchronous with the rest of the Music, and adjusting the pitch of the same (which can be incremented or decremented, depending upon one's requirement), the required synchronisation can be achieved with ease.

This brings us to the conclusion of our discussions on Music sculptor, MIDI as well as multimedia audio – as a whole.

10.8 Summary

MIDI files can be played back using windows media player and all other popular multimedia player software. Because of the complexities involved in MIDI recording, it pays to check out royalty free MIDI music libraries that are available on the Internet.

To build up a MIDI music studio, one needs to have a MIDI compatible synthesizer electronic keyboard, MIDI plug-in cables and MIDI sequencer software.

After the MIDI recording is over, the resulting MIDI data has to be edited to suit the specific requirements of the project. MIDI sequencer software is used to edit MIDI files.

PART IV

MULTIMEDIA TEXTS

PART OVERVIEW

Part IV explores the next media: texts.

Though texts are one of the oldest forms of communication mediums, they do manage to find a place in the fascinating world of multimedia. Multimedia texts are not so different from conventional texts – but depending upon the applications and contexts in which they are used, certain interesting situations may arise.

This part has only one chapter that deals with everything concerning multimedia texts - including titling and hypertexts.

Chapter 11

Designing Texts

CHAPTER OVERVIEW

In this chapter, we first introduce texts as integral components of multimedia projects.

Though they might sound pretty simple at the first glance, multimedia texts do involve lot of design and development considerations. You might be in for a surprise, as we discuss these strategies one after another.

Hypermedia and hypertexts get a neat focus in the pages that follow, and finally we get to know some of the tools available for editing multimedia texts.

Throughout the course of the chapter, several commercial CD-ROM titles have been references to illustrate various concepts.

11.1 Introduction

Texts play an important role in our lives.

Since the advent of editing programs like WordStar and MS Word, the influence of information technology on print media has only been increasing. Our scope, in this book, is however limited to the treatment of texts as an element - in multimedia projects.

The extent, to which texts are used in a multimedia project, depends upon three factors:

- The nature of the project (Multimedia CD-ROM, Presentation multimedia, Game etc.)
- The subject (Dinosaurs, War games or Corporate profits?)
- The treatment of the subject (Heavy graphics / Light text, Heavy text / Light graphics etc)

Examples

- Multimedia reference encyclopaedias like Microsoft's Encarta or the Grolier multimedia encyclopaedia may contain extensive text based information – since they literally replace multiple volumes of Encyclopaedia Britannica.
- Edutainment CD-ROMs like the learning company's 'Reading Blaster' – meant for teaching spellings and grammar to kids, relies more on visuals and audio than text – to deliver the contents.
- There may be few exceptional CD-ROMs like my favourite 'Tune land' (a very compelling nursery rhyme teacher) – from seventh level communications - that doesn't make use of any text at all!

11.2 Texts as a part of multimedia project

Texts can be used in multimedia projects for different purposes.

These include

1. Title texts
2. Body texts
3. Menu and navigation texts
4. Button texts
5. Miscellaneous texts

The design rules that govern multimedia texts, largely depends upon the context in which a particular text appears. For example, we can evolve some quick rules like title texts should be big in size and should employ some of the brightest colours and that body texts should be of smaller size.

The rest of this chapter is dedicated to discussions on the importance of proper text design, how to design texts for various kinds of multimedia projects etc.

Figure 47: Extensive multimedia texts in David McCauley's CD-ROM "The way things work". Notice the usage of various fonts.

Figure 48: On the contrary, my CD-ROM title 'Tales from Indian Mythology' – published by cybervalley systems, features very little text.

11.3 Text design basics

Designing text involves two important aspects of information that is being presented: content and display.

- ❑ Content covers **what** is the matter that is being presented – whether it is technical information or a sales update or news.
- ❑ Display covers **how** the matter is being presented – what fonts are used, what colours and backgrounds are being applied etc.

Rather than detailing what benefit a proper text design can bring in for a multimedia project - let us take another approach. Let us discuss the ill effects of poor content and display design, which, in turn, will emphasize the importance of text design in multimedia projects.

11.4 Effects of poor text content design

It is needless to over-emphasize the importance of content: poor contents fail to impress the user and result in loss of interest in the whole project. Careful attention should be paid, not only to the language, but also to ease of expressions.

A point of interest in multimedia text design is that, the display and content design should synchronise seamlessly, to produce successful results. The tone and 'effect' produced during the display can be greatly enhanced by achieving intelligent synchronisation.

For example, while discussing something that's ancient or something related to history, it's better to engage fonts that represent old manuscript characters. If the interface graphics designer is intelligent enough to give a very fine backdrop (say, that of ancient stone slabs), then naturally, the results are very impressive.

11.5 Effect of poor text display design

Poor display design affects every interface of the project. It spoils the general appeal produced by visuals and other media. This ultimately results in customer dissatisfaction and chances are high, that the user may not even explore the project well enough.

The degree of these adverse effects may vary, depending upon the immediate impression created in the mind of the user and the extent to which other media are trying to balance this failure. In the worst case, poor text display design may become the main cause of the failure of the project.

If you chance upon to see different types of multimedia projects, you can easily understand how intelligently the display parameters have been manipulated - depending upon their context, to have a lasting impact. You can also realise the consistency between various screen events and the relative texts that are being displayed.

For example, in an encyclopaedia project like Microsoft Encarta, the 'facts' box (that display texts with various facts and figures) will always open out an interface that displays the contents consistently - with similar types of fonts. Only the content changes accordingly.

Another example would be that almost all buttons would share same type of fonts and in some cases, even colours, to maintain certain degree of consistency and integrity throughout the project.

11.6 Parameters that control text design

There are three main parameters that control display designs of multimedia texts. They are

- Fonts
- Font colours
- Backdrop (or background)

While fonts affect the profile of the displayed texts, colours and backgrounds affect the overall appeal of the same.

11.7 Fonts - definition

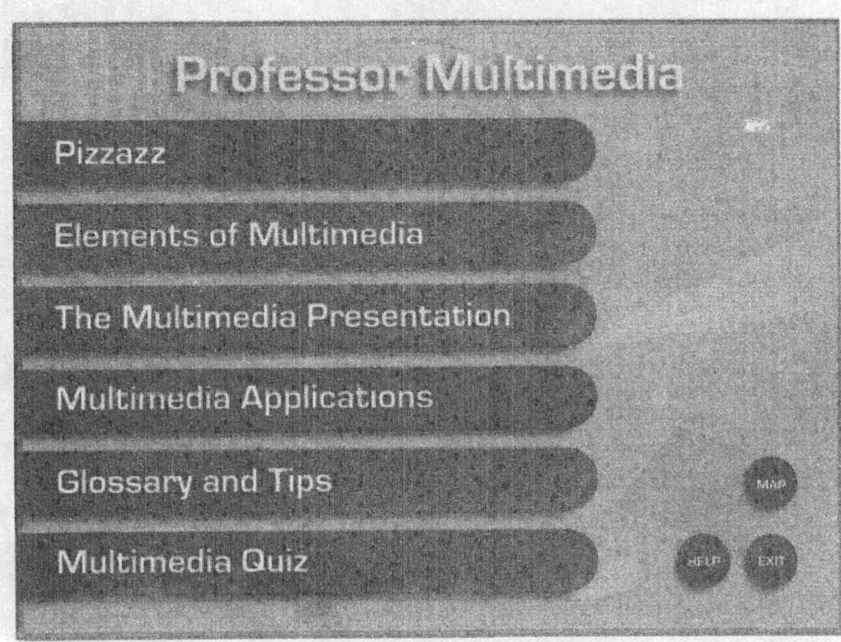

Figure 49: Notice menu texts and button texts in Individual Software's "Professor Multimedia"

Fonts can be defined as a collection of alphabetical and numeric characters, of similar or comparable profiles and which belong to a particular typeface family that's determined by a unique family name. The sizes of fonts can either be adjustable or not, depending upon the nature of the font family.

11.8 Types of font families

Two types of font families emerged as industrial standards, amidst hundreds of other proprietary standards. Apple first introduced both of these font families. They are

- Postscript fonts and
- True type fonts

We shall take up true type fonts for our discussions, as it's the preferred choice in a standard windows environment.

11.9 True type fonts

Fonts, that are scalable i.e. whose sizes can be altered, while maintaining the basic profile design of the characters, are called true type fonts. These fonts support windows 'WYSIWYG' (What You See is What You Get) technology i.e. these fonts will be printed by your laser or inkjet printer exactly in the same way, as they appear on screen.

They may sometimes, be generated as bitmap structures - depending upon the capabilities of the printer attached. These fonts are compatible with both PC / Windows and the Apple Macintosh environments.

To have a look at all the true type fonts supported by your computer, follow this procedure:

1. Double click on the fonts icon in the control panel. The lists of fonts that have been installed and available with your operating system are displayed.

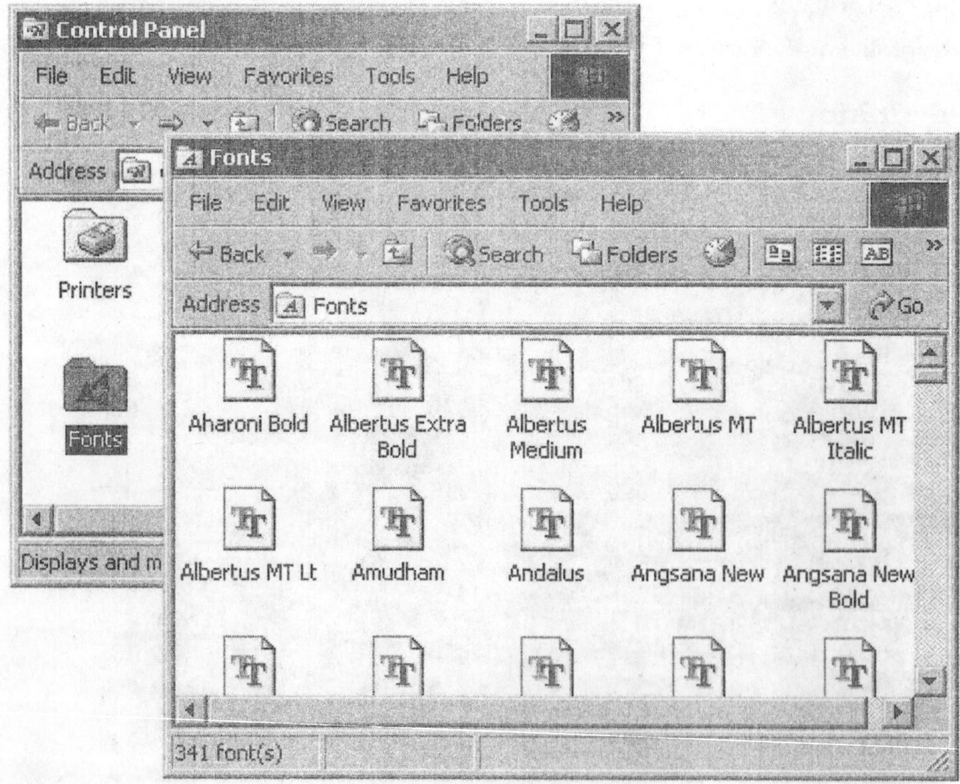

Figure 50: Various fonts installed on your computer

2. On double clicking the font file names, the font display is available under various sizes.
3. Options are available to add or delete the Fonts from the list. You can even customize the System to display only true type fonts.

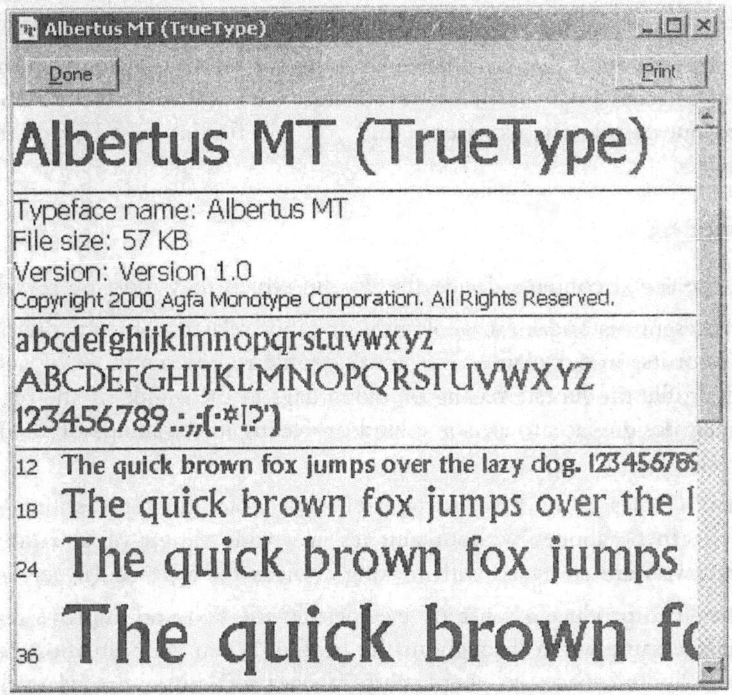

Figure 51: Details of a given font

4. If you want, you can install new fonts using the Install fonts dialog box.

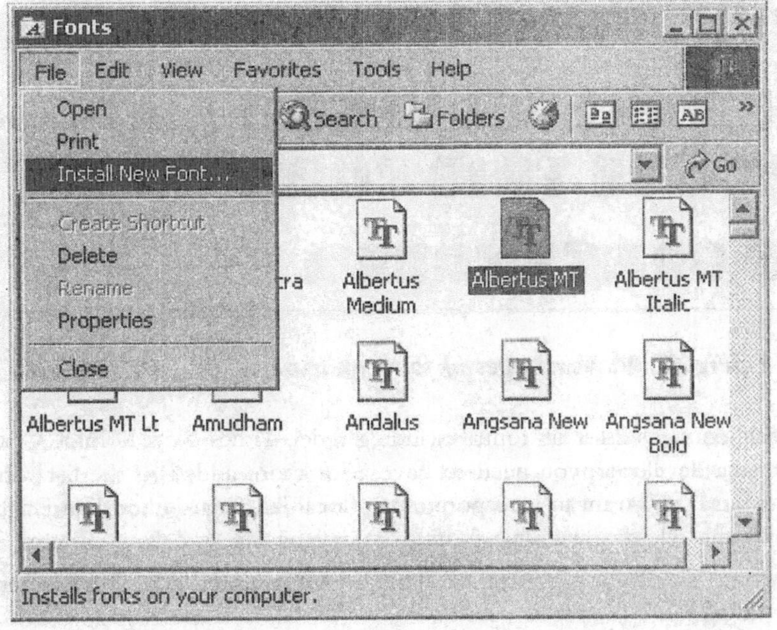

Figure 52: Installing a new font

11.10 Selecting the right font

Selecting the right type of font, for a given project at hand - may sometimes be tougher than selecting a life partner! This confusion is mainly because of thousands of varieties of fonts that are currently available for desktop applications. Worse still, a thousand more are being added every day on the Internet, thus compounding the situation.

Though there are no hard and fast rules that govern which fonts are to be used for a given situation, I am offering the following suggestions as indicative tips - rather than conclusive rules. True, they are not thumb rules...but most of them have been derived out of practical experience and you will find at least half of them relevant and readily applicable in your projects.

11.11 Designer's tips

- To a great extent, the actual contents decide the way, in which they must be represented.
- For example, to represent historical, archaeological or other related contents, the preferred choice is a font by name EmGraves or its various clones. This font's profile represents those of age-old English writings of the past. This very profile produces a feeling of olden days in the minds of the readers. Herein lies the true success of the display design - to arouse some kind of feeling in the minds of the readers, that's true to the context.
- 'Times New Roman' (Times in the Mac) is the preferred choice for representing 'Conventional' or 'News' type of contents. It can be applied without glitches in a wide variety of situations and you can seriously consider it whenever you are confused with making choices for a particular screen in your project.
- 'Ariel' and 'Helvetica' can produce a sense of evenness in the text and improve readability - because, these two fonts maintain the same width throughout the profile. When your situation demands packing of more information within a limited space, or where the font sizes to be used are relatively small - give these two, a quick shot! Most probably you'll be satisfied with the results.

Old English Writing !	→ EM Graves
CONVENTIONAL TEXTS!	→ Times New Roman
SENSE OF EVENNESS !	→ Arial / Helvatica
DON'T USE THIS FOR LONG SENTENCES !	→ Fancy Fonts

Figure 53: Various types of fonts and the effects they produce

- Windows OS itself contains a list of fonts, including Ariel, Times New Roman, Courier and System fonts. But, as a multimedia developer, you need to have a lot more added to the list. Check out the free stuff available via Internet. If you want to incorporate your local language (other than English) into your projects, you need to install the relevant true type fonts of your language into your system.
- Don't use fancy fonts like 'Tony White' or 'Weshollidays', for representing long sentences. At the most, they can be used for titling.
- Do not have too many font families - in your system. Limit yourself to best hundred or so, available with

you. When you are adding new items to your collection, take care to remove the older and unwanted ones, so that the total number available in your system is maintained. Removal of fonts from the display disk may not result in removal of fonts from your hard disk! You have to clearly specify your options in the message boxes. For details, refer Windows help system.

- Don't make use of too many varieties of fonts, within the same project. This may result in loss of integrity and fail to make an impression in the mind of the user. Particularly, maintain the inner contents with the same type of font. If you want to distinguish a particular portion of the text from others, use font attributes like *italics*, underline, outline and colour - instead of changing the very type of font. Also, the button bars and menu items must be consistent in their general appeal.
- A variety of special effects can be applied to the general texts and these are discussed under a separate topic called 'titling'.
- Font sizes also play a crucial role in elevating the appeal produced by a particular kind of font type. Do not use either very large or very small font sizes for representing long sentences or contents (Particularly in 'reference' type of multimedia projects like the encyclopaedias) - the optimal size would be 12 to 16 points.

Figure 54: Children's edutainment titles - like 'Reader rabbits Interactive reading journey" from the Learning Company - makes use of large sized fonts, for effortless reading.

- On the other hand, edutainment projects, particularly those meant for children - usually make use of large fonts, so that the child is able to read the text without much strain. Another point, which I'd mentioned earlier, should be remembered here: 'Children titled should not be packed with too much contents.' Thus, you're usually left with lot of free space at every instance of the project, thus enabling easy usage of large sized fonts!

- **Last point:** The best method to find out the right font for a particular project is to take out the background separately and try out different permutations and combinations possible. The best time to make decisions on font types is during storyboarding (Storyboarding process is explained in later chapters) rather during the actual stages of production...If need be, the background environments can be roughly developed for experimentation purposes, to try out the font faces. This exercise, though seems a bit complicated, is bound to reduce lot of time wastage during the actual production.

11.12 Font installation issues

The following discussions illustrate one of the potential issues while selecting a particular font for your project – not from a design perspective, but from a programmer's viewpoint.

You can use literally any type of font for your project. No authoring environment restricts this independence. However, there is one catch:

You have to ensure that all the variety fonts you are using are available in all client systems also!

Otherwise, the Windows environment replaces your font with the best alternative possible - which may deviate far from your choice. So you may have to find out whether your fonts are supported by the client system an **install them when you don't find one!**

The installation program that you supply along with your package usually handles this task. Writing out an installation program, that'll do the above functions is not only difficult but may invite other troubles.

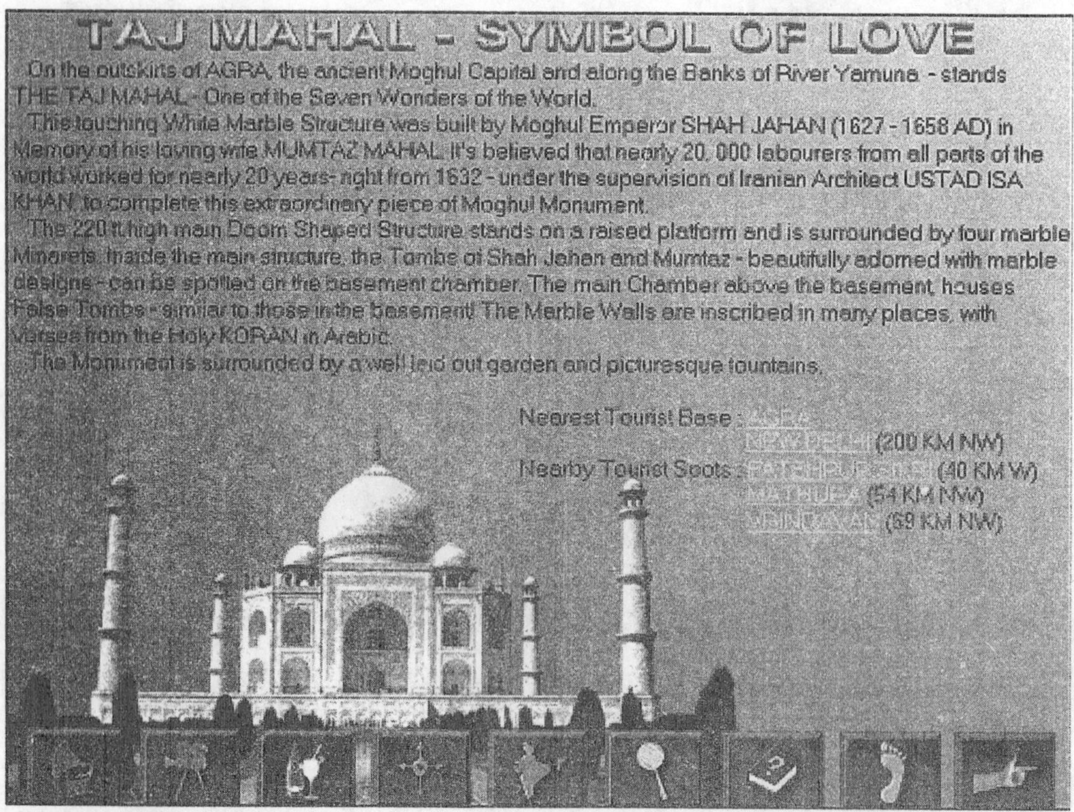

Figure 55: I ensured that I am making use of most common fonts in my CD-ROM title "Tourist's India – an Interactive Multimedia Guide" – published by cybervalley systems.

For example, chances are that you are using a particular font developed and sold by a company. If you are distributing this font with your package, you are violating the copyright of the font manufacturer! Refer the appendix titled 'IPR Laws in the Indian Context' for more details on copyright laws.

Because, the font manufacturer sold the particular fonts to you only for your usage and not for redistribution to others! Once you install the fonts in the client machines, it's available for him also and he can use the same for all of his purposes. Even if you take care to remove the fonts during un installation by painstakingly writing an uninstall program, if the client doesn't uninstall your package, then the fonts become available for his usage!

Apart from all these troubles, writing out an installation program that'll serve these purposes involves, not just adding a few files to the client's windows system directory - but also modifying certain system files in the client's operating system!

Any mistakes in such installation or un-installation programs may be very costly, because, if something goes wrong - with the system files because of our rewriting, the very system may crash down or may result in other unexpected consequences. It requires a hardcore windows system programmer to write such a program without a hitch.

So, are there any ways to get over such problems?

Well, here are a few suggestions, though not solutions - in a strict sense.

- ❑ As far as possible, make use of system fonts that come bundled with windows operating system, like 'Ariel' or 'Times new roman'. You can expect to have the same in all client machines and need not worry about them.
- ❑ Make all titles and other areas –hopefully few in number - that carry other varieties of fonts, as images or bitmapped pictures. Though it's a bit difficult to handle them, (refer my note on 'Anti-aliasing' in the discussions that follow) you need not worry about installing the font files, to maintain the display design!
- ❑ This suggestion is a bit more complex: To 'create' your own fonts with the help of font creation tools like 'The font studio' and distribute them freely without worrying about copyright issues! Of course, as a creator of the font you have to register your stake over the creation by registering the copyright, or otherwise, somebody else may do it! If you are not satisfied with the pre-installed fonts of Window, and have considerable time to spare, give it a shot!

11.13 Titling

Titling is an art by itself.

Particularly, the variety of 'supercharged special effects' can be applied only to titles and not other portions of the contents. Also, good titles often invite the readers to have a detailed look at the contents that follow...and that probably makes them more important in multimedia projects.

A variety of choices are available for designing titles - the options available are usually determined by the packages you are making use of. Nevertheless, what we are going to discuss here are available in almost all successful multimedia packages and can readily be applied.

11.14 Jaggies and anti-aliasing

One of the serious problems faced by text designers in the windows based environment or equivalent, is that of 'Jaggies' - or small edge disturbances created with true type font families. These disturbances are relatively low - rather, insignificant - when the font sizes are small, but assume significant importance with larger font sizes, as that in titles. To have a glimpse of what jaggies are, have a look at the figure.

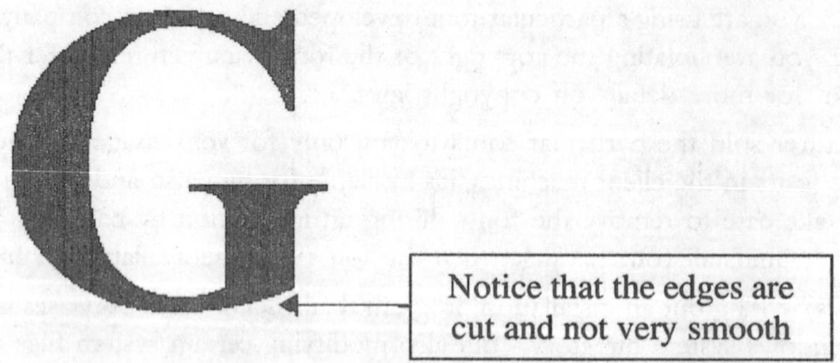

Figure 56: Jaggies – illustrated. You can actually have a better view of jaggies than the one I've shown, in your computer. Jaggies are smoothened out during laser printing.

These disturbances distort the profile of the fonts to such an extent that the beauty of the title totally stands spoiled because of them!

The serious victims are those alphabets and numbers that have some sort of curvature, like 'S' or 'C'. Those made up of relatively straight lines, like the letter 'L' often manage to present a decent look, even with jaggies.

This problem can be seen in most of the word processing packages like MS Word or Word perfect - but, since these disturbances are barely visible after laser printing at 600*600 dpi resolution, the problem is barely conceivable.

So, how do we get over the problem?

Shall we all try to restrict our contents to make use of only straight lined alphabets? Wow, that'd be too harsh and we may seldom succeed in trying to express what we want to! After all, we have got only 26 English alphabets at our disposal to joggle with... we may rather try to live with jaggies and restrict our font sizes to tolerable limitations!

But wait! The situation is not that worst, after all.

For the problem of jaggies, there is a very efficient solution called the 'technique of anti-aliasing'. Let us see what it is and how it can be used to get over jaggies.

11.15 Anti-aliasing texts

Anti-aliasing is the technique of tracing out the contour of the font profile using various shades of the font colour, in such a way that jaggies are reduced to the minimum and are barely noticeable even at large font sizes.

As mentioned earlier, most of the word processing programs do not have 'anti-aliasing' feature. We have to look out for some popular paint editing tools like Adobe photo shop to have a taste of how an anti-aliased text would look like. To have a glimpse of the same, look at the sample I have provided. Carefully notice the marked difference between an anti-aliased and non anti-aliased texts and the difference produced in their appeal, even when their sizes, content and colour are very much, the same.

Paint shop Pro is yet another software, surprisingly a shareware, that's supported by efficient anti-aliasing algorithms. It supports all true type fonts pre-installed in your system, and automatically traces out the profiles as and when you develop the contents. Paint shop pro also contains various other 'effects simulation' features that make the package, a highly recommended tool for designing multimedia titles.

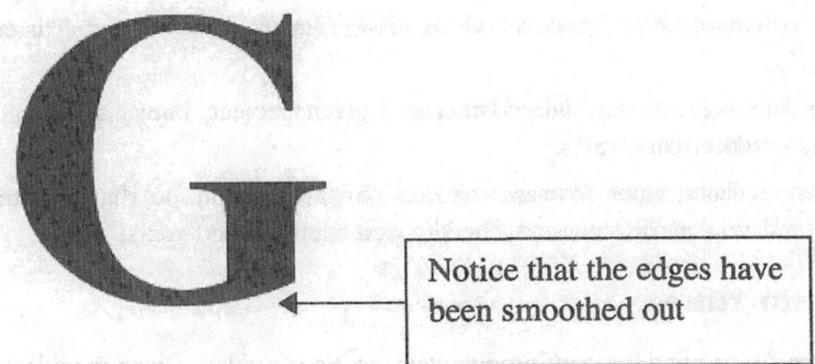

Figure 57: Anti aliased text – illustrated. If you cannot find any big difference between the earlier text and this one, use a magnifying glass – if you have one. These subtle edges are perceivable more in monitors than in print media.

11.16 Editing anti-aliased texts

With all it's advantage, you may most probably face one problem with all anti-aliased texts: since almost all tools meant for anti-aliasing texts store the resulting graphics only as images, there's no way to treat the contents as texts, once they are anti-aliased (unless your authoring environment supports it!).

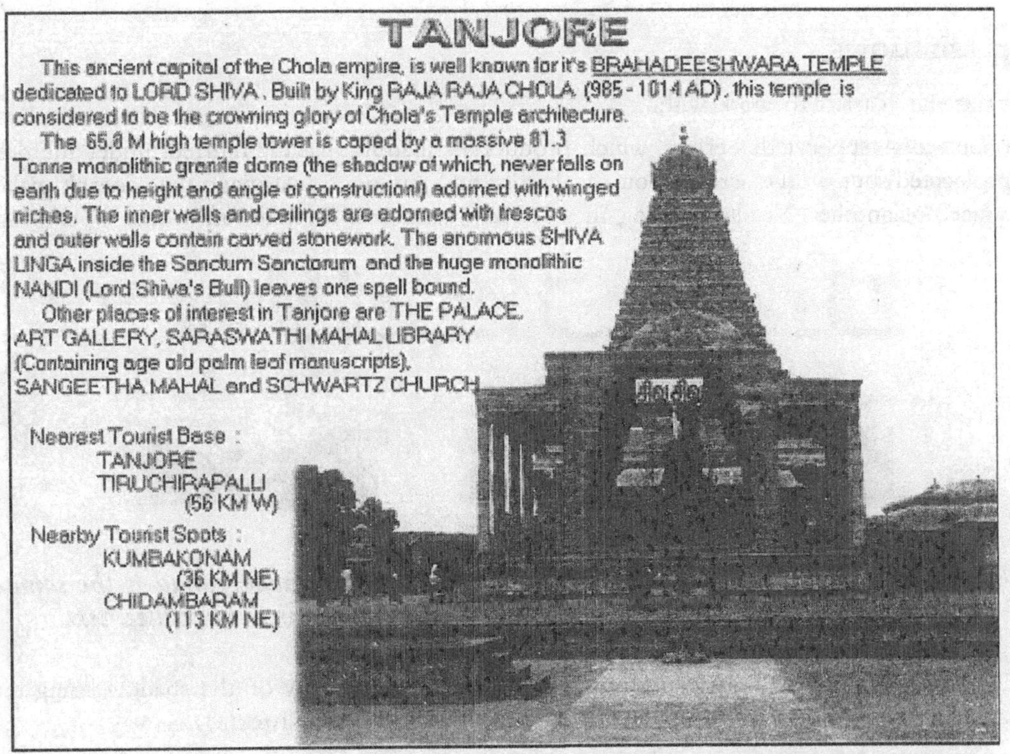

Figure 58: The titles are anti-aliased, but not the body text – in my CD-ROM title 'Tourist's India – an interactive multimedia guide', published by cybervalley systems.

That means, you can no longer open the anti-aliased texts in your standard word processors and do editing, if any. You may have to use graphic design tools such as Paint shop Pro or Adobe Photoshop – introduced earlier, to edit the contents. This invariably consumes lot of time as well as effort, apart from the expertise required to handle the packages.

So, it is better, not only limit the usage of anti-aliased texts in a given project, but also design it in such a way that they can be placed as images – rather than texts.

Also, it is better to keep all anti-aliasing work towards the end of production, so that all alterations are made only to the normal text contents and you hardly have any need to edit anti-aliased texts!

11.17 Special effects for titles

A variety of special effects can be applied to multimedia texts; to page titles – in particular.

The software tools he or she is using to create special effects, dictate the options available to a designer. Premier photo editing software tools like Adobe Photoshop and Corel Photo paint provide lot of special effect options. Paint shop pro, for its share, does provide a number of these effects and also has an interesting feature of recognizing Adobe Photoshop special effect filters.

With the help of such software, your titles can fly high.

If the tools you are using do not support some of the effects that are in your mind, you can even write programs using Windows 16 or 32-bit API! But, for that, you should either know windows graphics programming or depend upon somebody else, who knows that.

For the current discussions, we shall take up a few common special title effects, available in most graphics tools – including Paint shop Pro.

11.18 Drop shadows

Drop shadows are the easiest to work with.

Almost all famous tools support this effect, which produces a shadow -usually blurred, under the desired text, so that it looks 'projected' out of the screen. You can hardly find any good web page that doesn't make use of this effect, in one place or another. Needless to say, these effects work best for titles and other types of headings.

Figure 59: First is a fancy effect, wherein the body colour and the background is the same – white. In the second text, drop shadows have been applied over a bevelled text.

You can usually control the colour, degree of blur and the extent of opacity of the shadow, using the dialog box options that are thrown open, once you try to add this effect over a selected text.

Here are a few useful tips, for using drop shadows:

- ❑ Never make use of any colours other than black, for shadows...they seldom produce good appeal. Remember that no coloured shadows exist in nature!
- ❑ Drop shadow effects work best in white background, although some light colours may also work out well.
- ❑ Never try this at dark backgrounds...the shadows may barely be visible!

- ❑ By maintaining similar background and font colours, some fancy effects can be achieved, as shown in the illustration.
- ❑ Drop shadows have best chances of working together with 3D texts or bevel effects (discussed separately). Refer the illustration, which is a typical example of such a conjunction.

11.19 Bevel effects

Next to drop shadows, bevel effects and their clones are the widely used effect on titles. When applied, they make a projection out of the title area – so that the text protrudes out with some shine, as shown in the illustration. You can control parameters like the degree of shininess, bevel size, angle of bevel etc. This effect is relatively easy to apply and is very effective in titling, when the background is particularly a photograph or bitmap.

Bevelled texts, in combination with drop shadows can produce great results, when they are applied with suitable fonts over a very light or white backgrounds.

11.20 Three dimensional texts

Normal texts, as we see on the monitor, are all two-dimensional.

If we could add a space co-ordinate along the Z - axis, then the entire environment becomes three dimensional (for detailed discussions on two dimension and three dimensional fundamentals, kindly refer the chapter on multimedia animations)

Objects placed in three-dimensional environments look more real and present a 'physical entity' kind of look. For example, look at the three dimensional (henceforth represented as 3D) text in the diagram.

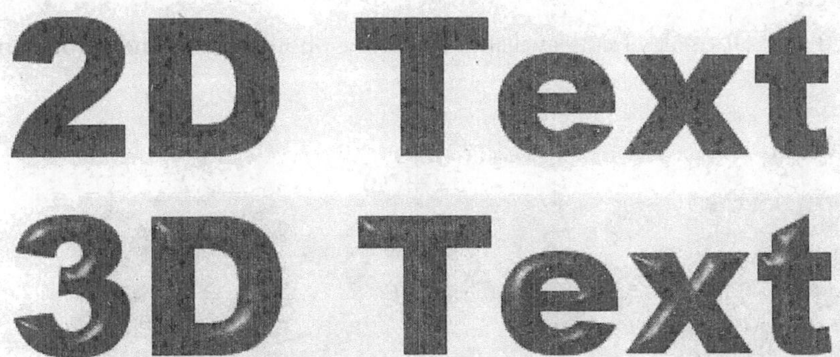

Figure 60: Using graphic tools, it is possible to apply a variety of special effects to titles – like the 3D text shown here.

For comparison purposes, the same text has been presented nearby, in the conventional 2D form. With 3D texts, much more effects are possible like controlling the intensity of light that's cast over the Text objects, altering the 'Surface Parameters' of the text objects etc.

In general 3D texts are employed only for representing very important texts in a project, like the project title.

11.21 How to create three-dimensional titles?

Three-dimensional texts can be created in two ways:

- ❑ To use advanced graphic tools with 3D text simulation capabilities
- ❑ To make use of 3D modelling and rendering software

The choice between these two depends upon your exact requirements and other constraints like time and budget. All advanced graphic tools are bundled with ready made 3D simulation routines, that mostly decide the type of 3D effect that's going to be simulated - but you do have control over a few parameters like colour, shading, light (in some cases) etc.

One great advantage with them is that they are very fast to work with. It only takes a few minutes to produce 3D effect of your choice over the given text and study the results. Thus, you can experiment with lots of permutations, until you achieve satisfactory output. If the original software is not endowed with the effects that are in your mind, you can look out for third party plug-ins (when the parent software supports such a feature) that'll provide the necessary effects you want.

Adobe Photoshop literally has thousands of such plug-ins that generate almost all conceivable effects - including a huge variety of 3D title effects. Some of them are even available free of cost or as shareware, over the Internet.

On the other hand, 3D modelling software gives you much more independence to work with - at the cost of more time and effort. Also, learning to work in 3D space is a bit more difficult than normal 2D.

So, here is the balance between these two:

When you want to create 3D effects over stationary multimedia texts, do prefer graphic tools and their plug-ins. Even if you don't find something that'll exactly match the one in your imagination, you'll at least find an equivalent - in most of the cases.

In the worst case, you may have to look out for an alternative effect!

3D Modelling tools are best choices for 'animated' texts (discussed in the following sub-heading). Some software even let you to produce 3D flying texts easily, without giving you the strain of working in 3D space. One such tool is Corel move that comes bundled with Corel Draw group of programs and is the preferred choice of many.

A number of other special effects are possible with graphic tools, but the ones discussed above - are especially applicable to multimedia titles.

In general, it can be stated that all other effects available for other photo editing and retouching, are available for texts also.

11.22 Text animations

Figure 61: A text animation featured in my CD-ROM title 'Six Sacred Temples', published by cybervalley systems.

Text animations include moving or flying texts, frequently associated with some graphics - that usually adorn the start-up sequences or the concluding titles.

Many multimedia producers make it a point to animate the first few sequences of their title, displaying their company name along with the logo, followed by the name of the title and the main screen. This initial warm up provides an immediate sense of satisfaction to the viewers and sets the tone for the rest of the project.

Text animations, along with graphics, may be difficult to create, as their development involves usage of three dimensional software platforms - supplemented by the skills and techniques demanded by such 3D environments.

If you want to animate texts alone, without much graphic effect - some software tools let you do that very easily. But, you may have to limit yourself to the animation systems supported by the package and may not enjoy the independence of working in 3D environments; the only advantage being the ease with which you can create such animations, thus saving lot of time.

Good 3D software development platforms are not so cheap and you may have to invest substantially for the same. One suggestion is that you can get this animation work done outside - through some third party developers who specialise in creating professional animations. Even reputed multimedia producers find this method economical and easy.

2D and 3D Animations have been dealt with in detail in later chapters and the basic principles remain almost the same for creating animated texts too.

11.23 Content design

Content design is, in a way, more important than display design.

Because, the initial spell produced by a good display design, is kept alive throughout the proceedings - only by the contents of the project.

Content design involves controlling both quantitative and quantitative aspects of multimedia texts. It not only demands an intelligent perception of the project - as a whole - but also the ability to present things in an interesting order.

11.24 Qualitative aspects of content

Qualitative aspects of content development, involves the following tasks:

- ❑ Developing the contents to be presented
- ❑ Deciding the language to be made use of
- ❑ Deciding the expected behavioural outcome on target audience
- ❑ Producing a sense of appeal relevant for the project, by controlling the tone of language used and the way of addressing the target audience.

The target audience of the proposed project influence nearly all of the above-mentioned aspects, either directly or indirectly. Any deviations from their viewpoint affect the degree of success of the project.

Thus a good content designer should be capable of shifting his or her paradigms to that of the general audience and proceed with the development process. This unique characteristic, not only demands a wholesome understanding of the audience thinking, but also of the society in which they dwell.

For example, all children titles should contain simple words and expressions – as a rule. This helps the child to explore the project on its own, without the help of adults. On the other hand, adult titles may follow one style or other, based on the project under production. This is what we mean, by controlling the 'tone' of the language.

11.25 Controlling quantitative aspects

Qualitative aspects involve the following tasks:

- ❑ Deciding upon the 'length of the text' - in each screen.
- ❑ Deciding upon the total quantity of matter to be distributed through the project and
- ❑ Dividing the contents, in required proportions, between the screens – for optimal distribution of content over the complete span of the project.

Quantitative aspect of contents, ultimately decide the total duration of the project.

Packing a lot of information within a single page may affect readability and presentation. On the other hand, if a core idea is scattered across several pages, then audience get bored or do not understand the point so well.

For corporate presentation, it is better to use bare minimal texts that fill the entire screen – office people never have enough patience to go through elaborate texts. Detailed explanations, if any, should be made either by the presenter (in case of live presentation shows) or by a gentle audio background (in other cases).

For Children edutainment titles, it is better not to pack too much stuff in one screen. They may find those old DOS games more interesting than your edutainment title…and since we use the term 'edutainment', do make good use of funny strips and light jokes, that'll make the presentation lively!

Even in reference titles like encyclopaedias, do not add much, in your urge to disseminate whatever you have got. You may most probably be giving more details than that required, which often irritates the user.

An intelligent way to address this problem is to provide necessary 'links' or 'hot spots' or relevant web addresses - so that those who need more information can explore further. This concept has been elaborated in the sections that follow.

Many a times, multimedia development companies find it a lot more useful to employ copywriters, for the purpose of content development. Some famous CD ROM producers in foreign countries even have expert consultations - particularly while developing children titles.

11.26 Hypermedia

One of the most interesting characteristics of multimedia project is its interactive nature. It is this interactivity, that gives multimedia - an edge over other forms of entertainment like television and video.

Interactivity is the feature that enables the user or the observer to participate in the ongoing proceedings, in some way or other. He is not a mere spectator of what is being presented before him, but is a participant. He can exercise some control over the flow of information or take part in the events that are happening.

All these things help him to have a personalised experience about the whole exercise. This is what interactivity is all about.

No other communication medium is bestowed with this level of interactivity.

One of the techniques used for making multimedia projects interactive, is hypermedia.

Hypermedia is a well-defined structural arrangement of information in the forms of audio, video, text, animation, graphics and other elements of multimedia - pertaining to a particular topic or related to it, with relevant linkages in between them.

As an example, let us try to list out various bits and pieces of information available in Microsoft's multimedia CD-ROM titled 'Oceans':

- ❑ Various facts and figures about oceans (text)
- ❑ Underwater photographs (graphics)
- ❑ Sounds recorder underneath the ocean (audio)
- ❑ An underwater video clip (video)

Now, let us see how this project tries to make use of hypermedia, to present a seamless blend of information to the user – using hypermedia.

Let us assume that the user is exploring the page titled 'sea shells'. Here, he is presented with lot of scientific information about seashells. If he is interested, he can try out some exciting photographs and / or video clippings of seashells using the nearby hyperlinks. He may also try to listen to some actual underwater audio recordings, as he proceeds. How does that sound?

Oh my, try it out for yourself!

And then you will know how different a multimedia experience is, from watching a documentary series on oceans - in the Discovery channel or National geographic!

Figure 62: Microsoft Dinosaurs CD-ROM, makes the best use of hypermedia - to present information available in various media - as a seamless blend.

Now, the linkages that exist between different forms of information are called hyperlinks. In the example that we discussed above, the following hyperlinks are present:

- Hyperlinks between information on seashells and photographs of the seashells
- Hyperlinks to seashells video clippings
- Hyperlinks to underwater audio clippings

Hypermedia can be broadly classified into hypertexts and hyper-graphics. In this chapter, we will be discussing hypertexts and reserve the latter to later chapters.

11.27 Hypertexts

Hypertexts represent all textual information in the project, interlinked to various other subtopics – by means of hyperlinks. Those words that carry hyperlinks to other sub topics are called hot words and are usually distinguished from other normal texts, either by a different font colour or by a different text style.

Almost every web page we see today on the Internet has hypertexts.

Hypertexts enable multimedia professionals to arrange their information into meaningful groups and present them easily, when the user requires it. Without proper organising, the entire project may present a chaotic look... and the best way to do it is by making use of hypertext methodology.

Hypertext feature is imperative to all titles, which contain lots of reference material - like the Microsoft Encarta or Cinemania. Children edutainment titles and those that generally contain very less text-based information, usually depend more on hyper-graphics and not hypertexts.

It can be concluded that, in general, it's very useful to adopt hypertexts in project, when the volume of information to be shared is on the higher side.

11.28 How to embed hyperlinks in multimedia projects?

It is easy to create hyperlinks in html web pages – but web pages are not our concern here. We are interested more in multimedia presentations and projects, which are not web pages, but live executable programs.

It is very easy to develop a hypertext system of your own, using any windows programming environment and use them directly into your projects. One way of doing this would be to develop a small database of hyperlinks - wherein all 'hot words' can be stored with the relevant linkage details. When the user clicks over a particular 'hot word', relevant hyperlink details are read from the database and the screen is updated with the appropriate information.

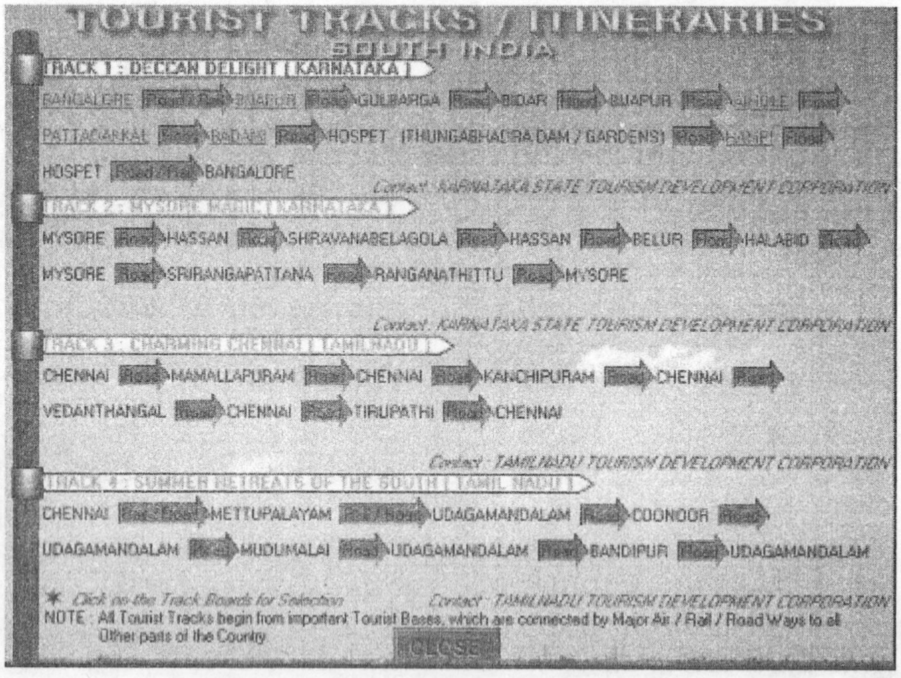

Figure 63: In 'Tourist's India Interactive Multimedia Guide' CD-ROM, I made use of an internal database to store all the hyperlink information - spread across several states and union territories!

Depending upon the requirement and your programming environment, you can try to achieve the same results, by various other methods. For advanced controls, you can look out for the appropriate Windows API routines.

Many premier multimedia-authoring environments, exclusively meant for multimedia programming, have these features built within the package. All you have to do is to inform the package regarding the hot words and the hyperlinks they connect to.

The package takes care of the rest and activates the hypertext system, on receiving relevant mouse clicks over the hot words.

11.29 Designing a hypermedia system

Designing the proper hypermedia system is a very important stage in multimedia project development. In fact, much of the time spent during story- boarding, is for organizing the contents into various meaningful groupings and designing the relevant hyperlinks between them. Improper hyperlink design leads either to several modifications during the course of project development or to improper distribution of contents throughout the title.

Hypertexts, in proportionate combination with hyper-graphics, make out a very successful hypermedia system that fills the users with thrill and contempt - as he proceeds to explore the project, stage after stage.

Here are a few thumb rules to adopt, in designing a hypermedia system:

- Divide the contents into meaningful groupings. A better way to organise the contents, is to adopt a 'Top Down Tree' approach - as illustrated in fig.11- 2. The top most level usually contains an index (or Titles) of all sub-topics, branching out to lower levels. As the levels come down, the depth of information also descends to more intricate details. The greatest advantage of this methodology is that it allows only those who are interested in a particular topic to explore further, and others to bypass them. Thus, the interest the user develops as the title proceeds is kept alive throughout the proceedings.
- For some titles, it's better to integrate Hypertexts and Hyper graphics and design the project just as an integrated Hypermedia system. In such a system, the 'Hot words' are usually linked to some graphic images and photographs and vice versa. In fact, it's this methodology that's currently being adopted in most of the titles, as the producers fell that giving more and more text based information, tends to reduce the tempo of the multimedia experience...But enough care should be taken to design a proper mix between these two powerful indexing systems.
- Enough care should be taken to provide an easy and unambiguous navigation system. Otherwise, the user may be caught at some point of the title and may not be able to return to the screen of his choice. This problem becomes compounded particularly with respect to Hypertext systems with lot of hyper linkages descending down to several levels of intricacy. To cope up with this problem, all multimedia titles provide you with the option of reaching the Main screen or Main menu from any sub-level - so that the user feels confident, even if he's unable to trace back his old navigation path.
- Another useful feature will be to provide a 'Back' option, at any point of time, so that the user can go back to previous levels of his navigation path, from the current screen. Of course, to achieve this - you may have to keep track of all the movements of the user carefully... the levels up to which the user can go back in the title being decided by *the number of levels you can keep track of!*

11.30 Text editing software tools

A variety of Software tools are available for creating texts for multimedia projects - the choice depends upon the requirement and usage.

- For content creation and development, any standard Word processing tools like Microsoft's Word and Corel's Word Perfect can be used. These tools even allow you to check up the spellings and grammar of your language, so that more time can be spent on developing the contents.
- For creating Title special effects, any Image editing Software can be made use of. Adobe Photoshop, as I had mentioned earlier, is the undisputed leader for PC platforms and the Mac, though Corel's Photo Paint and host of other software are not noticeably lagging in their features. Paint Shop Pro from is available free of cost, for the first 30 days usage, as a shareware.
- For 3D Texts and Text animations, packages like DOS based 3D Studio from AutoDesk or Windows based Light wave 3D from Newtek can be made use of. But, advanced 3D Modelling and Animation software are available only on Windows NT and Silicon Graphic's Irix platforms.

- For designing Hypertext Systems automatically, look out for multimedia specific authoring platforms like Multimedia Tool book from Asymetrix, which support built in Hypermedia interfaces.

11.31 Summary

Texts play an important role in many multimedia projects. These texts are different from the conventional texts in many respects and are called multimedia texts.

Designing texts for multimedia projects involve display and content design. Display design involves the correct choice of font style, font colour and also font size. Designing title texts involve other considerations like anti-aliasing and special effects like drop shadows, cutouts, 3D texts and text animations. Content design involves controlling both quantitative and quantitative aspects of multimedia texts.

Hypermedia methodology enhances multimedia projects. Hypertext feature is provided in titles with lot of text-based information. Hypertexts can be created either by proprietary programming or other supporting authoring environments.

Many text editing software tools are available for content development, title development and font design, under PC and Mac environments.

11.32 Keywords

- **Fonts:** A collection of alphabetical and numeric characters of similar or comparable profiles that belong to a particular typeface family.
- **True type fonts:** Fonts, whose sizes can be altered while maintaining the basic profile design of the characters.
- **Anti-aliasing:** The technique of tracing out the contour of the font profile using various shades of the font colour, in such a way that jaggies are reduced to the minimum.
- **Hypermedia:** A well defined structural arrangement of information in the forms of audio, video, text, animation and graphics- pertaining to a particular topic, with relevant linkages in between them.
- **Hyperlinks:** The linkages that exists between different forms of information in a hypermedia system.
- **Hypertexts:** Text based information, interlinked by means of relevant hyperlinks between various sub topics.

PART V

MULTIMEDIA GRAPHICS

PART OVERVIEW

Part V is devoted to multimedia graphics.

Graphics, in our context, includes still pictures, images and photographs alone and not those with dynamic movements like animations, which are reserved for another chapter.

It's needless to stress the importance of graphics in multimedia – but for catchy graphics and dynamic animations and video, it is impossible to capture the attention of the audience beyond few minutes.

This part begins with the first chapter on the world of colours – dealing with multi colour display systems like monitors and projection panels, followed by lengthy discussions on graphics creation, manipulation and editing methodologies.

Chapter 12

The World of Colours

CHAPTER OVERVIEW

In this introductory chapter on multimedia graphics, we begin with discussions on the hardware side of graphics viz. colour display systems.

Two main parameters that control the quality of display – colour depth and resolution are dealt with in detail. Then we move on to the task of striking a fine balance between these two parameters, resulting in a particular video mode configuration. The most famous display system for the desktops, viz. the colour monitors, get a brief introduction - followed by a step-by-step methodology to configure video controller cards to required video modes.

We conclude the chapter with discussions on relatively lesser-known display systems – like public information display systems and presentation display systems.

12.1 Introduction

Welcome to the wonderful world of colours!

But for those tens and millions of colours, which manifest themselves before our eyes in the form of eye-catching graphics, textures and patterns, multimedia would have been a boring alternative!

If you want to realise the importance of colours in multimedia, just try out your favourite CD-ROM, using a system with monochrome monitor. You will find it really frustrating to follow up the pale grey ball in the black and white fields, in Microsoft's title 'Golf'.

A variety of colour display systems are used to transport the viewers to the magical world of multimedia. The most widely used ones are the CRT colour monitors and of late – LCD monitors. Other kinds of display systems include touch screen monitors meant for multimedia kiosk applications and desktop projectors used for multimedia presentations.

Before taking a detailed look at these equipments, it would be worthwhile to spend some time on understanding the basics of colour display systems – what we mean by colour depth, resolution etc.

12.2 Basic concept of colour displays

If you ever thought that - after all, all colour monitors of same physical size are all one and the same - sorry! You may be wrong!

Apart from the physical size, there are actually a number of other parameters that ultimately govern how well Hollywood's Marilyn Monroe looks, in your 14" colour monitor - the most important parameters that govern being the colour depth and resolution of the monitor.

It is interesting to note that these two parameters are not actually controlled by the monitor – but by the AGP colour card or the graphics card that you use.

12.3 Colour depth

All colour display systems are capable of handling only limited number of colours, at any given point of time.

Systems with bare minimum configuration can manage to handle 256 different colours, for any given image and those with higher configurations can throw up to 16 million colours at any point of time!

It is interesting to note here that it's difficult for the human eye to recognise more than 256 different combinations of colours at any fraction of time. But please don't misunderstand me. This doesn't mean that we all can be content with 256 colours – there are other professional reasons to go for 16 million colours or more!

The total number of colours that could be handled by the monitor depends upon the memory capacity of the video controller card – often known as video random access memory or VRAM.

Video controller cards are also called as AGP card or Graphics card in certain systems. They all serve the same purpose i.e. to interface between the computer and the display device viz. the monitor.

Let us imagine that the entire monitor screen is made up of small dots, called pixels. Pixels are the acronym for picture elements.

The colours that are to be displayed by each pixel, at any fraction of time, are stored as colour data inside the VRAM. Thus, the total number of colours that could be displayed by the system at any point of time depends upon the amount of colour data that could be stored inside the VRAM.

The number of colours that could be stored by each bit in VRAM is obviously the total number of zero-one combinations possible. Ultimately, the total number of memory bits in VRAM dedicated to storing colour information, decides the total number of colours that would available for the display at any point of time.

Note: *Not all bits of VRAM can be used for storing colour data. We have to store another set of information called the resolution as well, which is explained later.*

Thus, we have the following sets of standard number of colours that could be made use of:

Table 18: Colour depth and the number of colours

Colour depth	No of colours
1 - Bit per pixel	2 Colours
4 - Bits per pixel	16 Colours
8 - Bits per pixel	256 Colours (also known as 8 bit colour)
16 - Bits per pixel	65, 536 colours (known as 16 bit colour or High colour)
24 – Bits per pixel	16.7 million colours (known as 24 bit colour or True colour)

Monitors equipped with a minimum of 8 Bit displays (i.e. with 256 Colours) are suitable for beginners, while 24 bit and 32 bit are recommended for professionals.

12.4 Resolution

Let us proceed further remembering our assumption the entire screen is made up of small dots called pixels. Now, how many such pixels are there on the screen, at any given point of time - is what is known as the resolution of the monitor.

Even these dots are stored as resolution data, inside VRAM. Thus, the available VRAM space is shared between colour depth and resolution data.

Another interesting point to note.

The pixels or dots over the screen, which we have been talking about all along, are logical pixels – and not physical ones!

But that does not mean that there are no physical picture elements on the monitor. It is just that these actual or physical pixels are different from the logical pixels that deal with colour depth and resolution.

The following table summarizes some of the popular resolutions adopted:

Table 19: Resolution and no of pixels

Resolution	Pixels
640 * 480	640 rows and 480 columns of pixels
800 * 600	800 rows and 600 columns of pixels
1024 * 768	1024 rows and 768 columns of pixels
1280 * 1024	1280 rows and 1024 columns of pixels
1600 * 1200	1600 rows and 1200 columns of pixels

The resolution of the screen ultimately decides the size of the picture, on the screen. A picture that occupies the entire screen, in a 1024*768 resolution looks 'chopped off' at 648*480 resolution.

Figure 64: On your left hand side, you see the picture of a bird of size 1024*768 pixels. On the right hand side, you are seeing the same picture on the same monitor – but at a different resolution – 640*480. Notice that the bottom portions – below the legs are not seen. They can be reached only by scrolling down the picture.

This actually tells you about a potential resolution problem that might occur in your projects. For example, if you have designed a project at 1024 * 768 resolution monitor and deliver the same for a client whose is using a colour resolution of 640*480, then you are going to have problems getting your invoice through.

Another problem, which is relatively less damaging – is the case of viewing a lower size picture on a high-resolution monitor.

Figure 65: Imagine the same bird picture to be of a lower size - say 640*480. When it is viewed on a monitor with 1024*768 resolution using graphics software such as Paint shop pro, black borders appear on all the four sides to fill the gap left by the picture.

Though small monitors can be adjusted to give better resolutions, it may not be relevant to employ very high resolutions on small 14" monitors – because, as you increase the resolution, the system font sizes also tend to become small. In fact, equilibrium should be stuck between the monitor size and the resolution. Refer the following table that provides recommended resolutions for monitors of various sizes.

Table 20: Monitor sizes and recommended resolutions

Monitor size	Resolution
14"	640 * 480 / 800 * 600
15"	800 * 600 / 1024 * 768
17"	800 * 600 / 1024 * 768 / 1280 * 1024
21"	1024 * 768 / 1280 * 1024 / 1600 * 1200

12.5 Monitor video modes

Number of colours as well as resolution data is stored in VRAM memory.

Since both are space hungry, sharing the available resource to optimum levels, becomes critical.

Both of them should be set to such values, so that they balance each other and provide a satisfactory output for all kinds of applications. Very high resolutions at very low colour depths or vice versa simply won't work.

To arrive at this balance, I'm providing a small table below, which details all the optimal combinations of resolution and number of colours – and the corresponding VRAM requirements.

Table 21: Memory and maximum resolution possible

Video memory requirements for various optimal combinations			
Resolution	**No of colours**		
	8 – Bit	16 - Bit	24 - Bit
640 * 480	300 KB	600 KB	900 KB
800 * 600	470 KB	940 KB	1.4 MB
1024 * 768	768 KB	1.5 MB	2.3 MB
1280 * 1024	1.3 MB	2.6 MB	3.8 MB

Considering the average user and standard VRAM sizes, which are 1 MB, 2 MB and 4 MB - we have the following popular combinations:

Table 22: Memory and maximum resolution possible

Video Memory	Maximum colour depth and resolutions possible
1 MB	640*480 with 24 Bit Colour
	800*600 with 16 Bit Colour
2 MB	1024*768 with 16 Bit Colour
	1280*1024 with 8 Bit Colour
4 MB	1024*768 with 16 Bit Colour
	1280*1024 with 8 Bit Colour

This combination of colour depth and resolution is usually called the video mode or colour mode of the monitor.

12.6 Impact of video modes on multimedia applications

When you are developing multimedia applications that are going to be distributed to the public, then the problem of resolution vs. colour depth takes problematic dimensions.

Since the users might have configured their system to any possible video mode listed above, there is no standard video mode to which we can design our application.

So, How to cope up with this problem?

There are two possible solutions, which we can adopt.

- The entire application may be so designed, that it's independent of the video mode or colour mode of the client system. This may involve usage of screen units that are independent of the monitor - i.e. something other than pixels. Certain specialised multimedia authoring environments automatically support this feature, so that the programmer need not worry about this problem at all. When compiling the executable module of the application, the software adds necessary codes that maintain integrity through various client platforms.
- The application can be designed for a specific optimal number of colours and resolution - generally 256 colours at 640*480 pixels - and add the necessary codes that port the application across various video modes. Such applications run normally under all resolutions and colours, but with a border surrounding the screen.

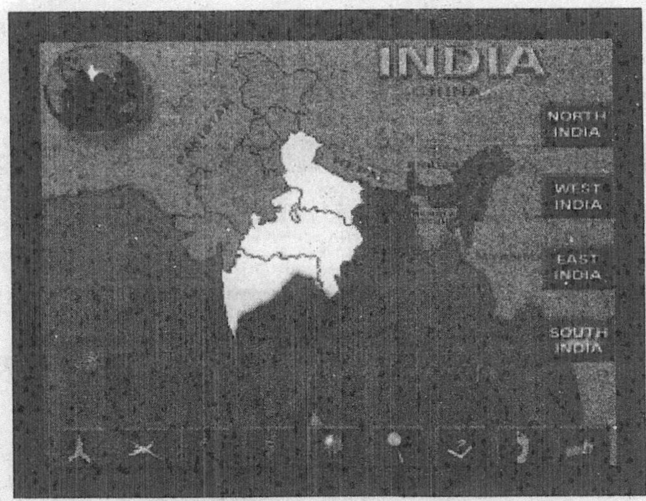

Figure 66: For Tourist's India CD-ROM, I created a black screen that filled the entire client system. Over this, I started placing the visuals at 640* 480. If you view the CD-ROM at this resolution, then you will just see the graphics without border. But on higher resolutions, you will see a black border around the screen.

12.7 Switching to different video modes

Now, let us see how to configure your system for a particular video mode and try out various other modes to find the combination best suited for your monitor and colour card.

- Right click on your desktop or laptop wallpaper and select Properties. The Display panel is thrown open.
- You've got the following screens on this panel: screensaver, appearance, web, effects and settings. Select the settings tab to open up the display settings screen.
- You have the following options in the settings screen, which configure the display system in various video modes.
- **Colours:** This setting controls the colour depth of your display. You have options like 256 colour, High colour (16 Bit), True colour (32 Bit) etc. The number of options available to you may be affected by the VRAM of your AGP card.
- **Screen area:** This setting controls the resolution of the display. You can choose various combinations – from 640 * 480 to 1600 * 1200.
- One important thing to note here is that – when you increase the resolution, you will find that your colours are adjusted automatically depending upon the overall VRAM memory available. For example, as I increase the resolution of my monitor to, say 1600*1200, I have only 16-bit colour option left in the colour panel and not 24 bit or 32 bit.
- When you click on the advanced options button, what you see is very specific to your display driver and manufacturer's utilities. Herein you may find many interesting options available to do finer control of your display settings. However, some experience is required to handle this and is recommended only for advanced users. *These advanced options will be enabled, only if you had installed the manufacturer's display drivers on top of default windows drivers.*
- Thus, it becomes important to install the right display drivers for your colour card. Otherwise, you may not be able to enjoy the capabilities of the display card to its fullest potential. Don't let your supplier go without the drivers for display card. The threat of not getting the display driver is more, when you purchase a system

off the shelf or ask some system engineer to assemble the system for you. Please ensure that all the device drivers are given to you along with the system itself – before you complete the purchase of your new multimedia computer.

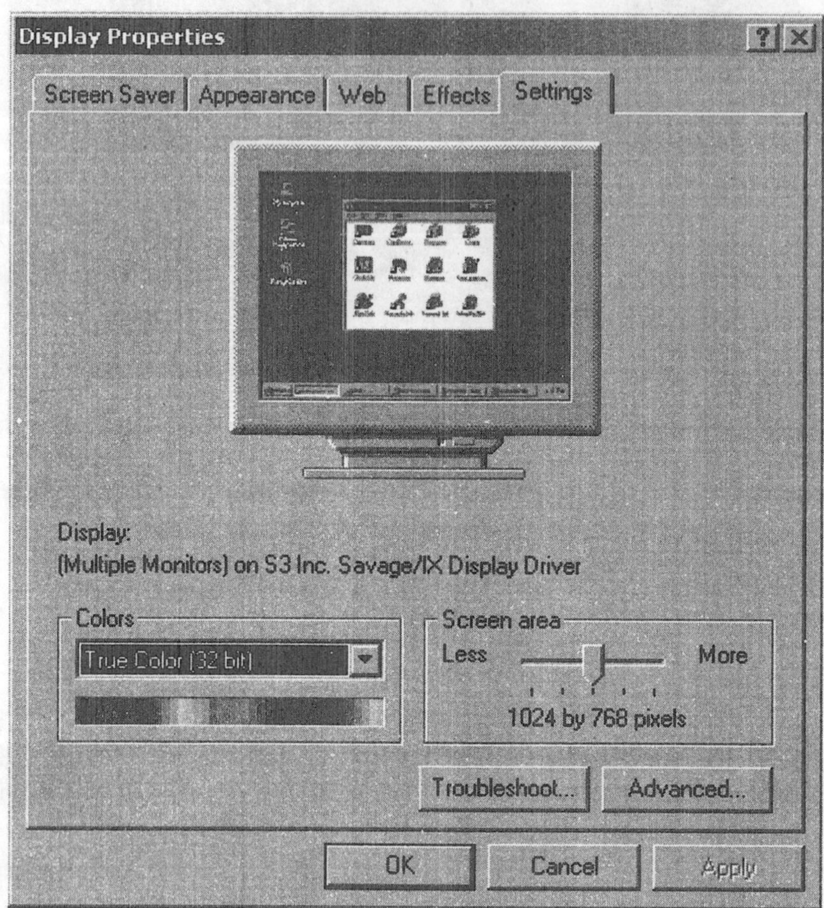

Figure 67: Switching to different video modes using display settings panel.

12.8 Colour monitors

Colour monitors are the most famous among the multimedia colour display systems.

Though colour monitors were introduced several years before, they could not make their way home to mass usage - until the dawn of the multimedia.

Today a large variety of high breed monitors sway the world market - and hundreds of types are available to suit the varying needs of the users, right from the simple desktop or office applications to complicated workstation or CAD environments.

Some manufacturers even bundle audio speakers in to their monitors and call them 'multimedia monitors".

Apart from resolution and number of colours, monitors are controlled by two other parameters: Dot pitch and Monitor refresh rates.

- **Dot pitch:** The dot pitch is the parameter that ultimately governs the sharpness of colour monitor. It is actually the physical distance between two actual picture elements (or actual pixels) on the monitor and is measured in millimetres. Normally, a dot pitch of 0.28 mm should be suffice for all 14" and 15" Monitors.

For higher sizes, typically a dot pitch of 0.26 mm or lesser, is most suitable. Unless you have specific reasons, it is better not to change to dot pitch of the monitor.

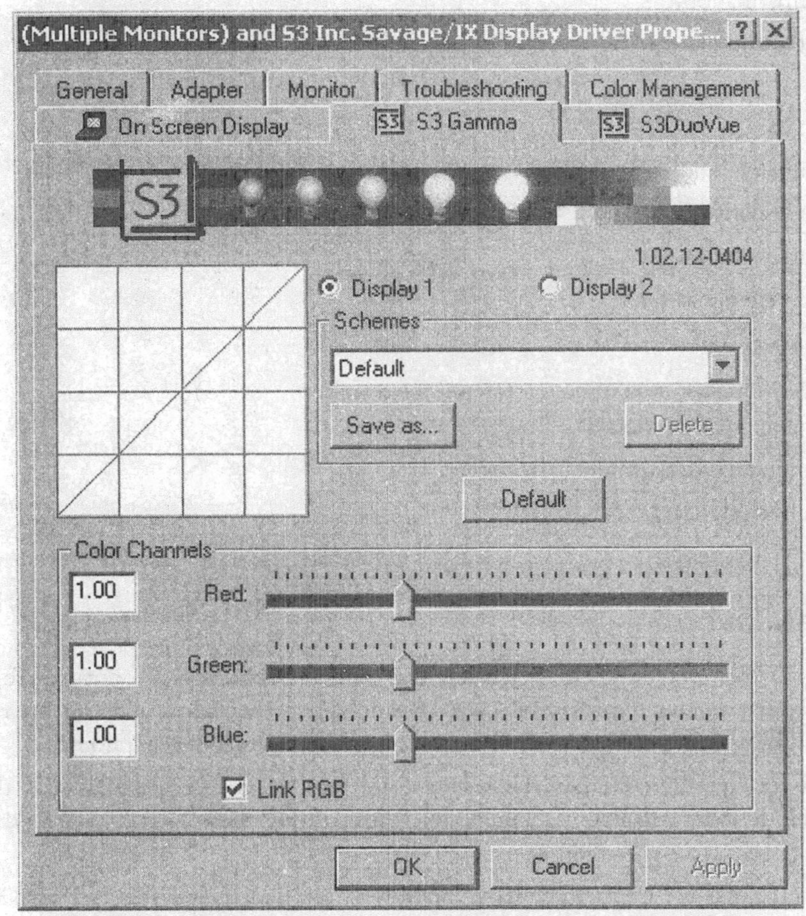

Figure 68: These are one of the advanced option panels available in my system. This panel is very specific to the SIS display driver I am using - you might be seeing a totally different panel, under advanced display options.

- ❑ **Monitor refresh rate:** If we are to imagine the entire screen to be made up of rows of picture elements (or actual pixels) and the screen display at any second as a series of illuminations of such rows, then the monitor refresh rate signifies the speed with which every line is illuminated, one after another, and is measured in terms of hertz (Hz). The typical refresh rates employed, range between 60 Hz and 90 Hz. Without specific reasons it is better not to change to refresh rate of the monitor.

Though colour monitors are best suited for desktops and associated applications, they cannot be employed very effectively for certain other multimedia applications like multimedia presentations (for a large group of audience) and multimedia kiosks.

So a whole new breed of display systems had to be developed to fulfil this need. These are known by various names like public information display systems and presentations display systems.

Let us briefly discuss what they are.

12.9 Public information display systems (PIDS)

Computer aided public information display systems (or PIDS) are those that are kept for general access - in places such as airports and star hotels – to provide necessary information to the public. PIDS usually take the form of multimedia touch screen kiosks, wherein the users can simply touch the relevant buttons on a touch screen monitor and seek the required information.

Some of the places that can make the best use of touch screen multimedia kiosks are:

- Tourist offices
- Start hotels
- International Airports
- School multimedia labs
- Museums and art galleries
- Exhibitions and seminar rooms
- Technological and IT fairs
- Corporate enterprises
- Video game machines at casinos
- Supermarkets and huge departmental stores
- Airports and railway stations
- Automatic teller machines

12.10 Multimedia kiosks

Though aided efficiently by computers, PIDS are meant for general public and are not just for computer literates. What follows naturally, is that a general information seeker cannot be expected to click on the relevant item in a list of perplexing menus boxes and buttons or to enter a bunch of command line parameters!

It's here, that multimedia technology comes to the rescue: simple graphic representations of the options available, associated preferably with sounds and texts, arranged as a typical hypermedia system makes things much easier to use.

Those PIDS that make effective use of multimedia technology are called multimedia kiosks. The most widely used display system for multimedia kiosks are the touch screen monitors.

Let us briefly discuss about them.

12.11 Touch screen technology

Touch screen systems come alive with the physical touch of a finger!

They need neither keyboard nor mouse, making them the best choice for public access.

Those who need information will simply have to touch the kiosk screen with their fingers, on the relevant area...and presto! The magic begins.

Internally, touch screens convert a user's touch to a mouse click – so there is no additional programming effort required, from a multimedia producer's point of view.

Touch screen monitors have the following advantages over conventional display devices, in the context of PIDS applications:

- Touch screen monitor sizes are usually much bigger than their counterparts, thus making them easier to use.
- Makes use of unambiguous input methodology - viz. a gentle touch.
- Touch screens are compatible with many operating systems and application software, thus making it easy to develop multimedia kiosk applications.

12.12 Composition of touch screen monitors

Touch screen systems internally have three major components:

- **Analog sensor:** Analog sensors recognise the touch of a person and send information to the computer, regarding the event and the place of touch. With this information, the multimedia application running behind the scene decides what the user is requesting and reacts accordingly.
- **Controller card:** A controller card is similar to all other multimedia interface cards. These cards manage to convert the incoming analog data from sensors to digital information. The X and Y coordinates of the touch point are identified and informed to the multimedia application. Both internal and external cards are available.
- **Driver software:** The device drivers make the digital information issued from the controller cards, available to the associated multimedia software applications. Drivers are available for both PCs and the MAC platforms.

Multimedia kiosk applications are getting widespread recognition worldwide, and consequently, the usage of touch screens is also on the increase.

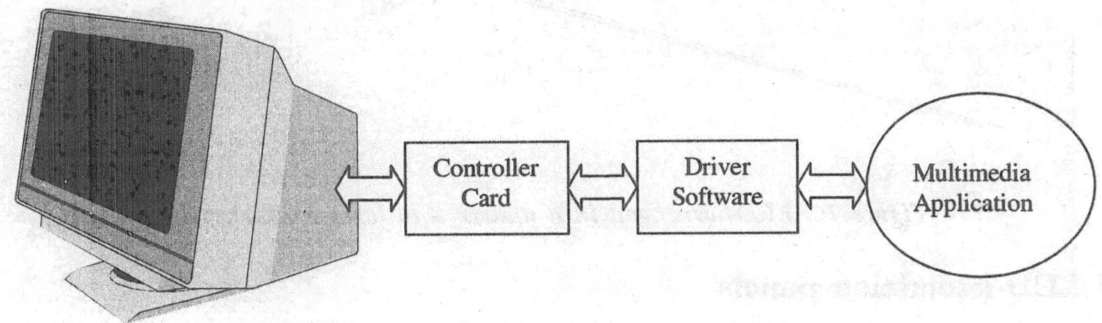

Figure 69: Components of touch screen kiosk system

12.13 Presentation display systems (PDS)

Presentation display systems – as the name implies - are those that are used for computer-aided presentations.

When the audience is very few, one can manage the show with a normal 17" Colour monitor. But as the number of participants increase, the choice for an alternative presentation system becomes imperative.

PDS display devices offer much higher screen sizes than the normal monitors.

The display is usually projected to a white screen, on the boardroom or seminar room. This latest technology is undergoing rapid metamorphosis; Of late, equipments whose resolutions are comparable to that of workstation monitors, are swaying the market.

Though all PDS display devices basically use of the same technology called LCD, they are offered in different flavours. Here, we shall take up the most famous among the lot viz. the LCD projection panels.

12.14 LED technology

A light emitting diode (LED for short) is an electronic device, capable of displaying any particular combination of RGB colours (The Red Green Blue system of colours used in computers) and is also transparent to light.

So, when a series of these LEDs are arranged in the form of a row - column matrix, they can represent computer display – much like the way pixels represent computer output in a monitor. Remember – pixels are also picture elements, arranged in the form of a row-column matrix.

Since LEDs are transparent, a normal overhead projection system can enlarge the image on this matrix and project it over a screen. This is the basic principle behind all LED projection systems and such LEDs arranged in the form of row-column matrix, are known as LCD panels.

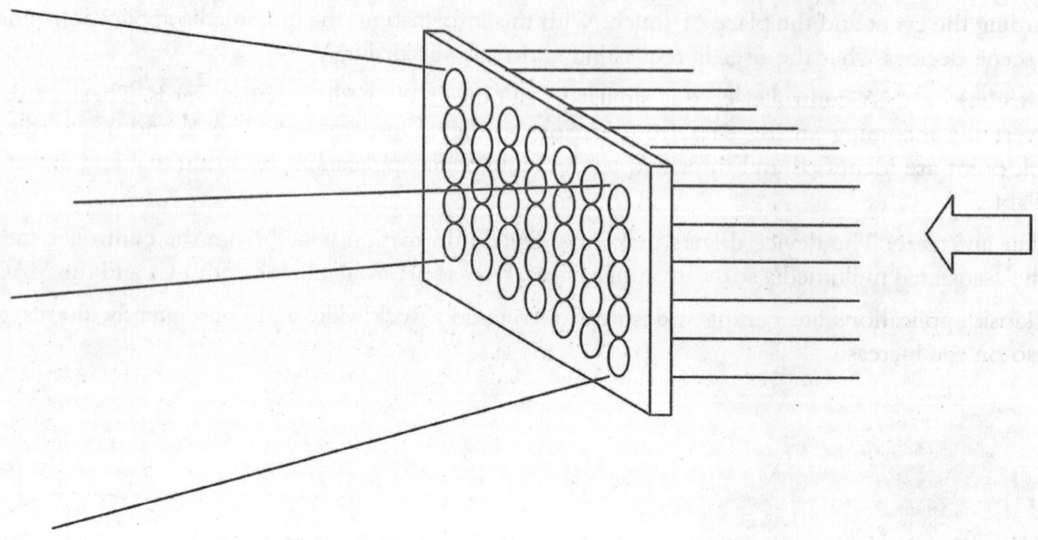

Figure 70: LEDs arranged in a matrix – to form LCD panel

12.15 LCD projection panels

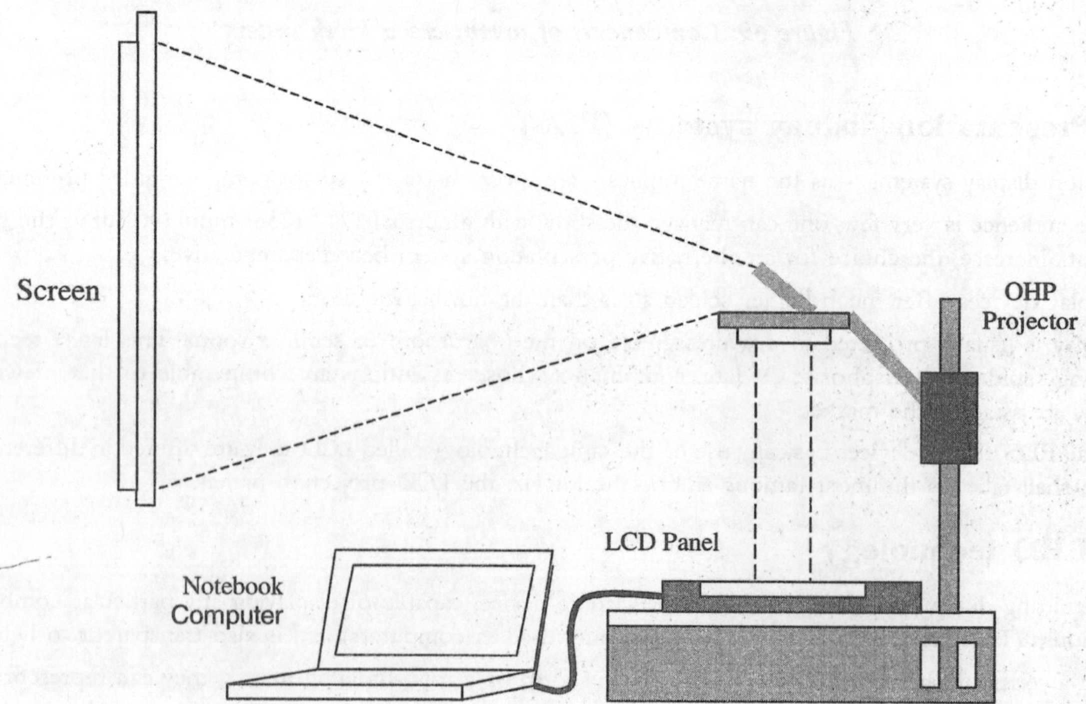

Figure 71: A multimedia presentation projected to screen through an LCD panel and overhead projector

In case of LCD projection panels, the output from computer is directed to a small and compact matrix of LCDs arranged in a specific pattern, which constitute the projection panel.

This panel is often kept over an overhead projector, in place of transparencies. And when the projector is illuminated, the graphics in the panel is projected over the screen, facing the overhead projector.

The advantages of LCD panels are their lightweights and smaller sizes. Most of them weight between 5 to 6 pounds only and can easily slide into a briefcase, which make them most suitable for travelling seminarians and presenters.

12.16 LCD panels - types and specifications

Two types of LCD panels are currently available - those with active matrix technology and the rest with duel scan passive matrix technology. Passive matrix panels suffer from lesser colour saturation/ contrast and slower response times than the active matrix - but passive matrix panels often cost less than their counterparts.

In general, passive matrix panels are more suitable for 'slide show like' presentations.... but once the presentation throws up a video or an animation sequence - it's much better to go for active matrix technology.

Almost all commercial panels are compatible with PC and MAC platforms. The device drivers - as usual, provide the necessary interface between the application and the device. Some panels even support sound projection facility, making your otherwise polite presentations rich in multimedia. Remote control mouse are the preferred accomplices, for such presentation shows.

In the introductory stages, the resolutions of most panels were limited to 640 * 480 - but now, situation has vastly improved – to 1024 * 768, 1600* 1200 or even higher resolutions.

But remember!

As the resolution increases, the supporting environment should cope up with the increasing standards - like, you may need to have a brighter overhead projectors - typically those with 4000 to 6000 lumens. Lumen is a unit for luminous intensity of the projector.

The number of colours is yet another criteria for LCD panels, and you have got systems with 512 to 16 million colours. Video is the ultimate test and the single most important reason for purchasing panels that support higher number of colours. With presentations involving extensive videos, it is better to have panels with 16 million colours. Computer graphic images with fine gradations of colour also look better in a 16 million-colour panel.

Typical panel screen sizes are 8.4 and 9.4 on lower ends and 10.4 on higher ends panels; and the projected image sizes can go even up to 300 inches - provided, the white screen is wide enough to accommodate.

12.17 Summary

Colour display systems like monitors, are used to display millions of colours in multimedia projects.

The way the colours are exhibited in a display system depends on two parameters: number of colours and resolution. The total number of colours that can be displayed as well as the resolution of the display depends on the memory capacity of the video controller card, also known as VRAM. A particular combination of colours and resolution is called the video mode.

Colour monitors have two other controlling parameters as well; viz. the dot pitch and monitor refresh rate. Colour monitors are best suited for all kinds of desktop applications.

Public information display systems make use of touch screen monitors, which can recognise the physical touch of a user. Those applications that make use of multimedia technology and touch screens are called multimedia kiosks.

Presentation display systems use LCD projection panels to project the display over a white screen.

12.18 Keywords

❑ **VRAM:** Video random access memory - The memory capacity of the video controller card, which serves as the interface between the computer and the display device.

- **Resolution:** Total number of logical pixels, in terms of rows and columns, supported by the display system.
- **Video mode** or **colour mode**: A particular combination of resolution and the total number of colours of the display system.
- **Multimedia kiosks**: Public information display systems that make use of multimedia technology.

Chapter 13

Digital Imaging

CHAPTER OVERVIEW

The chapter begins with discussions on various categories of multimedia graphics like interface design graphics, content graphics etc. Various sources of multimedia graphics and their distinctive attributes get our attention in the next paragraphs, followed by differences between raster graphics and vector graphics.

Graphics created with the help of 3 Dimensional utilities have been dealt with separately, as they form a separate class of still pictures. We also talk a bit about hyper graphics.

The chapter winds up with a bird's eye view on various kinds of software tools available for creating multimedia graphics. How these tools can be made use of for a given project – is the food for thought, in the next few chapters.

13.1 Introduction

What do we mean by graphics or multimedia graphics?

There can be no conclusive answer –as different people use this generic term to cover a wide variety of entities. Hence, it becomes important to understand the term multimedia graphics – as implied throughout this book - before we start our other discussions.

In this book, multimedia graphics represents a collective terminology that includes all kinds of still pictures like photographs, images and art works – as used in multimedia applications. It does not include any entities with dynamics and movement - like animations or videos.

Sometimes, the term graphics is used interchangeably with multimedia graphics.

With this discipline, we clearly come out of a potential misunderstanding of treating everything under the graphics umbrella. In later chapters, when we are dealing with animations, we will use specific terms like 2D animations and 3D animations - whenever possible, so that there is no ambiguity in understanding what we really mean.

Graphics play a pivotal role in all multimedia applications. The maxim 'a picture is worth a thousand words' is so factual that one cannot underestimate the impact of visuals over plain texts or audio – in the context of multimedia.

Since computers can seamlessly comprehend with millions of colours at any point of time, there are people who feel that computer based imagery is much better that other visual mediums like print or television.

13.2 Graphics in multimedia projects

Graphics employed in multimedia applications can be divided into two main categories:

- Graphics that are part of the application interface design and

- ❑ Graphics that are part of the contents presented

It's important that we clearly understand and distinguish between these two categories of graphics, before proceeding further. The following paragraphs will help you to do so.

13.3 Graphics for interface design

All multimedia applications present a graphical interface with which the user interacts.

Have a look at the interface of Microsoft Oceans CD-ROM. This is the first screen that greets the user – and throughout the title, the bottommost buttons are retained.

This is a classical example for the interface design graphics we are talking about.

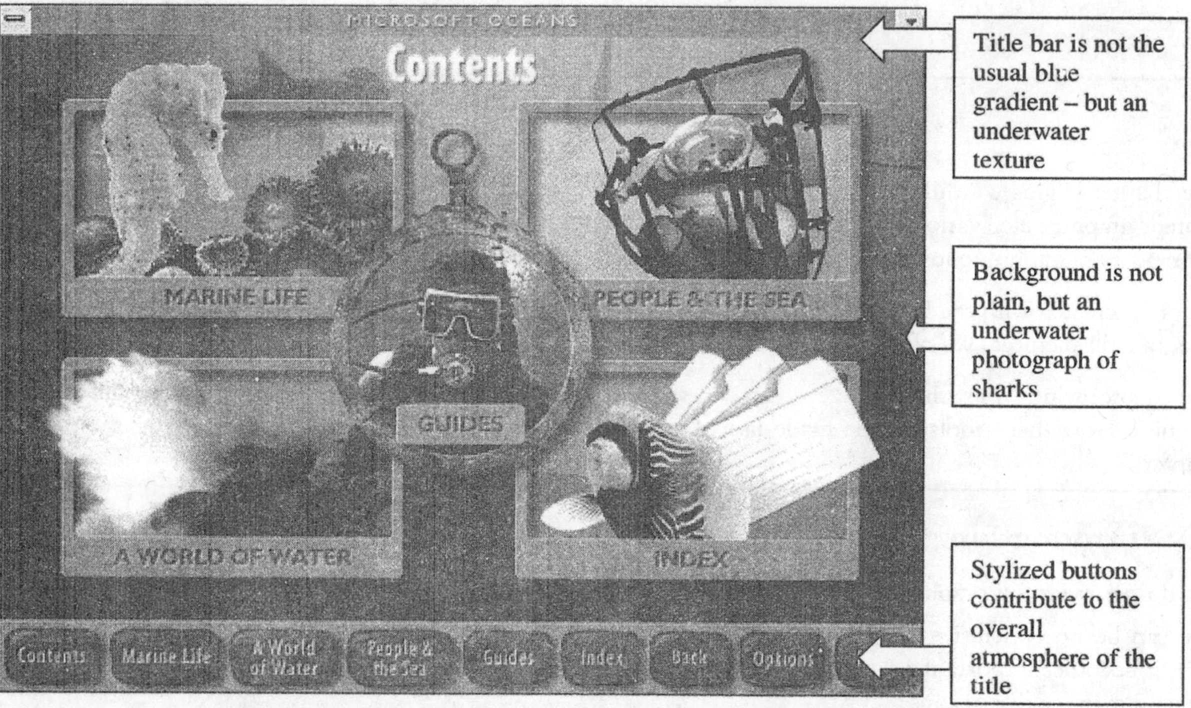

Figure 72: The main interface of Microsoft Oceans CD-ROM fittingly captures the mood and theme of underwater learning adventure. Take a close look at the buttons that have been modelled after underwater rock formations.

The interface graphics presents itself to the user throughout the course of the application. As the user navigates across various sections of the application, the contents may change a bit – but the overall theme of the interface has to be maintained consistently.

The user interface must be simple and friendly, with an attractive look - so that the user is inspired to explore the multimedia application further and further. In fact, interface design is an exclusive specialisation to some of the professionals in multimedia – who are frequently hired by companies, just to do the interface design.

Multimedia graphics play a vital role in evolving interface designs that appeal to all groups of audience.

Capturing the mood and theme of the title is probably the biggest task of an interface designer.

Suitable photographs or images can be added to the background as collages and texts can be super-imposed over them. Also, it is important to create the buttons and menus to capture the theme of the title as much as possible.

Have a look at the Microsoft Oceans interface, once again. See how the interface designer has created an appealing underwater or 'oceanic' appeal by placing appropriate images in the background and adopting rock formations for buttons and title bars.

Good interface designs blend so well with other contents of the project that many a times it's difficult to distinguish and differentiate the actual combination of graphics that has been made use of.

Of course, to achieve such a degree of seamless presentation, the original images may have to be manipulated and edited in many different permutations and combinations. Going back to the same example of Oceans interface design, you will be able to distinguish the following independent picture elements that have been blended seamlessly to produce the overall appeal you appreciate:

1. The title bar, which is an image by itself
2. The background underwater picture of sharks in the bay
3. The word "Contents" which is an element by itself
4. The four rectangular boxes that represent the chapters.
5. Collaged pictures contained inside these boxes - sea horses, diving equipments etc. Each of them, in turn, has been compiled from of more than one image.
6. The circular pendent in the centre and the diver in it.
7. The background for buttons
8. The buttons themselves

Now, you can see that – after all, the business that looked so simple a few moments ago is not that simple as it looks! Fortunately, the professional graphics editing tools that are currently available for PC and the Mac platforms present us with unlimited number of editing and special effect options that the ultimate design is limited just by your creativity and not by the capabilities of the tools.

To summarize, interface design graphics are characterized by the following attributes:

- ❑ They should be simple and appealing
- ❑ They should fittingly capture the theme and mood of the title
- ❑ There should at least be one background image or collage
- ❑ Buttons should be designed suitably, to fit the overall theme of the design

We will reserve further discussions on strategies and techniques for good interface design for a later chapter titled multimedia applications – project design, conception and execution.

13.4 Graphics for contents

Now, let us concentrate on the second category of graphics.

Graphics for contents include all photographs, clip arts and other kinds of still images that are made use of, as a part of the main contents presented. For example, in the same Microsoft Oceans CD-ROM, look at the following graphics under the topic 'Inflatable fish'.

Graphics are powerful companions to information, when presented suitably. Even in the example that we saw above, note that around 60 to 70% of the space is dedicated to graphics and only the rest has been filled with textual information. Hyperlinks have been provided at attractive places, for those who wish to explore more.

In general, each and every scene (or page) of multimedia applications should be filled with at least one main picture or image. Other contents and smaller images can be shown as hyperlinks or hotspots.

Figure 73: The same Microsoft oceans CD-ROM making use of colourful graphics to explain a topic.

Content design graphics are characterised by the following attributes:

- ❑ They are totally related to the topic under discussion and must be exclusively designed and developed for each project. For example, for its title Oceans - Microsoft should have either hired its own team of photographers to shoot all the pictures or more probably, should have acquired the copyrights for various photographs from oceanographic specialists.
- ❑ Content design graphics should be developed in exact concurrence with other forms of media presented – like texts and videos so that all these different elements fit together as one seamless stream of information. Thus it's imperative to decide exactly what photographs, pictures and clip arts need to be developed for the project, well in advance - so that there is no wastage of time, effort and resources.
- ❑ The more you plan, the better. For example, if you can decide exactly what sort of photograph or image should be featured in each page (or scene) of the title, then you can go ahead with the photo shooting or acquisition based on your specific requirements. But if you are unsure, you may end up accumulating loads of material which you might probably not make use of in the end.

With this, we conclude our discussions on categories of graphics and switch over to the other topics.

13.5 Types of graphic imagery

Types of graphic images made use of in multimedia projects, should fall under one of the following categories:

- ❑ Photographs (Either scanned or digitally photographed)
- ❑ Clip arts (Drawings drawn using specialised drawing packages)
- ❑ Three dimensional graphics (Images developed using 3D design packages)
- ❑ Miscellaneous variety (all other types of images)

Let us detail what they are and how they can be developed for a specific project at hand.

13.6 Photographic images

Photographic images include all types of photographs, stored as rastor bitmaps in the computer. They are either scanned from printed photos (scanned photos) using scanners or upload directly from digital cameras (digital photos).

Figure 74: Photographs are either scanned from physical printouts or uploaded from digital cameras, directly.

There are no hard and fast rules as to which one is the best. The quality of the images is mainly determined by the capabilities of the equipments used.

For example, using a high-end professional scanner, it is possible to scan printed photos and pictures to the finest detail. Similarly, using high-end digital cameras, it is possible to take professional photographs of great quality. However, there are limitations to both.

The quality of scanned photos is determined, not only by the quality of the scanner – but by the quality of the original photograph itself. No high-end scanner will be able to improve the colours or resolution of a bad photograph beyond certain limits.

While digital camera photos do not usually suffer from such limitations – unless the photographer wants to take a low-resolution photograph, there are other constraints. Digital cameras as on date are unable to offer the level / variety of zooms and filters as available in conventional SLR cameras. The net result is that there are limitations to what a professional photographer can do with a digital camera, in terms of creativity.

Photographic images find extensive use in almost all multimedia projects. They can be effectively used in interface designs as well as contents.

13.7 Clip arts

Clip arts represent digital drawings that are drawn directly in a computer, using drawing tools like Corel Draw.

Digital artists make use of digital paints and brushes provided by specialised drawing environments of such packages and gives life to his or her imagination straight through the monitor, instead of conventional mediums like paper.

These drawing are usually stored as vectors. We will be seeing what vectors are, in a short while from now.

There are many misconceptions about digital drawing process.

Many imagine that the skills required for traditional artists and digitals artist are different - which is incorrect. True, the methodology and techniques to be made use of are slightly different and digital artists seldom enjoy the 'free brush stroke independence ' of traditional artists - but the base creative talent required for artwork remains very much the same.

Figure 75: A simple line drawing, drawn using Corel Draw package

A digital artist may have to try out different painting tools and stroke options available, before deciding upon the exact combination that will result in desired output.

Software vendors, who are developing such packages, are ceaselessly updating their products to ensure that almost all possible brush strokes and other painting options available in traditional painting process are also available digitally. Professional tools like Adobe Illustrator, Corel Draw and Macromedia Freehand can bring out stunning outputs at the hands of experienced digital artists.

13.8 3Dimensional graphic images

3 Dimensional graphic images are those that are developed using specialised 3D software packages and tools.

Figure 76: A surrealistic mount kailash developed using 3D software tools - for cybervalley systems CD-ROM title 'Tales from Indian mythology'

We are grouping them as a separate category because, of late, there has been an increasing trend in making use of 3D tools for graphic imagery – particularly in those situations wherein conventional photography or digital drawing are not suitable or possible - like surrealistic landscaping, land and house modelling, imaginary worlds etc.

By placing various model elements in a virtual space and rendering them with a mixture of textures, lights and other environment variables – 3 dimensional artists are able to cross the limitations set by physical world and transcend to a different plane altogether.

Developing 3D graphics involves skilled expertise and time and hence must be sparingly made use of.

Advanced concepts of 3D graphics are reserved for later chapters - but, for the purpose of multimedia graphics, it would be suffice to note that realistic images of artificial entities can be developed using 3D graphic packages.

This characteristic is of immense use to graphics developers, in the following situations:

- ❑ When it's dangerous or impossible to take an actual photograph of the required entity or environment – like, say, a picture of a dinosaur or the close up shot of hot lava.
- ❑ Sometimes it is cost effective to construct a 3D model and develop images rather than going to the physical location, for the required images.
- ❑ Literally any view at any lighting and ambience, can be generated with 3D graphics.

But the decision to use 3D graphics should be taken, after considering the following limitations:

- ❑ It is not so very easy to develop and render 3D graphics.
- ❑ 3D environments demand specialised skill and expertise to work with; also, at times it can be highly time-consuming process.
- ❑ 3D packages are generally more expensive than other media packages and almost all high-end software demand robust system requirements.

It is the designer's job, to evaluate all these pros and cons of 3D imagery, before arriving at a final choice.

13.9 Types of graphics storage

We all know that computers store all kinds of information, as data.

Graphics that fill the entire 29" colour monitor with millions of colours are no exceptions. They have to be stored as some form of digital data, which the computer can understand and comprehend.

There are essentially two fundamental ways of storing graphical data:

- ❑ Rastor graphics and
- ❑ Vector graphics.

Let us explore these two a bit further.

13.10 Rastor graphics

Rastor imaging is the technique of dividing the entire image area into small logical dots called pixels and storing the colour information contained in each pixel. For example, for a picture of size 640*480, the rastor graphic should record colour information for around 307200 pixels!

These thousands of independent colour dots finally combine together to throw up the beautiful blonde you are staring at, in your colour monitor. If you can zoom-in on any portion of a rastor image, you will actually be able to see the independent pixels that make up the image.

This methodology of storing graphic data is what is known as raster imaging and the graphics thus stored are called rastor graphics. In Windows working environment, they are more commonly known as bitmapped graphics.

In the context of this book, we will stick to the term rastor graphics.

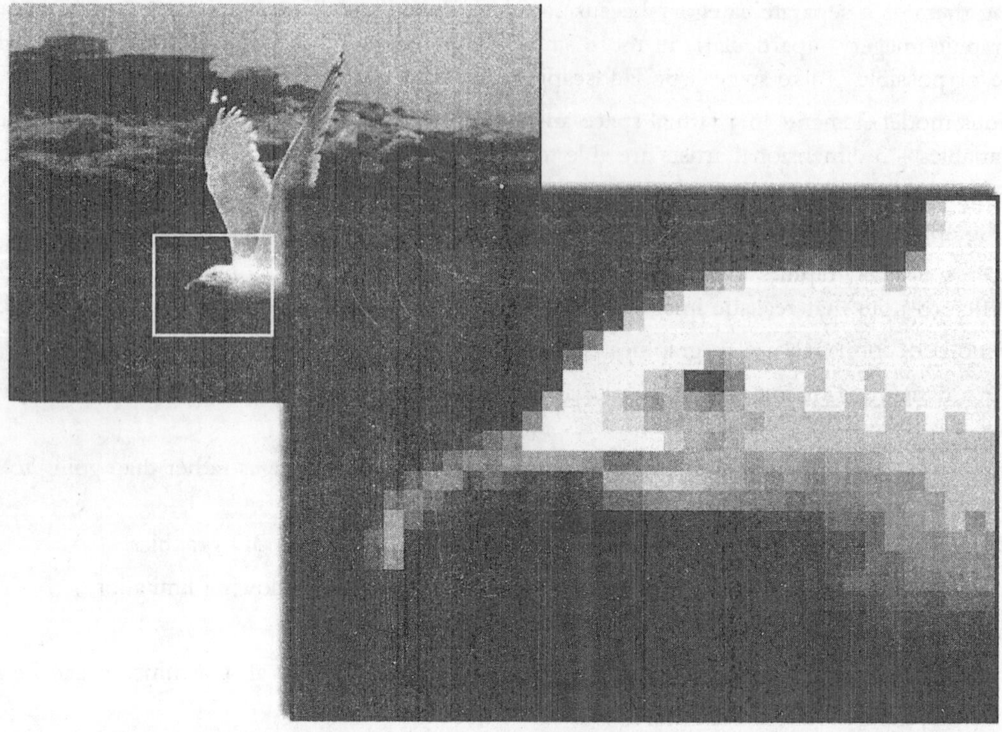

Figure 77: A small portion of a rastor bitmap, when enlarged several times, will reveal the underlying pixels that make up the graphic.

Rastor graphics is relatively a simpler form of storing image data. Many software manufacturers started coming out with different file formats of rastor graphics - to serve the needs of various applications.

The net result is that we currently have more than a dozen famous file formats or so to work with!

A good idea is to keep a software utility or package that converts an image, from one file format to another. These are called image conversion utilities and are available on the Internet, for free. However, if you are using one of the professional graphics editing programs like Adobe Photoshop, there is no need for such utilities – as the program itself recognizes many different file formats.

Among the different file formats available for rastor graphics, JPEG has evolved as the best among the lot – in terms of file size and quality. This format was evolved by Joint Photographic Expert Group and hence the name JPEG. It is one of the widely used formats in many multimedia applications.

On the flip side, JPEG is a lossy compression algorithm i.e. the image quality is sacrificed to some extent during conversion and this is unacceptable in certain situations like desktop publishing; and hence the need for using multiple file formats.

For a detailed list of various file formats available for rastor graphics, kindly refer the appendix.

Rastor graphics have their own advantages and limitations.

First, the positives:

- ❑ Almost all kinds of images - photographs, digital drawings, clip arts etc. can be stored as rastor graphics. In other words, there is no restriction on the nature of image that can be stored.
- ❑ They can be easily distributed across a wide variety of applications and are certainly in much wider usage than their counterparts: Vector graphics.
- ❑ Vector images can be converted to rastor images – but the contrary is not possible.

Now, the limitations:

- ❑ It is very difficult to modify the rastor images, once they developed. To change even a small curve, literally every pixel has to be erased and redrawn...thus, there is not much flexibility in modifying the image. All we can do is to alter the size, colours etc. This makes them inefficient for usage in digital art applications - wherein the artist, after painting a stroke or two with his graphic tablet, invariably wants to modify his earlier strokes little...without erasing and redrawing!
- ❑ Since every pixel or dot in the image has to be stored as data, generally the file sizes are very high. And the situation is much worse, if the file format used for storage adopts loss less compression algorithm. For example, a bitmap file (.bmp) with a single colour takes the same amount of space, 1.44 MB to be precise, as another with more than a million colours! This is because of the fact that, irrespective of the number of colours used, the colour information or data is recorded for each pixel!

13.11 Vector graphics

Instead of storing the graphic images as pixels of colour data, it would be better if we could identify the individual lines, arcs and curves that make up the ultimate image and store them as a group of such elements. This technique of storing image data is what is known as vector images the images thus stored are called vector graphics.

Vector graphics offer the unique advantage of modifying lines and curves, after they have been drawn – without affecting the quality of images. This capability is very significant for digital artists and designers.

Specialised graphic tools are available for developing vector graphics – Adobe Illustrator, Corel Draw and Macromedia Freehand are some of the prominent packages in the market. All these tools store an artist's creative strokes as lines, arcs and curves so that all modifications are possible at any point of time.

Vectors are not limited to just images. They are extensively used to construct 3D wire frame models as well. We will take a better look at this during our discussions on 3D animations.

Now, let us see the advantages and limitations of vector graphics.

Advantages

- ❑ Since vector graphics are stored as codes of lines and curves, they take up much lesser space than rastor images.

Figure 78: First, I drew this cartoon image using simple vector drawing tools. In the second diagram, I modified the first to evolve another character. Make a note that there is no loss of quality whatsoever, in this transformation. If you won't object, I'd like to call the first one a cow and the second one a pig.

- ❑ Vector graphics can be edited easily, without losses.

Limitations

- ❑ Not all types of images can be stored as vector graphics. For example, photographs and digital camera pictures, made up of many thousands of colours, cannot be stored as vectors.
- ❑ As already pointed out, no rastor image can be converted as vector graphics.

Like rastor storage, there are various file formats for storing vector graphics as well. For a list of file formats, please refer the appendix.

13.12 Multimedia graphic tools

Different kinds of software tools and packages are currently available in the market, for digital imaging applications. Though it is difficult to pin point any specific tool as the best one, some have emerged as the industrial standards, because of their quality and the features.

Multimedia graphic tools can be broadly classified as:

- ❑ Tools and packages meant for digital image editing and processing
- ❑ Tools and packages meant for digital artistry
- ❑ Tools and packages meant for 3 Dimensional graphics and
- ❑ Miscellaneous utilities.

The following table lists some of the famous software in each of the above-mentioned categories.

Table 23:Examples for various categories of multimedia graphics tools

Category	Tools and packages
Image editing	Adobe Photoshop
	Corel Photo paint
	Jasc Paint shop Pro
Digital artistry	Adobe Illustrator
	Macromedia Freehand
3D Graphics	Maya
	3D Studio Max
	Corel Bryce

13.13 Class - I :Image editing tools

This class of tools are mainly meant for retouching / editing and manipulating images that are already available as rastor bitmaps.

A digitised photographic image may have to be edited for several reasons like improving the quality of the image, removing unwanted portions, altering the size of the image, adding special effects or combining objects in one or more images.

Hardly there are any situations in reality, wherein a photographic image may be directly used in the multimedia project without any editing.

Adobe Photo shop and Corel Photo paint are some of the tools in the forefront. Adobe Photo shop supports third party plug-in software functionality, which extends the core capabilities of the program to new heights.

13.14 Class - II: Digital artistry tools

Apart from editing rastor images like photographs and images already available, a digital artist may want to create drawings on his own. Digital artistry tools are meant for this purpose.

These tools support a number of drawing options normally required by digital artists – like freehand drawings, colour gradients, geometric figures etc with the help of which, creative artists are able to give shape to their imaginations.

Figure 79: One of my simple drawing attempts, using digital artistry tools. The original clipart is available in Multimedia Magic CD-ROM.

The resulting files are usually stored in one of the vector file formats.

Adobe illustrator, Macromedia Freehand and Corel Draw are some of the famous software packages available in the market for digital artists. Paint shop pro supports limited but interesting set of vector tools.

13.15 Class - III: 3 Dimensional graphic tools

3D software tools are specialized environments in which one can model, texture, light and render objects. The skills and expertise required to master 3D are almost completely different to the earlier set of tools – handling 3D is much more complex and time consuming and hence must be carefully used.

3D software demand more CPU and RAM resources and are generally available only on high-end platforms.

Most 3D graphics packages demand muscular hardware because of intense mathematical computations involved in working with 3 Dimensions. Hence they are available mostly on high-end platforms, though PCs based 3D development is also getting popular.

Alias Wave front, SoftImage, Maya and 3D studio max are some of the software available for 3D graphics development.

13.16 Class - IV: Miscellaneous utilities

Miscellaneous utilities include small programs meant for converting graphic file formats, tools for organising and sharing images etc.

Often, while working with multimedia graphics, one has to toggle between various raster and vector file formats, because of the multiplicity of popular imaging standards available.

It is true that most of the Class I tools recognize a wide variety of image formats – but there might be situations wherein you need to use certain file format not supported by your tool. In this case, you may have to go for one of the suitable conversion tools available.

Organising and maintaining a catalogue of images can be come a menace over a period of time. Under such situations, it is better to use 3rd party tools meant for organising your graphics to various categories and groupings.

Such utilities are mostly available free, on the Internet. Check out www.download.com for the latest set of tools you want.

13.17 Summary

The term multimedia graphics represents digital photos, scanned pictures, digital artworks and 3D images. Multimedia graphics can be broadly classified as interface design graphics and content design graphics. Sources of images could be photographs, clip arts etc. Graphic data can be stored in 2 ways: as rastor and vector graphics.

Multimedia graphic tools can be classified as image editing tools, digital artistry tools, 3D graphic tools and miscellaneous utilities. Adobe Photoshop and illustrator, Corel Draw and Photo paint, Macromedia Freehand, Jasc Paint shop pro are some of the tools well known in the market.

13.18 Keywords

- **3 Dimensional graphic images:** Images that are developed using high-end 3D software packages or platforms.
- **Rastor imaging**: The technique of dividing the entire image area into pixels and recording the data on each pixel.
- **Vector imaging:** The technique of storing a digital drawing as a group of mathematical lines, arcs and curves.
- **Plug - Ins:** Programs developed by third party developers, to extend the core functionality of specific software packages.

Chapter 14

Scanning and Digital Photography

CHAPTER OVERVIEW

Scanning and digital photography are two indispensable sources of digital imagery.

In this chapter, we briefly look at the different types of scanners and the basic principle behind scanning, followed by discussions on professional scanning techniques.

Digital photography is a profession as well as an art and has hit the mainstream in recent years. We take a quick look at different types of cameras available and then concentrate on what makes a good digital photograph.

14.1 Introduction

Sources of multimedia graphics could be digital photographs, clip arts, 3 Dimensional graphic images or any other miscellaneous sources.

Digital photographs have to be developed - either by scanning or by digital photography.

While clip arts and 3 dimensional graphic images can be generated within the computer itself - using relevant set of software tools, digital photographs can be acquired only with the help of dedicated equipments: scanners or digital cameras.

Let us focus our attention first, on scanners since they predate digital cameras.

14.2 Scanners – an introduction

Scanning is a very simple process of converting any picture data in paper, to a digital image. Once the image is saved in the computer, it can be edited using relevant software.

Apart from photographs, scanners can also be used to digitise texts in paper, which can then be converted to an MS Word document or so – using a specialized technology called OCR (Optical Character Recognition). This is nothing less than a boon for converting voluminous load of textual information, in books - to a digital format, without the need of typing in the entire book, page by page.

Several types of scanners are available in the market to suit the needs of different applications. These include:

- ❑ Sheet-fed scanners
- ❑ Flat bed scanners and
- ❑ Hand Held scanners

Though these equipments look so different from one another, the basic principle behind them remain very much the same. A scanner head is used to read the image data with the help of light beams and the reflections are recovered by a series of light sensitive diode crystals, that ultimately transmit the corresponding digital information to the system - in the form of electrical signals.

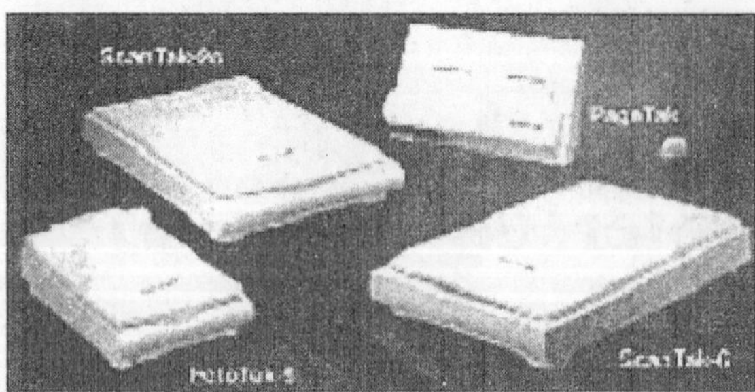

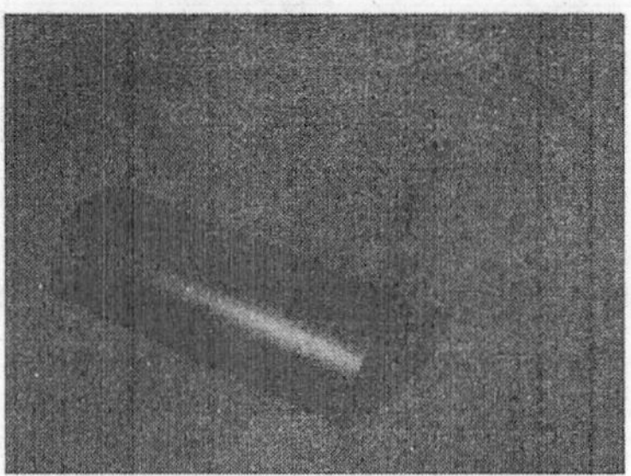

Figure 80: Different types of scanners are available in the market - to suit the needs of different applications

The major difference between these different types of scanners lie in the way the page containing the photograph and the scanner head that reads the picture data, move past each other.

14.3 Sheet-fed scanners

Sheet fed scanners, as the name implies, are used to scan sheets of paper.

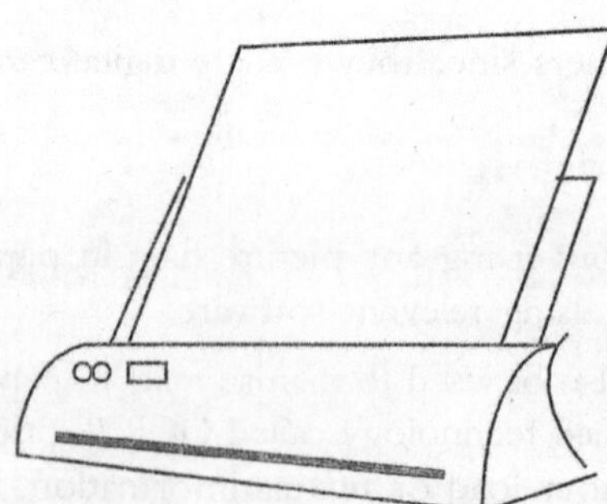

Figure 81: Sheet fed scanners

Here, the scanner head remains stationary, and a series of soft mechanical motors move the paper past the scanner head - slowly.

They are mainly used in office applications, where scores of pages may have to be scanned - every day. The results are pretty good, but the serious limitation that restricts their usage in multimedia environments, is that they cannot accept sheets thicker than a single page - and thus cannot be used to scan books etc. without destroying the latter!

14.4 Flat bed scanners

In case of flat bed scanners, the page containing the photograph remains stationary over a reflective glass plate and the scanner head moves over the plate, on the other side - scanning the picture data

Here also, the results are quite superior - and more importantly, they can be used to scan pictures from books, magazines etc. without a hitch.

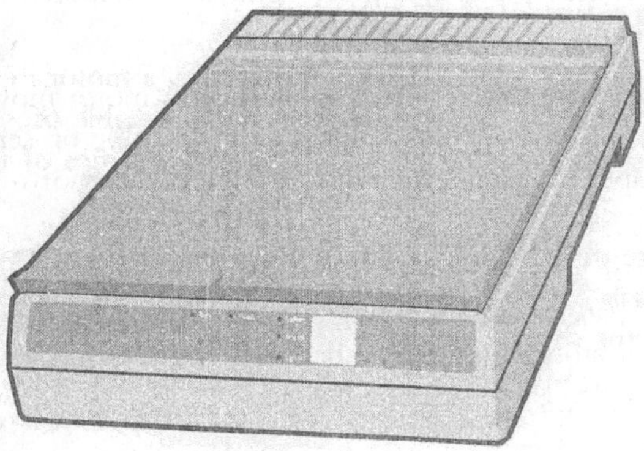

Figure 82: Flat bed scanners

The page that has to be scanned should be placed softly over the glass bed - much like the copiers – and the scanning process should be initiated in the software application that controls the scanner. The process is simple and straightforward.

One distinct advantage of flat bed scanners is that they can be used to scan even very large images - part by part.

Flat beds are the most widely used type of scanners – among the three.

14.5 Hand held scanners

In this type of scanner, the scanner head has to be moved manually over the paper – portion by portion.

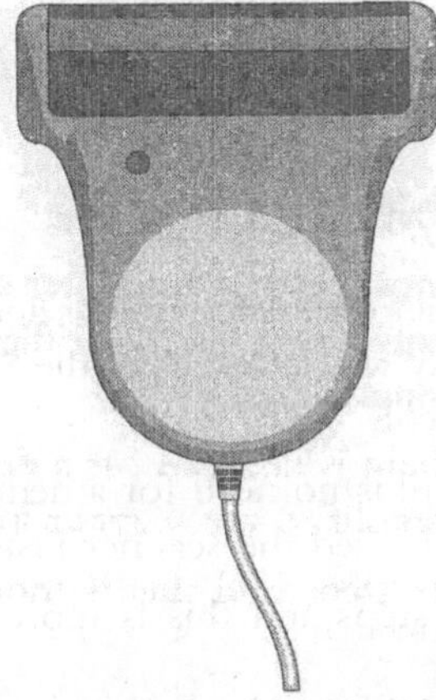

Figure 83: Hand held scanners

Since human hand movements cannot be expected to be even, the results are usually not comparable to that of flat bed scanners. However, the purpose of hand-held scanners is different and they generally do not require that high a degree of accuracy.

Such scanners can be spotted in places like retail markets – where they are used to read the bar codes in the labels.

14.6 Basic principle behind flat bed scanning

At the start of scanning process, a powerful light source illuminates the paper containing the picture data - placed upside down. The side adjacent to the glass window is the side to be scanned.

The idea is that the blank or white spaces will reflect more light, when exposed, than inked or coloured dots.

The scanning head is located right below the glass window.

When the scanning process is initiated using the scanning application, a motor moves the scanner head on the other side of the window, slowly from bottom to top. The scanner head, capable of sensing the light that's bounced off from the various portions of the paper, transmits the data through a series of mirrors - to a light sensitive diode matrix system.

These diodes react to the exposure of light, by transmitting electric currents proportional to the intensity of light falling on them. These electric signals are converted to digital data, as usual, by analog to digital converters - before being passed on to the computer for storage as graphic data.

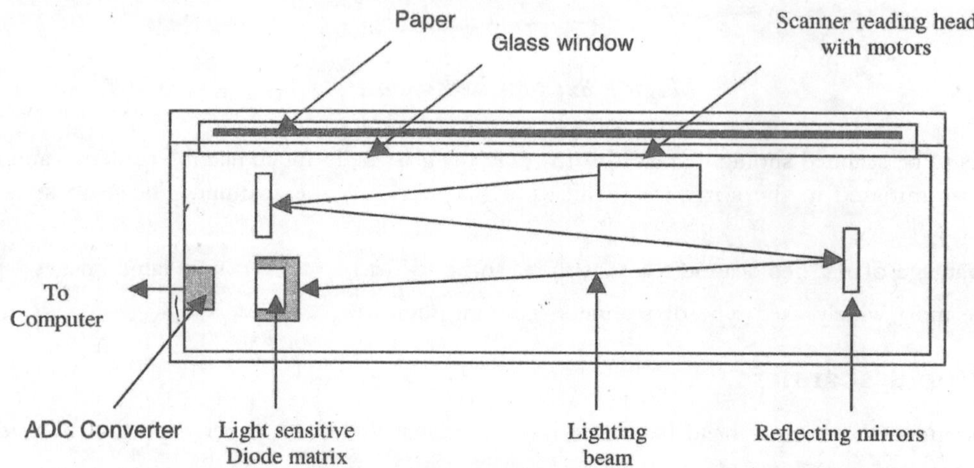

Figure 84: Principle behind Flatbed scanning

14.7 Hooking the scanner on to your computer

A few years before, the process of installing scanner on to a computer and establishing the communication protocols, use to be a complex exercise. The main complexity was in installing the SCSI scanner card that served as an interface between the computer and the scanning equipment.

But now, with the introduction of USB port, there is no need for a dedicated interface card and the equipment can directly be plugged into the system. This has simplified the scanner installation process dramatically.

The procedure can be explained in few simple steps and this is more or less the same for almost all brands of flatbed scanners.

The first step is to install the scanner software that comes bundled with the equipment. This software contains an application that can control the equipment as well as the device drivers required to recognize the hardware – when plugged in through the USB Port.

Once the drivers are successfully installed and the machine is rebooted, we can say that the system is ready to interface with the scanner.

In Windows 2000, you can directly plug-in the equipment through the scanner cable whose one end is connected to the computer and the other end is inserted into the machine's USB port. The Operating system immediately recognises the presence of a new hardware and configures the same for usage.

14.8 Scanning process

The actual scanning process is pretty simple.

- ❑ Place the required photograph or drawing on top of the glass panel and close the scanner with the white board cover.
- ❑ Initiate the scanning process using the application that came bundled with the scanner. If you are starting the scanner for the first time in the day, you may get "Warming up the lamp" message.
- ❑ After warming up, the scanner head traverses back and forth and the photograph is shown on the scanning application.
- ❑ At this point, you need to select the settings with which you want to do the scanning. You may have to set the DPI (Dots Per Inch - i.e. the sharpness or the resolution at which the pictures are scanned) of the picture. You don't need anything more than 150 – 200 DPI for normal applications, but if you are going to print the scanned photograph, you can go up to 300 DPI or even more.
- ❑ Do the actual scanning process and select where the resulting data should go. If you select file, then the image will be saved as a .bmp or .jpg file. It is better to save the scanned pictures as bitmaps first, before converting them to jpg images using some graphics application like paint shop pro.

14.9 Tips for scanning

- ❑ The quality of the scanned image very much depends upon the quality of the original photograph or drawing. Hence, use good quality photographs or drawings.
- ❑ The DPI of the scanning relies, to a considerable extent, on the quality of paper being used. Better the quality of paper, higher the DPI that can be employed during scanning! For example, if you are scanning colour photographs printed by photo studios, then you can easily engage a higher DPI; on the other hand, if you are scanning pictures from magazines or newspapers, you will find that higher DPI often reveals the RGB colour dots – thus making the image useless.
- ❑ While placing the paper over the glass panel, always try use the central area - leaving some gap in the edges. This will result in even pressure across the paper – when the white board presses the paper.
- ❑ Go for DPI above 200 only if the photograph is of exceptional quality.
- ❑ With some scanners, you can even zoom in on a particular portion of the photograph -during the scanning process.
- ❑ The scanned picture may have to be edited to suit the particular multimedia project under production, before embedding the graphics. Various image editing software are available for this purpose.
- ❑ Though a variety of filters and editing options are available in the image editing software, most of them are only capable of making a good picture look better – and not in making bad pictures look good! So, there is no point in banking upon them heavily. Not only the photograph, but also the quality of paper containing the photograph - plays an important role in scanning. Art paper and other high quality paper printouts achieve best results.

14.10 Digital photography

Digital photography is the process of taking photographs using specialized digital cameras and storing the images directly as digital data - without making use of any film at all!

Digital photography is currently revolutionising not just the multimedia industry, but also a whole lot of other sectors like printing and news - throughout the world.

For example, reporters now can take a digital photograph of an incident and transmit the data immediately via e-mail to his or her office - wherein, the editor can embed the same on to the paper directly and print it! Thus, superior quality pictures can be transmitted in no time, to the destination without getting troubles like 'exposure of film roll', 'washing the films' etc.!

As in the case of scanners, though a variety of digital cameras are available in the market, the basic principle remains almost the same, as illustrated below.

14.11 Basic principle of digital photography

The image that's focused with the camera lens, is cast over a special chip called a charged coupled device, whose face is studded with an array of transistors - that create electrical currents, proportional to the intensity of light that's cast over them.

Logically, each of these transistors ultimately makes up the pixels of the digital bitmap that's going to come to our monitor!

Note

Colouring information has to be recorded as a combination of Red Green and Blue intensities (RGB Values). To capture this information, one transistor is actually not enough. Hence, digital cameras actually make use of more than one transistor per pixel to capture all the millions of colour dots that needs to be recorded!

You can very well imagine the complexity of the circuitry - when the said camera is capable of taking, say, pictures at 1024*768 resolution!

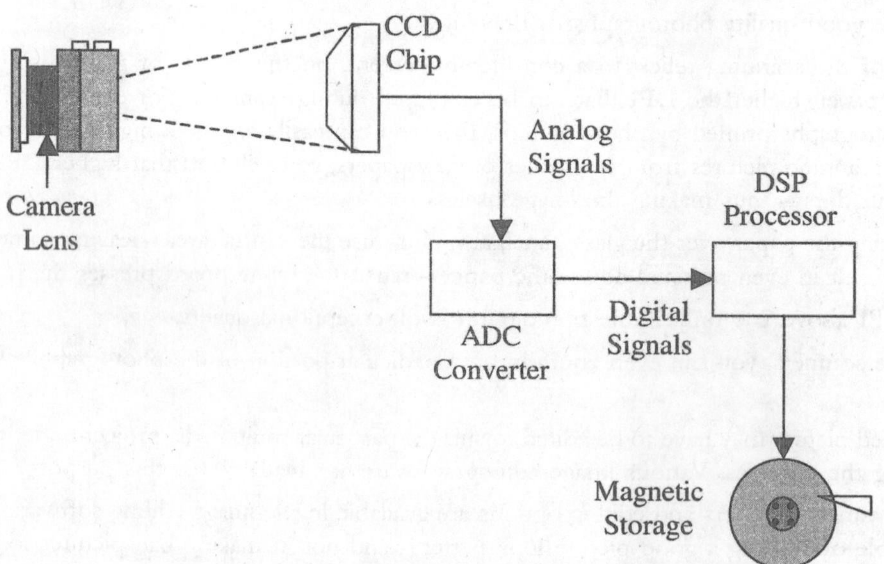

Figure 85: Basic principle of digital photography

The continuous stream of electrical analog signals generated by each of the transistors, move over to the ADC converter, wherein they are converted to digital zeros and ones and sent to a digital signal-processing unit (DSP) that has been already programmed to manipulate photographic data. The DSP adjusts the contrast and detail in the image to that perceivable by monitors, compresses the RGB pixel data that make up the image, and finally store the same in the camera's magnetic memory slot.

This memory may be a permanent magnetic memory or simply a RAM chip, depending upon the type of camera. Some cameras allow floppies to be inserted into a special mini floppy drive, so that the image data can be stored and then transferred to computers.

Digital cameras are available for both Microsoft Windows and the Apple Macintosh platforms. Depending upon the sharpness, quality of the picture and the associated storage space, the price may vary.

14.12 Camera specifications

We need to understand the parameters and specifications that dictate the capabilities of a digital camera and thus control the quality of the pictures taken.

They are:

- No of effective pixels (usually expressed in mega pixels)
- Different image sizes possible (directly proportional to CCD pixels)
- Optical zoom (expressed as 1x, 2x, 3x etc.)
- Digital zoom (also expressed as 5x, 10 x etc.)
- Image quality, type etc
- Memory card specifications
- Video capture / output
- Power / battery requirements
- Other camera specifications like exposure, shutter speed, aperture range, flash etc.

Here, we will discuss certain important parameters and specifications you need to know while purchasing a digital camera.

- **Effective pixels:** This is perhaps the most important parameter, which controls the quality of the pictures taken. The more the effective pixels are, the better. A 5-mega-pixel camera can capture more details of the shot taken than a 3-mega-pixel camera and hence better quality pictures. On the flip side, the size of the pictures will be big and hence we need more memory to store each picture.
- **Zoom:** Optical and digital zooms control the zooming capacity of the camera. The most important point to take note of is that, while optical zoom does not result in loss of quality, digital zoom does result in pixalation and other problems and hence results in loss of quality.
- **Image size and quality:** Images can be captured at various resolutions and colours, using a digital camera. The higher the resolution or number of colours, the better is the image quality. Popular resolutions are 1600*1200, 1024*768 and 640*480.
- **Memory specifications:** The flash card or the memory card that is slid into the camera, serves as the storage medium for pictures taken. Memory cards are available with 64 MB, 128 MB or 256 MB capacities. The capacity of the card dictates the maximum number of pictures that can be taken using the camera. Once the memory slot is full, you have to either insert a new flash card into the slot or download all the pictures into a PC and release the memory of the card for reuse. The following table gives you an approximate idea of how many pictures can be stored in a 64 MB memory card – at different sizes and quality.

Table 24: Number of pictures that can be taken using a 64 MB flash card – at various settings (approx.)

Resolution\ Quality	1600*1200	1024*768	640*480
Best	66 pictures	159 pictures	390 pictures
Medium	131 pictures	306 pictures	709 pictures
Basic	256 pictures	578 pictures	1301 pictures

- **Video capture:** Certain digital cameras, apart from capturing pictures, can also record videos without sound. This is a desirable feature, if you want to record small clippings for your projects. The movies are usually stored as mpeg files.
- **Power / battery capacity:** This is not as less important as it looks! Particularly when you use flash for each and every photograph, the power consumption is pretty high. Add the LCD display's power consumption on top of this! All this necessitates a very powerful battery capacity.

14.13 Summary

Scanning is the process of converting images and photographs on paper to digital imagery. There are three types of scanners: Sheet-fed, Flatbed and Hand-held scanners. Flatbeds are the widely used ones.

Results of scanning process depend on two parameters: the number of colours and DPI (dots per inch) used for scanning. High-end scanners can capture more details from a given photograph, than their low-end counterparts.

Digital photography is the process of taking photographs using a digital camera.

The parameters that control the results of a digital camera are number of effective pixels, optical zoom, digital zoom, resolution and number of colours.

Here again, high-end digital cameras can capture more details from a given scene than low-end cameras.

14.14 Keywords

Dots per inch (DPI): The total number of dots used to capture one square inch of a physical image. This parameter dictates the quality and resolution of scanned pictures.

Chapter 15

GRAPHICS EDITING

CHAPTER OVERVIEW

Having seen what are all the different categories of tools available for graphics editing and manipulation, we now need to take a detailed look at the different graphic manipulation options and how they can be put to use in a given project.

For illustration, we take Jasc Inc's Paint shop pro – a cute little image editing tool with the help of which, we can master all the fundamentals and gear up for complex editing tools like Adobe Photoshop.

Graphics editing and manipulation operations are literally unlimited in number – there are functions to edit the colour, orientation of the image, add special effects, enhance the quality etc. You will learn most of the fundamental operations and how to apply them in combination.

The chapter winds up with an introduction to various ready-made sources of professional digital images.

15.1 Introduction

We already saw in one of the previous chapters that sources of multimedia graphics could be photographic images, clip arts or 3 dimensional graphic images, apart from all other miscellaneous sources.

We also saw that the photographic images have to be obtained either by scanning or by digital photography and digital images thus obtained must be edited and manipulated, before they can be used in multimedia applications.

In this chapter, we are going to concentrate on the latter part of the story viz. digital image editing and manipulation. We will first understand some of the technical terms, terminologies and concepts, before looking at some of the actual tools that help us to do digital image manipulations.

15.2 Need for graphics editing and manipulation

All digital photographic images must be edited before being embedded into a given project.

Why?

Well, there may be more than one reason.

- ❑ We may want to improve the look and feel of the image, by altering some of its attributes like brightness, colour contrast etc (editing).
- ❑ We may wish to remove some of the unwanted portions of the image or might wish to add something from another photograph (manipulation)
- ❑ We may have to adjust the size, resolution and number of colours that make up the image. Refer the following section for more details (editing)

- We may wish to add certain special effects that are not available with conventional or digital photography. A variety of filters, functions and effect options are available with image editing software tools that enable us to try out hundreds of special effects (manipulation)
- We may wish to convert one file format to another.

15.3 Basic attributes of an image – size, resolution and number of colours

Before proceeding further, we should understand the three basic traits of any digital image. We have already come across these terms in the previous chapters – but under a different context.

They are:

- **Image size:** Every image has a width and a length – expressed either using as physical dimensions (cm, inches etc) or logical dimensions (pixels). If you are going to print the resulting image after editing and manipulation, then it is better to use physical dimensions. Otherwise, use logical dimensions.
- **Image resolution:** The number of dots that fill up a square inch or square cm in the image. As we increase this number of dots, the image size becomes pretty big – since it contains more details per square inch. Once again, if you are going to print the resulting end image – use higher resolution and if you are going to use them in pc multimedia applications, use lower digits.
- **Image colours:** Every image is made up of a number of colours. This number could be as low as 256 or as high as several millions of colours. This parameter indicates how many colours are contained in a particular image.

These parameters have a direct impact on the physical memory of the image. Higher size or number of colours implies higher memory requirements.

For a better understanding, I've drawn a table comparing the memory requirements of various images of various sizes, resolutions and no of colours.

Table 25: Memory requirements of a bitmap image – comparative study

Size (Pixels)	Resolution (Pixels / inch)	No of colours	Size (KB / MB)
640*480	72	16.7 Million (24 bit)	900 KB
	72	256 (8 bit)	301 KB
	300	16.7 Million (24 bit)	900 KB
	300	256 (8 bit)	301 KB
800*600	72	16.7 Million (24 bit)	1.3 MB
	72	256 (8 bit)	469.7 KB
	300	16.7 Million (24 bit)	900 KB
	300	256 (8 bit)	301 KB
1024 * 768	72	16.7 Million (24 bit)	2.2 MB
	72	256 (8 bit)	769 KB
	300	16:7 Million (24 bit)	2.2 MB
	300	256 (8 bit)	769 KB

You will notice that it is the number of colours that is the major decision factor that affects the physical size of the image. It is important that we understand this very clearly at this point of time.

15.4 Number of colours in an image

Each digital image may contain a few hundred or few thousand or a few million colours!

Technically, these are called 8 Bit, 16 Bit, 24 Bit and 32 Bit colour schemes. 24 Bit scheme can contain as many as 16.7 million colours and is sufficient for most applications.

Have a close look at the images shown.

I can guarantee you that one of them is an 8-bit image and that the other is a 24-bit. But you are unable to distinguish them.

Even if you were to refer the CD-ROM that comes with this book and have a very close look at the original colour images, you will still have difficulty identifying the 8-Bit image.

This is mainly because of the fact that human eye cannot distinguish anything beyond 256 colours.

Thus it is possible to reduce the number of colours of most images – if not all – to 256, without market difference in the resulting image. However, if you are going to print the resulting digital image, better stick on to 16.7 million colours – as printing machines are more sensitive than human eyes.

Before we conclude, let me break the answer: The image on the right hand side is an 8-bit image!

Figure 86: Can you tell which one is an 8-bit image and which is a 24-bit image?

15.5 Graphics editing concepts

Graphics editing tools we see in the market today were developed over a period of time. During this period, several concepts have evolved in this space and almost all professional tools make use of these concepts – in one way or other.

In this chapter, it may not be possible for us to discuss all the concepts – but we will see some of the important ones, listed below:

- Anti aliasing
- Layering
- Selections
- Masking
- Image filters

Let us discuss these concepts, one by one.

15.6 Anti-aliasing

The term anti-aliasing should not sound alien to those who have read one of the previous chapters titled 'Multimedia texts'. There, we saw that anti-aliasing is used to smooth out the edges (or jaggies) of the text by way of employing a series of colour gradients - in and around the sharp edges.

Figure 87: The figure on the right hand side shows just a portion of the image - resized by roughly 400 %. You can see the rough squares protruding out of the dome's edges. Technically, this is called pixelation.

The problem of jaggies comes into picture even with digital graphics and anti-aliasing is required to smooth out the sharp edges resulting.

Unlike text data, wherein jaggies develop even during the initial typing stage itself - graphic images are prone to jaggies only when edited…and more noticeably so, during the zooming or picture resizing operation!

Anti-aliasing pictures involve much more complicated algorithms than texts - something like pixel interpolations and replicating each pixel by a mathematical factor etc., and only professional photo editing software are endowed with the same. Without anti-aliasing, enlarged pictures almost become unusable in professional multimedia applications.

Figure 88: Here too, the right hand side image has been resized by roughly 400 %. But it looks much better than the previous one - at least without the square edges, because of specialized mathematical algorithms that are made use of during resizing operation.

If you are sure that the image is going to be enlarged and if the source of the image is in paper or photograph, then you can perform the zooming operation during scanning process itself. The results are better that software based zooming.

15.7 Layering

Layering is an important concept in the world of graphics editing – as it gives immense power to a creative digital artist.

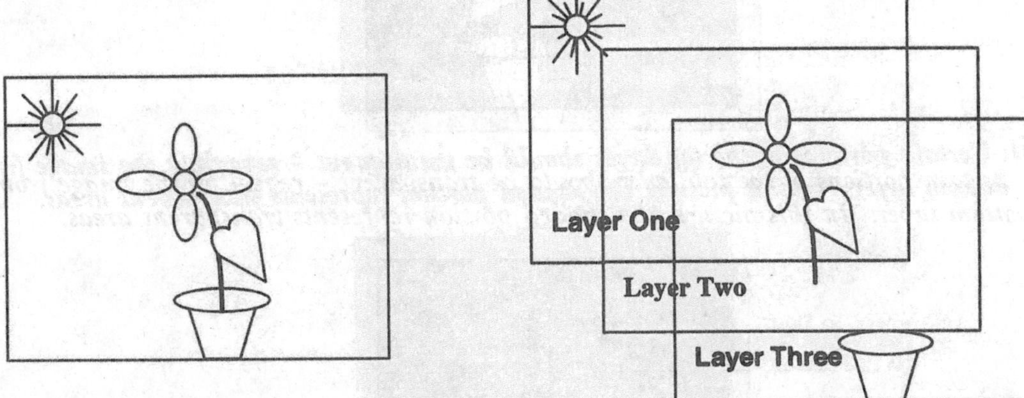

Figure 89: According to the concept of layers, each image is composed of one or more layers. In this sample figure, what you see as a single picture on the left hand side is actually composed of three layers – one containing the pot, one containing the plant and a third one containing the background.

According to this concept, each image is made up of one or more layers. What you see as an integral picture may actually be composed of several elements in different layers.

The biggest advantage of having layers is that you can edit a specific portion of the image, without disturbing the rest. For example, you can retain the same image as shown in the example – and just change the background to evolve a totally new picture with minimal effort.

Figure 90: The right hand side picture was evolved from the left – by simply replacing the background layer with a night effect.

For this reason, the bottommost layer below all other layers – is usually called the background. Digital artists use it to put a basic background for their pictures, on top of which - they add the image objects they wish to add.

To reveal the contents below, each layer should have certain portions transparent.

In the previous example, many portions were transparent – that is why you were able to see the night background – when the background image was changed. For your understanding, I've shaded the transparent portions in layers two and three.

Figure 91: Certain portions of the top layer should be transparent – revealing the image from the bottom layers. In this picture, the shaded portion represents transparent areas.

Figure 92: The opacity of the top layer has been set to 50%; hence all lines are visible only as dashed outlines.

Apart from transparency, each layer may also have an opacity element associated with it. If the opacity is 100%, then the layer is totally opaque and if it is 0% then the layer is totally transparent. In between zero and hundred, one can choose any degree of opacity he wants and can actually produce very cool effects with it.

Unlike transparency, which can be applied on specific portions of a layer, opacity has to be adjusted on a layer-by-layer basis.

15.8 Selections

A selection represents a particular portion in the whole image.

For example, in the image provided below, you can treat the sun, plant and the pot as independent selections. Once you select the sun alone, you can actually adjust its placement, control its colour or do other forms of editing and manipulation.

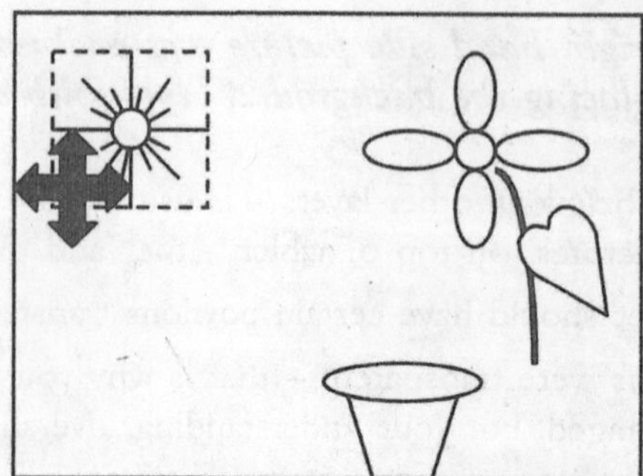

Figure 93: Selections help us to manipulate independent portions of the image.

It will be very interesting to compare selections with layers.

You may actually think that you can have the sun, the plant and the pot in independent layers and adjust the placement of the layer straight away, instead of making independent selections of the objects. In reality this is impracticable and cumbersome – for the following reasons:

- You cannot keep adding layers to every other object featured in the image. As the number of objects increase, it becomes very difficult to manage the image.
- Increasing the number of layers also increases the size of the image and it becomes difficult even to load the image due to heavy size. This is undesirable as it takes long time to save and load the image every time.

The right methodology is to strike a balance between the layers and the selections. When the numbers of objects are small, see if you can manage without a layer or with one layer.

Figure 94: In the image shown, how many layers you think you really need?

The key to arrive at this balance lies in understanding how selections really work and how different objects of a given image need to be manipulated.

In the example image provided, you may want to move the stars, moon, clouds, houses and the trees - independent of each other. In order to achieve this independence, will you keep all these objects in independent layers? If you were to do so, you may have to manage at least 20 different layers for such a simple image!

This is really not worth it and an unintelligent / resource intensive option.

Instead, try to think what are all the objects you can place in one layer and select them easily.

Let us assume we place the moon and the stars in one layer.

Can we select them at ease?

Very much! Since there are no objects around them, we can easily select them using the selections tools available with the software we are using. Most of the professional graphics editing applications feature various kinds of selection tools – to suit the needs of different projects.

For example, we can select the stars using rectangular selection tool, as shown below:

Figure 95: All the stars in the image can be easily selected using the rectangular selection tool.

How about moon and the clouds?

This is a slightly tricky affair, because the moon and clouds are linked with each other and they cannot be selected independently.

But the question is this: Is there a real need to separate clouds from the moon?

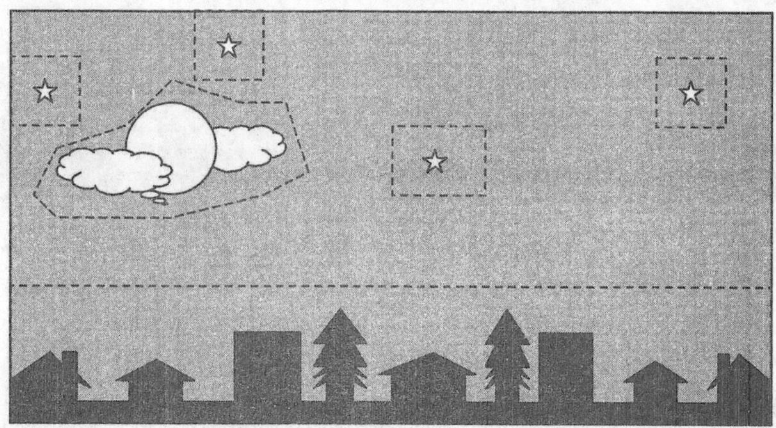

Figure 96: All objects, other than the background - selected using various selection tools.

There can hardly be a situation! The combination looks good; let us leave them as they are.

Now, we have ended up with one layer with moon, clouds and the stars.

Next, look at the buildings and the 'not so good-looking' trees. We can as well put them in the same layer as the moon and the stars – because they are featured in the bottom portion of the image and hence can be selected without disturbing the rest.

In order to get things clarified further, we've provided you an image with each of these objects selected using appropriate selection tools.

The selection tool used to select moon and the clouds – looks interesting. Unlike the rectangular selection tool that is used to draw geometric selections, this tool is used to select objects using irregular contours. Some applications call this a freehand selection tool. This freehand selection tool is probably one of the most innovative tools that you will frequently use in real life projects.

Now, we have ended up with a much simpler figure – with one background and one layer with all objects put together.

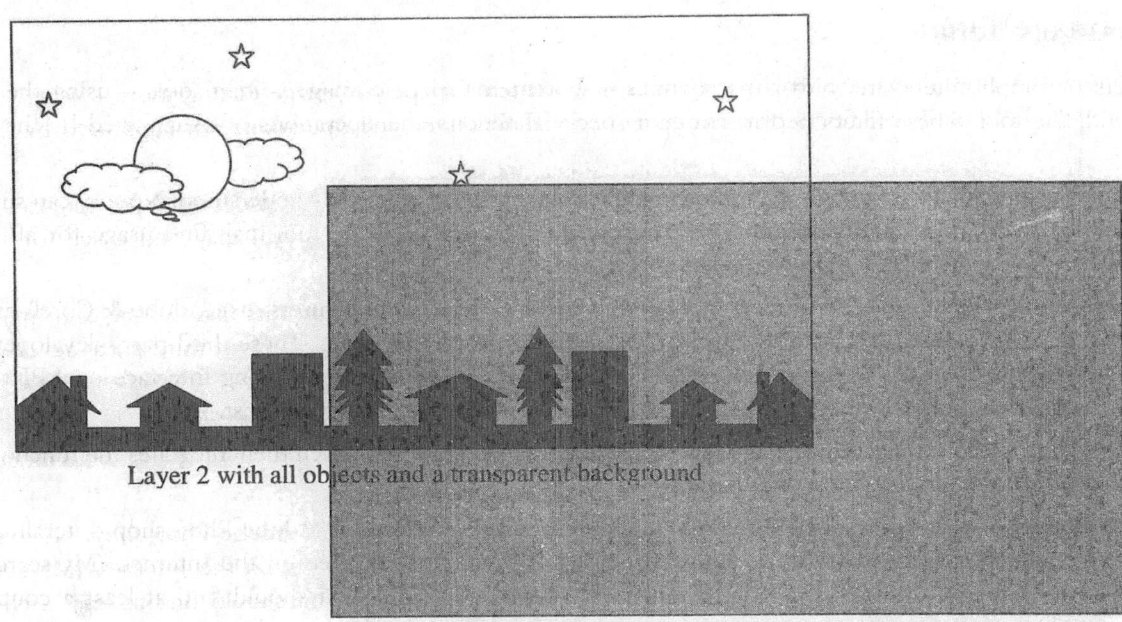

Figure 97: The final layers arrangement we have ended up with.

It will be interesting to note that all the objects could be selected in the second layer easily because we segregated the background. If we were to mingle the background with the objects, selections would have become pretty difficult – since the areas around the stars and the moon would not have been empty, by then!

15.9 Masking

Masks are special kinds of layers – which hide specific portions of the underlying image and expose the rest.

For example, let us introduce a mask - in the sample image we have been dealing with in the above pages. This mask exposes a circular portion of the underlying image – blocking the rest from the eyes of the viewer.

Masks can be saved and reapplied over any other image.

Like layers, masks also have the opacity element attached with them. This can be used create faces in-between the layers.

Figure 98: The mask over the image exposes selected portions of the image

15.10 Image filters

Image filters or simply filters, are third party routines – written for specific image editing tools – using the APIs provided with the tool. These filters perform certain special functions and operations not supported by the main tool.

The inspiration behind image filters and the reason behind their success can be easily understood: No tool can support all the possible effect and manipulation options; and not all who purchase the tool may find usage for all those options.

Hence, instead of developing all the effects by themselves, the core tool manufacturers (like Adobe & Corel) expose only certain limited number of effects and leave the rest to third party developers. These third party developers get hold of the image filter development SDK (which is a sort of application programming interface or API to the core tool) and develop optional effects, which can be purchased either free or for a cost.

These filters, when placed on specific locations, are identified by the core tool – which then integrates the functionality and operations of the filter with its own options.

The most famous tool, which has made the most out of these filters concept, is Adobe Photoshop. Literally there are thousands of filters available today for Photoshop and many are available free on the Internet. (My search on "Free Photoshop filters" in http://www.google.com yielded 169,000 pages! You should find at least a couple of them very useful!)

15.11 Basic editing operations

Digital artists make use of a variety of editing operations over the original image – in order to achieve the desired results. This section introduces some of the basic operations most commonly found in all graphics editing software.

15.11.1 Re-sampling or resizing

This is the process of changing the size of the image, to suit the needs of the application at hand.

It is always safer to reduce the size of the image rather than increasing it – because enlarging the original images almost invariably results in reduced image quality.

There are many different techniques involved in resizing like bilinear re-sampling, bi-cubic re-sampling, pixel resizing, smart sizing etc. Unfortunately, these topics demand in-depth analysis and discussions and are beyond the scope of this book.

Please refer the section on anti-aliasing – earlier in this chapter, to see how enlarging operation reduces the quality of the image.

Figure 99: Original image resized to 50% of its size

15.11.2 Dithering

Remember our discussions on the number of colours that make up an image – earlier?

Well, dithering operation is very closely related to that concept.

Each colour image has a colour palette associated with it. This colour palette contains the list of colours that are made use of, within the image.

For a 256-colour image, this colour palette will obviously have 256 different slots and so on.

When an image made up of millions of colours has to be reduced to another with – say, just 256 colours or so, then we obviously need a process by which the million colours in the colour palette can be reduced to just 256.

A mathematical technique called dithering is employed for this purpose.

Dithering reduces the number of colours by identifying all the basic colours and simulating the rest by intermingling pixels of two or more palette colours. If these simulated colours are not too close to the original colours, then the resulting image appears to be a bit grainier.

Figure 100: In order to produce this effect – that looks pretty amazing in the print medium, I used dithering to reduce the number of colours from 16 million to just 2! Process used was error diffusion. Certain details have been totally lost (like the sculptures on the left and right side of the first tier) – but the image, as a whole, looks like an Indian ink line drawing!

There are several processes of dithering - like reducing to nearest colour, error diffusion etc. Error diffusion is usually considered as a better option.

15.11.3 Flipping

Flipping is the process of producing a mirror image of the graphic image.

There are horizontal and vertical flip operations, resulting in horizontal and vertical reflections of the bitmap.

I frequently use horizontal flips to produce symmetrical images that look almost 'picture perfect'. To produce these kinds of images, we need to select one half of the picture, produce a horizontal flip of the same – and blend it seamlessly with the original half.

Figure 101: One on the left is the vertical flip and the other is a horizontal flip - compare them with the original image

Without referring to the previous page, can you tell me which half of the following picture is from original image and which one is the flipped half? Left, or right?

Figure 102: By combining one half of the original picture with a horizontal flip of the same - I created this interesting replica of the original temple. Challenge is to find out which one is the original half - left or right?

15.11.4 Rotating

This is the process of rotating the picture to required inclinations.

Perpendicular rotations like 90 degrees, 180 degrees etc. do not result in loss of picture quality, because they are as good as flipping pictures. The rest invariably result in slight loss of quality – mainly due to the development of jaggies.

Figure 103: First image is a regular rotation – 90 degrees. No loss of quality is noticeable. The second is a 30-degree rotation. The sharpness of the original picture has been lost a bit, but the quality is still tolerable.

15.11.5 Zooming

Zooming is the process of enlarging a particular portion of the image, either to have a better look at it or to do some editing in that portion.

For example, we could zoom in on just the top portion of the temple, in order to see the details and edit them a bit.

Figure 104: Image zoomed in using the zooming tool in Paint shop pro software

During zooming operation, the actual size of the image remains very much the same.

The process of enlarging a picture is totally different form zooming and was discussed under an earlier topic called resizing.

15.11.6 Colour corrections

Various parameters that define the colours of an image - such as brightness, contrast, intensity, hue and saturation - are editable.

Brightness is the level of illumination in the picture and contrast is the difference between the brightest and the darkest portions of the picture. By slightly increasing the brightness and contrast, we can actually improve the quality of most images.

I usually set contrast level to twice that of brightness level. For example, if I increase the brightness 6 times, I set contrast to 12 times.

Figure 105: Frankly, our sample picture does not need any serious colour corrections. For the sake of illustration, I slightly improved the brightness and contrast. The one on the right is the edited picture.

It's difficult to explain these different colour effects with words and black and white pictures. You may have to try them out yourself using relevant graphic editing tools like paint shop pro.

15.12 Advanced editing and image manipulations

So far we have been looking at relatively simple operations that did not distort the original image to a great extent. In this section, we are going to concentrate on certain advanced image manipulation operations that may well distort the original image to a very great extent.

Frankly, these effect operations are innumerable in number! For example, for Adobe Photoshop – a premier digital image-editing tool – there are thousands of 'filters' available… and each of these filters comes with one or more special effect operations!

Here, we will look at some of the special effect options available. The terminology used is pretty close to Jasc Inc. Paint shop pro – but you should be able to find their equivalents in Adobe Photoshop or Corel Photo paint – pretty easily.

15.12.1 Drop Shadows

This is probably the most widely used effect in the world of digital artistry.

The effect produces shadows below or above the contours we define. The contours are usually the edges of the whole picture – but that is not a strict rule.

For example, in the illustration provided below, the first image throws a shadow down the whole photograph whereas the second projects the temple out of the photograph!

There are many parameters you can control, with drop shadow effect – like the angle, length, blur and opacity of the shadows.

Figure 106: Drop shadows are usually cast downwards over the whole picture (left), but they can also be applied in many other ways (right).

15.12.2 Bevel Effects (Inner bevel / Outer bevel)

Bevel effects produce dramatic effects on ordinary images. They are responsible for the 3 dimensional projections you enjoy in most digital artworks.

By changing the brightness and contrast over the edges of the image (or selection), bevels produce effects, which project things out of the plain paper.

Look at the sample image I have provided. The bevel effect applied over the image is a type of inner bevel that gives frame like appearance to the image. To increase the overall impact, I've coupled drop shadows with this.

Bevels are at their best with multimedia texts – they can make any ordinary text look extraordinary!

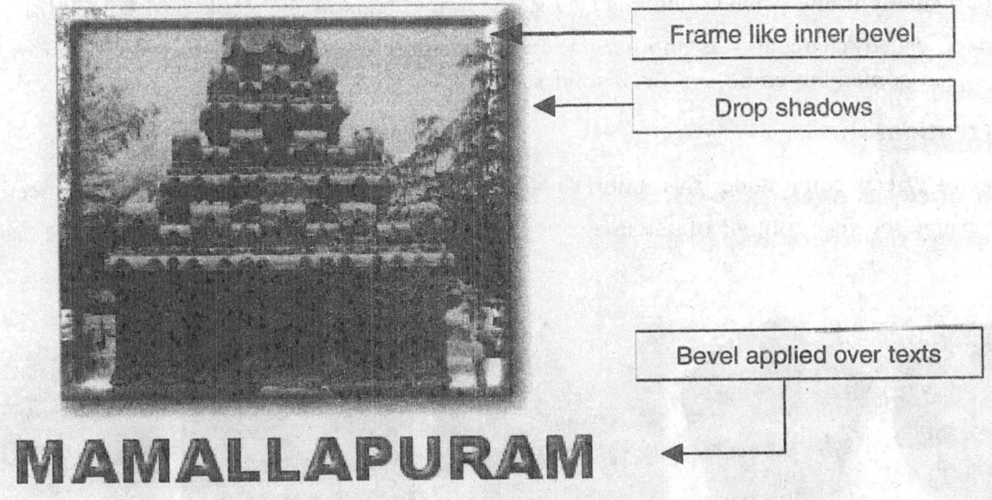

Figure 107: Bevels and drop shadows are excellent combination – when used appropriately, as illustrated here.

Remember our discussions on 3D texts in an earlier chapter on the same topic. Bevels are the ideal tools for producing 3D effect in texts.

The fonts over which bevel effect has to be applied, must be thick enough to accommodate the shades are light variations produced by bevels.

In the example shown, I used Arial black as my font. The results could have been much better, had I increased the size of the font; but since the image itself was pretty small, I had no choice.

Minor variations of bevel effects, like the buttonize option – also belong to the same family.

15.12.3 Emboss effects

Emboss – as the name implies – result in effects that seem to emboss the contour of the image over a metal plate or a stone surface.

Have a look at the two examples I've provided – in order to understand the effect.

Figure 108: Two types of emboss effects - sculpture and charcoal - applied over the original image.

In the first image, the original picture looks like a rock cut sculpture. One can choose the background and the texture colours. This effect is called sculpture.

This effect is particularly useful – when you want to show simple texts as archaeological epigraphs!

The second effect, called 'charcoal' – is another variation of emboss effect. This image looks more like a crayon pencil drawing, than something embossed on a solid surface!

15.12.4 Deformations

Quite a number of effects come under this umbrella – the famous pinch / punch, cylinder, perspective, skew etc. Deformations change the very contour of the image over which they are applied – as shown in the examples below.

Figure 109: Many types of deformations - circle, pentagon, pinch, punch and perspective - illustrated.

I have no hesitation in terming deformations as a sort of fancy effect – which is of lesser use in real life projects, as compared to drop shadows and bevels.

15.13 Jasc Inc Paint shop Pro

Having seen so much about the types of special effects that are available at the disposal of a digital artist, let us get hands on with one of the professional tools available in the market – Paint shop pro!

Note: What I will illustrated here is version 6.0, but I could see that version 8.0 is already available in the market – from their website http://www.jasc.com. But this is not a serious handicap for the overall understanding of the subject, since paint shop pro version 6.0 itself incorporates most of the features - we have been discussing all along.

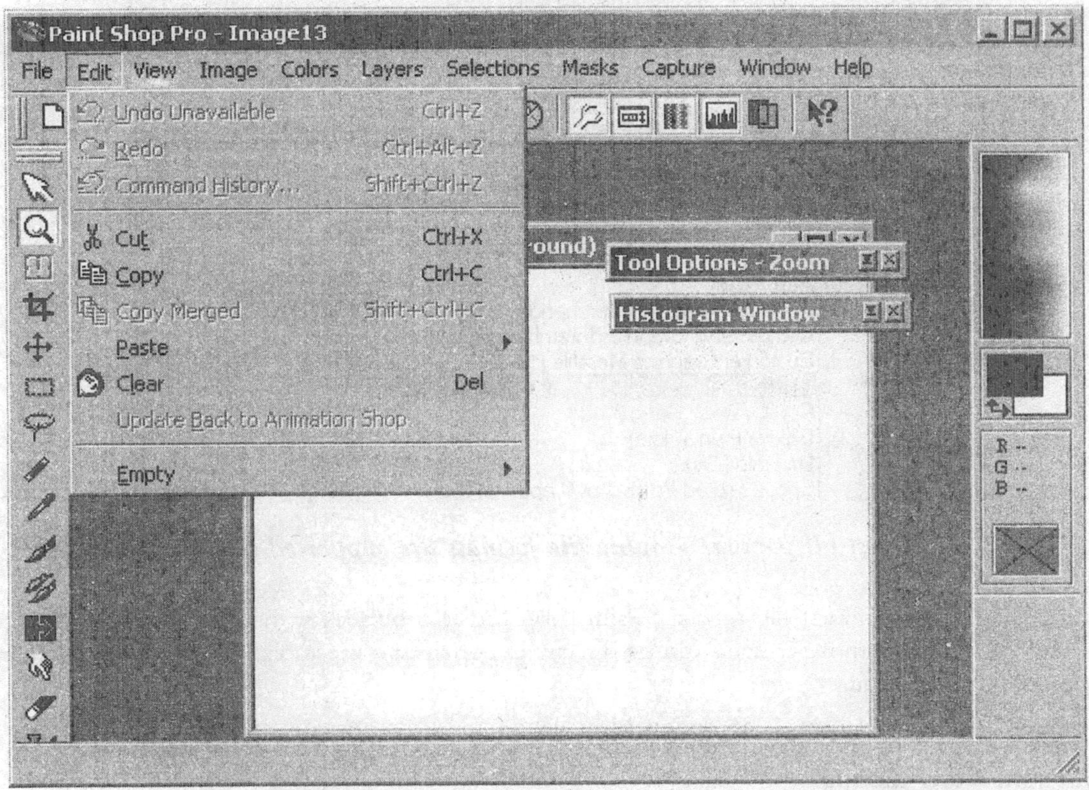

Figure 110: Jasc Inc Paint shop pro is a professional digital image editing solution.

Paint shop Pro can be used, either to create new pictures by digital drawing processes or to edit any of the existing digital photographs.

Apart from the usual File, edit, view, window and help menus – there are six other menus in which we are interested. They are: Image, colours, layers, selections, masks and capture menu.

15.13.1 File menu

The 'File Open' option can be found under the file menu item in the menu bar. Click the option, and the open dialog box is displayed.

Paint shop Pro supports almost all of the famous graphic file formats - including bitmap (.bmp), Corel draw graphics (.cdr), computer graphics metafile, CompuServe .gif, Targa .tga, .tiff, windows meta files (.wmf) and what not ?

Images in all these file formats can be directly opened and edited without a hitch.

What's more important, is that any of these files can be saved back in any other file format – using 'save as' option! Thus, apart from being a graphics editing and manipulation tool, Paint shop pro can also be used as an image conversion utility – suitable for most projects. This is one reason why I love this cute little tool.

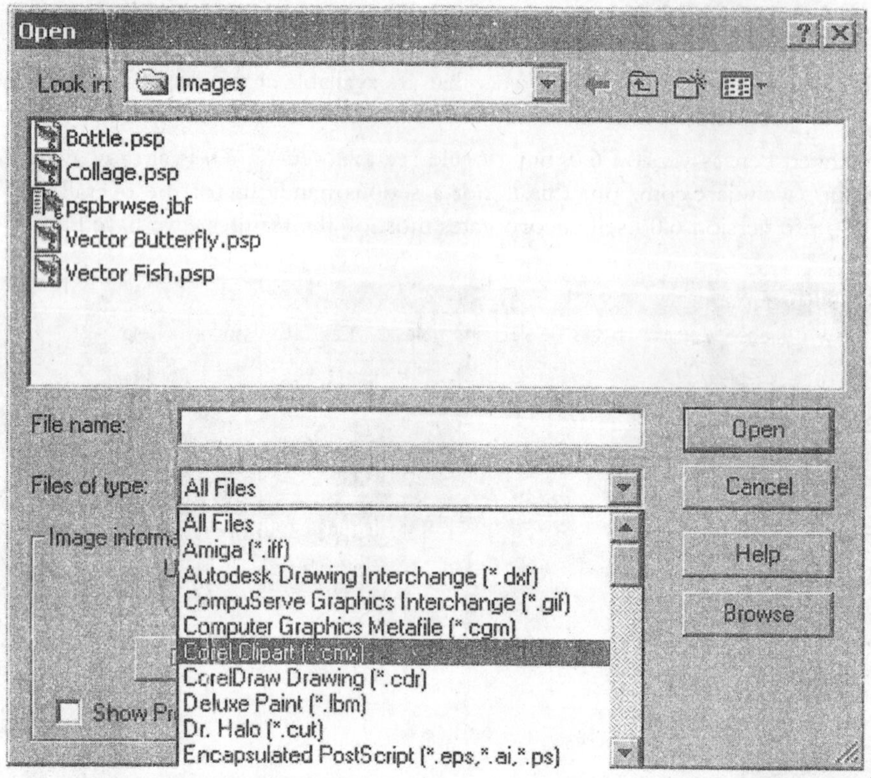

Figure 111: Almost all popular graphic file formats are supported by Paint shop pro

Apart from opening many different file formats, Paint shop pro also buckles with many versions of latest digital cameras- so that images from those cameras can be directly imported into the tool. These options are found under the Import button in File menu.

Note that support for digital cameras is an optional installation and does not come bundled with the core package.

15.13.2 Edit and View menus

Edit and view menus present all the usual options and I hope you can explore them yourself.

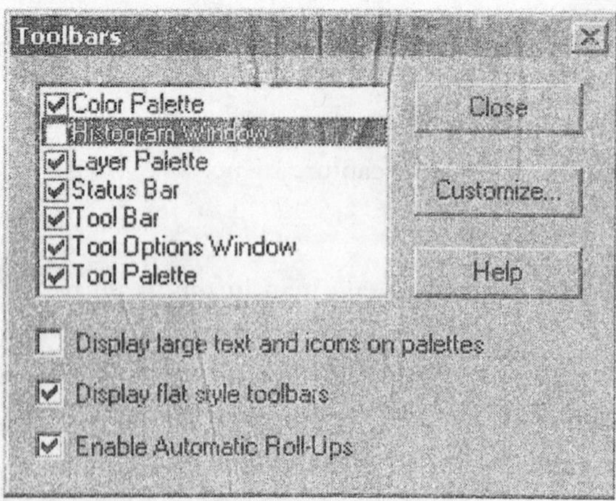

Figure 112: Toolbars window: Most of the palettes and windows are useful in Paint shop pro – and must be turned on, always!

I'd like to highlight the toolbar button in view menu – however. This button pops up a window that shows, which are all the toolbars that are currently displayed inside the Paint shop panel.

Do ensure that the options - as shown in the figure - are selected properly.

You will notice that we have switched all the toolbars on, but for the histogram window. This is because of the fact that most of these windows are pretty useful for our work.

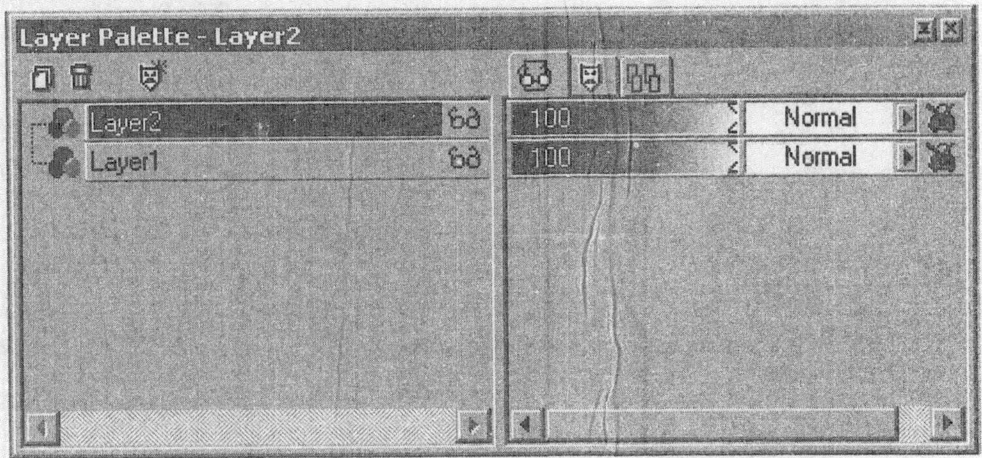

Figure 113: Layer palette that helps us to move between the layers...

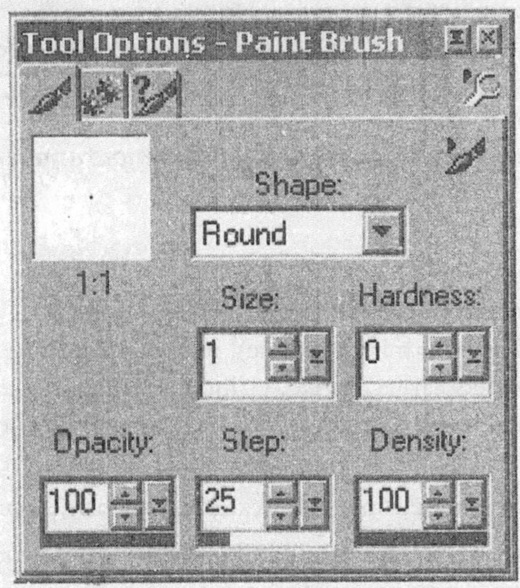

Figure 114: ... and tool options window that helps us to select various parameters for editing tools. Both panels can be made visible by clicking the right options in the Toolbar window.

In particular, the layer palette and the tool options window are two places where you need to go very frequently. Note that these two are floating panels and you may sometimes close them by mistake. If you are stuck up, come back to toolbars and switch the option on. The palette will be visible again.

Similarly, the image information button under the view menu helps us to view the different parameters associated with the current image – like the length, breadth, resolution, number of colours, number of layers, size etc. - in one place. The shortcut to reach this panel is shift+ i.

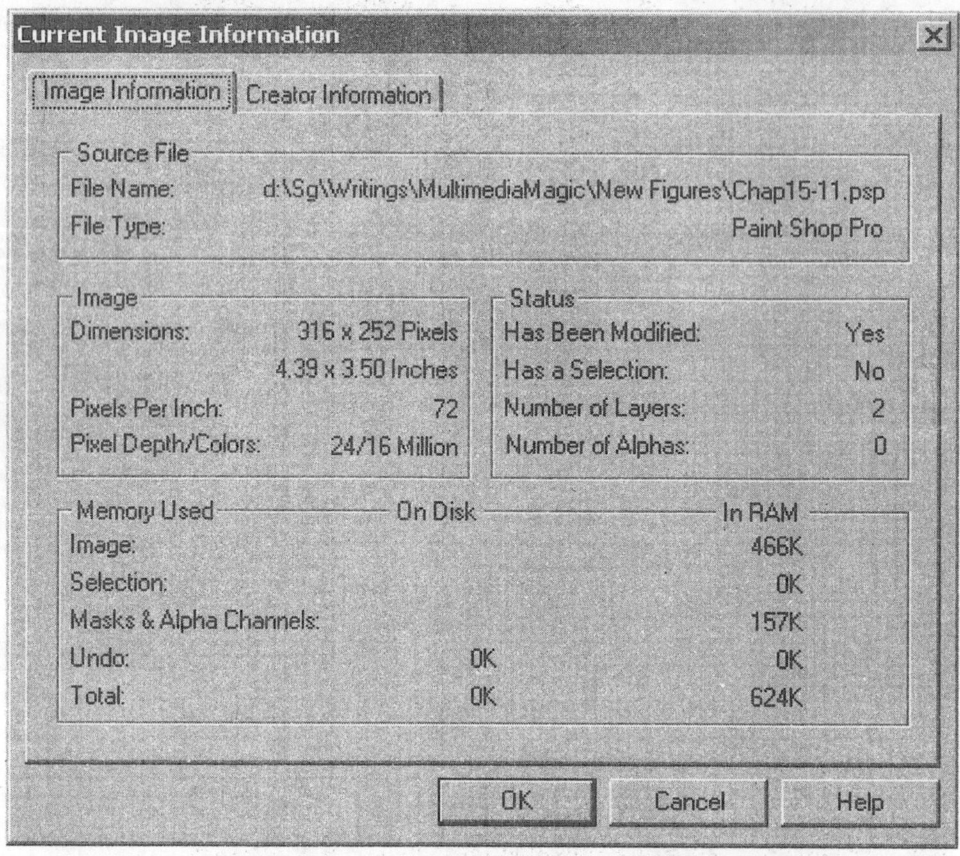

Figure 115: Current image information lists all possible parameters associated with the image.

15.13.3 Image menu

Quite a number of editing options are available under the image menu.

These include image orientation editing (flip, mirror, rotate), image size editing (add borders, canvas size, resize etc), all the deformation options we discussed earlier (circle, cylinder, pentagon skew etc.), all the special effect options under effects (drop shadow, bevel, embossing effects etc.) and the image correction options (blur, sharpen, noise etc).

The watermarking facility allows us to embed invisible watermarks inside our images, for copyright protection.

We haven't explored the picture frames as yet, but it could be a very simple and interesting effect to try out on your own. Essentially it adds a frame around any image; the nature of picture frame and the texture applied could be selected from the dialog box.

The next sections of effects are called 'filters' in paint shop pro. These filters are slightly different from the third party image filters we discussed about, in an earlier section in this chapter. These effects are organized under five different categories: blur, edge, noise, sharpen and other effects. The terms are self-explanatory.

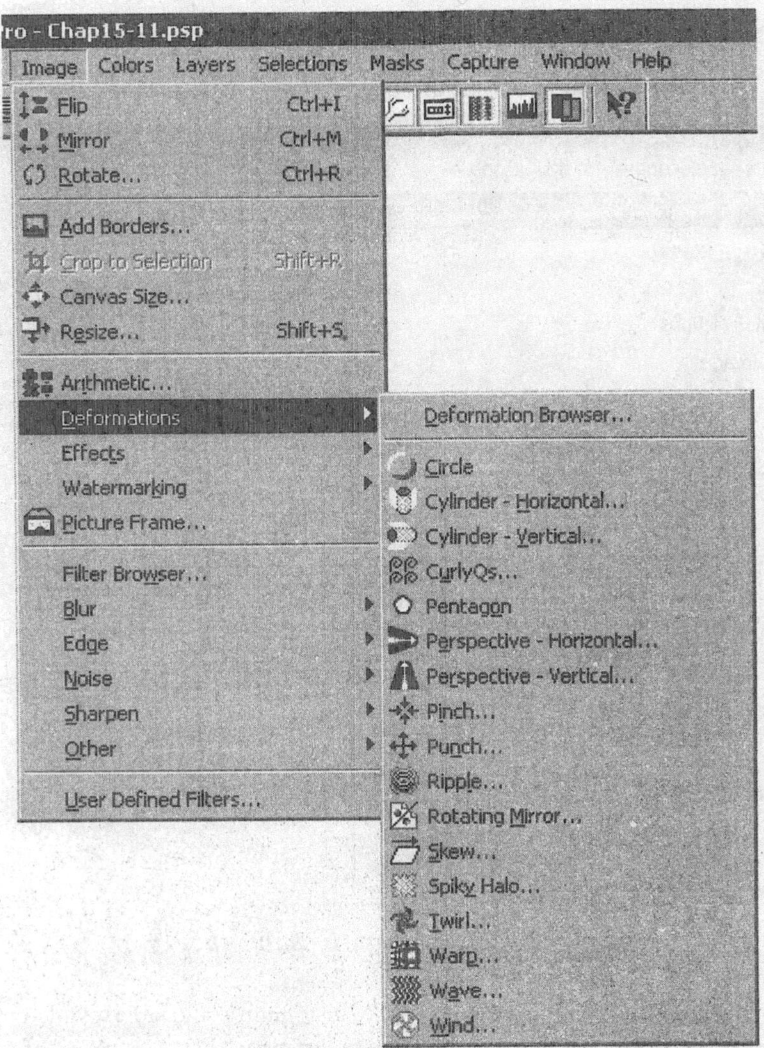

Figure 116: Options available under the Image menu item in Paint shop pro.

The filter browser is a convenient dialog box that lets you to experiment with various filters, before you actually apply them over the image.

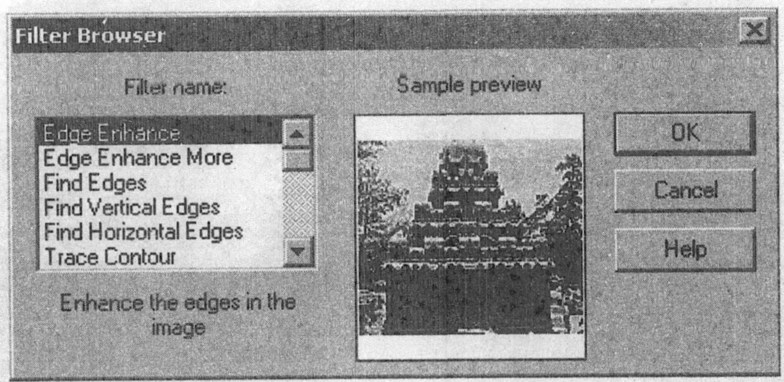

Figure 117: Filter browser gives you the option to try out all the effects before you apply them.

15.13.4 Colours menu

Colours menu is a sort of one-stop-shop for all the colour manipulations you can do with paint shop pro.

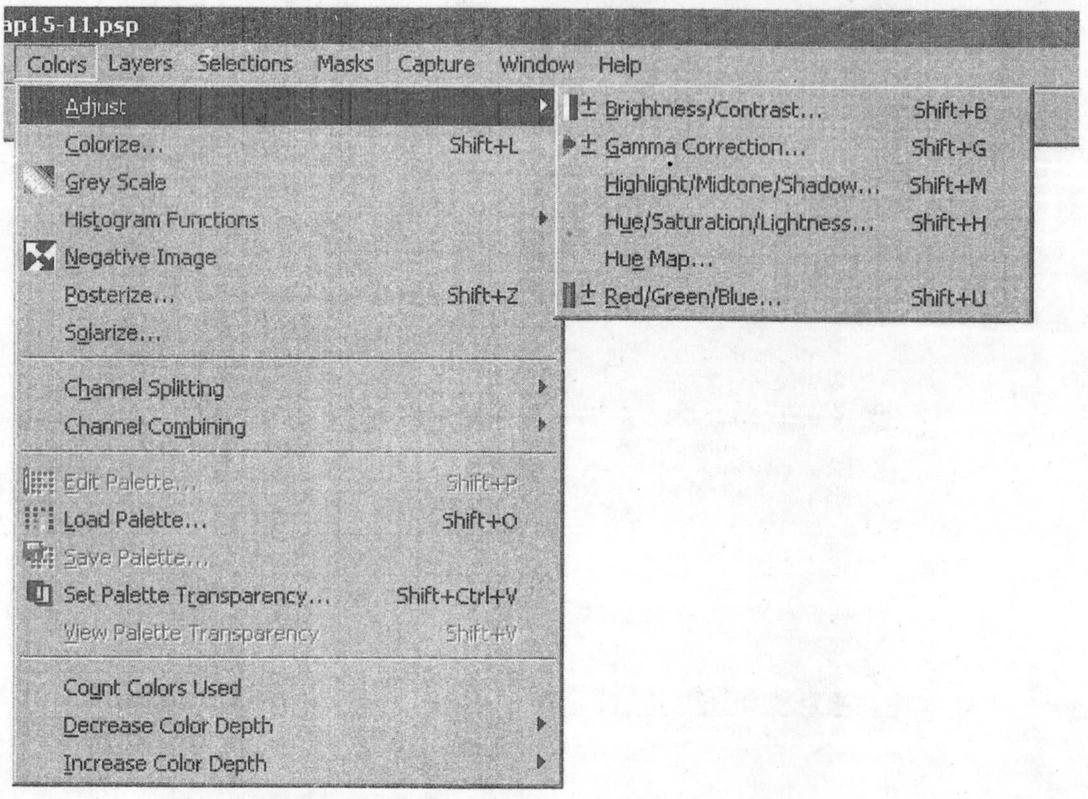

Figure 118: Colour menu in paint shop pro

The first set of options – including adjust, colourize, greyscale, histogram etc. enable a wide range of colour correction and manipulation functions. In particular, the colour adjustment panel has a number of options like controlling brightness/contrast, hue/saturation/lightness and red/green/blue. We can safely claim that these powerful tools can meet most of our colour correction requirements.

Greyscale is used to convert a colour image to a black and white image. I have used this option for almost all pictures featured in this book.

Figure 119: I used decrease colour depth function to 2 colours – to produce this effect

Channel splitting enables segregation of colours that make up the original colour picture to RGB or CMYK. These options are particularly useful for those involved with the printing industry.

Increase / decrease colour depth functions are probably the most frequently used ones in the whole colour menu options. We already discussed – earlier in this chapter, that any colour image can be made up of colours as low as 2 or as high as 16 million.

The colour depth function allows us to convert a picture with 16 million colour depth to just two colours or vice versa. More often than not, you will be juggling between 16 million and 256 colours.

In the example I've provided, I decreased a 16-bit colour image to a 2-colour image – and just selecting the blue channels during the reduction process. For the sake of better understanding, I'm also providing the exact set of options I used.

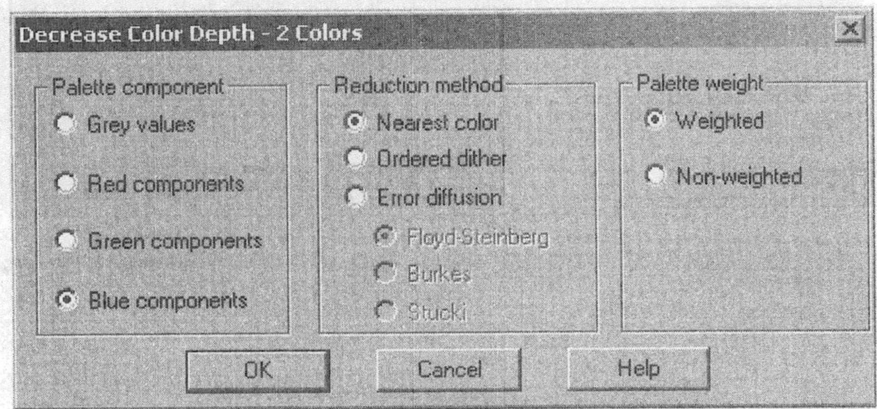

Figure 120: The options I used for reducing the number of colours to just 2 – from 16 million!

It is interesting to compare this with the dithering effect we discussed earlier. While dithering traced the basic profile of the image using a number of dots, decrease colour depth just identified the major colour regions and produced a different look for the same temple.

Which one looks better - dithering or decrease colour depth?

Well, the answer is a matter of one's taste and there can be no definite answers!

I'll conclude this section with one observation:

Most of the options like layering and effects will be available, only on a 16-bit colour image – in paint shop pro! So, even if your final image is of depth 256, work with a 16 bit image till you have completed all the imaging manipulations and finally convert the same to a 256 image using decrease colour depth option.

Note: I always have the habit of beginning all of my images as a .psp picture – the default file format in which paint shop pro saves its images. The .psp file format is of 16-bit colour depth and remembers all the multiple layers, masks and other information about the image. When all the manipulations are completed, I take a copy of the image (Ctrl+D) and save it as .jpg or whatever file format that is required for my project. I remember to save the original .psp in a separate folder – so that I can always come back to that original image, in case I need to do further manipulations on the same image. Many of the images featured in this book were originally saved in .psp file format and only a copy was used inside the book.

15.13.5 Layers menu

The next menu item that calls for our attention is layer menu.

Unfortunately, this is not of very great use – as we have a better and faster option for controlling the layers: The layer palette window!

The layer palette lists all the layers associated with a given image, identifies whether it is a masked layer or an invisible layer etc. and also displays the opacity of the layer. You can create a new layer, delete an existing layer and also change the order of layers…

Well, these are all the main options you really need, in order to work with the layers!

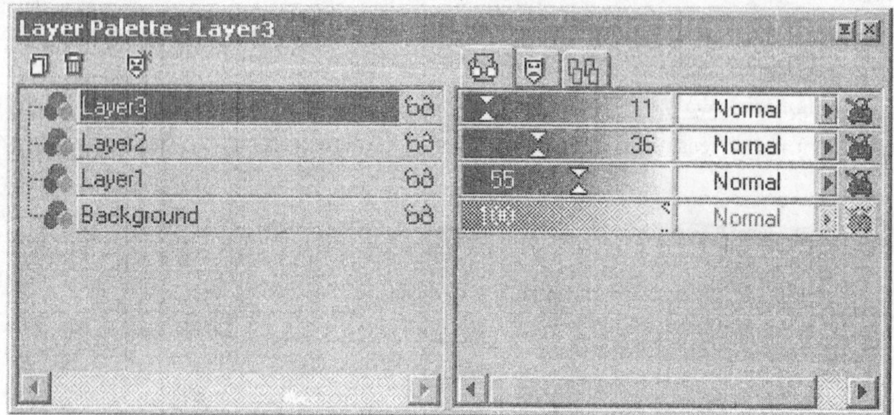

Figure 121: The layer palette allows you to control different layers in the image.

To illustrate the power of layers, I'm providing you with a simple example.

Figure 122: This "hazy" stuff is not a ready-made effect available in paint shop pro! It was done, purely with the help of layers.

I produced this hazy effect by super imposing same image multiple times – over different layers with slight offset. The only difference was in the opacity of the layers.

The exact options I am talking about, is already available in the earlier image on layer palettes.

15.13.6 Other menus

There are other menu items like selection, masks and capture – which you can try on your own. In particular, capture function is most useful for capturing screen shots in various modes.

This brings us pretty much to the conclusion of our detailed discussions on paint shop pro. What I have discussed here is but a tip of the iceberg. As you start using the tool and try out new effect options, you will understand that there is always something new to uncover – in this wonderful world of multimedia graphics!

15.14 Summary

The three basic attributes of an image are image size, resolution and colour depth. An image can be made up of colours as low as 2 or as high as 16 million. Anti-aliasing, layering, selections, masking and image filters are some of the important concepts behind graphics editing.

Basic editing operations include re-sampling, dithering, flipping, rotating, zooming and correcting colours. Special effect operations like drop shadows, bevel effects, emboss effects, deformations etc can be termed as advanced manipulation options.

Jasc Inc.'s paint shop pro supports numerous colouring and image manipulation effects - apart from providing layering, masking and other functionalities.

15.15 Keywords

- **Dithering:** The process of changing the RGB value of the colour pixels that makes up the image, to the closest matching colour in a predefined fixed colour palette, using complex mathematical algorithms.
- **Masking:** The process of blocking out selected portions of the Image, for a particular editing operation.

PART VI

MULTIMEDIA ANIMATION

PART OVERVIEW

We have now landed on an exciting chapter in our learning journey!

Multimedia animations are undoubtedly the most compelling among all the elements of multimedia. Animation means fun! And computerised animation means creativity unbound! 3D Animation means endless days of excitement!

Traditional hand drawn animations have long been in the race, ever since the advent of Walt Disney cartoons, but it was only after the introduction of computers – that multimedia animation hit the main streets and represents a multi billion-dollar industry today!

In the next few chapters, we will be doing really serious work and understand almost all the basic technologies and concepts associated with animations. Have a cup of tea, before you begin!

Chapter 16

Fundamentals of Computer Animation

CHAPTER OVERVIEW

This chapter serves as a curtain raiser for this complex technology.

We begin with the most fundamental question: Why do we need a specialized medium called animations in a multimedia project, after all?

A briefing on different types of animations popular in the industry follows these discussions.

It is important to understand and classify different types of animations – based upon technology, media and applications. Later on, this will be of immense use to us – because the strategies used to develop animations are very much influenced by the category to which they belong. The rest of this chapter is devoted to understanding two-dimensional and three-dimensional planes and what sorts of tools are available to develop 2D and 3D animations.

The purpose of this chapter is to wet you into the world of animations and prepare you for more detailed discussions in the later chapters.

16.1 Introduction

Multimedia animations or simply animations represent a series of drawings that are presented one after another to the user's eyes at those speeds that provide an illusion of movement.

Going by their basic concept, animations are not very different from films. The only difference is that while films are video graphed via a video camera or a camcorder, frames that make up the animation are created either with the help of drawings or specialized three-dimensional environments.

Animation, as a technology, was born well over a century before computers. But conventional animations took lot of money, effort and time to develop and were beyond the reach of mainstream entertainment. It was only after the introduction of computers that animation was able to evolve as a multi million-dollar industry and was able to stroll past dizzy technical heights hitherto unknown.

Our focus here is however limited to the fundamentals of computer based animation technology – and with special emphasis on its role, as a facet of multimedia. So, let us keep all other generic discussions aside and get down to business.

16.2 Animations in multimedia projects

Animations were incorporated into multimedia, primarily because of the need for dynamic graphics in real time multimedia applications.

Figure 123: It'll much more fascinating to see these balloons floating - instead of standing still.

For example, let us imagine that we need to show a balloon floating in thin air – in a children's edutainment title. With graphics imagery, what we can provide, at the best – is a high quality digital photograph of a big balloon. But if we were to use animations for illustrating the same point, then the balloon can be brought to life and may well be floating across the monitor – if not the big blue sky! Imagine how compelling it will be for a six-year-old child, staring at the monitor!

This is the power of animations and hence their respected position in the world of multimedia.

Do you get the point?

16.3 Need for animations in multimedia projects

Animations are engaged in multimedia projects, for one or more of the following reasons:

- ❑ To explain a concept or illustrate a point, better. Animations are perhaps, the best tools for illustrating what you are really trying to say.

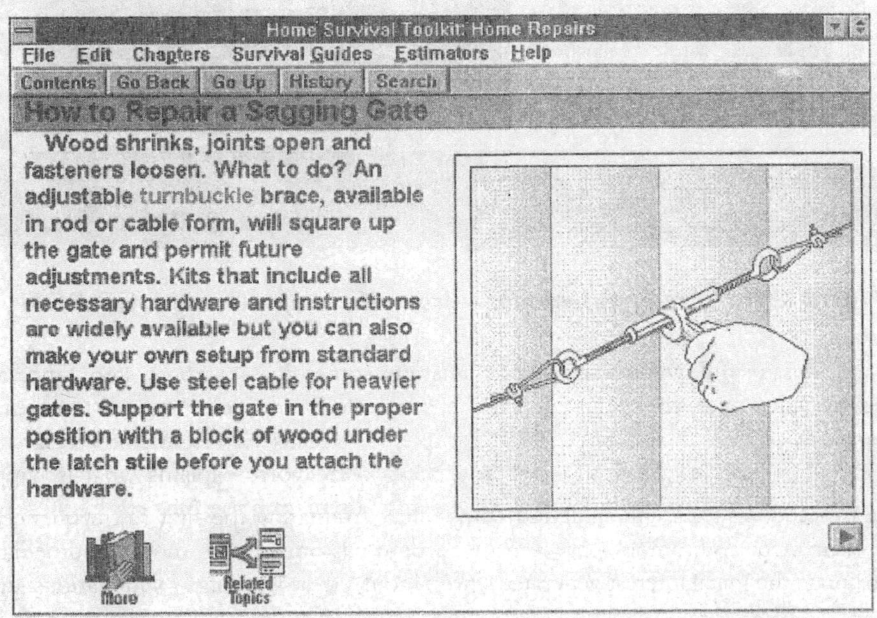

Figure 124: Usage of animations – from "Home survival toolkit" CD-ROM

- Look at the example provided from "Home survival toolkit " CD-ROM. This title explains how to use various types of household hardware for domestic purposes, how to do your own repairs within the house etc. Such details can be best explained with the help of computer animations, rather than pages and pages of photographs or texts.
- There are situations wherein, a given sequence cannot be photographed or video graphed. For example, in Andromeda interactive "Interactive space encyclopaedia" CD-ROM, various astronomical concepts - like the 'big bang' theory - are clearly illustrated with the help of computer animations. It may not be possible to video graph such a sequence, which is believed to have happened millions of years ago! A static digital photograph will hardly impress upon the viewers! An animated shot is the only viable alternative.
- A similar illustration can be provided from Microsoft's Oceans CD-ROM. In the section titled, 'How does a sub dive?' - instead of mincing up with words, the titles throws open a cute little animation, which illustrates the point beyond all conceivable doubts. The background voice over explains what is happening – as the animation proceeds.

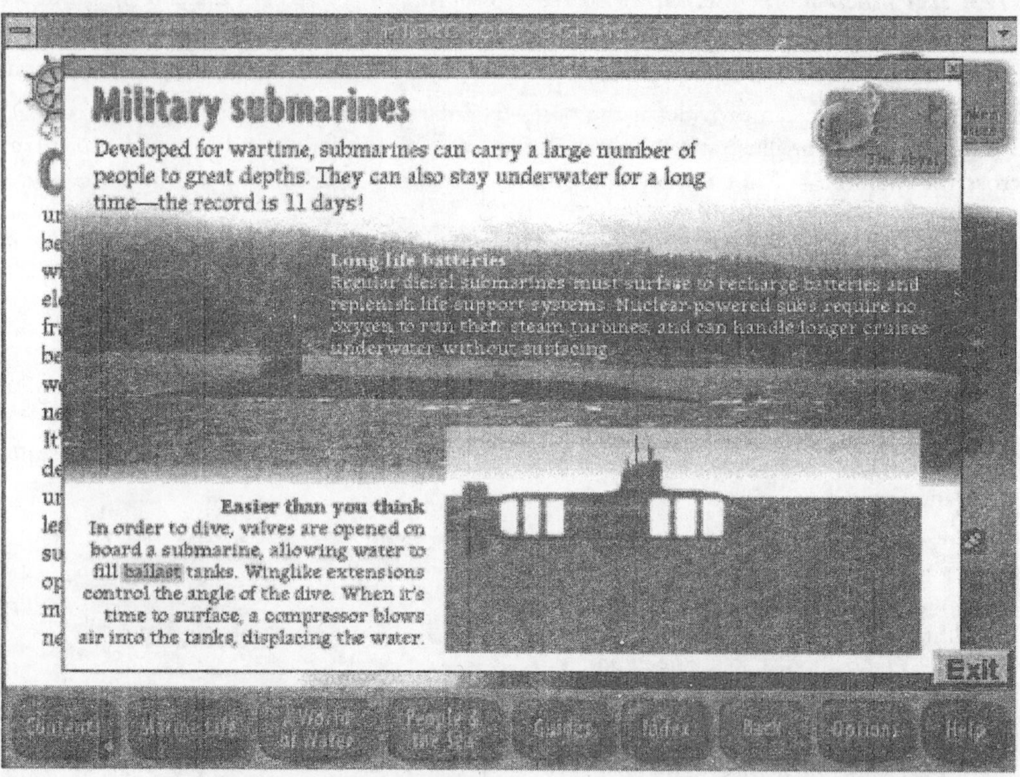

Figure 125: Usage of animations – from Microsoft "Oceans" CD-ROM

- Animations are most useful, when you need to illustrate something – step by step. Since animations can be accompanied by voice-over, the sequence can be controlled very well. You can look at all the examples provided above, to appreciate this point. For example, in Oceans CD-ROM, how clear it is to understand the basic principle behind a submarine – when a background voice explains what is happening!
- To make the proceedings rich, colourful and compelling. Animating the first few sequences of the title – to keep up the excitement and tempo – has almost become customary with most multimedia titles. Of course, good titles maintain the initial interest generated, throughout the proceedings - with various kinds of animations.

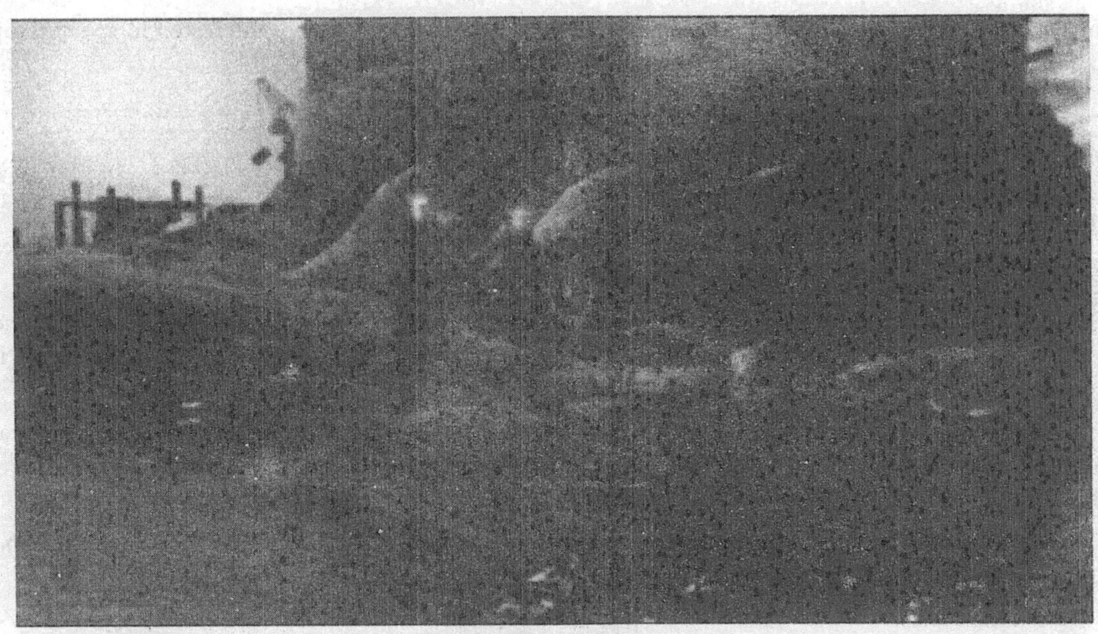

Figure 126: The compelling beginning sequence of Sid Meier's multimedia game 'Civilizations'

In short, animations are not optional elements in multimedia titles – but mandatory.

But the extent, to which animations are deployed - is dictated by the nature of the title under development. In general, children entertainment and edutainment titles and multimedia games make extensive use of animation technology, than other types of multimedia applications.

16.4 Computer animations - classification

The term 'computer animation' encompasses literally any kind of animation created using computers. Multimedia animations are those that are used in multimedia projects.

A simple classification of various types of computerized animations will be of great interest to us, at this stage.

Table 26: Animations - Different classifications

Classification	Based on	Animation
I	The basic philosophy of animation	Cel / Frame animation Object animation
II	The number of dimensions involved	Two dimensional animation Three dimensional animation
III	The nature of applications	Movie animation Television animation Multimedia & Games animation Net animation and others
IV	The technology used to create animated movements	Animations by programming – including Morphs Precompiled animations

Now, let us explore these categories without getting into the details. Those who are interested in specific topics may have to explore other specialized books on the subject.

16.5 Classification I

16.5.1 Cel animation

In cel or frame animation, the entire animation sequence is treated as a collection of independent frames or still images. Each frame differs from the previous one, by minor variations.

When these independent frames are displayed in sequence, they create the illusion of movement. When the images displayed are fast enough to fool the human eye (at around 25 to 30 frames per second) – the result is a very smooth animated movie!

This basic philosophy is not very much different from the technique adopted in cinemas. In cinema theatres, the filmed shots roll past the projector at incredible speeds, creating the illusion of a group dance or fight sequence on the screen.

The only difference between them and cel animation is that the individual frames are video graphed in movies, whereas they are developed using traditional drawings or by other means – in animations.

Figure 127: Each frame differs from the previous one by a small variation. When the frames are flipped at high speeds, the shot gets animated.

16.5.2 Object animation

In object animations, a static backdrop is maintained throughout a sequence – and the object to be animated is moved across the backdrop.

In the example provided, the kite is the object that is being animated.

Take note that I have carefully places only static objects like houses in the background. I'd love to add a tree – but then, during animation, if it remains still and the kite alone is moving – then it might not look natural. After all, when the blow of wind is so good that it lifts a kite, then it would move the tree branches as well!

You can have more than one animated object in the sequence. For example, I can have another animated kite in the same shot or even a bird or two.

One interesting question comes up: Kite is a static object and hence it can be animated here and there. But, how about birds? Will they not have their own animated movements – flip of wings etc.? I leave this question to you for the moment, with a hint: It has something to do with cyclic animations, covered in a later section.

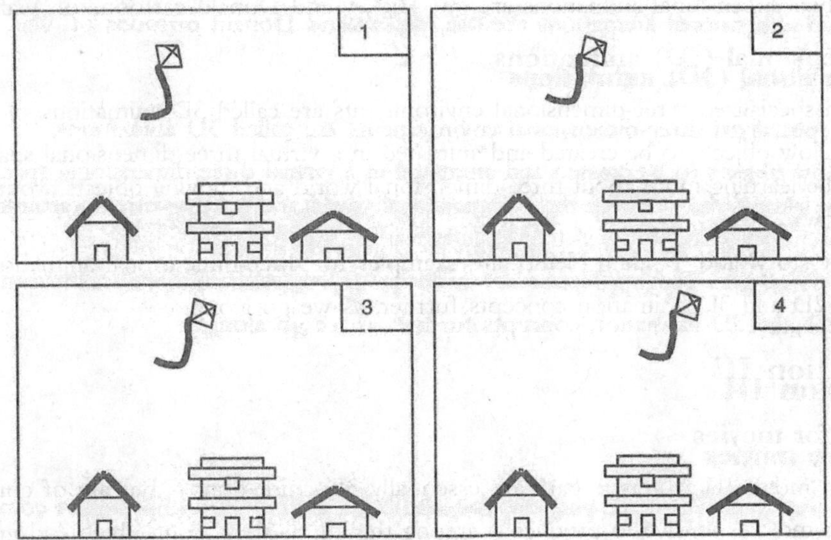

Figure 128: In this sequence, the background houses etc remain static, whereas the kite moves here and there...

Object animations can be created only with the help of software packages that support them. I cannot think of a better example than macromedia flash - for this.

Traditional Indian shadow puppeteers are known to make use of this technique for creating two-dimensional animated movements!

16.6 Classification II

16.6.1 Two-dimensional (2D) animation

Animations created in two-dimensional planes are called 2D animations.

Figure 129: Old Walt Disney films are classic examples of two-dimensional animations

Two-dimensional planes are characterised by two axes – X and Y - that define any point in that plane. A good example for a two-dimensional plane will be this very paper which you are reading.

Classic examples of two-dimensional animations are old Mickey and Donald cartoons of Walt Disney!

16.6.2 Three-dimensional (3D) animations

Animations created in specialized three-dimensional environments are called 3D animations.

These environments allow objects to be created and animated in a virtual three dimensional space -characterized by three planes. We will be learning more about three-dimensional world and moving objects around in virtual space – in the pages that follow.

Feature films like 'Toy story' and 'Finding Nemo' are examples for three-dimensional animations.

We will be exploring 2D and 3D animation concepts further, as we go along.

16.7 Classification III

16.7.1 Animation for movies

Animations we saw in movies like Jurassic park are essentially 3D animations – but are of complex nature.

They are probably the most expensive to produce – among the lot, as they require high-end graphic hardware and software to develop and render decent animations.

16.7.2 Animation for television shows

Conceptually, animations produced for television shows are not different from those developed for movies – but the main difference lies in screen size and the corresponding resolution/ rendering quality.

Whereas movie animations demand resolutions and rendering of the highest quality possible (and hence require expensive hardware / software), those meant for television shows require much lesser resolution (and hence, tolerate mid-end hardware / software).

Note: Terms like rendering may sound foreign to you, at this stage. Don't worry! We will be covering all these fundamentals, in later sections!

It is said that the animation rendering process for movie 'Titanic' was done on roughly 120 machines, simultaneously!

16.7.3 Animations for multimedia applications and games

A wide range of 2D and 3D animations are made use of in multimedia applications and games.

It is difficult to provide any basic grammars for such animations – as the nature of applications are too many.

The specific needs of the application, dictate the quality and complexity of the animation. In the examples we saw earlier in the chapter (Microsoft Oceans and Civilizations CD-ROM), we witnessed the usage of both 2D and 3D animations.

Animations for multimedia projects can be further sub-classified into

- Animations for content and
- Animations for interface design

Animations for content are those that are used to illustrate a concept or an idea, in the multimedia project. For example, the submarine animation we saw earlier in Microsoft Oceans is an animation meant for content.

There might be situations wherein the interface design may have to feature some minor animations. These are called animations for interface design.

As a rule, interface design animations are most simple in nature and in most cases, are 2D animations.

Figure 130: Magic software's Mahabharatha features small animated buttons that add flavour to the interface

16.7.4 Animations for the Internet

The most important characteristic of Internet animations, that set them apart from the rest of the lot – is their size. As a rule, they must be less than 1 MB or, preferably, less than even 500 KB.

Macromedia flash animations are becoming the de-facto standard for animations on the net. We will be learning more about Flash, as we go along.

16.8 Classification - IV

16.8.1 Animation by programming

From the computer's perspective, every animation can be thought of as a series of drawing commands. These commands are executed at such incredible speeds, that they produce the illusion of seamless movement across the screen.

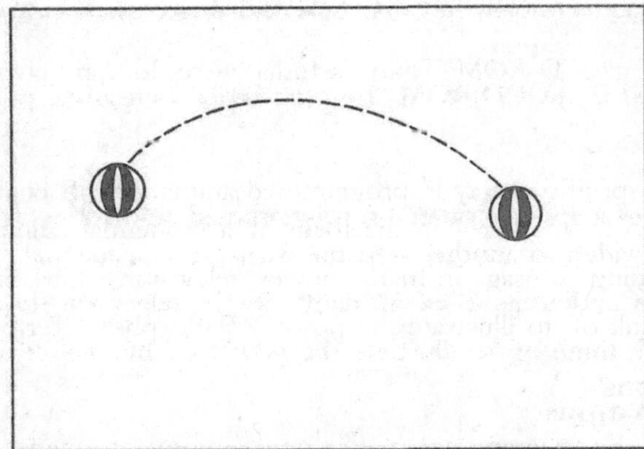

Figure 131: This movement of a ball can be produced, by writing a few lines of software code!

When one can write programs (using software languages like visual basic) that ultimately issue out a series of drawing commands, then that will result in animations – very similar to those produced by a series of images flipped one after another.

Let us say we want to animate the movement of the ball, in a predefined trajectory.

To the eyes of software program, the ball will be an image. You can then write a few lines of code to move the ball image a few pixels away every second – until it reaches the desired destination point. When this program is executed, it looks like an animation.

Animation by programming is very useful for producing bizarre effects with colours and curves. What cannot be achieved with the help of drawing tools can be achieved with the help of programming.

Figure 132: Simple animations like the flight of birds and the flow of flowers were created in 'Tourist's India' CD-ROM – using software coding.

Professional animation designers in reputed special effect studios like ILM (Industrial light and magic) are known for tweaking the software programs (mostly in C++) here and there, whenever they are obstructed by the limitations of the tool they are using.

Different bird flight animations in my CD-ROM 'Tourist's India' were done purely with the help of programming.

16.8.2 Morphing

Morphing can be categorized as a specific variety in programmed animations. It enables seamless transformation of one image to another or one video to another – in the form of a sequential animated movement.

Since its conception, morph is finding its usage in many movies, television shows and other entertainment media.

Probably the best movie I can think of, to illustrate the power of morphs is Terminator II – Judgement Day.

16.8.3 Precompiled animations

In an earlier section on animations by programming, we saw that movements can be created just during runtime – using relevant software codes.

But in most other cases, all movements are pre-drawn, flipped and compiled into specific file formats. These are called precompiled animations.

In real-time multimedia projects, we will mostly be using precompiled animations and only in very rare and exceptional occasions – will we consider animation by programming.

Almost all software tools meant for 2D and 3D animations render their output as precompiled animations – using one file format or other.

16.9 Understanding two-dimensional animation planes

Let us consider this particular page of the book. It possesses certain magnitude of area.

This area can be expressed as the product of length and width.

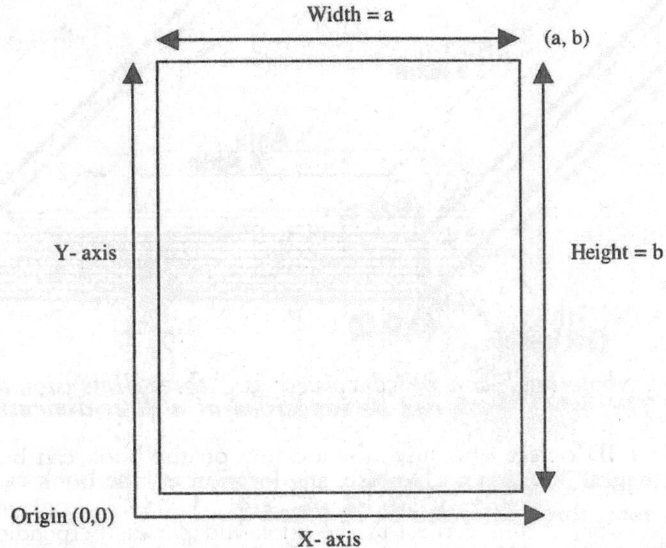

Figure 133: Two dimensional planes consist of X and Y axis

This page can be called as a two dimensional plane, because, any point (i.e. any location) within this page, can be represented using two coordinates - one on the X axis that runs horizontal to the page and the other on the Y axis that runs vertical to the page.

If we can draw, two such imaginary axes in this page, one on the extreme left (Y axis) and one on the bottom most part (X axis), then we can call the whole page as a two axis coordinate system or a 2 dimensional coordinate system.

Now, any point within this plane will have an X coordinate value and a Y coordinate value.

For example, if we assume that the total length of the page, to be 'a' and total width of the page to be 'b', then the top left corner can be represented as (0, a) - meaning that the X Co ordinate value is 0 and Y coordinate value is 'a'. Similarly, the top right corner will be (b, a) bottom left corner will be (0,0), and bottom right corner will be (0,b). These are extreme points of the page - any other point, will have X and Y values in between a and b.

Any figure, then, can be developed by filling up the points in the plane with the required colour. Consequently, each frame in the animation sequence can be treated as a 2D plane and the sequential movements of the object being animated can be recorded.

Two-dimensional animation files generally record only the deviations of the second frame from the first, and not the colour values of the entire screen used for animating the objects. Apart from saving considerable file space, this technique also helps the system to update the frames quickly, so that the movements appear to be natural.

16.10 Understanding three-dimensional worlds

Now, instead of a page, let us consider the entire book, as an object.

The book possesses not only area - but volume as well, because of its height. This volume can be expressed as the product of length, width and height.

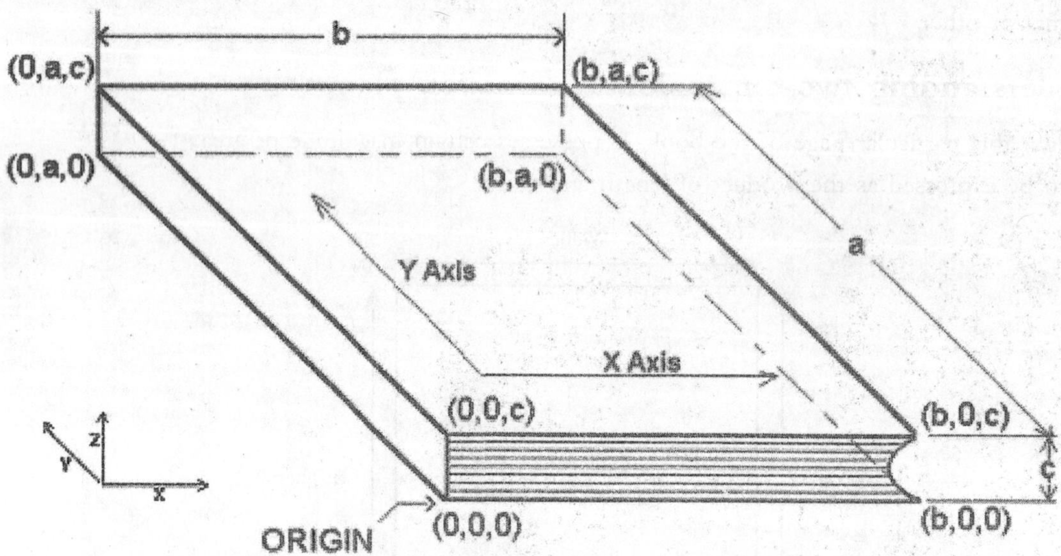

Figure 134: This whole book can be conceived as a three-dimensional object.

We can treat this book as a typical 3D object - because, any location on the book can be represented as a set of three coordinates – running along three different axis X, Y and Z.

X axis that runs horizontal to the book, Y runs vertical to the book and Z runs perpendicular to X and Y.

In three-dimensional coordinate systems, more than one plane comes into the picture.

The whole system has to be perceived as that space intersected by three different two-dimensional planes - the XY plane, the YZ plane and the ZX plane. Have a look at the figure that shows all the three different planes.

Coming back to the book example.

If we could draw three imaginary axes on the corners of the book,

- One on the extreme left (Y axis),
- One on the bottom most part (X axis) and
- One more along the direction perpendicular to X and Y axes (Z axis)

Then we could call the book as a three-axis coordinate system or a three-dimensional coordinate system.

Any point on the book will have an X coordinate value a Y coordinate value and a Z coordinate value.

As in the previous two-dimensional example, if we were to assume that the total length of the book to be 'a', total width to be 'b' and the height of the book to be 'c', then the top left corner on the bottom side of the book (i.e. at the back cover) can be represented as (0,a, 0) – which means that the X coordinate value is 0, Y coordinate value is 'a' and Z coordinate value to be 0 again.

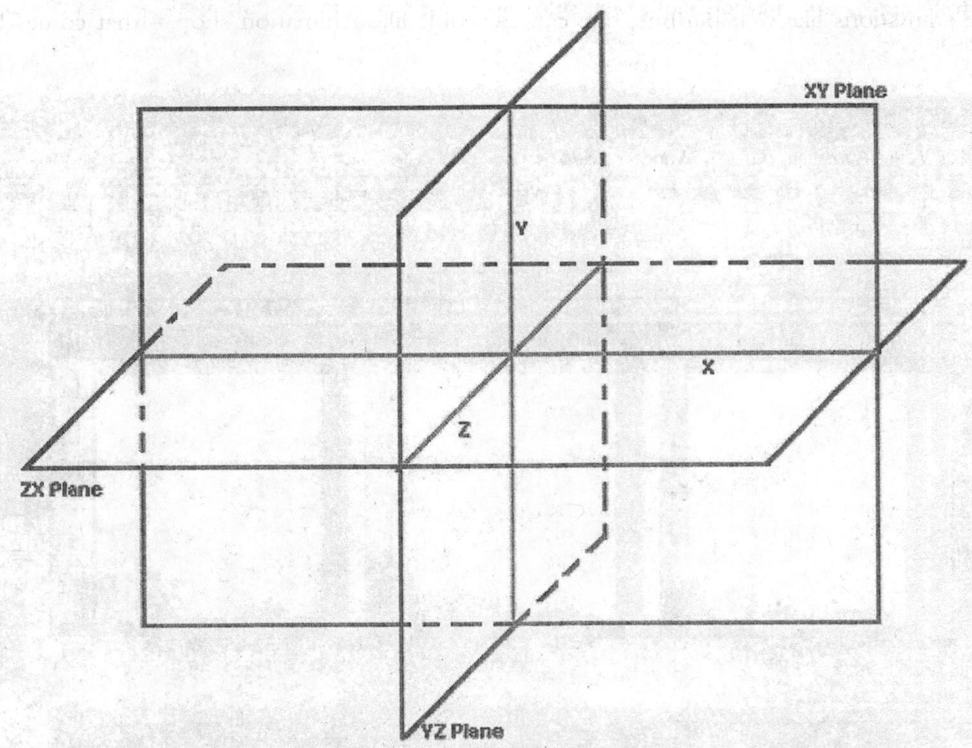

Figure 135: Three planes make up a three-dimensional world.

The very same top left corner, on the front side of the book (i.e. at the front cover) can be represented as (0, a, c) - meaning that the X coordinate value is 0, Y Co ordinate value is 'a' and Z Co ordinate value is 'c'.

On similar grounds, the following can be inferred:

On the front side of the book:

- The top right corner will be (b, a, c),
- The bottom left corner will be (0, 0, c),
- The bottom right corner will be (b, 0, c).

On the back side of the book:

- The top right corner will be (b, a, 0),
- The bottom left corner will be (0, 0, 0),
- The bottom right corner will be (b, 0, 0).

16.11 Animation tools

There are a number of tools available in the market – for designing and developing 2D and 3D animations.

As I had mentioned earlier, animation industry is worth millions of dollars and its potential has not yet been fully realized in countries like India. Hence, it should not surprise you to note that companies across the globe are throwing their money and time behind this lucrative market.

16.11.1 Two-dimensional animation software

Depending upon the project you are working on and its requirements, the tool you select for creating 2D animations could be simple, complex or professional.

To create simple animations like web buttons, one can use tools like Animation shop – that comes bundled with paint shop pro.

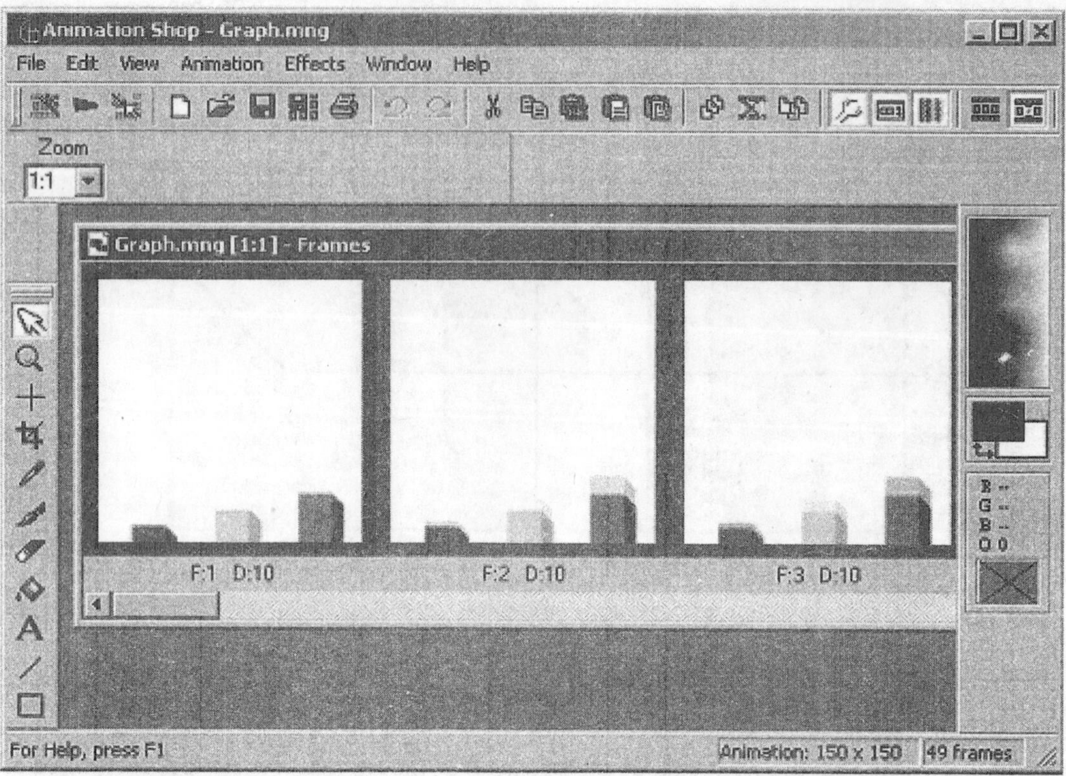

Figure 136: Simple animations can be easily done using Jasc Inc.'s Animation shop

If the animations are slightly complex, it is better to go for professional tools like Macromedia Flash.

If you want to do animation by programming, then you may have to depend on multimedia authoring packages like Macromedia Director and Author ware.

Talking about the fate of 2D in movie industry, we notice that traditional 2D animations are giving way to computer generated 3D animations. If you look at a list of all the animated feature films produced in Hollywood, this trend is evident.

Table 27:Tools for 2D animation

Product	Company	Website
Flash MX	Macromedia	http://www.macromedia.com
US Animation	Toon Boom Technologies	http://www.toonboom.com
RETAS	Celsys	http://www.retas.com
Toonz	Digital video	http://www.divideo.it
Animation shop	Jasc Inc	http://www.jasc.com

First, there were traditional hand-drawn 2D films; and then, there was a transitional period, in which 2D and 3D co-existed and now, we are almost in the third stage – wherein, 3D animations have captured the mantle.

To give you some idea about what sort of tools are available in the market for 2D animation, we've provided a table. This is just indicative – not exhaustive. Also, professional photo editing tools like Corel Photo paint are capable of editing animations – apart from still images.

The scope of this book limits us from discussing 2D animations any further. In the chapters that follow, we will be looking at Macromedia Flash and how to produce basic animations with that great tool.

16.11.2 Three-dimensional animation software

3D animation is a lucrative field that came into existence only after the intervention of computers in the animation industry.

It's then not very surprising to find a much more variety of tools available in the market, for generating 3D effects and animations. There are specialized packages for modelling, rendering and even for painting over 3D models!!

A brief listing of some of the tools I am aware of is provided below for your reference.

Table 28: Tools for 3D modelling and animations

Product	Company	Website
Maya	Alias systems	http://aliaswavefront.com
SoftImage	Avid Technology Inc	http://www.softimage.com
Light wave 3D	Newtek Inc	http://www.newtek.com
3D Studio Max	Discreet	http://www.discreet.com
Houdini	Side effects software	http://www.sidefx.com
True space	Caligari Corporation	http://www.caligari.com
Bryce	Corel Corporation	http://www.corel.com
Cool 3D	Ulead	http://www.ulead.com
Deep Paint 3D	Right Hemisphere	http://www.deeppaint.com
Poser	Curious labs	http://www.curiouslabs.com
Photo realistic	Render man	Pixar http://www.pixar.com
Rhino 3D	Robert McNeil & associates	http://www.rhino3d.com

Once again, the scope of this book and the chapter limits us from detailed discussions on the concept of 3D. There is one dedicated chapter on 3D software later in this part – which will introduce you to many basic concepts.

However, you should remember that 3D animation technology is an ocean by itself! Once you are into it, there is no way out!

Its fascinating swirls and depths will absorb you for the rest of your life!

16.12 Summary

Animations are artificial movements created by flipping a series of images at specific speeds. The need for animation as a media arises mainly because of the limitations of conventional videography. Computer generated animations can animate even those things that do not exist – in a virtual world.

Animations can be classified as 2D and 3D animations, cel and object animations, programmed and compiled animations and so on. Two-dimensional animations are developed on 2D planes and three-dimensional animations are developed on 3D virtual worlds.

Many software tools are available in the market – for developing 2D and 3D animations. The number of tools available in the 3D category is much more that for 2D.

16.13 Keywords

- **Cel or frame animation:** Animation sequence produced by displaying different Frames of movements, one after another, rapidly.
- **Object animation:** Animation sequence produced by, movement of an object over a general picture that's maintained as a backdrop.
- **Two-dimensional animations:** Animation sequence created in two-dimensional planes.
- **Three-dimensional animations:** Animations created in three-dimensional environments.

Chapter 17

Developing Animations for Multimedia Projects

CHAPTER OVERVIEW

This second chapter on multimedia animation technology provides a very reliable grounding for all enthusiastic and budding 'would be' animators, to really put their hands on to the very heart of core animation techniques and tools.

Fundamental concepts have been carefully discussed so that they are not limited to specific animation package, but applicable to most industry recognized professional animation environments. Some expert advice, programming tips and decision issues on choosing between two-dimensional and three-dimensional software have been pepped along the way.

17.1 Introduction

Our previous chapter was an introduction to this interesting world of animations – we understood some basic terminologies like 2D and 3D and wetted our hands with different kinds of animations.

In the current chapter, we will be getting down to more serious business and start discussing what are all the different stages of planning and execution – in developing an animation sequence for a project. These different steps detailed may not be followed word-by-word – but an understating of the overall workflow is required for any budding animator.

An important question to be answered, as a part of the planning process: Should we go for 2D animation... or 3D?

17.2 Animation process workflow

Professional animation development is a sequential and well-defined process.

In some cases, a step or two may overlap or be neglected altogether, but the general workflow is almost consistent between different development environments. The process we have detailed here is flexible enough to accommodate even very large animation projects like 3D movies.

We will address the topic in three different phases, for the sake of convenience.

- The first phase, which is the planning stage for the animation sequence to be developed
- The second phase, wherein we make a choice between 2D and 3D
- The third phase, which is the execution phase – wherein the animation sequence is developed using relevant software tools

Look at the project flow diagram provided – and do not be disheartened by the complexity of the diagram! As we proceed from stage to stage, you will realize why we need such a streamlined flow of work. Teams, which do not bother to do proper planning and desperately begin their work in great urgency – are brutally punished by rework, as things mature! Remember that animation is world of imagination and what is in your mind may be strikingly different from what the team leader expects in the sequence!

For the sake of simplicity, we take up a single example as our illustration, throughout the proceedings. And it is this:

We are in the process of developing a multimedia animation for an edutainment title on chemistry. A simple chemical reaction viz. the formation of water compound from hydrogen and oxygen – needs to be illustrated by means an animation sequence.

Hydrogen and oxygen gases react in the ration 2:1, to produce water.

$$2H_2(g) + O_2(g) \rightarrow 2H_2O(g)$$

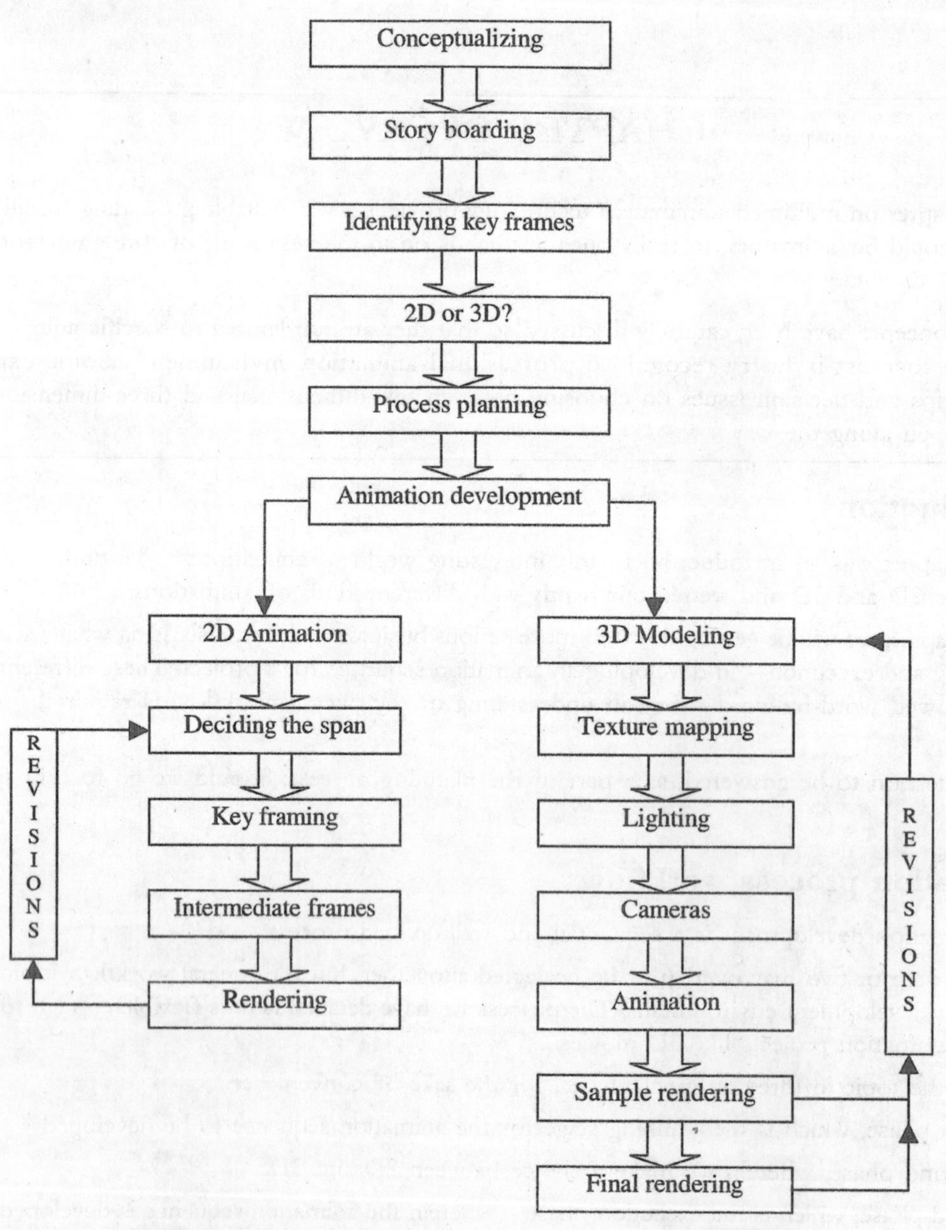

Figure 137: Animation development – process workflow

17.3 Conceptualizing

The given scenario, which has to be expressed as an animation sequence, has to be first conceived as an animation concept. By animation concept, we mean an approximate imagination of the actual animation sequence that's going to be developed.

All sorts of wild and strange imaginations cannot be translated into animations! Also, if you are working as a team, each team member will have their own imagination about the sequence!

The process of conceptualising is to put down all ideas in paper and to decide upon those themes that seem to satisfy the requirements of the project. Typically it begins with a brainstorming session with the team involved and the project manager should be the one to decide what should go into the concept.

For smaller projects, this session may well happen within the minds of the animators before the work is actually begun.

Talking about major animation projects like 3D films, this process of conceptualising is much more complex – since strategies and themes have to be evolved, both for the overall picture under production as well as the individual sequences that make up the movie.

Since we have kept our sample scenario pretty simple, we can easily evolve the animation concept as follows:

'Oxygen and hydrogen elements will be represented in the form of circles /spheres. Two hydrogen elements from each direction cross oxygen and get attracted to it as the cross. May be the attraction can be represented by love hearts. They come together and result in water.'

Note that we are trying to add some amount of creativity and drama so that even a chemical reaction looks vibrant – when animated! You will understand this better, as we go along.

17.4 Story boarding

Story boarding is a simple and yet, intuitive technique - which, when put to proper use - will result in increased productivity and shortened development time.

It is the process of visualising all the important shots (or 'frames') in an animation sequence and putting them down as rough sketches on paper.

Thinking about our sample scenario, we know that we have to illustrate the important happenings like

- ❑ How oxygen element needs to be displayed?
- ❑ How hydrogen elements approach oxygen?
- ❑ How they combine together?
- ❑ What is the resulting compound?

Figure 138: Imaginations can be different - but this is how we perceive the sample scenario.

Now, our storyboard will decide which element has to come first and from where, which element comes next and how they all combine and form the compound.

For the sequence at hand, we will dramatize the situation as follows:

- ❑ The beginning shot in which the Oxygen element waits in the centre – not knowing what to do
- ❑ One hydrogen element makes an entry from the left hand side and moves across the screen with small jumps – oxygen looks at it
- ❑ Another hydrogen element enters from the right hand side – oxygen looks at it as well
- ❑ Both hydrogen elements stop slightly after crossing oxygen
- ❑ "Love" waves
- ❑ Hydrogen mixes with oxygen
- ❑ Water!

Along with this, we may also have to think about other details like background colour system, camera angles etc. and try to note them down on the storyboard paper. These details will help the animators understand our overall expectations from the sequence – better.

Once the storyboard is ready, multimedia animation sequence is all set to progress to the next stage!

17.5 Identifying key frames

Key frames in an animation sequence can be defined as those important frames in which the movements of objects mature from one stage to another.

Identification of key frames helps animators to proceed with the sequence development in a very methodical manner. It also enables smoother integration of various parts of an animation sequence.

The animated portions in between the key frames are called 'slots'. These slots can be of varying lengths, depending upon the movements of the objects under animation.

Certain animation tools provide the flexibility of automating the movements within the slots. For example, in Macromedia Flash, you can specify an object's starting point in the first key frame and its end point in another key frame and the movements in between these two frames will be automatically generated by Flash.

In our example, some of the key frames will be...

- ❑ The frame in which oxygen waits for the hydrogen elements
- ❑ Entry point of first hydrogen element
- ❑ Different movement points of this element (may be many key frames)
- ❑ Entry point of second hydrogen element
- ❑ Different movement points of this element
- ❑ Stopping and looking at oxygen
- ❑ Combining with oxygen
- ❑ Water formation etc.

17.6 Decision between two dimensional and three dimensional animations

After deciding upon the key frames, we are stuck with a rather serious question: Are we to develop this sequence as a 2D or 3D animation?

We need to consider the following points, before deciding our choice.

17.6.1 3D may sometimes be a simpler option!

On the outset, 2D animations seem to be relatively simple and 3D, all complex.

Unfortunately, this is not entirely true.

There are many situations wherein, the required 3D models (i.e. three dimensional wire-frame structures) are readily available or can be developed easily. In such cases, it may be much easier to develop the animation sequence in 3D instead of 2D.

For example, if you want a ball or box or any other regular geometric shapes to be animated, then it is lot easier to work with 3D than 2D. By applying techniques like texture mapping, that are peculiar to 3D environments, striking results can be obtained with ease.

Thousands of ready-made 3D wire frame models are available on the market and the web. And most 3D software tools also pre-package a wide variety for models within their core distribution package. For example, Newtek's Light wave 3D ships with hundreds of ready-to-use wire frame models that can be used in a wide variety of scenarios.

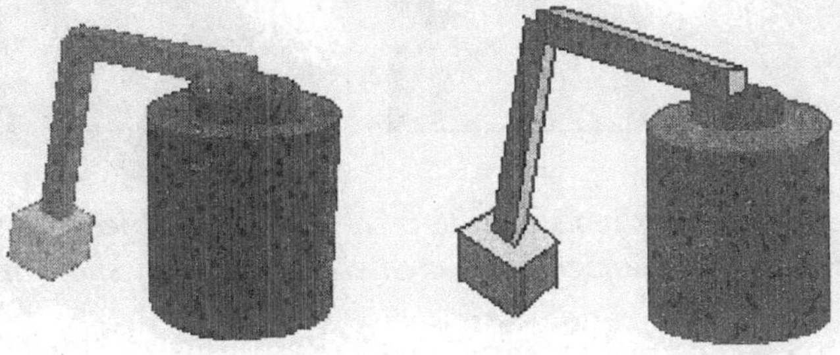

Figure 139: Look at these objects. The one on the left is 3D and the other is 2D. I took more time to draw the 2D model than develop the 3D; and if I were to animate the lever above cylinder, 3D may take a lot less time than 2D!

17.6.2 Character animation is a complex business in 3D!

It's rather difficult to model and animate live characters like human and animals and plants in 3D environments, as compared to 2D.

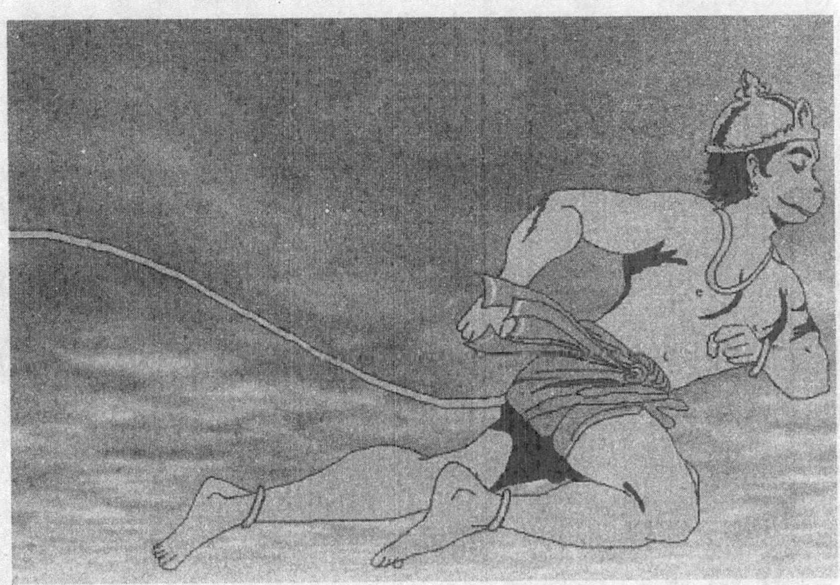

Figure 140: 2D character 'Hanuman' looks pretty dynamic in 'Tales from Indian Mythology' project CD-ROM, published by cybervalley systems.

Even 2D character animations are difficult - but can reasonably manage to bring out acceptable results with experienced animators on the job.

17.6.3 3D effects with 2D tools

Sometimes, the desired 3D effect can be achieved with the help of few intelligent digital brush strokes, within the 2D animation or painting tool! For example, the characteristics shades of light behaviour over the object can be brought out over 2D objects with advanced painting tools.

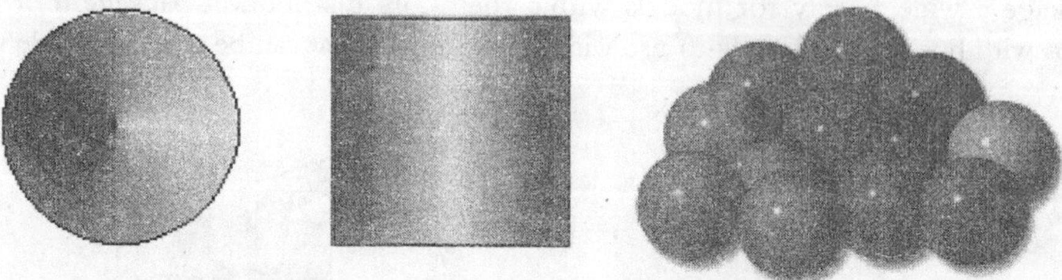

Figure 141: Digital painting tools enable creation of 3D objects to some extent. The group of balls on the extreme right was created using paint shop pro's picture tubes.

In such cases, instead of going 3D, we can consider 2D with advanced painting options. On the flip side, this may demand experienced animators and their patient effort.

17.6.4 Consider the relevance of the situation

Creating certain kinds of animations is simply not possible in 2D.

For example, consider an architectural walkthrough animation in which the entire building has to be animated in different angles. It is rather impossible to think of 2D for such cases.

Figure 142: Building walkthroughs like this can be done only with the help of 3D tools

17.7 Process planning

In case extensive animations are involved in a particular project, it's important to plan the entire animation development process.

In typical multimedia projects, critical paths (i.e. those activities, which, when delayed – will result in the total delay of the very project) are recognised well before the production of the title - because of the complexity involved in making various kinds of media ready, and integrating them into meaningful forms.

17.8 Animation development

When we reach this state, it means we have gone through the pain of proper planning procedures and are all set to take the graphic tablet on our laps and really 'start doing something'. The process of developing 2D and 3D animations are so different from each other, that they necessitate different treatments.

17.9 2D Animation development

❑ First, decide the total number of frames to be engaged for the particular animation sequence. This is what is called the span of the animation. The more the number of frames, the better - because, with gradual transition, the movements of the objects tend to be natural and smooth. On the flip side, this also means that we have to develop more number of frames!

❑ Tools like Flash provide flexibility to the users, to increase or decrease the number of frames between the key frames. However, it is better to plan as much as possible in the beginning rather than doing alterations during development. A proper projection on the number of frames required for a given sequence comes only with experience!

❑ It is better to plan for lengthier animations and then reduce the frames as we go along.

❑ Since we have already identified which are all the important key frames in which critical transitions are going to occur, we need to divide the span across the key frames. For example, if we are planning an animation with a span of 70 frames and if we have 7 key frames – then we may plan to distribute 10 frames between each key frame.

❑ The movement of the object(s) between two key frames dictate the number of frames to be inserted between them. If the movements are long, more frames are to be allocated in-between key frames.

❑ Develop the key frames. For the very first key frame, you may have to draw the objects to be animated or import them from files. But for subsequent key frames, it is enough if you show the relative movement of the object with respect to the present.

❑ First key frame development involves drawing the actual figures over the frame, using one or more drawing tools available with the environment. Sometimes, it may be felt that the drawing tools supported by the animation environment are simply not enough...in such cases, the frames have to be stored as individual bitmaps and manipulated using any of the advanced image editing software - till the desired results are obtained. This is a cumbersome process.

❑ In professional animation studios, it is customary to leave the key frames to be developed by experienced animators and leave the frames in-between to budding professionals.

❑ Once the key frames are done, the frames in-between can either be automatically generated or hand drawn using relevant tools. The nature of transformation or movement determines the choice.

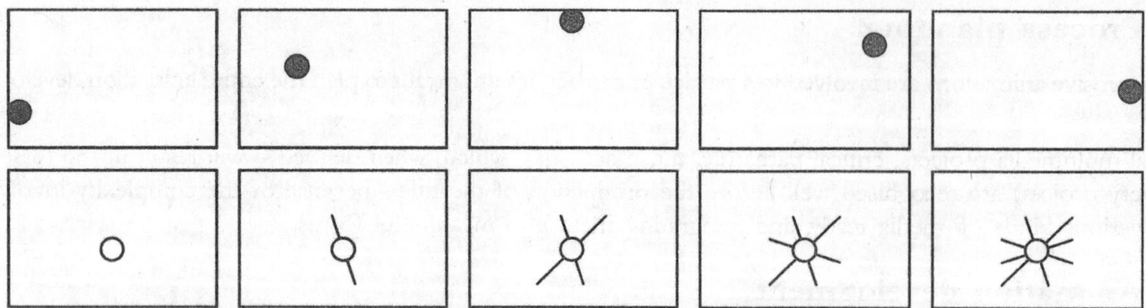

Figure 143: Two types of simple animations are provided as examples here. Which one, do you think – can accommodate automatic generation of frames in between key frames? And for which one, should we draw all the frames in-between key frames?

- Tools like Macromedia Flash have extensive capabilities for transforming objects across the frames, provided the objects are vectors.
- The speed at which the transformation between key frames occur, determines the number of frames. This speed can be easily controlled in tools like Flash. We will be seeing some of these capabilities in the next chapter – so, don't worry much about Flash for the moment.
- Once the frames are completed, they can be played back using the playback feature.
- When all the slots in between the animation have been completed, then they have to be linked and rendered together.
- At this stage, you may have to go back to some of the previous key frames and do the required editing – so that the overall animation looks like one seamless flow of movements instead of a chain of animations linked together!
- The final stage of animation development process is to plug-in the animation thus developed into the project slot. We need to ensure that the animation developed integrates well with the project and serves the purpose. If you have gone through the pain of proper planning which was detailed elaborately in the earlier pages – you will have little to change at this stage!
- There are two ways of plugging in the animation into the project slot – they are linking and embedding.
- Linking is the process of maintaining the animation file outside the multimedia core program and making relevant calls to the animation media file for playback - whenever required. This is the most preferred means of plugging-in animations into the project. The only flip side is that the animations can be seen by the users outside the program and may even be copied and reused!!
- Embedding is - 'literally' - the process of bundling the animation as a part of core multimedia project file. Professional multimedia authoring programs have something called resources – and once you specify all the sounds, videos and animations as resources, they automatically manage them and make them available to the executable program during runtime.

So THAT was two-dimensional animation!

In the next chapter, we will be looking at Macromedia Flash very deeply, which will help you to translate all these ideas to real-time action!

17.10 3D animation development

When it comes to 3D, the development process is almost completely different from 2D! And much more exciting too…

This process consists of several steps, which are sequentially detailed below.

17.10.1 Modelling

Modelling is the very first step in 3D animation development.

Models are wire frames that represent certain 3D shapes in the virtual world. Even simple objects like spheres and cylinders look pretty scary as 3D wire frames.

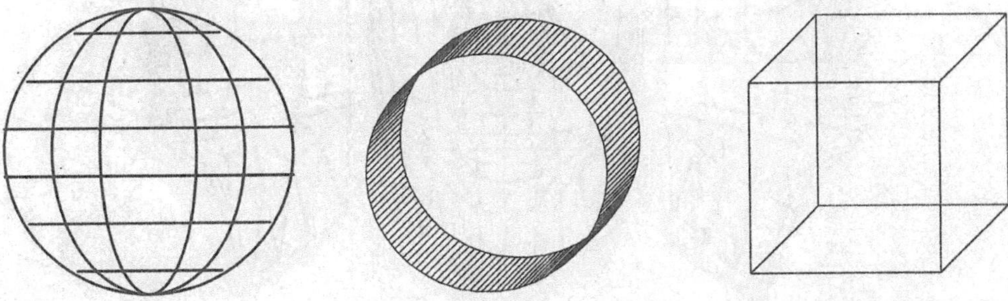

Figure 144: Even simple objects do not look that simple, when you look at their 3D wire frame models! Each model is made up of a number of lines and curves.

The reason is that 3D wire frame models are actually mathematical curves, which construct the 3D models in a virtual 3D space. Models of objects like plants, animals, mountains and landscapes are made up of much more complicated curves and are scarier than spheres - to look at.

Since simple mathematical curves cannot define such complex contours, 3D software programs make use of curve equations called splines. When several splines are put together in a three-dimensional co-ordinate system, complex surfaces can be created.

There are several varieties of splines in use – these include linear spines, cardinal spines, bezier spines and b-spines. One of the most complex objects to model viz. the human face - is defined using a special breed of splines called Non-uniform rational B splines (or NURBS!). When you are buying new 3D software programs for yourself or for your company, you should ensure that the software supports NURBS.

All the objects required for the animation sequence have to be modelled – either using the tools that come bundled with the 3D software or using specialized modelling tools. All basic geometric shapes like sphere, cylinder, box, tarsus and cone can be readily generated to required sizes - with most 3D tools. Some tools also support Boolean operations like add and subtract – with the help of which, two or more geometric shapes can be combined together and new shapes can be evolved.

For very complex models (like dragons!) 3D modellers resort to 3D laser probes, which, by making use of laser sensors arranged in all the 3 axes, capture the 3 dimensional data that make up the object. However, for this method to work, a physical model of the object needs to be created (in wood or plaster-of-paris) – over which the 3D probe can pass through!

Considering all these troubles, it is worthwhile to look at the 3D models and model libraries that are available in the market. Type "3D model libraries" in www.google.com and look out for the appropriate companies that sell the model you are looking for. To my knowledge, the digimation collection (http://www.digimation.com) is well worth a visit.

It is rather astonishing and even humiliating to realize that the creatures of Jurassic age that terrorized the explorers and movie fans alike – as actually complex mathematical equations!

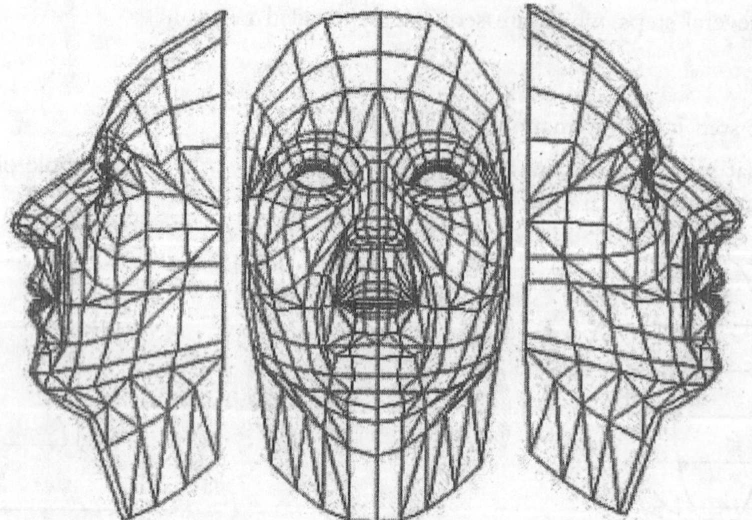

Figure 145: NURBS modelling is used to define the complex contour of a human face!

Modelling is the most important step in 3D animation sequence development.

17.10.2 Materials and texture mapping

Professional 3D software allows different kinds of material attributes to be applied to 3D wire frames. For example, one can 'apply' gold's properties to a model, so that it behaves like a gold, during rendering. Explicit characteristics of gold like shininess, reflectivity and refractivity, can be controlled so that when lights fall on the model, they behave accordingly. This gives a more realistic and natural look to the models, when rendered.

Texture mapping is even more interesting: It is the process of wrapping 3D wire frame models with 'textures' – which are nothing but 2D bitmaps. For example, the texture of, say mosaic, can be wrapped over a 3D floor in a virtual house – so that it looks very natural! Some 3D software allows even 3D projections or 'bumps' to be present over the wire frames, so that the looks are even more astonishing!

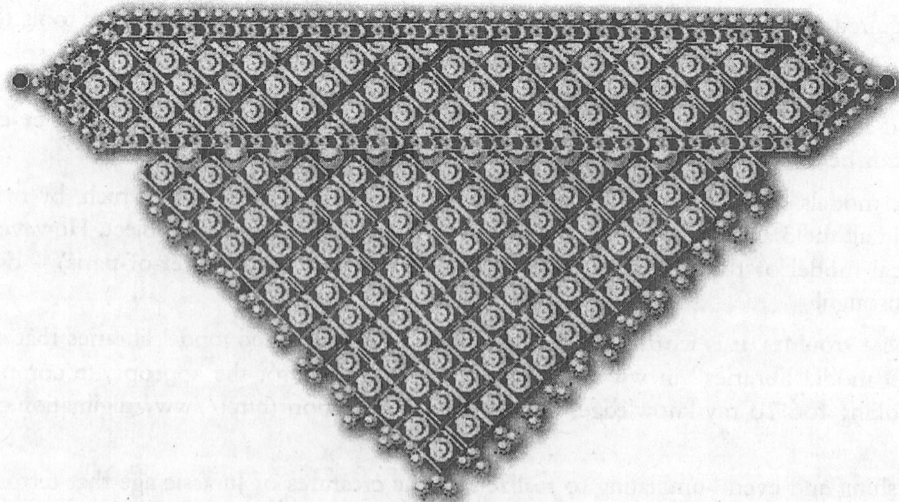

Figure 146: For a jewellery design project, I crafted this choker almost entirely with 3D! In full colour rendering, it is indistinguishable from a photograph – thanks to materials!

Figure 147: This was one of the surrealistic environments created for the CD-ROM "Tales from Indian Mythology". Look at the bumps visible on the floor and on the rocks.

17.10.3 Lighting

Once we have modelled the required wire frames and applied material and texture over them, we need to 'illuminate' our world with proper lights!

As you begin working on a project, there is a default lighting mode that is already available – but this will illuminate all objects with even lighting. You can override this behaviour by adding spotlights, ambient lights and other kinds of lights - within the 3D universe.

The luminescence, colour and various other characteristics of light, are controllable. There can be more than one light, in any scene. And with some advanced software, the light intensities can even be of negative value, so that they actually 'absorb' light that is already present!

Figure 148: Application of light over the sphere in a virtual 3D world – and its ultimate behaviour during rendering.

Your lighting arrangement and the reflectivity /shininess of the material you are using, will ultimately determine the look and feel of the 3D objects – during rendering.

17.10.4 Cameras

Cameras, in a 3D environment are used to 'view' the objects that are placed in the 3D world. You can also view the objects without cameras – but you may not have much flexibility in viewing. Moreover, if you are going to move around the object and see different portions, then cameras become inevitable.

Note: Please understand that the camera movements are different from the object movements. For example, when a 3D ball is animated from one end to another, then that is the movement of the object. You may either stand still and watch this movement or move along in certain other direction! This movement of your viewpoint is what is called the camera movement. I have tried to give an example to illustrate this idea – but the best place to know the better is a professional 3D tool!

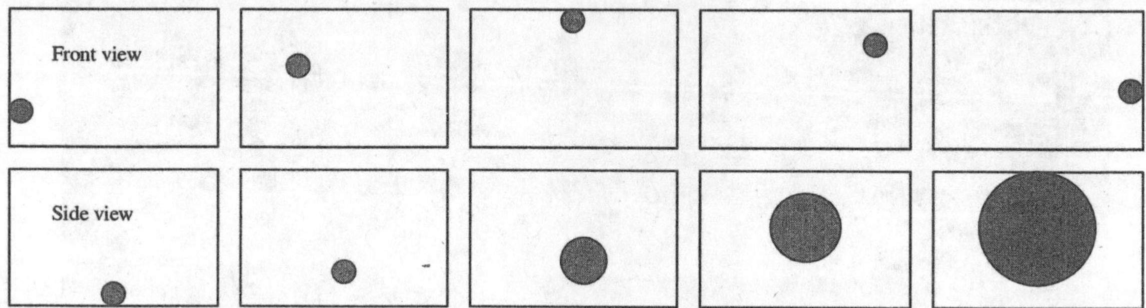

Figure 149: The front view and the side view illustrated.

Look at the example. In the first case (front view), you are a mere observer, just observing the ball going from one end to the other. In the second case (side view), you are standing right in front of the ball and the ball is actually coming towards you! These two examples illustrate two different viewpoints a camera can take – while observing the object movements. If you want you can also move the camera you are holding on your hand – and traverse along with the ball.

Cameras can be used to 'walk through' a 3D model of the building, to generate an illusion that the viewer is actually taking a walk inside the building – room by room!

When an object has to be viewed at several angles, one can make use of the cameras. Instead of rotating the object, it's much easier to rotate the camera at desired angles and take 'snapshots'.

Cameras, like lights, do possess several attributes like the field of view and focus that decide the ultimate behaviour of the camera. There can be more than one camera, in any given scene.

Figure 150: These two shots illustrate two different sequences from an architectural walk through done by 3D experts at cybervalley systems. A singe camera was allowed to wander all along the corridors of a virtual factory that was going to be built by the clients.

17.10.5 Key framing and animation

One of the significant advantages of 3D software is their ability to generate frames in-between key frames automatically. Once the key frames are defined in the timeline, the software automatically generates the intervening movements.

To give even more flexibility in movement of objects, 3D software allow the models to traverse along a trajectory or 'path' – during animation. For example, in the throw ball animation we illustrated earlier, it is possible to define a path for the movement of the ball and allow the object to traverse along that path – for the required amount of time.

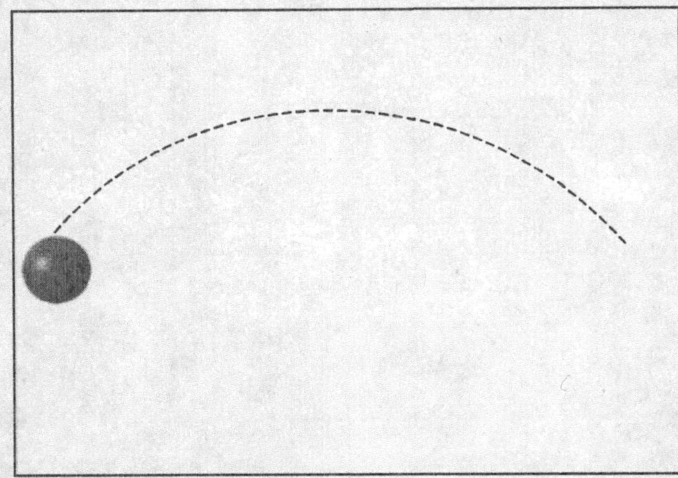

Figure 151: 3D models can follow a 'path' or trajectory, while moving in the virtual 3D world.

This path need not be just a simple curve – it can be any spline that can be defined on a 3D space! This gives immense flexibility to the animators to make the models traverse the way they want. One of the initial movements to be tried is spiral – it is wonderful even to see a simple object like ball rolling along a spiral curve with smooth flow!

Many 3D software tools have advanced motion control capabilities like inverse kinematics and bi-pedalling, with the help of which, it is possible to generate realistic walking and even dance movements. For example, inverse kinematics allows you to 'connect' various polygons- say, the limbs of a man; when the developer 'pulls' the hand, the rest of the body responds naturally, so that he need not bother about animation each and every part of the model!

For more complex movements, it is also possible to capture the movements of a live human using electronic circuitry and apply the same over a 3D model. This technique is frequently used in many feature films and is called 'motion capture'.

17.10.6 Rendering

Rendering is the last and final step to be completed, before we can actually see the wonderful movements we created in 3D environments. It is the process of applying lights, materials, textures, camera and animations to the given 3D scene - frame by frame - and capturing the output as individual images.

During rendering, all the relevant colours and shades are applied over the model – based on our lighting, texture arrangement and other necessary details. Internally, these are nothing but mathematical calculations. Since all these computations need to be done frame-by-frame, rendering process takes considerable time to complete.

The time required for rendering a particular sequence is governed by factors like

- ❑ Complexity of the scene (textures, lighting etc)

- ❑ Computational power of the machine(s)
- ❑ Resources available (RAM etc.)

For this reasons, it is best to start the rendering process (after sufficient back up and UPS arrangements) at nights and leave the system open for computations over the night. To save power, you can just switch off the monitors.

Figure 152: For rendering this scene titled 'Vaikuntha' for 'Tales from Indian Mythology' CD-ROM, we spent nearly 3 hours for each frame on a Pentium 1GHz machine with very decent RAM and swap space! The results speak for themselves.

In highly complex projects like 3D animations for movies, rendering becomes increasingly complex and we may have to go for network rendering! Network rendering is the process of rendering a single 3D sequence in a network of computers – in which each frame can be rendered in a different machine. The software co-ordinates rendering tasks across the machines – based on their capacity and availability.

Network rendering is supported by most professional 3D software today.

Note: It is said that – for rendering the sequences of movie 'Titanic', roughly 120 Linux servers were networked on a huge framework – often called the 'network farm' or render farm!

There are several algorithms available for rendering – like gouraud shading, phong shading and ray-tracing. Ray tracing offers good results but it is also the most time consuming, among the three. Hence 3D tools make use of phong shading for previews and ray-tracing for final rendering process. If you are buying a 3D package for yourself or for your school/college, make sure that it supports ray tracing!

Radiosity is an advanced form of rendering which can produce stunningly realistic images. But the concept and algorithm are pretty complex to understand and not many tools in the market, can boast about this capability.

17.11 Cyclic animations

Cyclic animation is a very simple animation technique, capable of producing stunning results.

In a cyclic animation, the frames are looped - so that, after the last frame, the first frame follows once again and the process continues till the user deliberately stops it.

The serious limitation of cyclic animation is that it cannot be applied to all the sequences and can be adapted only to those object movements, which are repetitive in nature. For example, let us consider that the required animation sequence is that a girl is walking down the lane. Now, her leg movements, after all, are repetitive in nature - as far as the animator is concerned...so, he just limits himself to seven frames of animation, and still manages to make her walk, over and over again!

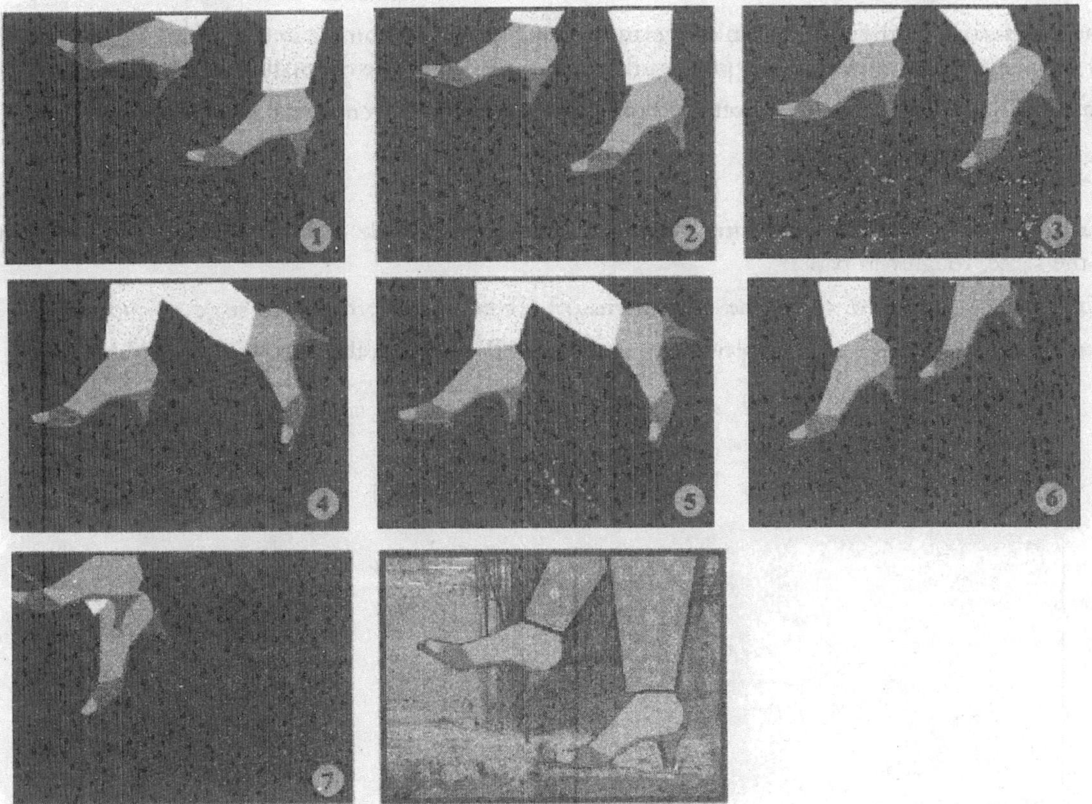

Figure 153: Cyclic animations can be used for movements that are repetitive in nature.

Look at the example. All the seven frames required for the animation have been displayed. Note that the last frame of the sequence has carefully been designed, so as to blend seamlessly with the first frame, which will follow - when looped.

The playback speed for this particular animation is 8 frames per second.

Pretty good 'cat walk'...isn't it?

Certain other scenarios in which cyclic animations can be put to use:

- ❑ Movement of fire flames
- ❑ Movement of birds
- ❑ Movement of clouds etc
- ❑ Character movements like walking and running
- ❑ Eye lid movements

17.12 Summary

Animation development is a seamless workflow that has definite number of steps – right from planning to execution. Planning phase includes conceptualising, story boarding, key frame identification, 2D / 3D decision-making and process planning. Execution phase includes 2D or 3D animation development and linking / embedding.

2D animation development process is almost completely different from 3D animation. For 2D, we need to fix up the total span of animation, define the key frames and develop them, fill the in-between frames with appropriate movements – either automatically or manually and finally render the animation.

For 3D, one needs to do modelling, material and texture mapping, lighting, camera setting, fixing key frames, animating and finally rendering. 3D software tools posses advanced capabilities – as compared to 2D packages.

Cyclic animation is a simple technique useful for animating repetitive movements.

17.13 Keywords

Story boarding: The concept of visualising the animation sequence to be developed - as a series of frames, and exhibiting the same, roughly in paper.

Key framing: Those frames in which, the movements of objects mature from one stage to another.

Texture mapping The technique of applying (or wrapping) 2D images (called maps) over 3D wire frame models.

PART VII

MULTIMEDIA VIDEOS

PART OVERVIEW

Digital video adds colour and pomp to multimedia projects. Without full motion videos, it is difficult to imagine successful multimedia.

But handling videos is a tricky issue and needs quite a bit of conceptual understanding. This part is dedicated to this single purpose. Right from understanding the basic technologies and concepts, this part contain detailed chapters that expose all the professional video editing and manipulation techniques frequently made use of in studios and production houses.

This part has two chapters: First one details all fundamental concepts associated with digital multimedia video technology and the second concentrates more on the editing aspects of the same.

Chapter 18

Introducing Digital Video

CHAPTER OVERVIEW

This Chapter is mainly concerned with the fundamental concepts of Digital multimedia Video Technology. Everything concerning multimedia Video - From Quarter screen Video clippings to MPEG standards, from Video for Windows to Apple's Quick time Player - has been discussed in sufficient light.

This Chapter lays the foundation for an exiting journey into the Jargons of multimedia Video - in the next Chapter.

18.1 Introduction

Digital videography is the order of the day.

From Video CDs (or VCDs) to Digital versatile disks (or DVDs), digital medium is dominating the landscape. Even television broadcasts are becoming digital, offering excellent quality in pictures and sounds.

Digital video has been recognized as a medium in multimedia technology – along with texts, audio and animations. There are many challenges in running video movies within multimedia applications. This chapter and few others that follow will expound this topic at reasonable depths.

18.2 Role of digital videos in multimedia projects

It is interesting to think about situations in a multimedia project that demand digital videos.

For example, let us consider 'Tourist's India – Interactive Multimedia Guide' CD-ROM. The product features important tourist places all across the country. It will be nice, if we could show some video clippings filmed on specific locations – while talking about that particular tourist destination. This will help the user to visualise things and imagine the look and feel of that particular location.

As a second example, let us look at Microsoft Oceans CD-ROM. It will certainly be a value addition, if we could add a few video clippings filmed underwater – right inside the oceans. It will nicely supplement the facts and figures we are presenting about oceans.

Now, let us consider a third example – where digital videos are unnecessary.

Tales from Indian Mythology CD-ROM features animated tales for children. The whole CD-ROM, from end to end, is full of digital animations. If we were to feature digital videos in-between, it will most certainly interfere with the aura created by fantasy worlds created with the help of 3D and 2D animations. Hence it should be avoided.

Figure 154: Digital videos provide value addition to Tourist's India – Interactive Multimedia Guide CD-ROM.

If we consider all other multimedia application scenarios like this, we will see that digital videos are relevant and useful under the following circumstances:

- ❑ The project has certain relevant sequences/ material that can be presented only by means of digital videography. Example: Underwater sequences for Oceans title.
- ❑ The project provides good scope for digital videos. Example: A black and white footage of Mahatma Gandhi – for a CD-ROM on India's freedom struggle.
- ❑ The project must feature live lectures / demonstrations / other pre-recorded material. Example: The chairman's annual shareholders meeting speech for a corporate presentation.
- ❑ The project has to feature sequences that are not viable or economical to produce by means of animations. Example: Lip and face movements of a presenter, in a multimedia-shopping kiosk.

18.3 Video Playback

Most windows operating systems can playback all the basic forms of video like .avi and .mpg via the Windows media player software. Media player 9 about which we elaborately discussed in an earlier chapter has very good support for videos.

Windows media player recognizes the following video file formats:

- ❑ MPEG files like .mpg, .mpeg and .m1v
- ❑ Windows media files like .asf and .wmv
- ❑ Windows audio-video file .avi

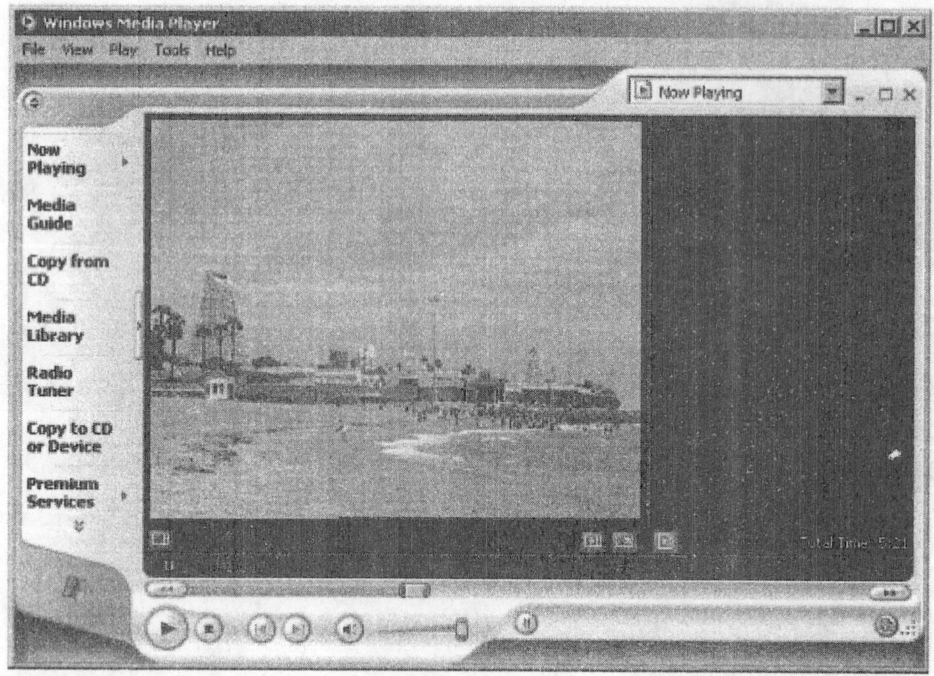

Figure 155: Media Player 9 playing back a digital video file from CD-ROM title 'Six Sacred Temples', published by cybervalley systems.

18.4 Quarter screen and full screen videos

In most multimedia applications, you will see that the videos featured do not fill the entire screen – mostly they will open out in a small window, which is approximately one fourth of the total screen area. Refer the example we provided in the beginning of this chapter and note that the videos are not full screen.

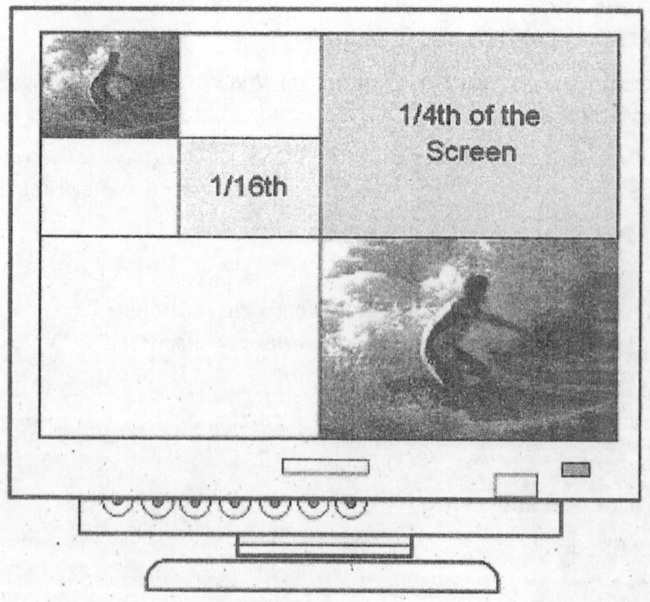

Figure 156: Quarter screen video - illustrated

Try another experiment. Take a movie VCD disk and try to open any of the .dat files under the mpegav directory using windows media player. You will be surprised to see that the movie opens up in a small window and does not fill the entire screen.

Try to right click on the movie screen and in the menu that pops up, choose 'Full screen'. Presto! The movie is now running full screen... But, wait! The quality of the movie is not very good, right?

You might be surprised at this behaviour, because the VCD looks so nice full screen in a television! If you move yourself away from the monitor, the results are lot more tolerable.

What is the reason behind this behaviour?

Remember our talks on resolution of the monitor, earlier. Actually television monitors have much lesser resolution when compared to computer monitors. Hence, relatively lesser pixels are required to fill the entire screen. But a computer monitor has at least 640*480 resolution – demanding more pixels for display. That is why you are watching television, only at a distance whereas you sit much closer to a computer monitor.

Moreover, while featuring video contents on a multimedia project, one has to give room for play, pause and close buttons which the user is likely to click. It is also possible that you may need to display some text along with the video contents – possibly some explanatory notes or supplementary information.

Because of all these reasons, multimedia producers often present the video contents as quarter screen videos or even less.

18.5 Full motion video

Multimedia videos that display pictures at the rate of 25 to 30 frames per second (fps) are called full motion videos.

Television displays pictures at the rate of 25 to 30 fps. 25 fps is a PAL standard, which is the broadcast standard adopted in most Asian countries – including India. 30 fps is the NTSC system, which is mainly adopted in USA and certain other countries.

25 fps results in very quick transition of still frames – resulting in smoother movement.

In the world of multimedia video, there were some problems initially in handling 25 frames per second – due to limitation of the processor and other resources. Hence videos with 15 to 20 frames per second were adopted – but this resulted in lot of jerks and other issues.

But now, with advanced multimedia video compression technologies like mpeg, 25 fps is not an issue anymore.

18.6 Video compression algorithms or CODECs

Raw videos without any compression will occupy huge file sizes – even a small video clip spanning a few seconds will consume several megabytes of storage space. For example, let us consider a video clipping of size 320 * 240 (which is a quarter screen video, when the resolution of the monitor is 640*480) playing at the rate of 30 frames per second (full motion) in true 24-bit colour.

In such a video, each frame would consume approximately 225 KB. Since we need to store 30 frames per second, we need at least 6750 KB per second or 6.59 MB! Imagine how much memory we will need to store 10 seconds of such data! It becomes impractical to handle raw videos of that size.

Hence, digital video professionals came out different kinds of compression algorithms to handle raw video. These compression algorithms have grown in number over a period of time, and it is most likely that even in your own desktop computer – at least a dozen video codecs may already be installed!

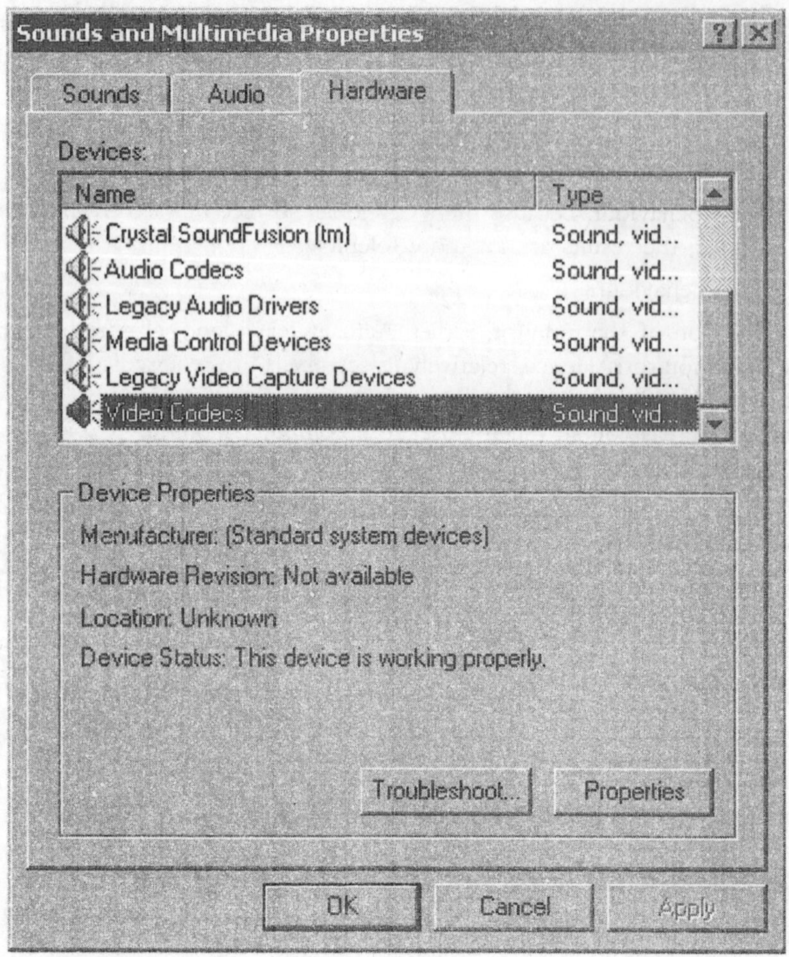

Figure 157: Many video codecs are pre-installed on windows 2000 operating system

To view what are all the video codecs installed on your win2000 desktop, go to Control Panel à Sounds and Multimedia Properties à Hardware and double click on the video codecs item. It is interesting to note that even audio has its own compression algorithms – registered under the title audio codecs.

The dialog box that pops up, lists all the different video codecs installed on the system – with all the necessary details. If you want to explore any particular codec further, you can do so by clicking on the same and choosing the properties button.

Each of these codecs may handle different types of file formats. For example, in the image displayed below, Intel Indeo codec handles a specific type of avi compression, Microsoft MPEG-4 Video codec handles .mpg videos and so on.

When a particular codec is not installed on the system and when you try to play a video file, which uses that codec – windows media player reports an error and tries to download the codec from the Internet. If the attempt succeeds, then the downloaded codec is installed on the system and the video is played back; but when the attempt fails, media player reports that the video file cannot be played back.

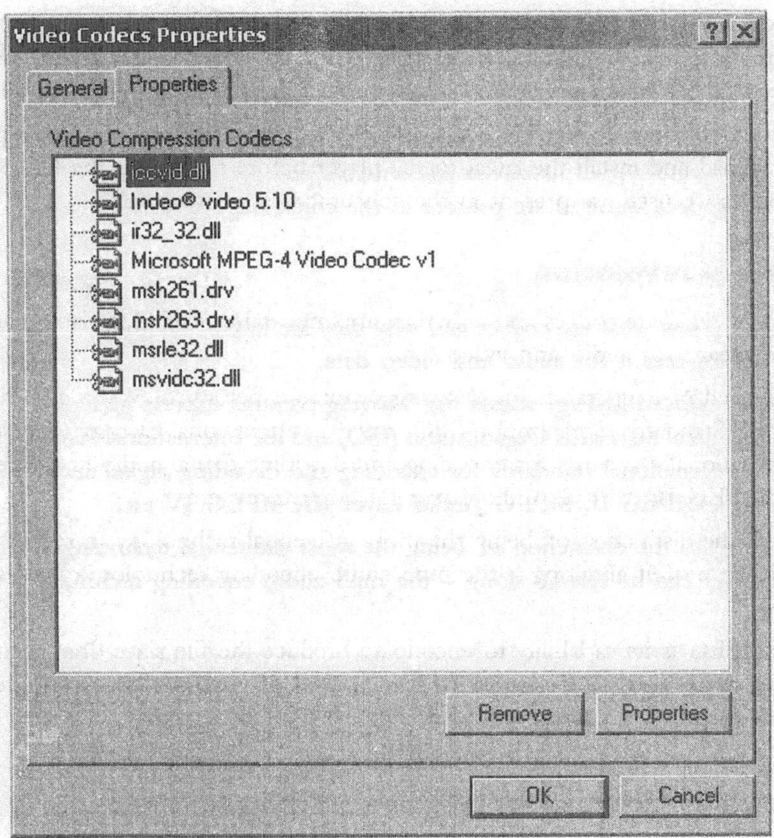

Figure 158: Details of different video codecs installed on a system

Some famous Video codecs are provided in the table below:

Table 29: Popular video codecs

Product	Company
Intel	Indeo Video Drivers
Microsoft	Microsoft Video1, Microsoft RLE, Microsoft MPEG-4
IBM	Ultimotion
Supermac	Cinepak drivers
Creative	Spigot
Moving Picture expert group	MPEG

The process of compressing raw video, using a particular compression algorithm is called *encoding.* The process of interpreting the encoded information and understanding the audio or visual information contained in them is called *decoding.*

For encoding our videos, we may need specialized software encoders available from various vendors. However, for decoding, we can use Microsoft Media player or Apple's quick time player that contain decoders for all commonly used codecs.

While speaking about codecs, I need to highlight one potential problem that might arise – particularly in multimedia CD-ROM projects meant for consumer market. In such projects, the video editor of the project or the program manager needs to ensure that the video codecs used in the project are the ones that are available on most systems.

The safest alternative is to adopt one of the codecs that come bundled with Windows media player and recommend the end consumer to download and install the latest media player before trying out the CD-ROM title. In this way, we ensure that all the codecs we used are present in the consumer's system as well.

18.7 The MPEG revolution

In the earlier section, we saw what are codecs and why they are important. MPEG is also an advanced compression-decompression algorithm meant for audio and video data.

The term MPEG (pronounced M-Peg) stands for 'Moving pictures experts group' – a committee that works under the direction of International Standards Organization (ISO) and the International Electro-Technical Commission (IEC). It represents a set of international standards for encoding and decoding digital audio and video data. Thus we have standards like MPEG I, MPEG II, MPEG Audio Layer III, MPEG IV etc.

MPEG can rightfully claim the distinction of being the most influential technology in recent times, in the world of digital videos. Its impact can be felt all along – the mp3 audio encoding technology, the VCD and DVD format videos etc.

The major advantage of MPEG is its capability to encode and reduce the file sizes dramatically, without sacrificing the quality of audio/video data. How MPEG achieves such a level of compression is a topic of detailed academic studies and is beyond the scope of this work.

For those who want to pursue studies about MPEG further, www.mpeg.org is a very good starter. The official home of MPEG committee is located at http://www.cselt.it/mpeg

18.8 Summary

Video is incorporated into multimedia projects to zap up the contents and present a media rich experience to the user. They are mostly meant for contents and not interface design.

The file sizes of digital videos are necessarily very large and this leads to popular usage of small video clippings. Hence, multimedia videos may be quarter screen videos or even lesser.

Digital video files played back at 25-30 frames per second are called 'full motion videos' - meaning that the motion is pretty smooth.

Compression-decompression algorithms are used to compress the videos for storage and uncompress them at runtime. Flavours of Microsoft windows operating system comes bundled with the relevant codecs to handle most digital video file formats.

The MPEG technology is revolutionizing the digital video landscape.

18.9 Keywords

- ❑ **Codec:** Acronym for compression-decompression algorithm for digital video files.
- ❑ **Full motion videos:** Digital video files played back at a speed of 25-30 frames per second.
- ❑ **Mpeg:** motion picture expert group

Chapter 19
Digital Video Production Techniques

CHAPTER OVERVIEW

This extensive chapter builds over the fundamental concepts of digital video we learnt in the earlier chapter.

First we understand various steps involved with digital video production process – right from equipments, location, video shooting and video capture. The process of digitising videos with the help of video capture cards is detailed at length.

Once digital video clippings are available, the arduous task of digital video editing and post-production begins. The chapter provides a very good overview on this subject, detailing all the fundamental concepts – one by one – with specific examples and later on, illustrating the same with Adobe premiere – one of the frontline suites meant for video post-production.

19.1 Introduction

In the previous chapter, we have developed a conceptual understanding of what makes up a digital video file. In this chapter, we will learn how to produce the same, edit / apply post-production effects and make it available for our projects.

19.2 Video production for multimedia projects

Producing digital video elements for multimedia projects involve the following steps:

- ❑ Shooting the necessary video sequences using a video camera
- ❑ Capturing or digitising the video data
- ❑ Video editing and post-production
- ❑ Embedding into the projects

We shall focus on each of these steps, in the pages that follow.

19.3 Video shooting

Shooting the required sequences for a multimedia project involves relevant equipment, people, location, storyboard and money! Depending upon the specific requirements of the project and the budget available, it may turn out to be a simple handy-cam shooting on a nearby location or a complex shooting involving different locations and characters.

19.3.1 Equipments

You can either buy a latest digital personal handy-cam or camcorder for yourself or you can hire appropriate equipment for the required period of time. If it is a low budget project or a personal production, I recommend that you stick on to your own equipments and people. But if it is a corporate or a film/ television project wherein you have sufficient funds, you can extend the arms as much as you can – for better results.

If you are going for personal handy cams, I recommend that you go for the one that has digital USB output. This might be slightly higher than the conventional equipments with standard DV In and DV Out – but the money you invest can be recovered during video capture process. You need not buy dedicated cards, if your digital handy cam itself comes with USB Out feature – all you need to do is to ensure that your motherboard has a USB or USB2 port on the back of your system. The results are also much better than their counterparts.

During video shooting, you can take the help of your friends who have some knowledge of videography. Quite a number of variables are involved in a shooting process - lighting, shooting angles, location, colouring, movements – all play their role.

If you decided to go for hiring professional cameras, you need to hire good videographers too.

Pay specific attention to the recording format used by the equipment – there are video standards like VHS, S-VHS, U-Matic, Hi-8, Beta cam SP and the superior Component digital / Composite digital recording formats... these recording formats govern the quality of recording to a considerable extent. Beta cams offer acceptable quality and are available at reasonable rentals.

Figure 159: Digital handy cams and personal camcorders are becoming more professional, powerful and packed with features – day-by-day.

Whatever may be the equipment, remember that the data has to be either recorded as digital data or should have the capability to be digitised. For example, if you are recording using a beta cam camera, you should have a service provider who can convert this beta cam recording to digital format for you. Such facilities are available in most cities and metros which have some kind of ongoing movie / television industry activity.

Also, pay attention to the broadcast standards like NTSC, PAL, and SECAM and decide which will be most suited for your purpose.

19.3.2 Backgrounds & landscapes

Remember this as a thumb rule: The lesser the number of colours the better your video output is going to look like.

What do we mean by this?

Let us say you are going to shoot a landscape with a river stream, trees, rocks and the sky. Here we can say that three to four colours are going to dominate – Blue (sky, river etc), Green (Trees), Brown (Rocks, tree trucks etc.) – and this is very much acceptable. But let us say you are shooting a rainbow or something like that – here, more than 7 colours, quite unrelated to each other – are going to come into play.

You will not see any major problems with both these scenes during the video shooting or preview – but colouring issues will arise during video encoding. This has something to do with the way video encoding is done in MPEG. When multiple, unrelated colours are used in a single frame – something called bleeding occurs along the edges of the image, thus pulling down the quality of the frame.

The second point to be considered with respect to the background is whether the background is going to be replaced or edited during post-production. For example, if you are shooting the speech of a company chairman against the background of a wall, you may want to replace this with some other decent graphics during video editing.

If this is the case, remember to shoot the videos under a salient blue background. During post-production, this blue background can be replaced with whatever background you choose to use. This technique is called chroma keying and is quite popular among the professionals.

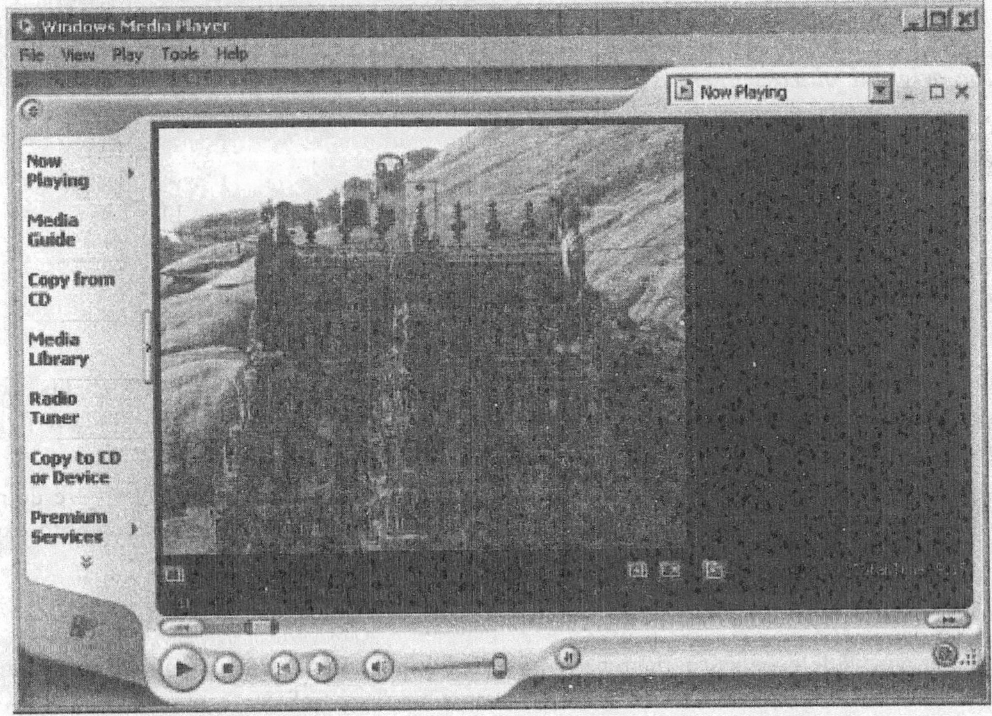

Figure 160: Colour bleeding invariably creeps in, when the number of different colours in a shot, is more. This temple tower features so many contrasting colours near one another - resulting in bleeding.

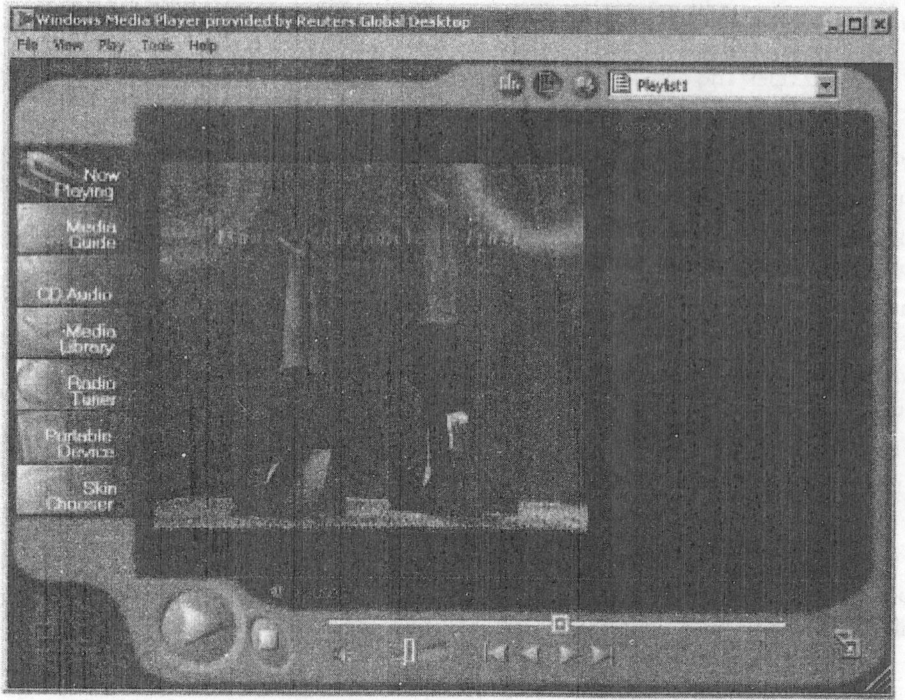

Figure 161: Chroma-keying technique is used to replace the background with which the original video sequences were shot in Cybervalley system's Yoga CD-ROM

19.3.3 Controlling camera movements

While shooting video sequences, the following combinations of movements are possible:

- Camera stationary, objects moving.
- Object stationary, camera moving.
- Objects as well as camera moving.

The safest option is to limit the movement of camera and let the objects do the required movements. This is because of the experience required in handling camera movements without causing jerks or shakes. These jerks cannot be corrected even during post-production and hence becomes a difficult problem to tackle.

Professional recordings make use of rails to restrict the movement of cameras – but if you are doing your own personal recordings, the control very much lies with your hands and shoulders. This requires both experience and practice.

19.3.4 Lighting

If you are a beginner with little experience, then it is best to shoot in daylight. Understanding of light and its impact on videography comes with experience and till then it is best to stick to ambient lighting.

Experienced professionals can handle light in the best possible manner. They can use light as a part of story telling process – using it efficiently to create the mood they wish to portray.

Lighting errors can be adjusted in post-production to some extent.

With these limited discussions, we will conclude our notes on video shooting. Videography is a technique as well as an art and cannot be learnt in one day – that too by just reading books. It requires considerable fieldwork and experience to master this art.

For multimedia professionals who wish to make out a career in post-production and videography, I'll seriously recommend some real training under an expert guidance.

19.4 Video capture process

Video-capture or video digitising is the process of converting analog video signals to digital data. The signals, once converted, are fed into the computers and stored as digital video files.

The process of video capture varies, depending upon the equipment used for video shooting.

- ❑ If you have used a camcorder or handy cam with digital video out option using USB, then the videos can be captured directly – without the need for external interface.
- ❑ Some handy cams support fire wire interface instead of USB, in which case you need a fire wire card for video capture.
- ❑ If none of these interfaces are supported, then you need a dedicated video capture card – which will accept the audio and video signals from the camcorder and do the digital conversion process using dedicated chips.
- ❑ If you have rented the equipment, then the output will be available to use as a Hi8 or beta cam tape – in which case, you need a relevant player to playback the video contents and capture the data using dedicated video capture board.

Thus it is not absolutely necessary that you should purchase a dedicated board – in order to capture videos into your computer. The equipments you have used for videography dictate the choice and options available for you.

On the application side, you certainly need dedicated software to capture the video signals coming into the computer and store them as digital video files in appropriate formats. Most video post-production software like Adobe Premiere, Ulead Video studios etc have facilities with which video capture can be accomplished with ease. If you do not have any of the above-mentioned software, try out some of the free tools available on the net. One problem with these tools is the file format in which you are going to capture – which we will discuss in a short while from now.

Let us draw a flow diagram to illustrate what we have been discussing till now.

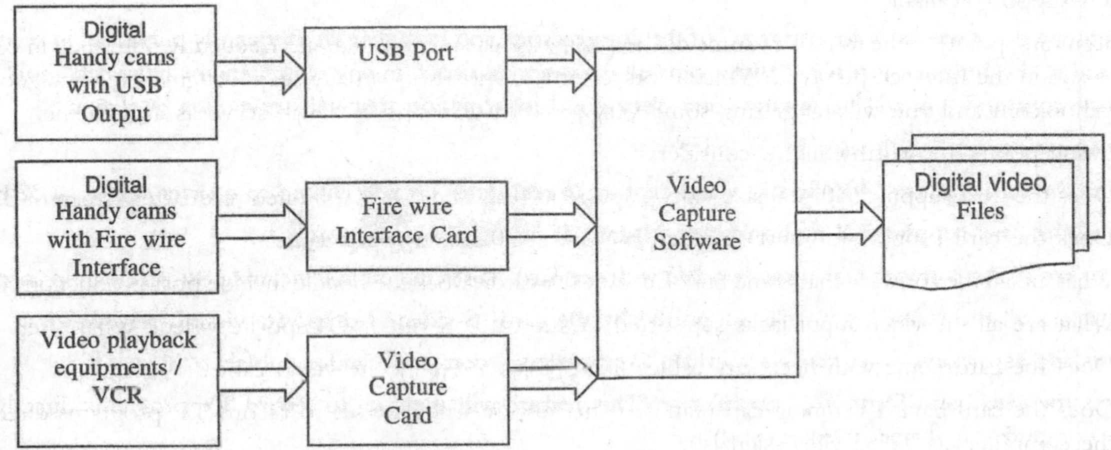

Figure 162: Process of video capture

19.4.1 Video capture cards / equipments

A video capture card is a specialized electronic circuitry that is capable of converting analog video signals to digital video signals. These cards usually fit into the 32-bit slot of the motherboard with all the video in and out jacks projecting on the rear side of the cabinet.

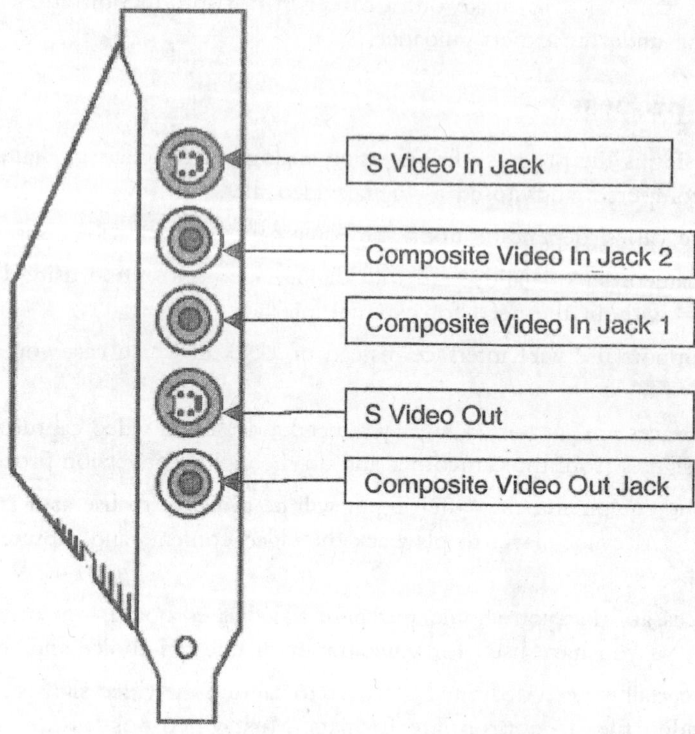

Figure 163: Rear side of a typical video capture card

Quite a number of video capture cards are available in the market and making a purchase decision is not easy. The purchase should be governed by many factors like the requirements of your project(s), capabilities of the equipment, budget and support available.

A good beginning point will be to look at some of the comparisons and tests that are frequently published in computer magazines and in the Internet. Just type "Video capture cards comparison" in any search engine like www.google.com or www.yahoo.com and you will be getting some very good information that will serve as a guideline.

The following points are worthwhile to consider:

- ❑ Does the card support 640*480 size video capture in real time? Or is it limited to quarter screen or 320*240?
- ❑ Does the card support full motion video capture at 30 frames per second?
- ❑ What are all the software that come bundled with the card? Does the bundle include post-production software?
- ❑ What are all the video input jacks supported by the card? S-video? Composite video? What else?
- ❑ Does the card come with necessary cables like s-video / composite video cable?
- ❑ Does the card have TV tuning capabilities? (This feature will allow us to record TV programs directly into the computer, as digital video signals!)
- ❑ What is the general performance of the card – when compared with other cards?
- ❑ How about the processor and memory resources required?
- ❑ What are all the digital video file formats supported by the card? Does it have real time MPEG video encoding capabilities?
- ❑ What are all the video standards supported by the card? NTSC? PAL?
- ❑ How easy it is to install the card and make use of the software for video capture?

The above questions would have given you some idea, which will guide you through the right purchase. It is best to check up the net and find out those vendors who ship their products internationally. Even for the very same cards, some vendors will offer very good deals. The only problem with net purchase is that local warranty and support will not be available.

Apart from capture cards, there are also dedicated equipments available for video capture. These are like set top boxes with relevant cables for input and output. They capture signals from video sources and relay the digital video data into the computer - using USB ports.

19.4.2 Different steps in video capture process

Equipments required:

- ❑ A Multimedia computer with video-capture card/ equipment, an audio card and with relevant software installed
- ❑ A video input source (VCR, Camcorder, Beta cam player etc)
- ❑ Necessary cables (prefer S-Video over composite, if you have a choice!)

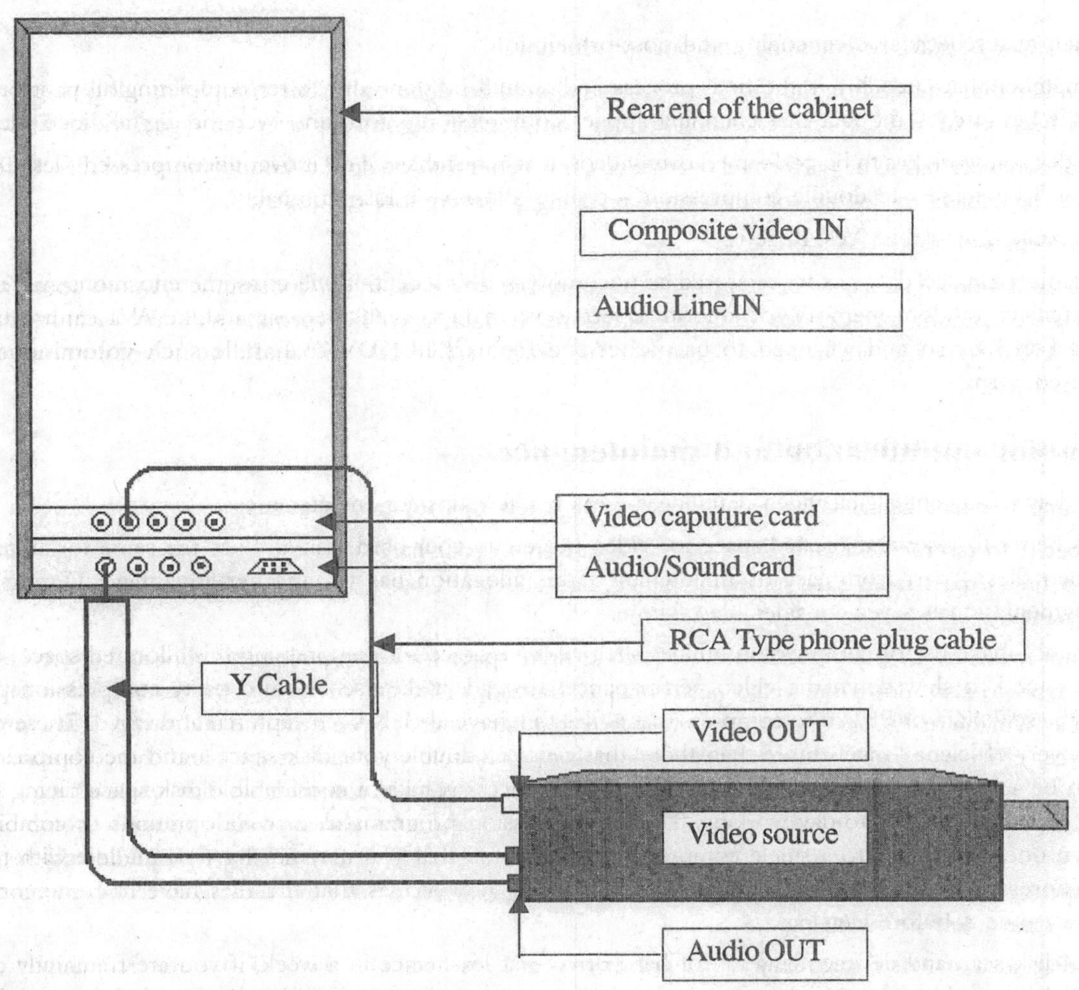

Figure 164: Video capture process detailed

Follow these steps in sequence, to capture video data:

- Connect the 'video out' jack of the input video source to the 'video in' jack of the video capture card, using relevant cables.
- Connect the 'audio out' jacks of the video source to 'line in' jack of the audio card. If your video equipment is giving out stereo audio (the two channels plugs are distinguished by two different colours) then you need to have a special 'Y' cable - that accepts 'audio out' from the left and right channels of the equipment and feeds them into the audio card.
- Play back the recorded tape from the video source. If your connectivity is correct, you can see the video - probably in a smaller window - in the digital video capture software window you are using.
- Fixing up the relevant capture parameters like the screen capture dimensions, compression ratios etc.
- Press the 'capture' button. The video data will be recorded onto the hard disk. This recorded file can be later saved in the required digital video file format.

19.4.3 Video capture file format

You might think that you can actually choose from various file formats available for capture. But this is not entirely true.

The problem arises because of encoding and post-production.

Always remember that encoding is the final process and should be done only after completing all post-production work. This is because of the fact that encoding applies compression algorithms over the digital video files.

If post-production work has to be performed over videos, it is better that we do it over uncompressed files. Otherwise, the videos will be subject to double compression – resulting in severe loss of quality.

Is there a problem with this? Yes, there is.

Since the captured video data has to be stored as uncompressed raw data, it will consume enormous space and will demand extensive random memory for smooth operations. In fact, even file formats like AVI cannot hold data more than 1 GB or so and we need to use other file formats like DV to handle such voluminous data in uncompressed form.

19.5 Tips for optimization and maintenance

If you are doing frequent digital video handling, here are a few tips for maintenance:

- It's better to reserve dedicated space for video buffers in your hard disk and use the same for all temporary video files. Apart from ease of maintenance, this allocation has yet another advantage: During disk de-fragmentation it saves considerable of time.
- Do not make use of compression utilities such as drive space for compressing this allocated space - because, they tend to slow down the video performance. Instead, make use of third party compression programs such as WinZip or PKZip to compress those files that have already been captured and saved. These programs are very efficient - much more than those that claim to double your disk space - and the compression that can be achieved is also of the highest order. This process results in considerable disk space saving - enough to cope up with day-to-day working. These compression programs also provide options to combine more than one video file into a single compressed .zip file - so that you may not have to muddle with too many compressed files. One disadvantage of this method, however, is that the files have to be uncompressed every time – before viewing.
- Do disk scan and de-fragmentation of hard drive – at least once in a week, if you are frequently capturing and editing video data. (De-fragmentation is the process of consolidating the file clusters containing the data as well as the empty clusters. For procedure on how to de-fragment your hard disk, refer Windows help). Disks that are frequently scanned for errors have much lesser chances of crashing down under heavy read-write operations.

- All video capture applications are memory hungry. Ensure that you have at least 256 MB of RAM. Also, ensure that you have allotted enough swap file space for the Windows operating system.
- Windows 2000 adjusts the swap file and temporary file space as and when required. But when it increases the file space, all operations may be suspended for considerable amount of time. Please do not disturb this process – wait till the operating system completes its task and the performance will improve from them onwards.
- Store all the back up files and other resources on a CD-R / CD-RW disc so that they can be brought back to the life, when the need arises. Keep only those files that are required for the current projects, on the hard disk.
- Finally, make use of higher capacity hard disk - Minimum 20 GB in case you are frequently muddling with digital videos. Because, you need a lot of disk space before editing and encoding the video data files.

19.6 Digital video post-production

Digital video post-production is the process of editing and mixing videos within the computer, using relevant software tools. Video post-production has grown over these years into a multi-million dollar industry.

There are many things you can do during post-production. Some of them are:

- Adding, removing and rearranging different portions of the video clippings shot
- Resizing video
- Mixing and remixing audio
- Editing colour, blend, lighting and other attributes of video
- Adding special effects / titling etc
- Interlacing 3D animation with live video shoots
- Interlacing still photographs with live videos

To do all this, you need rugged video post-production software that is rich in features. There are quite a number of post-production suites available in the market – like Adobe Premiere and Ulead Video studio. Before we could put our hands on these software suites, we need to learn certain fundamental concepts about video post-production that will help us to understand and appreciate various options available in the suite.

I've taken particular pains to present only the generic concepts so that they will be useful to you, irrespective of the tool you are going to use, later.

19.7 Post-production concepts

In this section, we will be uncovering some of the fundamental concepts associated with digital video editing.

Why concepts - without delving directly into the tool?

Because tools change over time, but concepts mostly remain in place. Rather than learning how many menus and options are available in any multimedia tool, a novice should understand the fundamental concepts that make up the tool. Later on, when time comes wherein he or she has to migrate to a different tool this learning will be of great use.

19.7.1 Understanding video clippings

In the world of video editing, we learn to conceive a lengthy video shot as a sequence of short clippings. Let me illustrate this with a mini video project we did for Tourist's India CD-ROM.

For a feature on Madurai, a temple city in south India, we had shot quite a lengthy video clipping. Now, we could not show all that we had shot for half an hour because the slot allotted to Madurai was just three to five minutes! Hence we had to pick out some of the best sequences we had shot and arrange it in a sequence.

We decided to illustrate just the main temple within the time slot. This temple was most famous for its temple towers rising on all the four sides of the temple – studded with colourful images of gods and goddesses. Now this process of prioritising what you really want to present, is very important. When half an hour video is edited to just three minutes, you can afford to show only the best and most important details.

The following sequences were selected from the lengthy clipping:

- Temple entrance and temple towers – outer view
- Temple tower – zooming in
- Details of statues studded in temple tower
- Temple entrance – people moving in
- Temple interiors and stucco decorations
- Temple walls

We actually did a few more, but these are enough for our illustration.

Now, all we had to do was to cut out the sequences we want - from the rest of the video clip. Video post- production suite allowed us to do this by means of a cut operation.

Figure 165: Cut operation can be performed using post production tools

All video suites will display the original video clipping (say video00.avi) as a series of bitmaps that stretch across the timeline – as shown in the figure. What we did was to specify the starting point and end point of the clipping and the rest of the video was removed. We saved the first clipping as Video01.avi.Repeating this operation for different clippings across the original video, we ended up with six different sequences of small clippings – just containing the shots we wanted to display.

Figure 166: Different video clippings arranged in sequential order – in the post-production suite

The second task was to arrange those clippings in the order we want and to make the integrated shot as a single video clipping. This was also easily achieved using the video suite – all we had to do was to import the necessary video clips in proper order and place them next to one another. During rendering, the suite will integrate all these independent clippings into one single video.

19.7.2 Concept of video and audio tracks

In the earlier illustration, we made one important assumption. We assumed that all the different clippings were coming from the same source movie video00.avi. What if the assumption is not correct? What if the clippings we need come from different sources? Are we to open and cut clippings each and every movie and save it? That could be a cumbersome and time-consuming process…

Video production suites offer a solution to this by means of video tracks. Theoretically, we can compare this concept of tracks with that of layers in image editing software tools. According to this concept, each video editing project can consist of multiple video and audio tracks. Video tracks will contain just the visual information and audio tracks will contain the corresponding audio information.

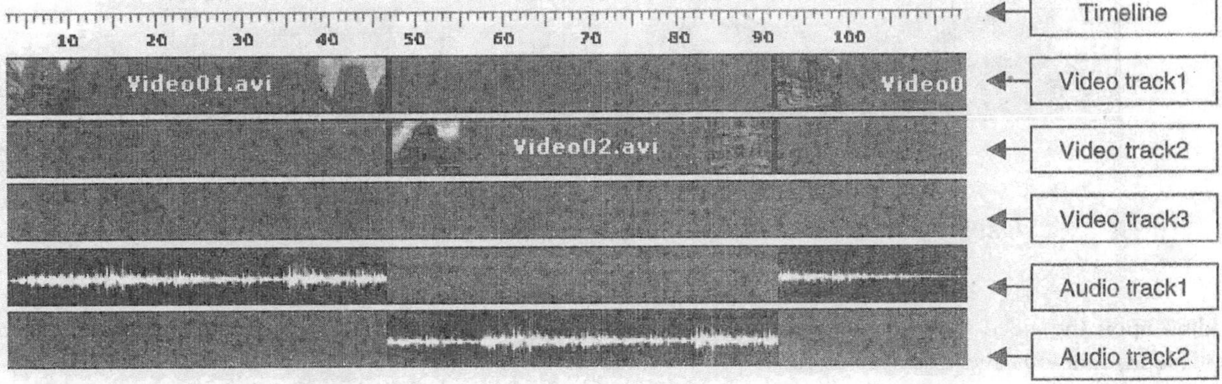

Figure 167: Multiple tracks of video and audio data can be combined together in video production suite environments

Each of these tracks can contain information from different files. For example, in a single project, we can have clippings coming out of different video source files. During video rendering process, the output of all these different tracks will be merged together.

Do note that video02 begins where video01 ends and video03 begins where video02 ends. If there is any overlap between the videos, the top most video will override all others – just as in layers – unless we define some special effect options.

19.7.3 Video special effects

Till now, it all looks like a neat little business: Cut different portions of video you want and stitch them as a single clip. Fine. How about some special effects? How about those dissolve and blind effects between the clippings? What if the first video is to fade into the second in a seamless manner?

In the world of digital video terminology, these effects are called transitions.

Transitions can be applied between two different video clippings. For example, in the above example, video01 stops at some point of time and video02 begin. Normally, the shift will be sudden and spontaneous – but if you want to smoothen out, you can apply a transition between these two clippings at some point of time when video01 ends and video02 starts.

In order to apply transition effects, some portion of video01 as well as video02 has to be sacrificed.

Let us say we want to blend the last five seconds of video01 with the first five seconds of video02. The two seconds of video clip should be kept one over the other - so that, in the timeline, there are at least five seconds in which both clippings interlace.

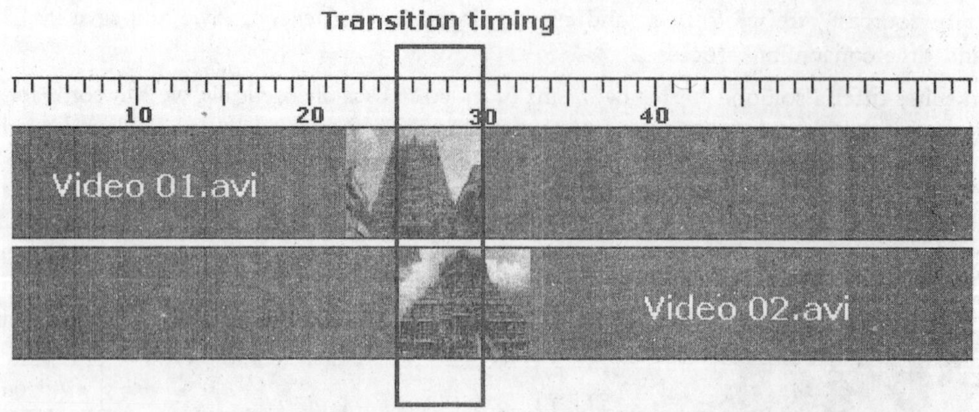

Figure 168: The five second interlacing gives us room to apply some transition effects between the clippings

Depending upon the video suite you are using, you can choose from many different transition effects – right from blinds, fade-in, fade-out and dissolves to more sophisticated deformations.

Figure 169: Fade in transition effect applied between video01 and video02

19.7.4 Image pans

Image panning is the process of treating the output window as a camera and making movements across the video. It is best for generating wonderful video clippings out of still images.

Let me illustrate this with an example.

Let us say we have the still photograph of an ancient and yet beautiful statue. You can very well feature this as an image in your project – but let us say you want to show this as part of your video clipping on, say, the architecture of ancient India. What you want to show is the complete details of this figure – inch by inch.

Would it not be nice, if you could pass the camera over the statue from top to bottom?

Well, that is exactly what image pan is all about. Using the utilities available in post-production suite, you can define the size of the camera window you are going to run over the still image as well as the direction of the camera movement.

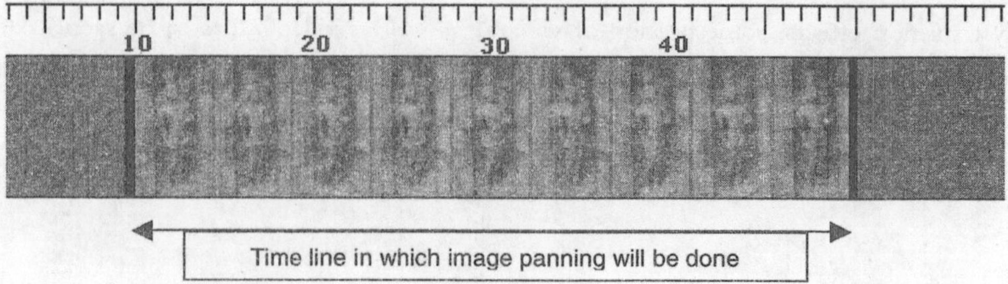

Figure 170: The still image is copied multiple times over the video track to provide working space for the camera panning

To do image panning, you first need to copy the still image over the video tracks multiple times – across the timeline. This will give you a virtual video clip over which you can run the camera.

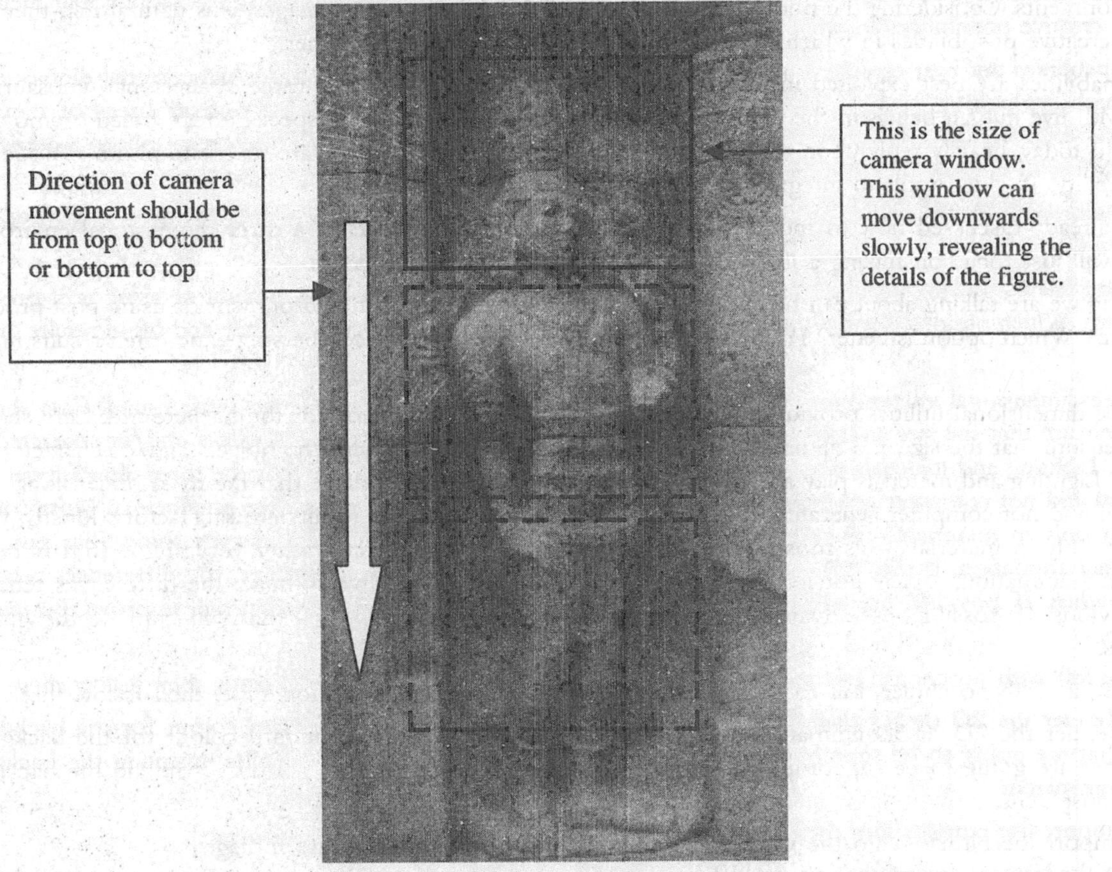

Figure 171: Image pan effect can be used to provide a bit by bit coverage of this beautiful statue in a video clipping

Once the video clip is ready, we can actually apply the image panning special effect over the video clip and achieve the desired results. The speed at which the camera moves will be determined by the timeline allocated for the panning process. If the camera movement is too slow, reduce the timeline; and if it is very fast, increase the timeline by adding a still images for a few more seconds.

Apart from moving from top to bottom and left to right, some suites also allow you to do other operations with image pan like zoom in / zoom out and deformations. Putting it all together, image pan can be a very effective tool at the hands of a skilful video composer.

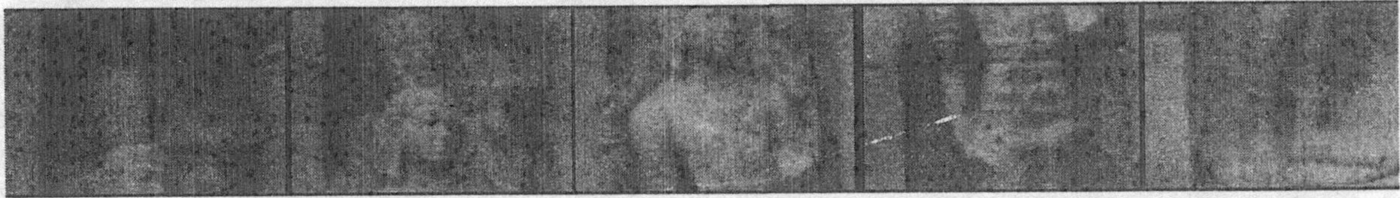

Figure 172: Resulting frames of image pan effect

19.7.5 Mixing videos with animation

We saw earlier that two-dimensional and three-dimensional animations can be developed using specialized packages and environments. Considering the photo realistic nature of 3d characters and images, it is natural that there might be many creative possibilities in which the both have to be mixed with each other.

These capabilities are best exploited in feature films. For example, we saw how three-dimensional dinosaurs could interact with live human beings in the Jurassic Park movie series. The so called 'special-effect' breed of movies that are abound today, heavily reply upon the capabilities of three-dimensional software to create photo realistic scenes and the ability of video tools to integrate them seamlessly with live footages.

We have already discussed how to model and render characters and objects in a three-dimensional environment. Here we will just focus on mixing a live video footage with animation clippings.

The mixing we are talking about can be done either in the three-dimensional environment or using post-production video suites. Which option is better? I'd prefer the first one because it is less cumbersome and often results in decent output.

Most three-dimensional utilities provide room for defining bitmaps and videos for the background. Care should be taken to ensure that the size and nature of the video clippings blends well with the objects and/or characters being animated. Lighting and materials play a critical part in making the viewers believe that the three-dimensional objects are natural and not computer generated. Do a trial rendering and see if the results are satisfactory. Mostly, you will be caught only in materials – as most animators tend to make their objects rather very shiny. In a pure three-dimensional animation, it may not look bad, but when interlaced with a live footage, the differences tend to be rather obvious. If possible, use advanced renderers with facilities like radiosity - that will improve the quality of renderings.

If you are left with no choice, but to do the blending via a video post-production suite, then follow these steps:

- ❑ Render the 2D or 3D animation as a series of bitmaps, adopting a standard colour for the backgrounds that are going to be superimposed with live footages. If the software permits, maintain the background transparent.
- ❑ Import the bitmaps into the video suite in a video track – above the life footage.
- ❑ If the bitmaps are transparent, the underlying video is exposed through the gaps. Otherwise adopt the chroma-keying technique to cut off all the unwanted colours in the bitmaps. This could turn out to be a rather cumbersome and time-consuming process if you do not have the right set of tools.
- ❑ Once the transparency is completed render the final output and check the results.

19.8 Adobe premiere video post-production suite

Adobe premiere is one of the most famous tools for video post-production, particularly on the windows platform. The tool is from Adobe Inc. (http://www.adobe.com), the creator of some of the frontline multimedia editing tools like Photoshop, Illustrator and Acrobat.

Premiere, as a post-production solution is pretty complex with numerous options and control panels. What we will be presenting here is, but a brief preview of the product – enough to wet your hands and get going. Most importantly, we will be concentrating on some of the concepts we learnt in the earlier pages.

The version we will be using for illustration is version 5.0 and it is not the very latest. But it is enough to illustrate all the concepts we had discussed earlier. For details about the latest version premiere pro, please log on to http://www.adobe.com.

19.8.1 Project options

As you open the premiere application, you will be asked to choose the settings for the new project. These settings and options alone are enough to confuse you for a lifetime!

There is nothing much to worry about, in this dialog box. All it says is that your video settings will be of size 640*480 (which is the default), using cinepak as the codec algorithm, with millions of colours and 100% quality (best). The audio settings indicate that the audio currently being used is of frequency 44.1 KHz and is of size 16-bit stereo – considered to be very good. The time base indicates that you are working on NTSC standard – which is 30 frames per second.

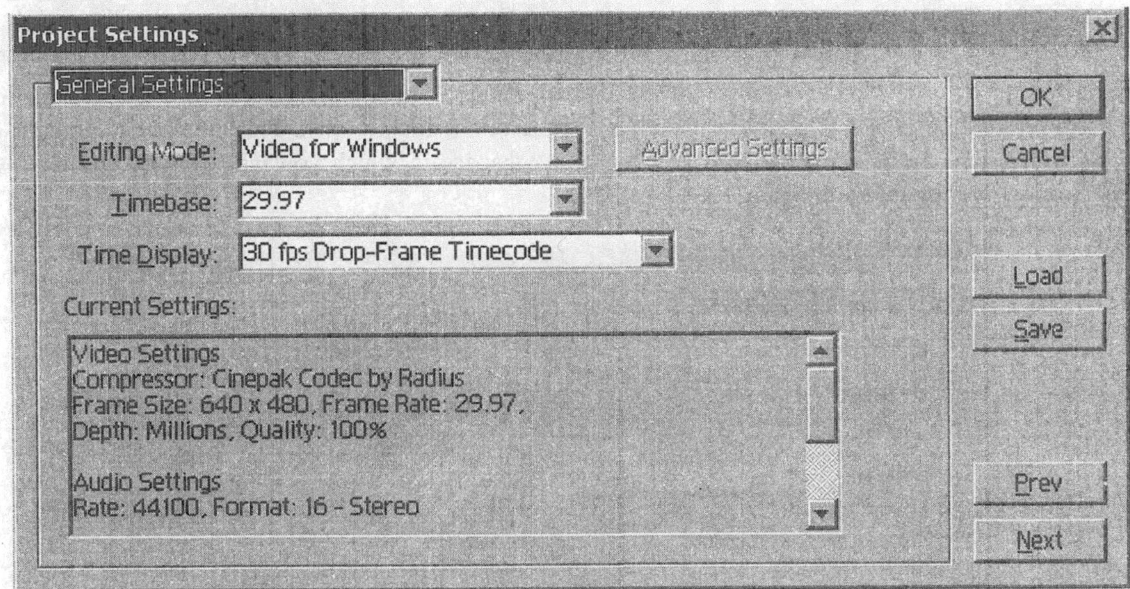

Figure 173: Premier project – general settings

Figure 174: Premier project – Video settings

If you want to change these default settings, click the general settings drop down box and choose the panel you want to change. For example, if you choose the video settings, you are presented with the option of changing the default video size, codec algorithm, number of colours etc. You should carefully choose these options to represent the requirements of your project. For example, if your source videos are of 320*240 size, then there is no point working with a size of 640*480 and you may decide to change this parameter.

Similarly, under audio options, you can choose to increase are decrease various parameters that control the quality of audio.

One very important thing to remember is that these are just project options and not the options that must be applied to the output video. While exporting the project as a movie in final stages, we will be presented with enough options to control the parameters during final rendering. Hence it is advisable to keep the project options to the best quality possible.

Once all these settings are provided, premiere main interface screen is thrown open. This interface has quite a number of windows, panes and menu items and this will be the workspace in which you will be spending most of your time while working on premiere projects.

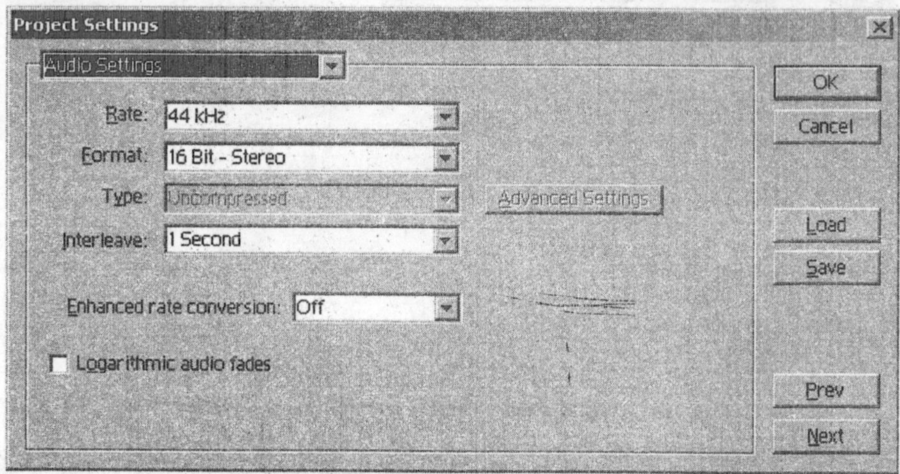

Figure 175: Premier project – Audio settings

Figure 176: Premiere – Main interface

19.8.2 Timeline & assets

Look at the main interface of adobe premiere.

The timeline window in the bottom will be the one you will be using most – in fact, all other panels are only meant to assist the activities happening in the timeline. The different audio and video tracks, which we discussed in the concepts section, can be seen in the time line. Take particular note of the transition track amidst the video tracks – all transition options are to be defined here.

Before you begin, save the project as it is under any given name. This project file will contain references to all the audio and video clippings you are using in the project.

To begin with, you need to import all the necessary raw videos and audios into the project. In the file menu, select Import à File and then choose the files you want to bring into the project, one by one. Mostly you will be importing video files, audio clippings and adobe Photoshop image files. Once these files are imported, they are available as assets in the project panel. But note that they have just been imported into the project – they have not been set against the timeline. It is you, who will be doing these arrangements in the required order.

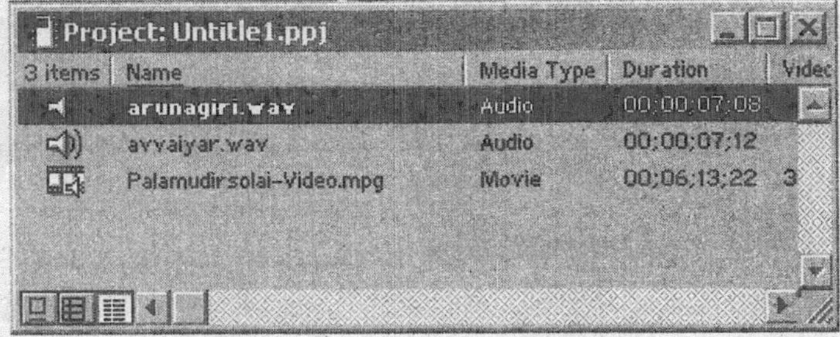

Figure 177: Few of the audio and video files imported into the current project

Once you have imported all the required files, the task of compiling the video and audio begins. Drag and drop the required video clippings into the timeline. The audio element that is tagged along with the video will be imported into corresponding audio tracks. You can either choose to use this audio or can replace the audio with some other clippings.

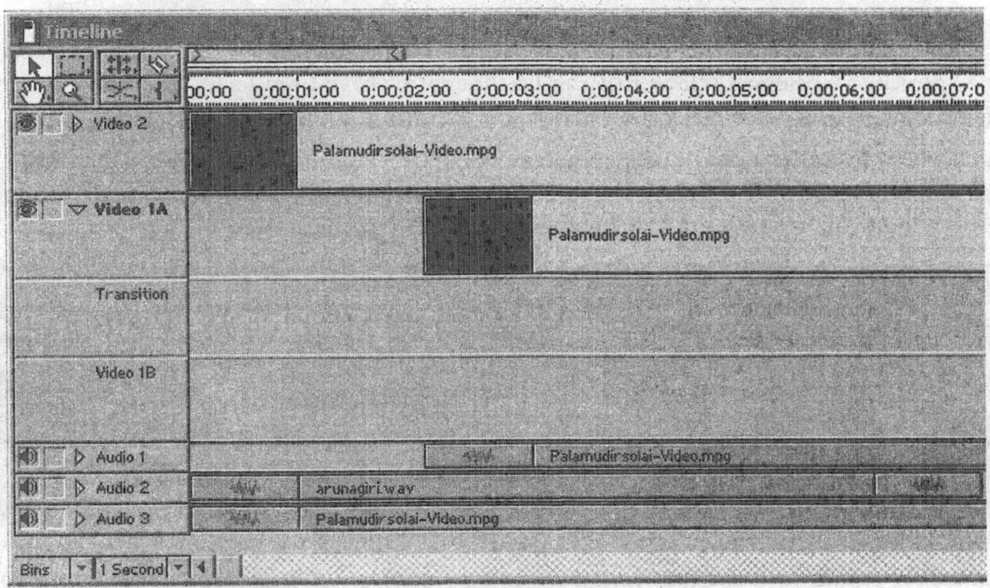

Figure 178: Video and audio clippings arranged along the timeline

In the picture showing video and audio clippings along the timeline, you see two raw video clippings and few other audio clippings being arranged in the timeline panel. Can you see any reason why the same video has been imported twice?

Remember that the videos we are importing are raw videos. We might want to take a clipping from the first few minutes and another clipping from the next few minutes. So, from the same raw video, you will be extracting several clippings and arrange them along the timeline. Remember our earlier example about the temple video – we actually chose six sequences spanning few seconds to few minutes, from a raw video of half an hour.

Thus you will find that the same clip has to be dragged down into the timeline multiple times and cut to required lengths. Now, if we were to apply some transitional effects across the clippings, it is best that we import them in two different video tracks. Once we have two videos interlacing each other, it will be possible to apply some transitions between them. This is what is shown in the figure.

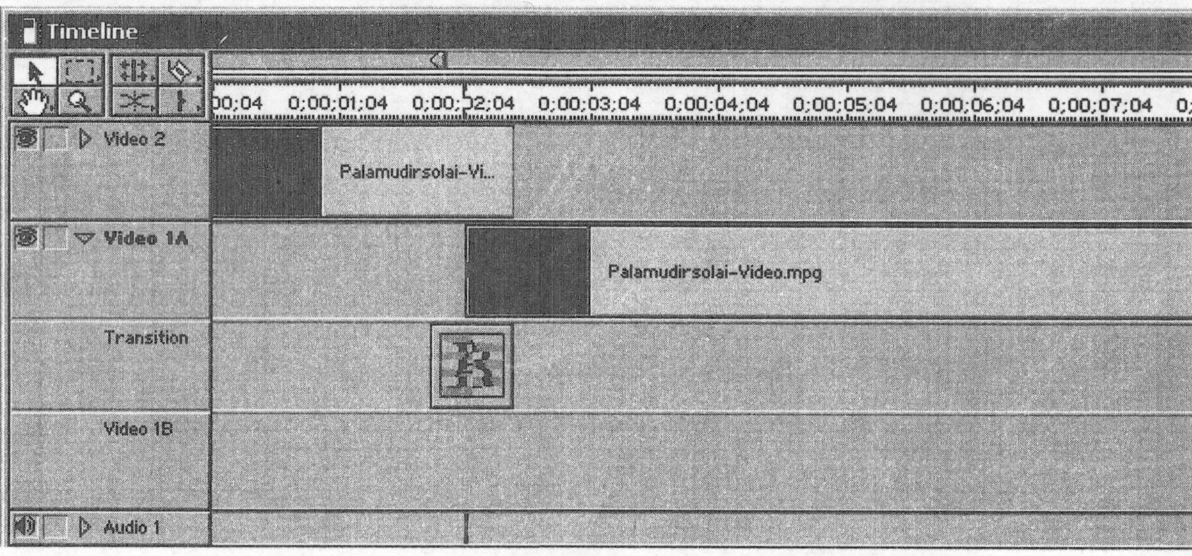

Figure 179: Transitions being applied between the videos

Talking about transitions, it is difficult to remain unimpressed by the wide-ranging transition effects provided by adobe. Almost all possible transitional effects that can be thought of have been included. Each effect, when applied over the transition track, opens out a dialog box that lets us control the sequence of mixing.

After arranging all the different clippings in the required order, the audio has to be edited. You may choose to use the audio that was recorded along with the video, decide to replace the same with music etc or you may even want to add a voice over the existing audio. All these combinations are possible within the audio tracks.

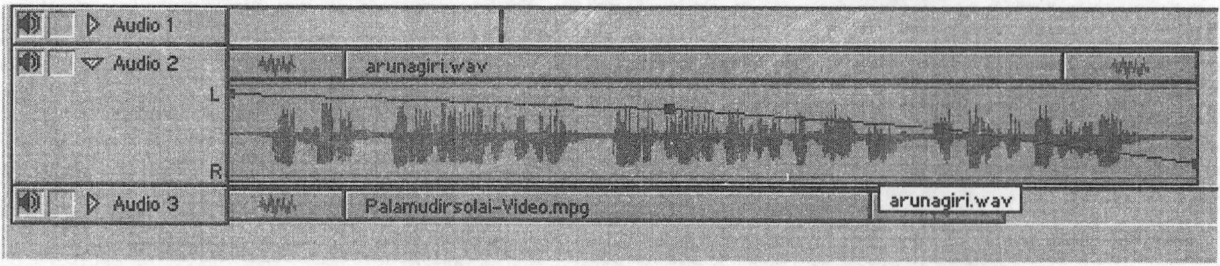

Figure 180: Audio fade-ins and fade-outs can be controlled with the rubber band tool

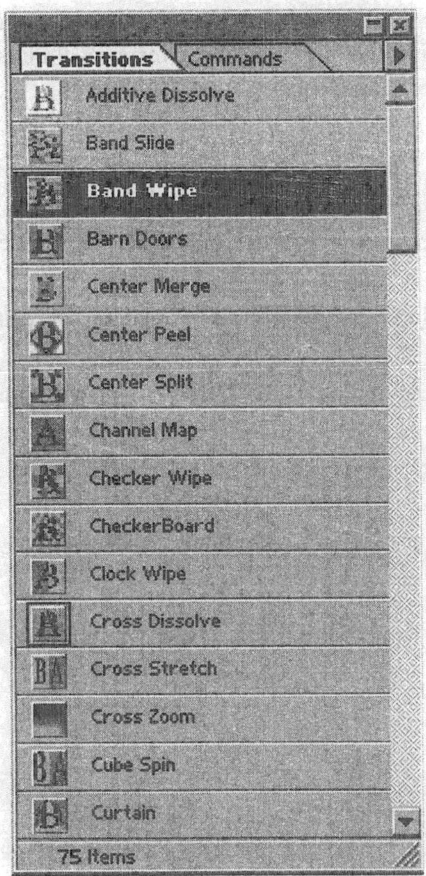

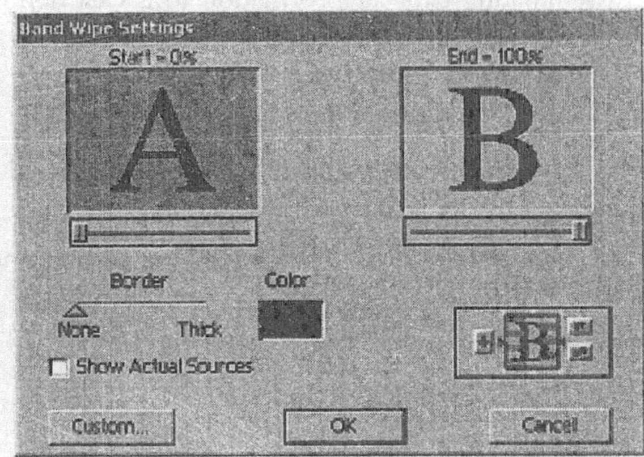

Figure 181: Transition effect options available. Each effect opens out a dialog box as shown here, which allows you to control the degree of transitions

As you expand the audio tracks (with the help of the small triangle near the wordings Audio2), you can see a red line going through the waveform. This is actually a rubber-band tool, which is most useful for providing effects like fade-in and fade-outs. Rather than providing a standard fade-in/out with gradual control of volume, this rubber band based tools provides more control over the volume of the audio clipping.

Premiere also provides a variety of audio filters that can be applied over the clipping. Just right click on the specific clip over the timeline and choose 'filters' option.

Adobe premiere, as a post-production solutions, is pretty advanced tool and there are many more operations and capabilities to be learnt. But we have to stop here since it is meant to be a preview, rather than an extensive discussion on the tool. Those who want to proceed further can take up relevant book detailing the capabilities of adobe premiere in depth.

19.9 Summary

Digital video production for multimedia projects consists of shooting the necessary sequences with relevant equipments, capturing and digitising the analog video data, video editing and post-production and finally embedding the same into the projects.

Before the shooting process one has to take care of equipments, backgrounds, what are all the camera movements to be used and appropriate lighting required. Video capture can be performed with the help of video capture cards.

Video post-production and editing consists of arranging the required clippings in the desired order and doing appropriate changes on the associated audio. It is possible to super-impose digital video over two-dimensional or three-dimensional animations, with the help of video post-production suites.

19.10 Keywords

- **Multimedia project:** A typical software project, making use of multimedia technology - with specific aim of disseminating explicit information to a well defined homogeneous or heterogeneous market segment - using various media technologies and interactivity.
- **Chroma keying:** The process of shooting videos with a blue background and replacing the same with static pictures or dynamic videos in editing room
- **Video capture / Video digitising:** The process of converting analog video signals to digital data so that computers can be used to edit the data
- **Video post production:** The process of editing and mixing videos within the computer, using relevant software tools
- **Image pan:** The process of treating the output window as a camera and making movements across the video

PART VIII

MULTIMEDIA PROJECTS

PART OVERVIEW

This part is pretty much the heart of this whole book.

So far we have been focussing on individual media elements and tools that enable different media content creation and editing. But multimedia cocktailing is all about combining different kinds of media together and delivering contents all at one go!

This has four detailed chapters - each riveting on the disparate aspects involved with multimedia project production. At the end of these chapters, you will understand what makes multimedia technology so wonderful and compelling and the challenges associated with producing the same.

We can pretty much write a whole book talking just about multimedia project production – but we will focus on all the important aspects to get a wholesome view of this topic.

Chapter 20

Project Conceptualization, Design and Development

CHAPTER OVERVIEW

This chapter focuses on the multimedia project design and development.

First, we understand what is meant by a multimedia project, followed by different stages that constitute the design and development of a typical multimedia project.

Each stage is explained in detail, followed by typical examples and discussions from real life projects. It is hoped that this important chapter will help all the students to understand and appreciate the actual project development process that happens in multimedia production houses.

20.1 Introduction

So far, we were concentrating mostly on individual elements of multimedia – like texts, audio, animations and video. We understood how to produce and edit them to specific requirements. In this chapter and subsequent chapters, we will try to assemble them as a single integrated multimedia project.

We will be discussing the different stages of multimedia project, what are all the different kinds of planning and resources required, how a project translates from vision to reality etc.

Let us begin our discussions by reviewing our understanding of multimedia projects.

20.2 Multimedia projects - definition

Multimedia project is a typical software project, making use of multimedia technology - with the specific aim of disseminating explicit information in an entertaining and compelling manner, to a well defined market segment - using various media technologies and interactivity.

Multimedia project distinguish themselves from all other types of information technology projects, in the following aspects:

- Creative and artistic capabilities become more important than the programming expertise required for the projects.
- The software suites, utilities and programming environment differs much from the conventional programming environments. The only common factor that can be sighted – in terms of software - is the operating system.
- The hardware capabilities and requirements are much higher, even during the development process.
- Conventional projects go through development, user acceptance test and production deployment. Multimedia projects also go through a similar cycle, but production deployment is often replaced by product distribution.

- ❑ Wide-ranging and heterogeneous mix of skills is required to effectively tackle different media utilized in the project.
- ❑ The market segment which multimedia addresses tends to be end-consumer market whereas conventional IT project are built for the business and enterprise markets.

20.3 Project conceptualization

Every project begins with a project concept or an idea. Multimedia is no exception.

Let us understand what it is.

A multimedia project concept is the concise definition of a project, that can be produced (or improved, if such a project already exists) and which will satisfy specific requirements of certain class of people.

Let me explain this with some examples.

- ❑ An interactive multimedia CD-ROM on places of tourist importance in India
- ❑ An interactive multimedia presentation of ABC Company and its activities
- ❑ An interactive multimedia website for an architectural firm

All these are multimedia project concepts. Each addresses the needs of different segments of people.

For example, the project on Indian tourism tries to present some useful information to all inland and foreign tourists who are interested in various tourist spots in India. The second project tries to project a proper image of ABC Company, probably to the eyes of potential investors, shareholders or offshore partners. The third one is meant for all visitors of architectural firm's website – to know their various offerings for them.

The project concept is perhaps the key decision taken, with respect to multimedia projects and enough thinking must go into it. Since multimedia is a relatively expensive affair, it is but logical to think of better options. The capabilities as well as limitations of multimedia technology should be fully understood, before adopting the same for certain requirements.

In case of multimedia presentation and websites, the decision making process lies with the corporate or business customers who should see whether there is any value addition by bringing in a new technology. For example, let us say there is an ABC software firm, which is eying on offshore projects from other countries. Now, it will make lot of sense and value addition for ABC to go for multimedia because the end consumers are IT literates and the presentation can boost the image of the company among their viewers.

But in case of multimedia CD-ROMs meant from end consumer market, the decision-making becomes much more complex. In real life scenarios, lot of discussions take place - necessarily in the form of meetings... before a decision is taken to go ahead with the project.

If such a decision making process hangs before you, ask the following questions to yourself:

- ❑ Does the topic or concept enjoy innate ability to capitalize on multimedia and interactivity?
- ❑ Do we have enough information available or is there any research required?
- ❑ Do we have enough manpower and resources to execute a project of this magnitude?
- ❑ Have we rightly identified and understood the market for which we are developing this concept?
- ❑ Has the project been developed before? If so, what is the scope for a second project?

During these discussions, it is best to involve all would-be-customers or a sample group of potential customers and do some sort of market research.

It's the proper development and understanding of the concept that stands behind every successful project – apart from skills and resources.

20.4 Project development - various stages

Once the project has been discussed and taken up for development, the arduous project development cycle starts. The following list provides an overview of various stages to be crossed:

- Data gathering
- Navigation maps structure design
- Media contents design and development
- Interface design and development
- Storyboarding
- Integration (also known as multimedia authoring) and
- Delivery

Expanding upon each of these stages, we end up with a complex diagram that details all the stages and sub-stages. We will be going through each of these stages in detail, as we go along.

At this stage, it is worthwhile to have a sneak preview or review of chapter one – to understand various types of multimedia applications; because, most of these stages are heavily influenced by the nature of application under production.

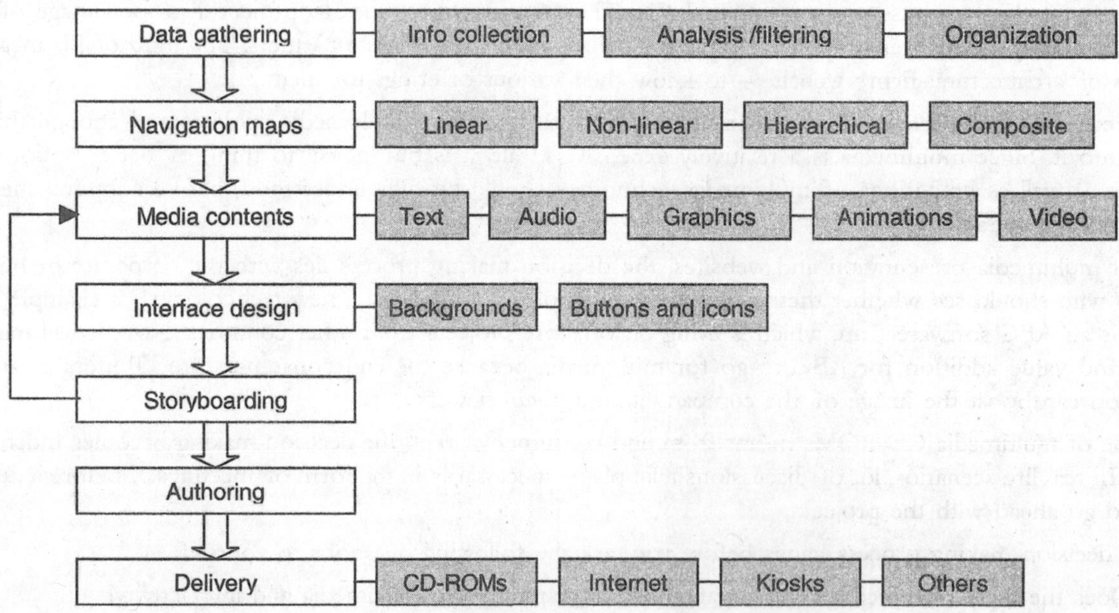

Figure 182: Project development cycle – various stages

20.5 Data gathering

Before we begin the project, all the required information with respect to the project to be developed, must be collected, analysed, filtered and organized. Irrespective of the nature of project, this phase is an absolute necessity.

In the initial stages, we tend to gather whatever we could grab – on the said topic. Then we will sit down and analyse what are all the primary sets of information that must be presented and what are all auxiliary information. The data collected must be organized in a logical sequence – and must be verified for authenticity.

Based on the above activities, we can identify the following phases, in data gathering:

- Information collection
- Analysis and filtering
- Organization
- Verification.

20.5.1 Information collection

At this stage, you start collecting all information relevant to the project at work.

The sources of information vary, depending upon the project under development.

For consumer CD-ROM projects, you have to rely on relevant books/library, magazines, video interviews and the Internet. It is better to pay some attention to the quality of information collected at this stage itself, as it will save time later. For reference multimedia titles – in particular, this exercise turns out to be rather extremely complex and some production houses prefer to outsource this task to agencies and individuals.

For corporate presentations and multimedia websites, the information has to be collected from the business establishment itself. There might be some brochures and pamphlets available, but in many cases, you have to talk to several individuals in order to collect the information you want.

For Cybervalley system's Tourist's India CD-ROM, we had to rely on the following information:

- Books, books and more books… reading the extensive range literature available on Indian tourism
- Collect all the different brochures, pamphlets and information material available from various regional tourism offices. This provided many interesting local information, not available in books
- Collect royalty free photographs and videos from, as many sources as possible – even friends and relatives were not spared!

20.5.2 Information analysis and filtering

Not all the information collected is going to be useful for the project. Data needs to be edited, modified and even deleted altogether!

Some information might be copyrighted and cannot be used as it is – it may have to be rewritten or rephrased. A good idea about the end product to be evolved will be very useful in deciding the volume and depth of information you need to have, under any given topic.

Filtering is the process of deciding which information is reliable / authentic and which is not. It is generally undertaken by the field expert - in coordination with the project manager.

The filtered data needs to be keyed into the computer for further processing.

20.5.3 Organization

The huge volume of information collected has to be organized in a logical and sequential manner. This organization forms the backbone for the navigation map structure, about which we will be talking in a short while form now.

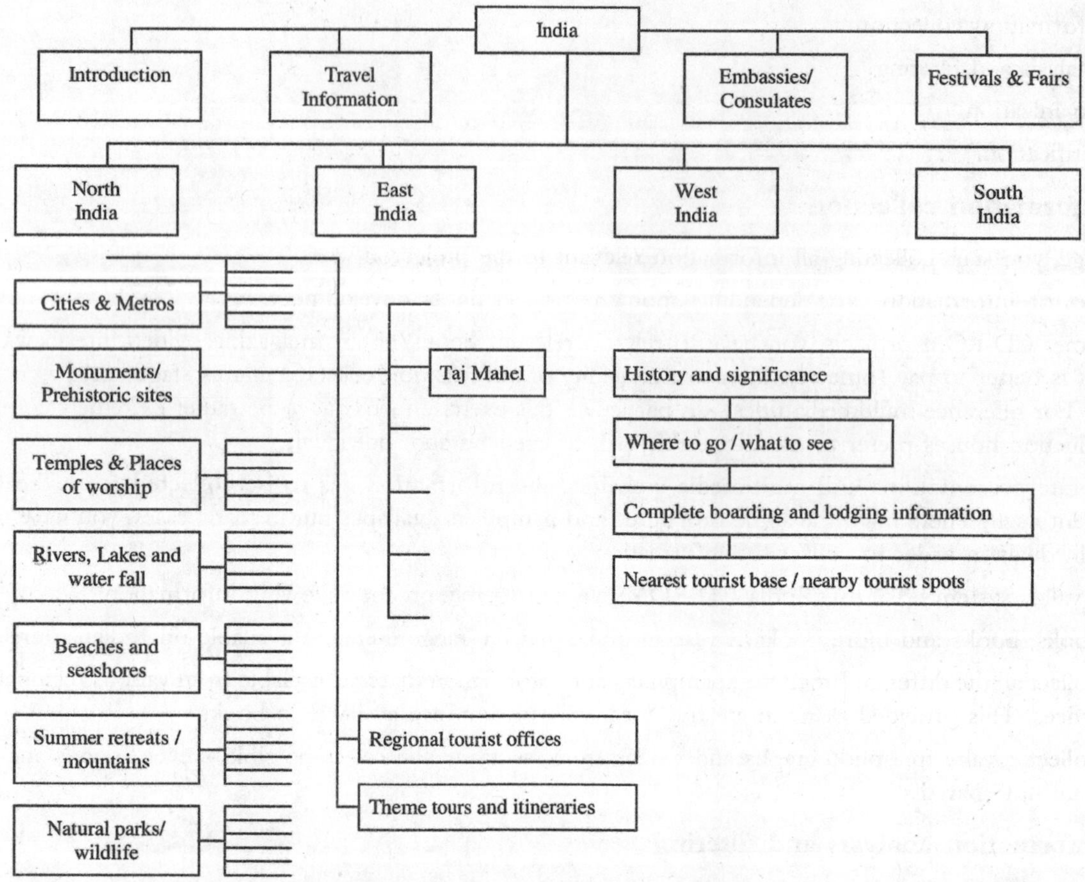

Figure 183: Organizing information for Tourist's India CD-ROM. Not even one fourth of the total information has been represented here - for sake of simplicity

The introductory topics will naturally get precedence, followed by the specialised topics.

For Tourist's India, the topics were arranged as shown in the diagram. As indicated earlier, in reference titles like this, the business could get extremely complex – as attested by this complex map. Not even one fourth of the information has been represented here – we have just depicted north India and just one tourist spot (Taj Mahal). Imagine how complex the actual data organization would have been!

20.5.4 Data verification and authentication

Once all the necessary information has been collected and organized, it needs to be verified and authenticated. It should also be checked for possible copyright violations etc.

For web-based projects, it is simple to make corrections – since web pages are always editable – but for multimedia CD-ROMs, this becomes a problem.

Once this operation is completed, we can arrange all the material into a master information booklet – which will serve as a blueprint for further development of the project.

20.6 Navigation maps

The end consumers usually browse through the multimedia project in stages. Not all information can be presented to them at any point of time. The power of multimedia is to provide different levels of information to different types of users – based on their interest and other criteria. Hence, the sequential presentation of material via a navigation map – or a system that would allow the users to navigate across the project – becomes necessary.

Navigation facilities bring great value addition to multimedia projects.

- The users can interactively select and view those areas, which they wish to explore – a very unique advantage which only multimedia projects can offer
- Even complex information structures like encyclopaedias can be presented in a simple and methodical manner – in this way
- Traversing across the project – from one portion to another – becomes a child's play. This is also very unique to multimedia projects
- Users will not be bored with the volume of information presented – since it comes in capsules or manageable bits.

Navigation maps or simply Nav-maps can adopt any one of the following structures:

- Linear structure,
- Hierarchical structure,
- Non- Linear structure and
- Composite structure

Let us start discussing each of these structures, as all of your projects must fit into one of these nav-maps.

20.6.1 Linear structure

The linear nav-map structure is the simplest among the lot.

In linear structure, the user moves through a sequential straight lined path - one portion after another. There is absolutely no independence to move freely in between the portions. At the most, the user may be given the option to move one step, forward or backward.

It is quite constrained – but a powerful navigation structure that is widely used in many applications. For example, most of the corporate presentation programs adopt a linear structure - because, they are meant for a group and not individual. Moreover, such presentations are usually accompanied by a lecture, in which case, the navigation must be obviously simple. Also, some edutainment titles meant for kindergarten children go linear - because such a small child cannot be expected to navigate through complex routes and it may even be confused, with such an option. Liner structure results in simplicity of the project – and brings down the overall budget as well!

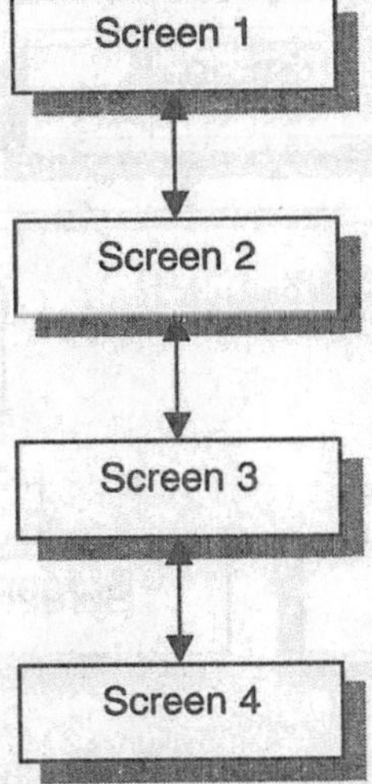

Figure 184: Linear navigation map structure

To some extent, a Microsoft PowerPoint presentation, without any hyperlinks to other slides, is also a good example for a linear nav-map structure.

Figure 185: Take particular note of the simplicity of navigation provided in this edutainment project. Previous and next buttons (simple arrows would have been better?) allow the child to traverse either way. The menu item will take them to the main screen from where it all began...

20.6.2 Hierarchical structure

Hierarchical structure provides a top down tree design - as shown in the figure. Typically, in this kind of mapping, the first main link branches out to different portions, which, in turn, branch out, further.

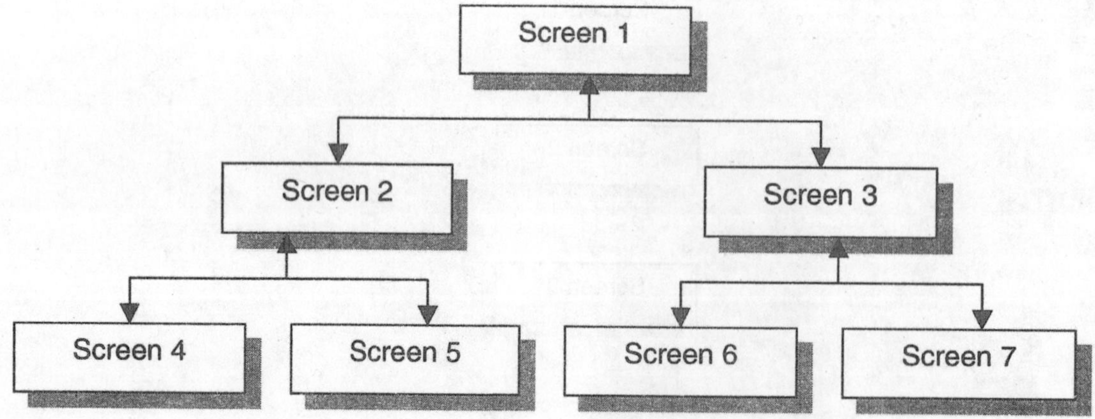

Figure 186: Hierarchical navigation map structure

Integrity is maintained by limiting the users movements within various branches. To move over from one branch to another, the users may have to come over to that portion where the branch starts and then make the next move. Many of the multimedia projects in the market today, are making use of this methodology.

Hierarchical design provides certain amount of freedom, and yet, retains certain integrity over the flow of information - by selectively restricting the pathways. With such a methodical structure in place, programming is also less complex. Professor multimedia CD-ROM, which was introduced in the first chapter - makes use of a simple hierarchical structure as its nav-map.

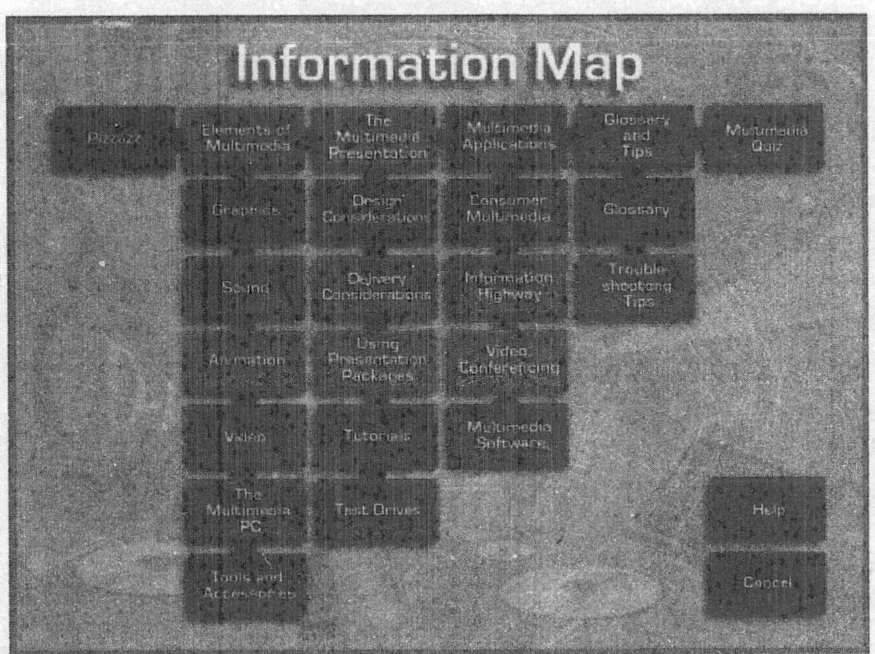

Figure 187: Professor Multimedia CD-ROM hierarchical navigation map structure

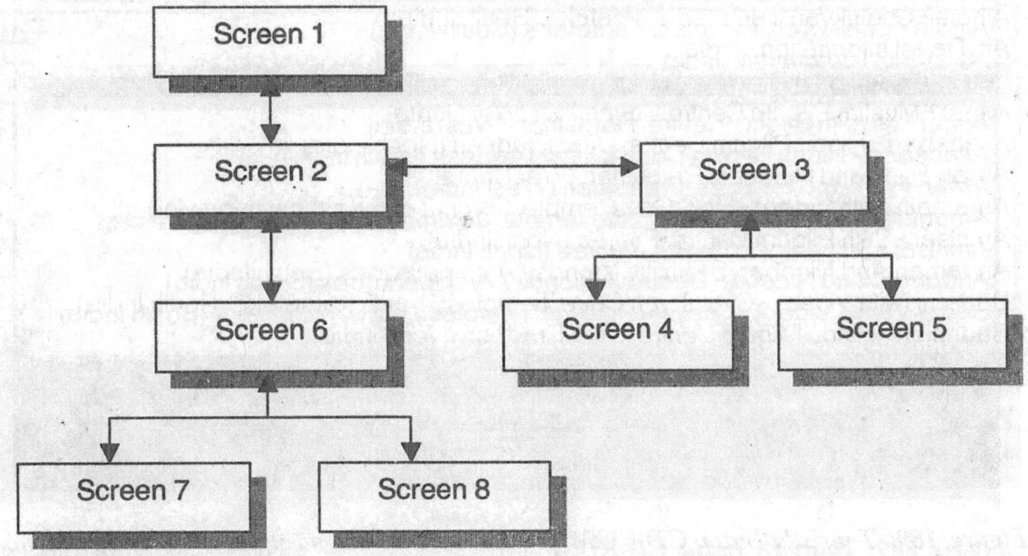

Figure 188: Non-linear navigation map structure – quite complex to handle

20.6.3 Non-linear structure

Non-linear structure is not bound by any restrictions and the users can freely navigate through any portion of the project - at their discretion. Navigation from literally any portion of the project - to any other portion, is very much possible, apart from the normal forward and backward options.

The underlying project that's adopting this type of navigation structure should be so designed that each and every portion of the project are not dependent upon each other and every single portion provides certain quantum of information -pertaining to the project.

The biggest advantage of non-linear structure is that it gives complete freedom to the end user – who can navigate freely across different portions of the screen.

As a rule, all projects that make use of non-linear nav-map structure provide a 'search engine' instead of the usual map structure for navigation. Or in other words, any multimedia projects that provides a search engine option to navigate across different portions of the project is most likely to adopt a non-linear structure.

Programming (or authoring) projects with non-linear structure is not simple and may demand proper strategy, knowledge and experience.

Having got your minds convinced with linear and hierarchical structures, there might be some difficulty in understanding what sort of projects adopts non-linear structure. If this question has already come up in your mind, then the next section is going to be most interesting.

20.6.4 Feature: How we provided a navigation structure for Tourist's India CD-ROM?

I thought it would be worthwhile to discuss the problems we faced while programming the navigation structure for Tourist's India CD-ROM.

The CD-ROM was to feature hundreds of tourist places across India – spanning four regions: north, south, east and west. Users can reach any given spot by one of these routes:

- They may know the name of the place already and wish to reach it, straight away (Example: Most people know Taj Mahal as a famous monument and try to search for it)

Figure 189: Tourist's India CD-ROM provides complete navigational independence via its search engine

- They may go through the regions and states, browse for specific categories of places and then reach the same (Example: North India → States → Monuments → Taj Mahal)
- They may look at some of the theme tours and itineraries page and reach the place (Example: North India → Theme tours → Golden triangle → Taj Mahal)
- They might be browsing some other place in the region, see that Taj Mahal is nearby, and hence try to reach it. (Example: North India → Cities → Delhi → Nearby tourist spots → Agra → Taj Mahal)

Thus, we understood that we had to provide room for multiple ways of accessing the same information!

And to add to this complexity, we had to provide room for a back button by which the user can go back by a few screens. With a non-linear structure, this is also complex because you should not only know the previous page – but should also understand the navigation route taken by the user! This ultimately resulted in the usage of a database to remember all the references to different bits of information.

20.6.5 Composite or compound structure

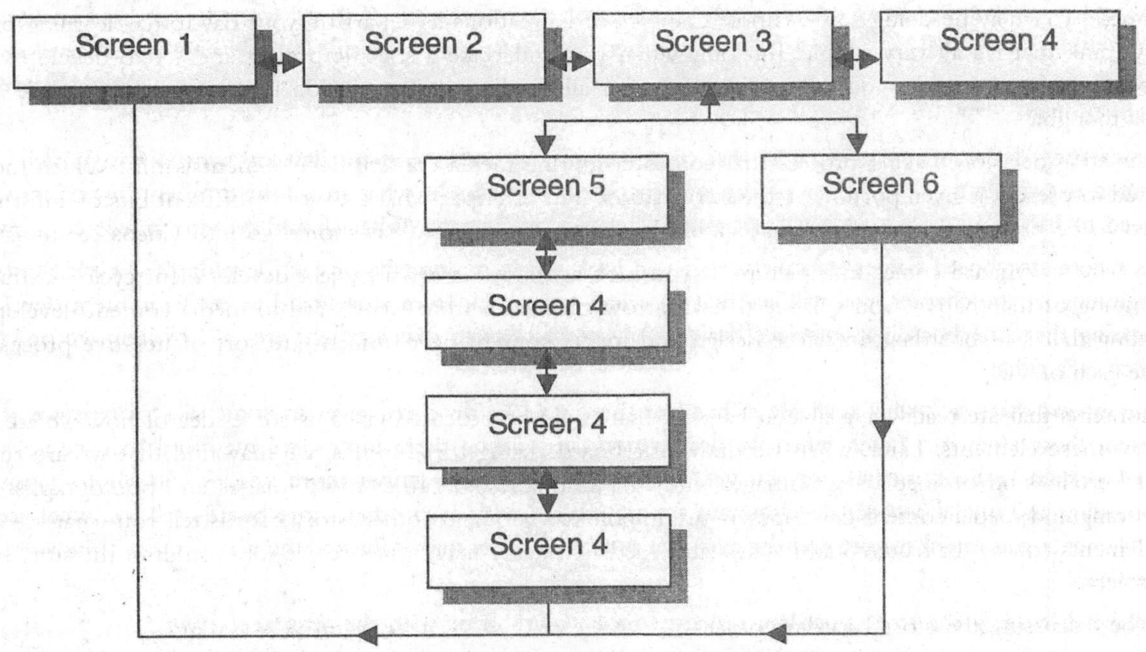

Figure 190: Composite navigation map structure

Composite structure is a combination of any of the three structures discussed above. The usual mix is linear and non-linear structures resulting in a nav-map that allows the users to navigate freely -but for certain portions, wherein, the movements need to be linear.

Composite structure enjoys the benefits of more than one structure – but programming is complex.

20.7 Developing media contents

Once we have the contents well organized and navigation structure ready, we are all set to develop various multimedia elements required for the project. This includes elements of audio, video, graphics and animations. The following table provides a summary of these elements to be produced, in a typical project.

Table 30: Various media elements to be produced for a multimedia

Media elements	Typical contents
Audio	Background voice over, music, button click sounds & project specific contents
Video	Mostly specific to given projects
Animations	Button movements, titling & project specific contents
Graphics	Backgrounds, Interfaces, Navigation menus, buttons etc.
Text	Project specific contents

Throughout this book, we have been discussing how to produce and edit various kinds of media elements for different kinds of applications. It is easy to develop media without any purpose, but when the requirements become specific, you'll realize that the task is not that simple.

For example, you may be doing some sample graphics or animations as a part of your day-to-day learning process and may think that it's all very simple! But only when you undertake a specific project and try to develop various media contents for the same – do you realize that, after all, media content creation is at least not as simple as you originally thought.

One interesting decision making process that comes up during media content development is this: Which media is best suited to present a given portion of the information? For example, what are all the different bits of information that need to be presented, as audio? What should be featured as text? What should go into videos & animations?

This is where storyboard comes into picture. If you look at the multimedia project development cycle illustrated in the beginning of the chapter, you will see that an arrow goes back from storyboard to media content development – indicating that storyboarding, interface design and media content development are sort of iterative process that influence each other.

Media contents that are readily available at hand or that could be procured gives us some idea of how we are going to present these elements. Later, when we draw storyboards using these inputs, we may find that we are running short of certain kind of media – say images, and may find ways to gather more images and photographs. Thus, storyboarding and media content development are interlinked with each other: story boards tell you what are all the media elements you might require and the available media contents may influence the way you draft the story boards for a project.

We will be discussing the story boarding process, once we are done with the interface design.

20.8 Designing interfaces

The interface is the screen over which any multimedia project is presented. Interface consists of graphics, animations and background music – if any. In short, interface is the front-end of the project. Though it may sound fairly simple, proper interface design sometimes becomes the most complex part of the project to handle!

Interfaces should be simple as well as attractive: after all, the user is going to be looking at the interfaces all the time – irrespective of what portion of the project he is browsing through.

The primary inspiration behind an interface design should be to produce an ambience and an atmosphere that is most suited for the title. In order to really appreciate the role of interfaces, take a look at any of the multimedia games in the market: Look at the buttons, menus and the background music that flows out of the speakers – you'll understand what I mean.

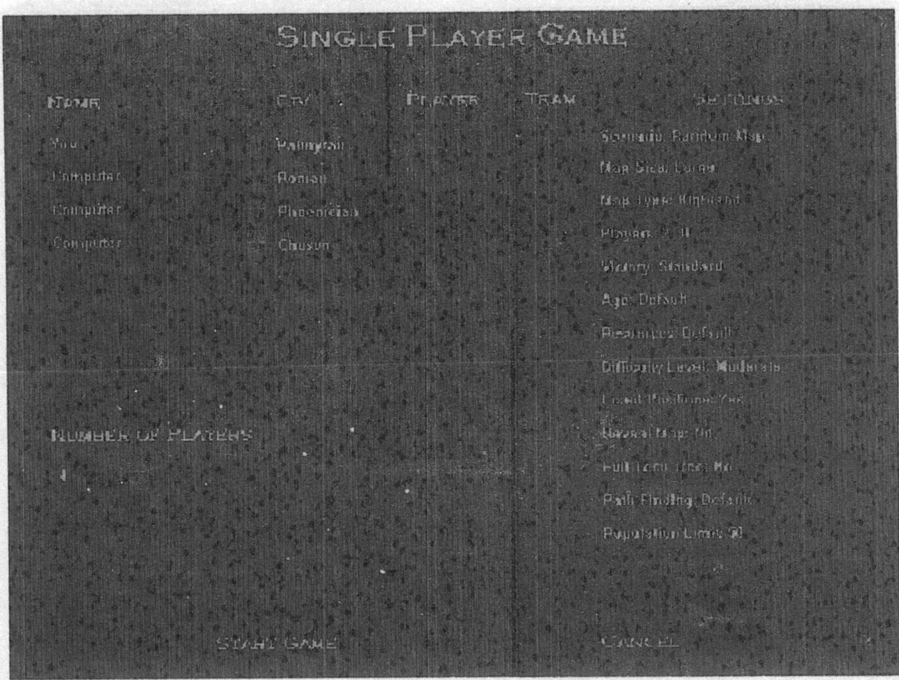

Figure 191: Multimedia gaming studios are particularly good at creating the ambience required for the game, by means of appropriate music, backgrounds and buttons. This interface is from Age of Empires from Microsoft.

Interfaces include the following items:

- ❑ Backgrounds (graphics / animations)
- ❑ Buttons and menus (graphics / animations)
- ❑ Background music (audio – wav/midi)

20.8.1 Backgrounds

Backgrounds provide a graphical platform or a backdrop, over which the whole project is presented. It is the plate that holds different media items that are being served to the user at different points of time. Backgrounds, along with buttons and menus – are visible the user throughout the project proceedings.

Backgrounds are mostly still images. A standard image may be used throughout the project or different backgrounds can be used for different portions of the project. It is not advisable to use animations as backgrounds – unless you have designed a very ingenious way of presenting it nicely.

Strategies for designing good background graphics were discussed in the earlier chapter or multimedia graphics, under the title 'Interface design graphics'. Here, we will just touch upon a few tips & techniques for designing good backgrounds.

- ❑ Let the title – and not the capabilities of the graphic designer at work - dictate the complexity of the background
- ❑ Children titles should necessarily have simple yet rich backgrounds.
- ❑ Multimedia kiosks and touch screen applications should have relatively simple backgrounds
- ❑ It is not necessary to have backgrounds at all stages. Look at the example provided from Tourist's India CD-ROM.

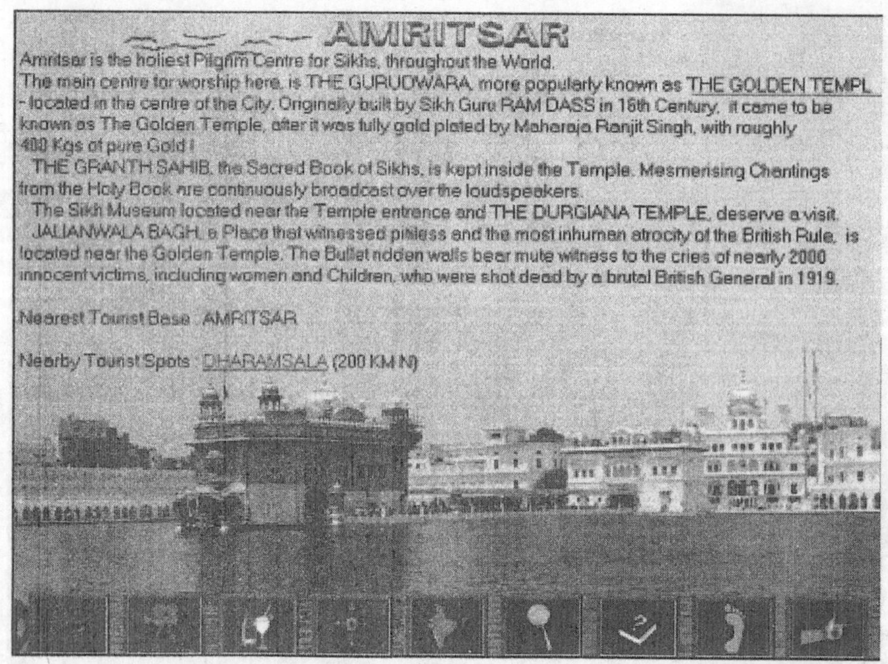

Figure 192: Backgrounds are not compulsory for multimedia projects – but buttons and menus are! This screen shot is from Tourist's India CD-ROM. The content itself provides a background over which information is presented.

20.8.2 Buttons and Icons

Buttons and icons help the user to navigate within the project.

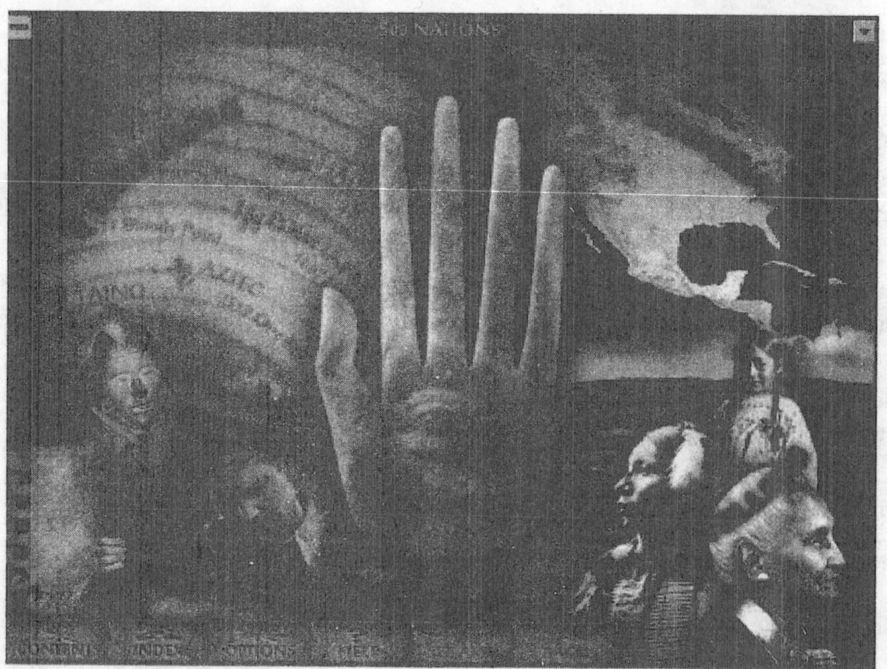

Figure 193: Look at the buttons and a rich graphical interface provided to Microsoft 500 Nations CD-ROM

Instead of providing the usual windows environment interfaces like grey menu bars and OK / Cancel buttons, most multimedia designers resort to fancy buttons and icons, as seen in many examples - throughout this Book.

Buttons can be of plain colour; they can be simple rectangles / letters or graphics with three-dimensional effects. They may 'react' to a mouse over event or mouse click event – by glowing or by moving 'in' and 'out', with the help of shading effects.

Points to be kept in mind, while designing buttons are as follows:

- Button texts should be very clear and legible. Complex textures and font designs should be avoided
- Button design should reflect the mood and ambience of the title. Look at the examples provided
- Small animations can be added over the buttons for mouse over events
- Buttons should integrate well with the background graphics – in terms of theme and colour.

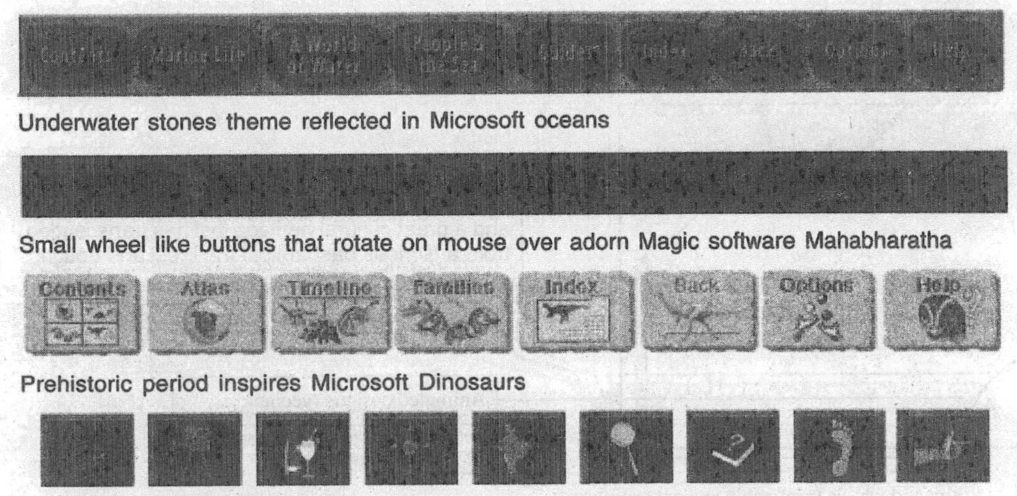

Underwater stones theme reflected in Microsoft oceans

Small wheel like buttons that rotate on mouse over adorn Magic software Mahabharatha

Prehistoric period inspires Microsoft Dinosaurs

Simplicity and ease of use were kept in mind for Tourist's India buttons

Figure 194: Examples of buttons from four different CD-ROMs

20.8.3 Background music

It will be good to have a theme music running in the background, throughout the proceedings of a multimedia project. This music can stop when the user starts exploring something or content related audio starts playing.

Backgrounds add lot more ambience and atmosphere to the titles and should be given a serious thought.

Since backgrounds must play on and on, it is not a bad idea to adopt a lengthy midi piece as the background. On the other hand, the limitations of midi over digital audio may force you to take up the latter, in spite of CPU and memory requirements.

20.9 Storyboarding

Media contents are ready. We have organised them with the help of a navigation map. Backgrounds, music, buttons and menus have also been designed.

Now comes the most important part of the project: presentation. How are you going to present the contents you have gathered? Navigation map and contents organisation help us to decide what should be presented first, and what should go next etc. But when the question becomes 'how' the contents should be presented, we need to resort back to the storyboarding technique, which we discussed earlier in multimedia animations.

Though the technique is very much the same, multimedia project storyboards differ significantly from animation storyboards. Whereas project storyboards concentrate on how different media contents blend together in every screen, the latter, as you may remember, record the details objects, characters and textures featured in the animation.

The following details must be discussed and finalized for each screen (or scene):

- Nature of background music
- Background graphics
- How menu and buttons should be featured
- Content graphics
- Content animations and videos – if any
- Hyperlinks
- Content audio
- Voiceover – if any

Let us look at a typical storyboard and you will understand what I mean.

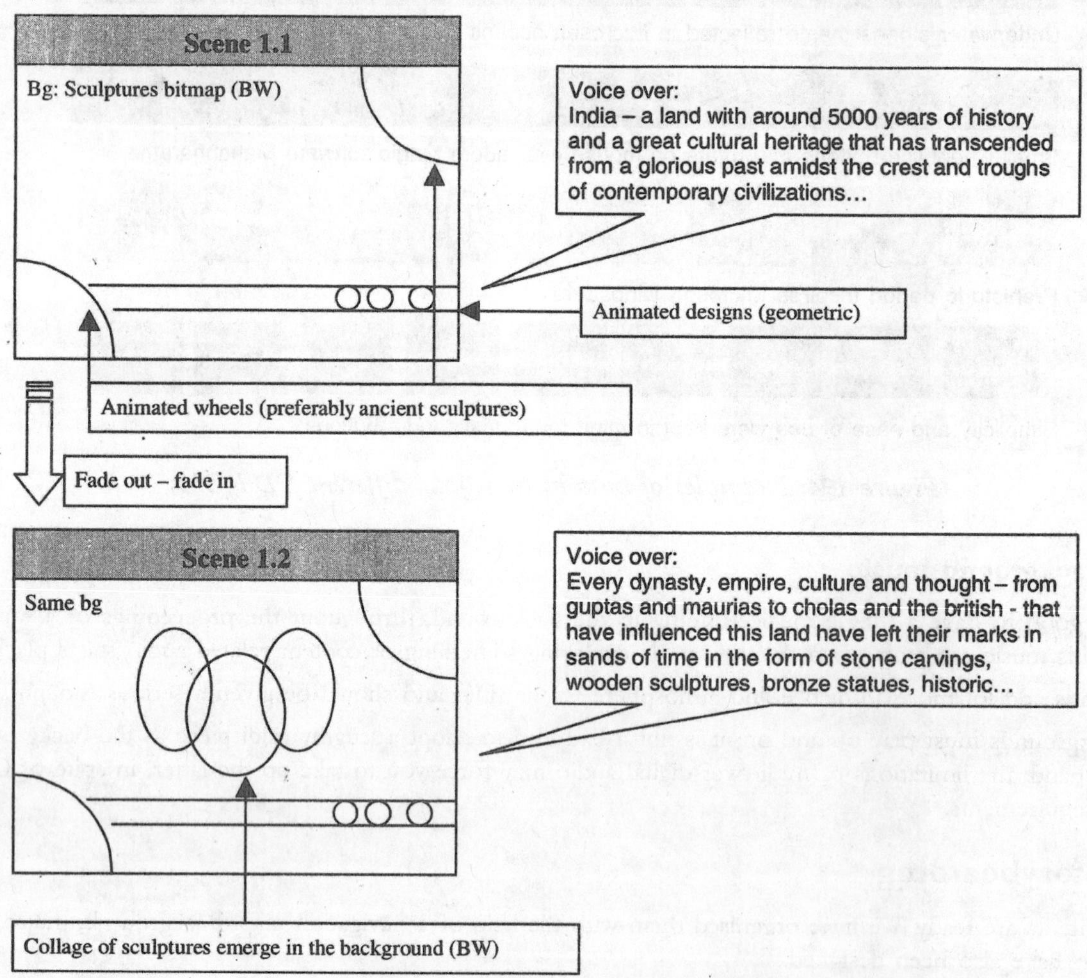

Figure 195: A sample storyboard from a multimedia presentation done at cybervalley systems

For the sake of simple discussions, I have just provided two shots from the storyboard. There are quite a number of things you should note, from this storyboard.

First, notice that the entire presentation has been arranged in the form of sequences and shots – 1.1, 1.2 etc. The first digit stands for a logical sequence and the second number represents the individual shot. To the eyes of the viewer, the entire movie will be a single sequence. The background voice over will be of immense use, in deciding which shot should go first, which should go next etc.

Secondly, take note of the skeletal animation details provided. This gives you some idea about the kind of animations that need to be developed for the project. Take note of the geometric animations that have been added – purely to enhance the visual effects.

The details of transition from one sequence to another have also been recorded. Sometimes this could be mouse click, but in this case, it is an automatic fade-out/fade-in transition.

Now, look at how this storyboard has been turned into a reality with the help of multimedia software.

Figure 196: Compare these screen shots with the storyboards we prepared earlier and you will understand how ideas translate to reality

As you look at more and more real life multimedia projects, you will begin to appreciate the art of developing compelling storyboard. I have termed it as an art, rather than a technique or a tool – because storyboarding requires enormous imagination and creativity to visualize the blending of different media in right proportions.

Good storyboards can tell you how the project is going to look like – after production. Lot of time can be saved in revisions, if sufficient time is spent in creating good storyboards...but, alas! Nearly half of multimedia projects produced do not do complete this exercise properly – resulting in wastage of time and resources at a later stage.

20.10 Multimedia programming (authoring)

Multimedia authoring is the process of making use of software tools, to assemble the media contents and deliver them as a single integrated project. We are going to discuss this topic in the next chapter – in detail.

20.11 Delivery

The media, in which the project is going to be delivered, also forms a part of project design. In most cases, the choice is limited to CD-ROMs - because of the sheer volume of the project material. However, if the project is based on Flash and is without huge videos, it is possible to host the same on the web.

If the project is going to be distributed as CD-ROMs, due considerations must be given to the file sizes, compression schemes to be adopted etc. Details of the CD replication have been included in the chapter on CD-ROMs.

20.12 Summary

Multimedia projects require creativity, artistic as well as programming skills. The project needs to be conceptualised first. Then it has to go through various stages of development that includes data gathering, navigation maps structure design, media contents design and development interface design and development, storyboarding authoring and delivery.

Data gathering includes information collection, analysis, filtering and organizing. Navigation maps represent organization of data and could follow linear, non-linear, hierarchical and composite structure. Interface design includes background design, buttons, menus and background music. Storyboarding is the process of putting ideas in paper, which will help us to organise and present media contents.

Multimedia project could be delivered as a CD-ROM or via the web.

20.13 Keywords

- **Multimedia project:** A typical software project, making use of multimedia technology - with specific aim of disseminating explicit information to a well defined homogeneous or heterogeneous market segment - using various media technologies and interactivity.
- **Navigation Maps or Nav-maps:** A map containing all possible navigation paths of the project.

Chapter 21

Multimedia Authoring

CHAPTER OVERVIEW

Multimedia authoring is the software capability to stitch different media elements together.

Authoring can be achieved with the help of dedicated tools or you can do your own programming to assemble different media elements together. This chapter details both the approaches, highlighting the pros and cons of each approach.

In depth discussions on how to select the right tool for the given project - proceeds to give a very good coverage of all of the fundamental characteristics that can be expected in a typical authoring system. The chapter also contains a curtain raiser for some of the leading authoring tools, available in the multimedia market today.

21.1 Introduction

Multimedia authoring comes at the tail end of the project, after all the media contents have been produced and storyboard has been developed. It is important that you understand various stages of project management cycle at this juncture. Hence, please ensure that you have gone through the earlier chapter on multimedia project design and development first – before exploring this topic on authoring.

Like media development, authoring is also accomplished with the help of various software tools available in the market. These tools adopt different strategies for assembling media contents – we will be looking at these different strategies as we go along.

All alterations, modifications, revisions, reconsiderations and redesigning - ends with this phase of the project. So, maximum attention has to be bestowed on every stage of multimedia authoring

Let us begin our discussions, by getting to know what exactly do we mean by multimedia authoring.

21.2 Multimedia authoring - definition

Multimedia authoring can be defined as the process of assembling or integrating different types of media contents like text, audio, animations and video - as a single stream of information – with the help of various software tools available in the market. The output of authoring process is mostly a multimedia software program that can be executed on any client machine with required libraries installed.

21.3 Multimedia programming versus Multimedia authoring

It is worthwhile to spend some time understanding the difference between multimedia programming and multimedia authoring. Though these terms are used interchangeably in many contexts, I think there are significant differences between the two – that sets them apart.

Multimedia programming refers to the process of writing codes - using one or more programming environments, languages and/or tools - that will handle multimedia contents and present them in an interactive manner to the end user.

Example: A multimedia CD-ROM done exclusively using languages like C++, C# or Java can be termed as a multimedia programming project.

On the other hand, multimedia authoring refers to the process of compiling multimedia projects using specialized software meant for handling various kinds of multimedia and presenting the same as a single integrated project.

Example: A multimedia presentation done with Macromedia Flash authoring environment.

The confusion between the two arises mainly because of one reason: Most authoring environments support some kind of programming using one or more scripting languages! For example, Macromedia Director comes bundled with a scripting tool called lingo. Similarly, Macromedia Flash supports Action script. But you should always remember that these are scripting tools meant for adding some sort of logic into the package and are not full fledged programming languages like Java and C#.

21.3.1 When to go for multimedia programming?

For all normal applications, it is best to make use of one of the multimedia authoring environments. They provide great flexibility, adoptability and give you the ability to change the flow of contents at any point of time. It is easy to compile and distribute multimedia data with the help of authoring tools.

On the other hand, multimedia-programming languages require tremendous initial effort and exposure to system level APIs. Of course, the degree of flexibility is great – you can literally do whatever you want, but this comes at the cost of extra knowledge and effort.

In spite of these arguments, multimedia programming is still preferred in certain occasions – particularly when you want to have first hand control over system level resources. For example, most multimedia games are developed using programming and many adopt their own rendering engine for better performance.

21.4 Authoring methodologies

Every authoring tool, package, environment or platform, makes use of some fundamental methodology, for assembling different media elements together. Some even go one step above the rest and offer flexibility to switch over from one methodology to another - whenever the need arises.

Based on the methodology they adopt, authoring tools can be classified as:

- ❑ Frame or page based authoring tools
- ❑ Time based authoring tools and
- ❑ Icon based authoring tools.

21.4.1 Frame or page based tools

Page based tools visualise every multimedia project as a sequence of *frames* or *pages* – which contain media elements embedded in them. And a whole multimedia project is nothing but a collection of pages or frames – often called as a *multimedia book*!

Every page of the book may contain many media elements - sounds, videos and animations. As the user starts viewing the project, the pages present themselves – one after another, in sequence. One page may have a hyperlink to another page that comes at a much later stage – and by clicking on the same the user might have effectively skipped several pages in between.

Like a physical book, these multimedia books can also be organized into different chapters. The navigation map may contain links to different pages or chapters of the book.

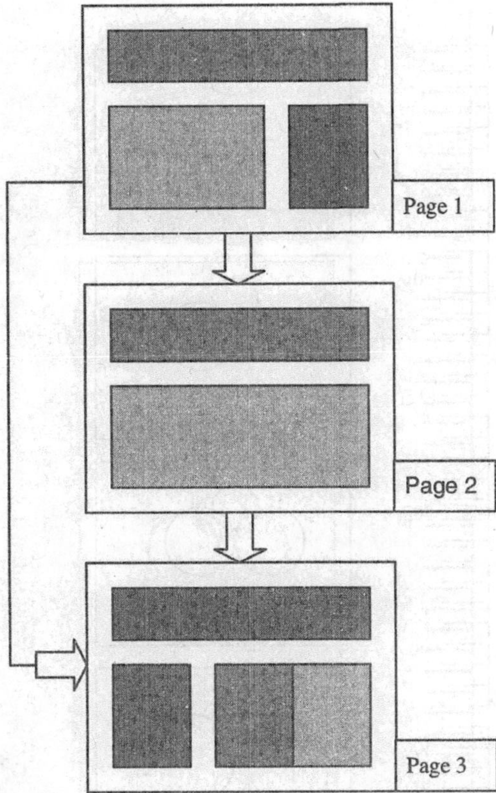

Figure 197: Page based multimedia authoring methodology

This authoring methodology is best suited for those projects, whose contents can be conceived as a sequence of pages or frames.

Asymetrix Multimedia tool book is a commercial authoring tool that makes use of this methodology. Microsoft PowerPoint, though not a full-fledged multimedia authoring environment – is another very good example for page based authoring tool.

21.4.2 Time based tools

Time based authoring tools allow the designer to arrange various media elements and events of the multimedia project - along a well-defined time line. By time line, we simply mean the passage of time – very similar to the timelines we saw earlier in our discussions on video post-production concepts. As the time advances from zero seconds (which will be the starting point of the project) - the events begin to occur, one after another.

The events may include media files playback as well as transition from one portion of the project to another. The speed, at which these transitions occur, can also be accurately controlled. These tools take the help of a software timer - which is a typical clock - that starts at the beginning of the project and graduates - minute after minute. The events happen, one after another - following this timer.

This type of authoring methodology can be very well adopted for those projects, wherein the information flow can be directed - from beginning to end - much like the movies. Macromedia's Director and Flash are excellent examples for time based authoring tools.

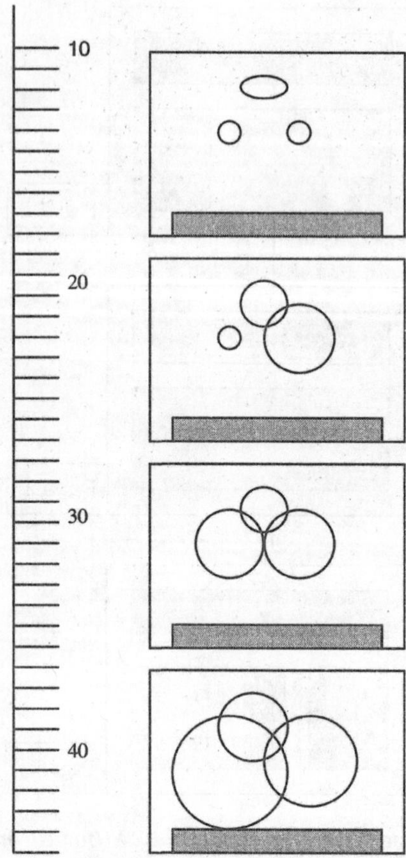

Figure 198: Time based multimedia authoring methodology

21.4.3 Icon based authoring tools

These tools allow each and every event and elements belonging to a particular multimedia project, to be arranged sequentially in the form of icons. These icons are arranged as per the basic navigation map structure adopted - and are driven from one phase to other, by means of events.

Icon based tools can effectively handle even complicated flow of information, with conditional loops. The projects can be quickly created and delivered. One of the leading products in this category is Macromedia's Author ware.

21.5 Characteristics of authoring tools

Apart from the methodology they adopt for integrating media contents, authoring tools also distinguish themselves from each other by means of other features. These include:

- ❑ Ability to handle different kinds of media
- ❑ Bundled multimedia library
- ❑ Mapping features
- ❑ Programming features and environment
- ❑ Segmentation functionality
- ❑ Compilation capability and runtime players
- ❑ Media embedding capabilities

To locate the right tool for a given project, we need to look at all these different features as well. Let us briefly discuss them.

21.5.1 Ability to handle different types of media

Most authoring environments and packages exhibit capabilities to edit and transform different kinds of media they support. For example, Macromedia Flash comes bundled with its own sound editor and manipulation utilities, which is satisfactory for most projects. This eliminates the need for buying another dedicated software to edit sound data. Another advantage of using these bundled utilities is that they enjoy better coherence and understanding with the main authoring environment and can eliminate duplication of work. Turning back to the same example of Macromedia Flash, sound embedded into Flash projects can automatically be transformed to mp3 files during compilation. This eliminates the need for buying dedicated mp3 encoders etc.

Certain other authoring tools come with external media editors bundled with them. These are separate editing programs, but are bundled with the authoring environment as a package. These programs may not have all the capabilities of a dedicated media-editing environment, but their basic features can still be put to best use.

While evaluating the media editors and the ability of the tool to handle different media, keep the following points in mind:

- ❑ How many different types of media editors are bundled with the tool? Most tools come with sound editors; so look at the other media – how about MIDI editing? Any video / animation editing capabilities are available?
- ❑ How effective is the media editor(s) – when compared to professional editors in the market?
- ❑ Does the authoring tool come packaged with some of the professional media editors, instead of their own editors?

21.5.2 Bundled multimedia library

Almost all authoring tools - contain lot of royalty free media clippings. These clippings are particularly useful for many occasions and are certainly value additions to the package. As a bundle, they are known by a common term: multimedia libraries.

Multimedia libraries usually contain:

- ❑ Digital audio clippings under different themes
- ❑ Photo libraries – arranged under various topics
- ❑ Clip arts
- ❑ Animations
- ❑ Videos

The combination and quantity of clippings offered in each category may vary from vendor to vendor. The more the clippings are the better.

21.5.3 Mapping features

As discussed earlier, various media contents have to be arranged as per the navigation map structure adopted, and the storyboard has to be developed.

Some authoring environments provide features to develop navigation maps and structuring of contents with ease. Instead of starting this exercise from the scratch on a paper, these tools provide some interface - with the help of which - a flow chart or a storyboard can be easily developed.

This feature is nothing short of a boon, because the navigation structure so developed can then be used for the project directly. It saves time, results in ease of work and permits revisions and additions without much taboo. Do look out for this feature with the eyes of an eagle!

21.5.4 Programming features and environment

Earlier in this chapter, we discussed the differences between multimedia programming and authoring. We also saw that some of the authoring environments support scripting languages. The nature and capabilities of this scripting or programming environment is also a feature to be considered for evaluating various multimedia-authoring tools. As the scope and capabilities of the scripting language increases, it invariably becomes complex. Also, there is a learning curve associated with their usage. This is particularly a challenge, because multimedia programmers often have difficulty learning conventional programming languages. They are usually good at making the best use of ready-made tools and features – rather than bothering about classes, instances and inheritance!

While evaluating the scripting environments, keep the following questions in your mind:

- ❑ How easy is the scripting language to use?
- ❑ Is it capable of performing low level system calls and APIs?
- ❑ How difficult it is to teach this language to a new bee?
- ❑ Is the scripting language available outside the authoring environment?
- ❑ Is it possible to do authoring without this scripting language?

The following table lists all the scripting languages supported by different authoring environments:

Table 31: Scripting languages supported by different authoring environments

Tool	Script
Macromedia Director	Lingo
Macromedia Flash	Action script
Asymetrix Tool book	Open script

21.5.5 Segmentation functionality

No multimedia project can be completed in one go - because of the sheer volume of work involved and the complexity associated with authoring.

In actual multimedia production environments, the projects progress - from one stage to another - in a sequential manner. These individual groups of frames or elements of a project are called *segments* of a project. The number of segments in a project is determined by the size of the project and the professionals involved in authoring.

Now, these different segments have to be compiled and tested individually, and then, they have to be integrated as one seamless stream of content. Also, the segments that work well as individual sequences should be consistent in their behaviour - when integrated with other segments.

In the authoring environments, these segments can be understood as sub-projects, which are ultimately integrated to deliver the bigger project. How efficient the tool is, in supporting this kind of segmentation and integration is the point to be considered.

21.5.6 Compilation features and runtime players

Once the project is done, it has to be compiled and delivered. Compilation is the process of generating machine specific codes and compressing the program. Authoring environments compile multimedia projects in three formats:

- ❑ As a stand-alone executable program
- ❑ As an executable program with dependent libraries
- ❑ As proprietary compilations with run time player programs

A stand-alone executable is the best among the three. It is very easy to distribute and maintain. It does not need dedicated installation programs. Also, it can be distributed on the net as a single download. A good example for such a program is Macromedia Flash whose compilation results in a single .exe file.

The second choice is not as good as the first. These tools also compile the project as an .exe file – but these executables require certain libraries to be present on the client machine. To make things more complicated, windows requires that some of these libraries be registered under windows registry so that they are available to the operating system as and when required. An installation program is necessarily required for installing and registering the dynamic link libraries (dlls). All these complexities can be tolerated, if the authoring tool itself provides features for creating an installation program; otherwise, we need to buy external installation programs like Install shield – which is going to cost money.

The third choice is a stand alone run time player, which actually plays the compiled project. These players come with the authoring software and are freely distributable. The compiled project will be in a proprietary file format and only the run-time player can understand and comprehend this data. This is preferable for corporate presentations etc. and not for large-scale consumer level distributions.

21.5.7 Media embedding feature

Multimedia projects make use of many audio, video, animations and graphic files. These content files can be bundled into the project by two ways: Linking and embedding.

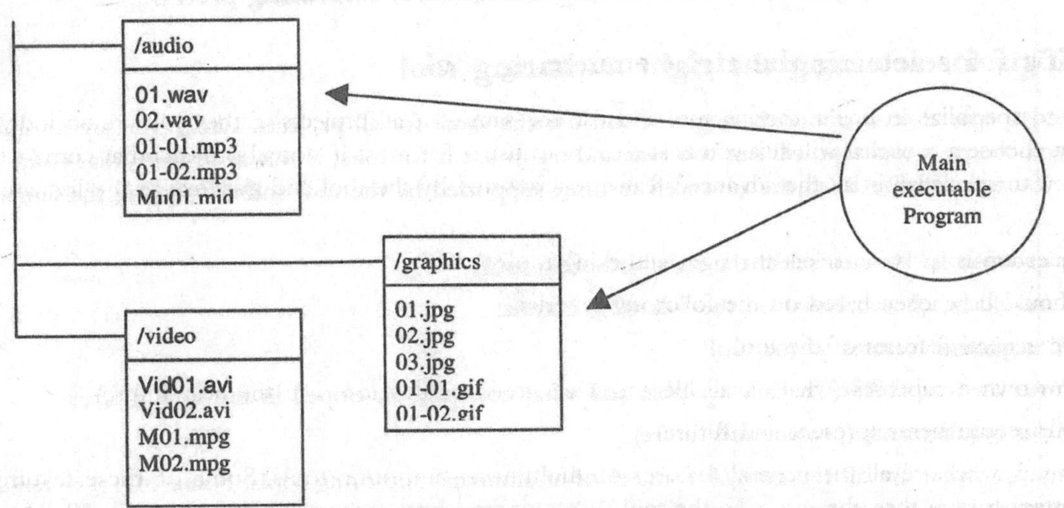

Figure 199: Schematic representation of linking process

Linking is the process of keeping the media contents as separate files in independent directories and calling them as and when required. In many projects, you can see directories like audio, video, graphics etc that contain independent media files. The problem with linking is that the end user will be able to see all these different media elements and start using them for their own purposes. If you don't mind this, then it's OK but if you want to safeguard the copyright of your media elements, linking is not a preferred choice.

Embedding is the process of compressing all the different media files and bundling it either with the exe or keeping it as an asset file and distributing it with the project. Media files embedded into the project are not visible to the end user as independent files – and it is not possible to decompress and decipher them. Windows provides cab files, which are files of similar nature. Embedding provide watertight security over the media content files.

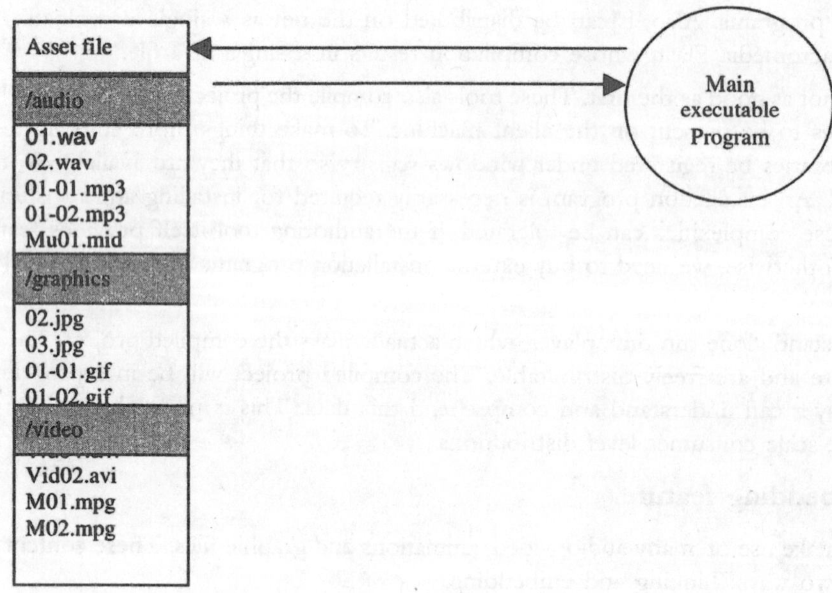

Figure 200: Schematic representation of embedding process

21.6 Tips for selecting the right authoring tool

It is better to specialize in one authoring tool and use the same for all projects. Either you are an individual or a consultancy, choose a tool that will suit you best and try to use it for most if not all projects that come to you. This will help you to specialize in all the advanced features supported by the tool and also realize the limitations of the tool.

Now the question is: How to select the right authoring tool?

The tool should be chosen based on the following criteria:

- ❑ The general features of the tool
- ❑ Your own capabilities (what's available and what could be developed in the near future)
- ❑ Your requirements (present and future)

We already saw what are all the general features of multimedia authoring tools. Some of these features may be more important to you than the rest – so the tool that supports those features must be given precedence over the rest. For example, you may think that you can collect all the different media elements required for the project by other means – hence the bundled media library may become less important or less useful. On the other hand, your specific project may require some sort of device handling capabilities which are available only in certain advanced scripting tools – in this case, scripting becomes very important feature to be considered and so on.

Whatever may be the features available with the tool, you – as a user – must have the capability to take advantage of those features. For example, if you have little or no exposure to programming languages and think that programming is too difficult for you – then obviously all the scripting features lose their importance. You should then concentrate on ease of usage and the power of auto compilation and so on. On the other hand, if you are already familiar with technologies like object oriented programming, then you would naturally like to take advantage of that knowledge and try to capitalize on it. In this case, all the scripting and system level capabilities of the tool assume importance.

And lastly, you should consider what sort of projects you are trying to do and what sort of activities you are likely to be engaged - in the future. Are you trying to specialize in corporate multimedia presentations or multimedia websites? Do you want to hit the commercial multimedia market or are you satisfied with specialized market segments? Are you product oriented or service oriented? All these questions need to be answered clearly. There is no harm in not knowing very clearly what you are going to do – in most cases that will be the situation! In that case, specialize on a tool that is most versatile and adoptable to different kinds of projects.

21.7 Commercial authoring tools - a curtain raiser

Few years before, when multimedia made its appearance in the horizon, there were at least a dozen big time players offering authoring solutions – apart from countless small players. Now, during the passage of time, the industry has settled down and market leaders have emerged.

Macromedia is the company leading the show, with its group of authoring solutions. It's Flash MX, originally indented to be a vector based animation system, has revolutionized the way multimedia contents are created – particularly for the web.

In this section, we will try to have a brief preview of the authoring solutions currently available in the market. As you can understand, the data presented here is very much volatile and was verified at the time of this writing. Please double confirm the information I've presented with that available on the web.

Table 32: Preview of some of the multimedia authoring tools available in the market

Tool	Company	Platform	Website
Director MX	Macromedia	Windows / Mac	http://www.macromedia.com
Flash MX	Macromedia	Windows / Mac	http://www.macromedia.com
Author ware	Macromedia (Playback only for Mac)	Windows	http://www.macromedia.com
Tool book Instructor	Asymetrix	Windows	http://www.asymetrix.com/en/toolbook/toolbook_instructor.asp
X Builder	Acrux Software	Mac	http://www.acruxsoftware.com
iShell 3	Tribe works	Windows / Mac	http://www.tribeworks.com/products/ishell/index.asp

I will be highlighting only the salient features of the product. In order to have better understanding, it is best that you download a trial copy of the tool you want and start playing around. IT magazines publish periodic reviews of authoring solutions from time to time. Do check them up for a comparison on various features between the products.

21.7.1 Macromedia Director

A heavy weight industry leader in multimedia authoring, Director has been in existence for several years and has maintained its leadership in both Windows and the Macintosh worlds. Though its positioning has somewhat been disturbed by the introduction of Flash, Director continues to be one of the most comprehensive solutions for multimedia authoring.

Director works through Lingo, a well-advanced scripting language that lets you add logic to the flow of contents. Automated effects like transitions are aplenty. But the working environment and the tool as a whole is slightly complex and requires reasonable time to master..

Table 33: Director functional specifications

Specification	Detail
Developer	Macromedia(http://www.macromedia.com)
Supported platforms	Windows 98, 2000 or XPMac OSX10.1.2 and above
Latest version (at the time of writing)	Director MX
Media support	Around 40 + media types including all graphic formats, WAV, mp3, AVI, AIFF, QuickTime, mpeg, Shockwave, Flash, Real Media etc
Scripting language	Lingo

Director works in two modes. In overview mode, elements are arranged as icons in the required sequence and executed - without user interaction. In studio, all the media elements - called casts - are arranged in different channels and played back in the stipulated time period. The tempo of playback can be controlled. The scripting language allows us to add interactivity and navigation control.

Lingo contains built in script editor for debugging the user code. Once written for a particular element - or cast - it can be copied and pasted across different casts, thus making transfer of behaviour across the elements easy. Apart from this, Lingo also uses special code segments called X objects - that can control external media devices.

All director documents can be linked or imported and the same elements can be shared amongst the casts, in one project.

Studio is the environment wherein the assembly takes place. Media elements or casts can either be created exclusively using director's tools or can be imported. Once the casts are ready for a segment, then they are assembled in a sequencing environment - called the score, which arranges different media elements in different channels and plays them back on the stage - at required speeds.

The synchronisation of various channels, results in sequential flow of information.

21.7.2 Macromedia Flash

If there is any tool that is groundbreaking and which has revolutionized multimedia – particularly on the web, it is Flash. When companies were struggling to pull different types of media contents and effects over the web, Flash made web multimedia a reality. Apart from web, flash has also become a tool of choice for multimedia presentations, CD-ROM projects and kiosks.

Table 34: Flash functional specifications

Specification	Detail
Developer	Macromedia(http://www.macromedia.com)
Supported platforms	Windows 98 SE, 2000 or XPMac OSX10.2.6 and above, 10.3
Latest version (at the time of writing)	Flash MX, Flash MX Professional
Media support	Most graphics formats, videos (AVI & Quick time), audio (mp3, ADPCM Wav etc.), Adobe Pdf, EPS
Scripting language	Action script

In flash, different media elements are arranged along the time line in different tracks. As the timeline advances, events occur and contents migrate or change. Most of the animations are done as vector graphics, so that they are not heavy for the processor. It is also possible to animate bitmapped graphics. Flash has advanced capabilities for organizing media contents in the form of libraries. One of the most powerful features is to store independent vector animations and drag and drop them over the main project.

Events are controlled with the help of action script. For example, in order to react for a mouse click event over a button object, one has to invoke action script and write few lines of code.

Transition effects are accomplished using alpha channels (fade-in / fade-out etc.). Videos can be manipulated and rendered online. All the various audio tracks can be rendered as mp3 during compilation.

In short, flash is a wonderful tool that is hard to resist.

21.8 Summary

Multimedia authoring is the final stage of multimedia project production.

Multimedia programming offers a slightly different approach to assembly – as compared to authoring tools. Different methodologies adopted for multimedia authoring can be grouped as Frame or page based authoring, Time based authoring and Icon based authoring.

Characteristics to look forward in an authoring tool or environment are: Media handling features, bundled media library, mapping features, programming features and environment, segmentation functionality, compilation feature and runtime players and media embedding feature.

Some of the famous authoring tools, available in the market are: Macromedia's Director, Macromedia Flash and Macromedia Author ware.

21.9 Keywords

- **Multimedia authoring:** The process of developing a software program, that will accept all of the media elements involved with the multimedia Project under production, put them up in their respective places - as advocated by the Storyboard of the Project and evolves as an integrated source of Information - many times supplemented by the interactivity, provided by means of Navigation paths.

Chapter 22

Project Planning and Costing

CHAPTER OVERVIEW

So far, we have been laying heavy emphasis on technology and technical aspects. Let us take a break and take a look at the managerial aspects involved with multimedia project design.

To some extent, most of these discussions are relevant for not just multimedia – but even for all other kinds of projects. But there are few things that are very specific to media development and we will be uncovering the same.

It is interesting to compare this chapter with an earlier chapter on multimedia project conceptualisation and design. They take different approaches to the same project development – one concentrating on technical aspects of the same and the other looking at the same from a managerial perspective.

22.1 Introduction

This chapter differs from all the previous ones in that it is not very technical in nature. Instead, it talks about multimedia project planning, execution and costing strategies. It is particularly meant for managers and team leaders who are handling multimedia projects.

However good may be the technology, a project will fail without proper managerial strategies. Enough time should be spent on aspects, which normally miss the attention of technical manager. Improper project planning is noticed even in large corporations and millions of dollars are wasted due to poor managerial decisions.

Apart from discussions on various issues that need to be taken care of, the chapter also provides some mathematical approaches from operations research methodologies to effectively manage multimedia projects.

22.2 Multimedia project planning

Multimedia project planning involves the following phases:

- Idea generation
- Market definition and segmentation
- Planning the required skills and resources
- Building the team
- Planning the project phase: Pert and CPM techniques
- Time estimates and cost estimates
- Pilot projects and prototyping
- Production - design and development

- ❑ Alpha and beta testing
- ❑ Delivery planning

Each phase can again be subdivided into several distinct stages. A schematic representation of these stages has been provided in the diagram.

Let us start discussing them one by one.

22.3 Idea generation

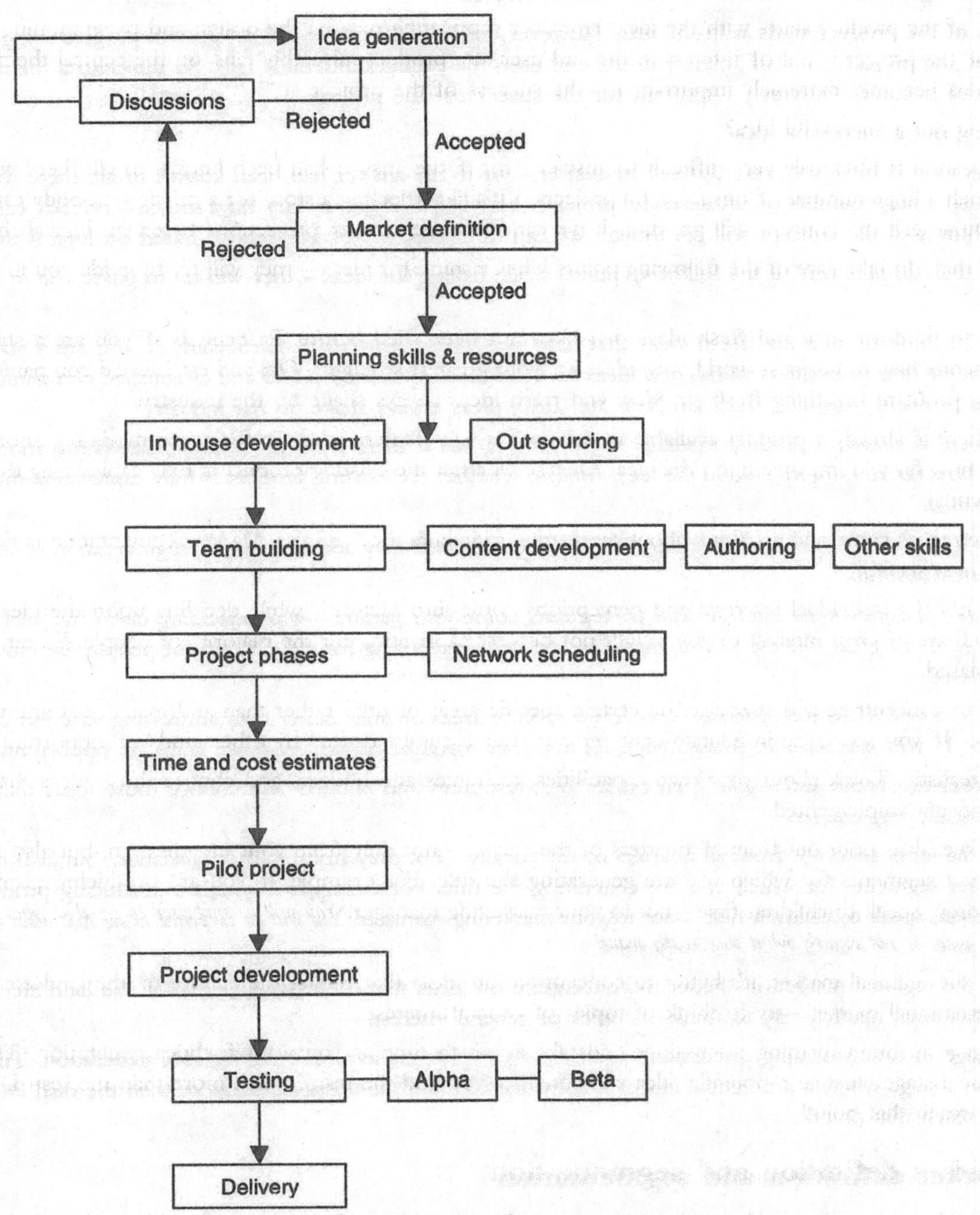

Figure 201: Different phases of project planning

Every multimedia project originates with an idea or concept. We already dealt with this earlier during our discussions on project design, but here, we look at it from a slightly different perspective.

For those projects, which are developed for specific customers, the concept is available from the customers themselves. For example, if we are designing a multimedia touch screen kiosk for a five star hotel - the hotel authorities themselves will give you some idea as to what they expect out of that project. Of course, the concept has to be polished and improved by interacting with them – but the basic idea is available.

On the other hand, if the project is product oriented, i.e. say if it is a multimedia CD-ROM meant for public at large, then idea generation becomes very critical and complex.

The success of the product starts with the idea. However captivating may be the design and programming work, if the theme of the project is not of interest to the end user, the product miserably fails. So the central theme of the project or idea becomes extremely important for the success of the project.

How to bring out a successful idea?

Well, this question is obviously very difficult to answer - for if the answer had been known to all, there would not have been such a huge number of unsuccessful projects...! It's like selecting a story for a movie – nobody can predict in advance how well the concept will go, though we can do some sort of projections based on logical thinking.

Having said that, do take care of the following points while fishing for ideas – they will try to guide you in the right path.

- ❑ Try to think of new and fresh ideas that have not been tried before. Particularly if you are a start-up or someone new to business world, new ideas are your greatest strengths. Old and established companies always have problem breathing fresh air. New and fresh ideas always shake up the industry.
- ❑ If there is already a product available in the market, see if there is scope for accommodating another one. See how far you improve upon the idea. Analyse whether the existing product is fully capitalizing the market potential.
- ❑ When ideas come and go, think about the market segments they address, Market segmentation is detailed in the next section.
- ❑ Let not the individual interests and perceptions come into picture - while deciding upon the idea. Topics, which are of great interest to you, might not be very captivating for the majority of people. Be rational and unbiased.
- ❑ Try to concentrate and specialize on certain specific areas or titles rather than addressing vast and unrelated areas. If you specialize in edutainment, let not your focus be drifted by other kinds of opportunities.
- ❑ Be realistic. Think about your own capabilities, resources and budgets and choose those ideas that can be practically implemented.
- ❑ Let the ideas pour out from all quarters of the society - not only from your organisation, but also from the market segments for which you are generating the title. For example, if you are producing products for children, speak to children first – not to your marketing manager! *You will be surprised to see that what you think they want is not exactly what they really want!*
- ❑ For the regional market, it's better to concentrate on ideas that reflect the culture of the land etc. and for international market - try to think of topics of general interest.
- ❑ Engage in brainstorming discussions and take as much time as you want for idea generation. There will come a stage wherein a potential idea will convince you and the team, much more than the rest! Debate till you reach that point!

22.4 Market definition and segmentation

Once the idea is generated, the expected market segment must be identified, so that the title can be designed and produced accordingly. Market segment refers to the group(s) of people with certain basic traits/characteristics or tastes - who may be interested in the product.

For example, let us try to identify the market segments for a CD-ROM that will teach English nursery rhymes to schoolchildren.

Shall we say 'all kids aged between three and eight' are our end users?

Ushhh… wait!

The kids who are going to buy our product should have access to computers either at home or at school. Hence we need to modify our definition of end users: 'All kids aged between three and eight, who have access to computers'.

Even this seems to be rather vague. How do we know how many children in a particular country are having access to computers? It will be difficult to project any figure. Let us see if we could be more specific.

First, children who have access to computers only at schools will hardly buy a CD-ROM. They need to have a computer – that too, a multimedia PC at home. Now, we need to search for newspapers and magazines for some statistics on these areas.

Looking at the last year sales figures of multimedia computers, let us assume that we have the following figures:

- 60 % of those families, whose monthly income is above Rs.30, 000 have purchased multimedia computers at home
- 40 % of those families, with monthly income above Rs.20, 000 have purchased computers at home, and 10% more are seriously considering a purchase in the near future
- Less than 10% of those families with monthly income less than Rs.10000 have purchased a computer.

Note: These figures have been provided purely for illustration and do not represent any real statistics available from market research.

Now, the mist begins to be getting cleared and you are beginning to get more and more specific. Let us assume another set of statistics, for the sake of our discussions:

- Around 50% of those who own multimedia computers, purchase multimedia CD-ROMs
- Around 30% are content with free CD-ROMs that are distributed with magazines and those that are available from friends
- Around 20% do not use multimedia CD-ROMs at all

Now, the scenario is much more clear - than it was, when we began this discussion. Let us try to redefine our user: 'Kids aged between three and eight, whose family income is above Rs.30000'. You can go on like how many of those will be learning English and how many will be interested in learning rhymes via a multimedia CD-ROM and so on.

Though kids might be interested in our product, unfortunately, the purchasing decision is going to be made by the parents! This is where the second statistics comes handy – remember that only 50% of those who have computers are prepared to spend money on CD-ROMs!

We can go on with this exercise until we can arrive at a ballpark figure as to how many people will be really interested in purchasing this CD-ROM. The actual purchase – in a most pessimistic projection – will be less than 25% of the total purchasing potential available.

If the market segment is not big enough or too big to address, then you have to go back and take a fresh look at the idea you are exploring… may be it needs to change.

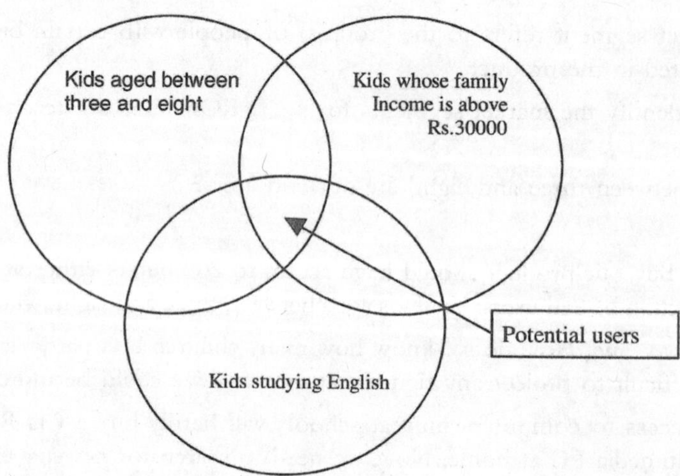

Figure 202: Identifying the right market segment

22.5 Planning skills and resources

Once the idea of the project and been conceived and proper market understanding is done, it is time to think about how to make the idea a reality. This is the stage where we critically evaluate the skills and resources required for the project.

Do we have sufficient skill set, resources and bandwidth required for the project? Will it be economical to do the project in-house or should we outsource it? If we were to take up this project in-house, what is the delivery schedule we are looking at?

These are some of the questions that come up at this stage. Many companies and individuals who are undertaking multimedia project work for the first time, under estimate the amount of effort and time involved. This is mainly due to lack of experience. There is no harm in consulting the experts who have prior experience in handling such projects – in fact their inputs will be of great use.

Some projects may demand intricate programming or authoring skills while certain others may demand more artistic skills. Skills required to develop a project meant for teaching music is almost certainly different from the skills required to develop a project on – say touch screen shopping kiosk.

All these things need to be given proper thought, at this stage.

22.6 Building the team

If we decide to do the project in-house, then we need to form a project team, identifying the professionals who will be involved in the project. This topic will get detailed coverage in the next chapter and hence will not be discussed here.

22.7 Project planning: Pert and CPM techniques

Project planning is a very detailed topic and there are people who specialise in just this topic. The mathematical approach that's available on this subject is called 'Operations research' and it offers highly scientific approach to project management.

Operation research, as a subject, is a vast area - encircling wide varieties of theories and techniques. Most of the theories are available in the form of mathematical models. Here, we shall concentrate on some of the models that'll be of direct use to those involved in project planning.

The topics we have chosen for our discussions are called network-scheduling theories in operations research.

22.8 Network scheduling

Network scheduling is the technique generally used for monitoring large-scale projects of any nature - such as constructions, installations and developmental work. It can also be used for multimedia projects of any size.

The technique mainly aims to minimize some of the common areas of lapse in projects - such as delays, interruptions, production bottlenecks etc. by identifying the critical time factors and activities associated with the project and coordinating the same.

One distinct advantage of network scheduling is that the processes are represented diagrammatically as arrows and activity lines. This helps us to identify and understand all the problematic areas of the project.

The two basic techniques of network scheduling, which we are going to discuss are:

- Program evaluation and review technique (PERT) and
- Critical path method (CPM)

CPM is the ideal choice - when the time taken by individual activities of the project are known well in advance or can be determined. Pert is suited for those projects wherein the activity timings cannot be judged accurately.

We will have to look at both of these techniques; - because Pert can adopted, when the type of the multimedia project undertaken is quite new and no such similar projects have been executed in the past; and CPM can be adopted, in other cases.

22.9 Network representation

Before plunging on to Pert or CPM, let us understand how to draw a network representation diagram of a project.

The first step is to arrange all of the activities - in the sequential order. For example, the multimedia concept development should come before storyboarding; storyboarding should come before animation development and so on.

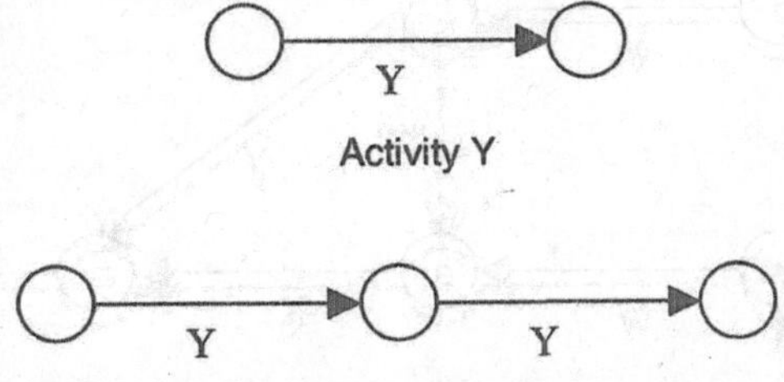

Activity X precedes activity Y

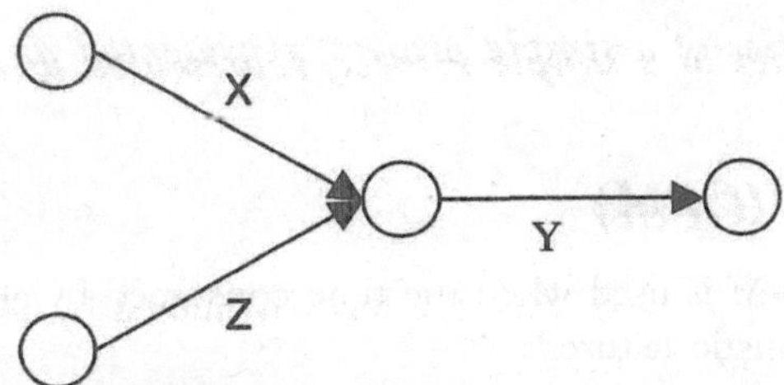

Activity X and Z precede activity Y

Figure 203: Network representations

Some activities may be interlinked with each other. For example, if there is an audio content associated with an animation, then that activity and animation development is interlinked. Certain activities may have a high degree of dependency on certain other activities. For example, authoring activity cannot be started before all the media content development activities are completed and so on.

This kind of interdependence is what is known as precedence requirement. An activity 'Y' is said to succeed activity 'X' - if, in any given time slot, 'Y' can be undertaken only after the completion of 'X'. Thus, X can be said to be the predecessor of Y, in operations research terminology.

Have a look at the figure.

- Each activity of the project is represented as an arrow. The circles at the end of the arrows denote completion of that activity, and are called 'nodes'.
- The precedence of activity X over activity Y, can be represented as shown in the second case
- If a particular activity has got two predecessors, then the representation will be like the one shown in the third case

It is assumed that the project starts with a single node: project concept development.

For the sake of mathematical computations, it's better to name the nodes, apart from activities. The naming convention is as follows:

- The first starting node - where the project starts - will have the number 1.
- Delete all the arrows emerging from node 1. This will create at least one new starting node, out of the remaining nodes. Name them as 2, 3 etc.
- Repeat the earlier for all other nodes in the network diagram and number all of them.

To make our discussions fairly simple, let us consider a not-so-complex network diagram as shown in the figure. All activities as well as nodes have been numbered, using the methodology detailed above. This network diagram will be used to apply Pert and Cpm techniques over the project.

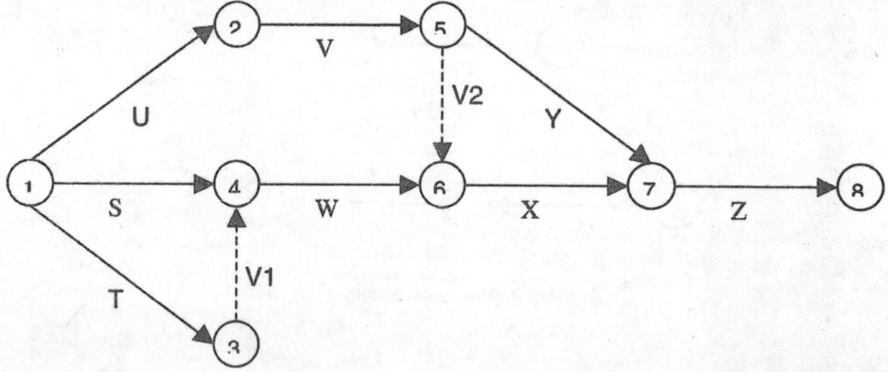

Figure 204: All activities of a simple project, represented as a network diagram

22.10 Critical path method (CPM)

As stated earlier in our discussions, CPM is used when the time consumed by all of the activities of the project are known beforehand or are of deterministic nature.

CPM technique helps us to find out the following data:

- It computes the earliest possible start time / finish time for each activity
- It computes the latest possible start time / finish time for each activity
- It identifies the critical path of the project and

❑ It computes the slacks or floats for activities other than those in the critical path.

Critical path of the project is that path, wherein the activities assume more significance than the rest. Any delay in executing the activities of the critical path will result in overall delay of the project. Hence, the project manager should ensure that all the activities of the critical path – also known as critical activities – should be completed well within the stipulated time. Identification of critical path is one of the biggest value additions of CPM.

Slacks or floats are time periods, for which, the particular activity can be delayed - without affecting the project. An activity with a lower slack value should be executed more carefully than that with a higher slack period. Critical activities always have zero slack.

Dummy activities are those that are introduced for the sake of computational convenience – they do not represent the actual work done and hence do not consume time. Have a look at the network diagram once again – dummy activities have been represented with broken arrows.

22.11 CPM computations

The first step in CPM computations is to identify the time consumed by each activity. Remember that one of the prerequisites of CPM technique is that the time consumed by all the different activities can be accurately projected even before starting the project. In practical situations, this translates to those projects in which you have prior experience. For example, if you have already done a multimedia presentation for business X, then you can accurately predict the timings of individual activities for another multimedia presentation project for, say, business Y. The modified network diagram shows all activities with their respective time values. For example, activity U consumes 7 working days.

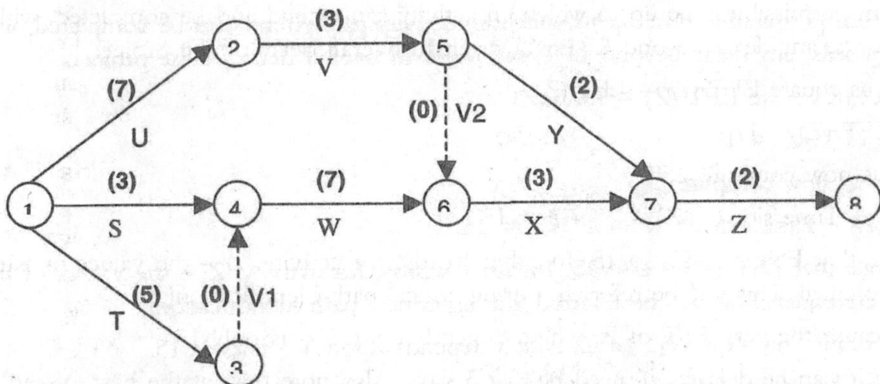

Figure 205: Identifying the time slot for each activity – modified network diagram

Having identified the time slots, let us concentrate on some of the variables that can be calculated with the help of CPM.

22.11.1 Early start time (EST)

The time at which the activity can be started at the earliest - EST - depends upon the predecessors of that activity. Activities without predecessors have zero EST.

In our example, EST of activity 'S' - denoted as EST (S) =0

Similarly, EST (T) = EST (U) =0.

But activity 'V' depends on the completion of 'U' - is it not? Thus EST (V) = Completion of activity 'U' = 7

22.11.2 Early finish time (EFT)

The time at which the activity can be finished at the latest - EFT - depends upon it's own time duration, as well as it's EST.

Thus, EFT (S) = EST (S) + Time slot of 'S' = 0+3 = 3

EFT (T)=0+5=5

EFT of dummy activity V1 will be EFT (V1) = EST (V1) + Time slot of 'V1' = 5+0 = 5

What will be EFT (V)?

Well, it's also EST (V) + Time slot of 'V' i.e. EFT (V) = 7+3=10

Now, getting back to EST… can you find what will be the EST (W) - which has 2 predecessors?

It's like this: EST (W) = Maximum of (EFT (S), EFT (V1)) = Maximum of (3,5) = 5!

The EFT of the last activity - 'Z' will represent the completion time of the project - at the earliest. From calculations, it can be evolved as 17 - in our example.

Thus, by shuttling between EST and EFT, we can very well find out the earliest start and finish times of all activities. Now, these will represent the best case - wherein activities start - as early as possible.

22.11.3 Latest start time (LST)

LST is the maximum permissible time up to which an activity can start and proceed without affecting the project. In other words, any delay beyond LST will result in overall delay of the project.

LST has to be computed - after computing LFT - in the reversed order i.e. we start with the last activity and end up in the first.

22.11.4 Latest finish time (LFT)

LFT is the maximum permissible time up to which an activity can extend and be completed, without affecting the project. In other words, any delay beyond LFT will result in overall delay of the project.

For best results, let us equate EFT (Z) = LFT (Z)

Thus, EFT (Z) = LFT (Z) = 17.

With this data, let us now compute LST.

LST (Z) = LFT (Z) - Time slot of 'Z' = 17 - 2 = 15.

Note: Kindly notice that EST (Z) is also 15. In other words, for activity 'Z' - the values of latest start time and earliest start time are equal. This will be referred, during critical path identification!

LFT (Y) = 15 - because the very EST of Z, which depends upon Y - is only 15.

That means, activity Y can be delayed, if need be, for 3 days. Also note that, at the best, Y can be finished in 12 days i.e. EFT (Y)=12

How about LFT (V)?

Well, here it's the minimum value between LST (V2) and LST (Y)

LFT (V)= minimum of (13, 12) =12!

You can compute LST and LFT for all other activities in a similar manner.

22.11.5 Critical path

Activities whose LST and EST are identical in values - like activity 'Z' - are the critical activities i.e. they do not enjoy the slack allowance and any delay in those activities will result in overall delay of the project.

A path, which contains all such critical activities - is the critical path. Maximum attention is to be bestowed on those activities that occupy the critical path.

22.11.6 Slacks

Slacks or permissible delays for any activity can be computed as the difference between LST and EST of any activity.

For example, slack of activity 'U' is LST (U) – EST (U) = 2

So, that was critical path method!

If we could develop a similar network diagram of our Project - which will naturally be a bit complex than that discussed - then the critical path of the project also can be identified easily.

Let us try to evolve a simple network diagram for our own chapter - i.e. various phases of multimedia project planning.

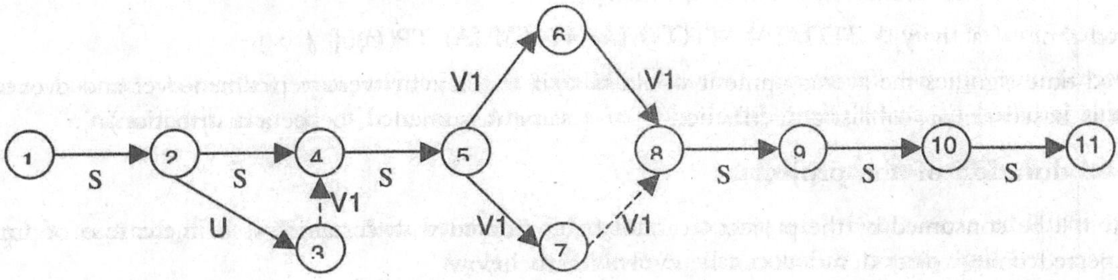

Figure 206: Various phases of multimedia project planning represented as a network diagram

We may have to give names for all activities involved, like this:

Activity A - Idea generation

Activity B - Market definition and segmentation

Activity C - Planning the skills

Activity D - Building the team

Activity E - Project planning: Pert and CPM techniques

Activity F - Time estimates and cost estimates

Activity G - Pilot projects and prototyping

Activity H - Production - design and development

Activity I - Alpha and beta testing

Activity J - Delivery planning

The precedence relationships are as follows:

Team building (D) can be taken up, only after B and C.

Pilot Projects can be taken up, only after the completion of E and F.

All other activities follow, one after another.

Now, by filling the necessary time slots, for the specific project, the critical path can be evaluated, in the same manner.

22.12 Program evaluation and review technique

Pert calculations are much more complicated than CPM - because, here, we have to struggle with much more number of variables. This method is particularly useful for projects, the activities of which cannot be accurately slotted for time.

Instead of one time slot for a particular activity (which is unknown), three time estimates are made use of. They are:

- ❑ Most likely time - The time most likely to be consumed by a given activity, under normal conditions
- ❑ Optimistic time - The time duration of the activity in the best possible situations
- ❑ Pessimistic time - The time duration of the activity under worst possible situations – when everything seems to go adverse

22.12.1 Expected time

The most probable time duration of the given activity, also called as the 'Expected time of activity', is evolved as below:

If TM (A) – Most likely time duration of Activity 'A'

TO (A) - Optimistic time duration of Activity 'A'

TP (A) - Pessimistic time duration of Activity 'A', then

The expected time of activity A TE (A) = {TO (A) + 4TM (A) + TP (a) } / 6

This expected time signifies the average time it would take, if the activity were performed over and over again; and the formula is based on probabilistic distribution of the same (assumed to be beta distribution).

22.12.2 Total duration of the project

Total time that'll be consumed by the project - cannot be computed with certainty, as in the case of Cpm. Instead, only the expected time project duration can be evolved as below:

First, compute the expected time for all activities of the project.

Then, use CPM to calculate the critical path of the project - using the expected time for all activities.

The total sum of all expected times, along the critical path - will be the most expected time duration of the project.

22.13 Time estimates and cost estimates

In any given multimedia project, the time involved and the cost of the project bear an inverse relationship. The more the time spent - the less is the cost involved, and vice versa.

22.13.1 Types of costs

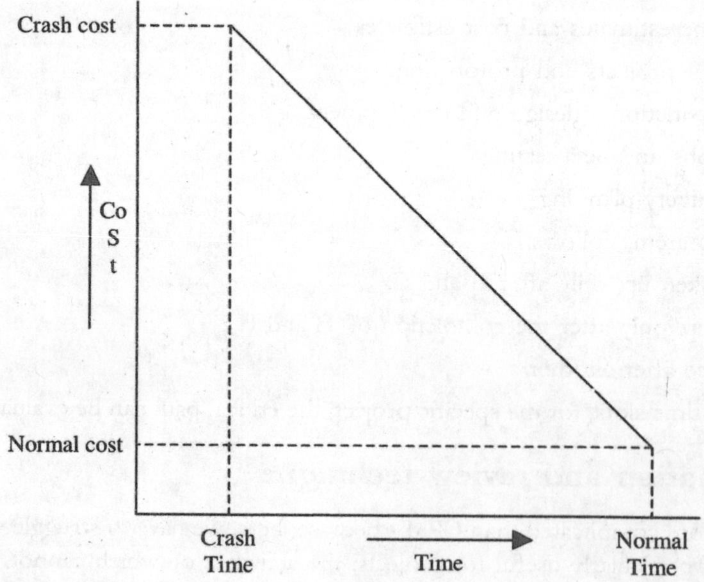

Figure 207: Time and cost involved in a project, have an inverse relationship

The projects costs can be generally classified into two groups:

- Direct costs and
- Indirect costs

Direct costs are those that are consumed directly by the project. For example, the cost spent for the technical manpower engaged for the project or for the rental charges associated with the computers used etc. - can be called as direct costs. One distinctive characteristic of direct costs is that, if we increase the same, the multimedia project time consumption can be reduced.

Following the above example, if we engage more man-power and / or more machines on the project - the project time consumption is sure to come down. On the other hand, indirect costs are the standard overheads associated with the project, including the loss of revenue due to delayed completion of the project. This cost will decrease directly with the project time.

22.13.2 Crash cost

Crash time is the minimal possible time duration, in which a given activity can be successfully completed. The cost associated with crash time is called crash cost.

22.13.3 Normal cost

Cost incurred by the activity, under normal time duration. For economising the project costs, the sum of direct as well as indirect costs should be minimised.

22.13.4 Optimum project time

The time duration, for which the sum of direct and indirect costs will be minimum, is called optimum project time.

22.13.5 Project crashing technique

The technique of finding the direct activities cost - when project duration is reduced by one unit time, each time and thus arriving at the optimum time duration - is called the project crashing technique.

The cost of crashing a given activity, by a unit time, can be calculated as follows:

[Crashing costs - Normal Costs] / [Normal time - crash time]

Crashing technique calculations are complicated and beyond the scope of this work. Those who want to know more can refer any good books operation research or network scheduling.

22.14 Pilot projects and prototyping

In case the project is of new type, it's better to go in for a prototype of the project. The prototype should include all intricacies of the project - as far as possible. The interface designs can be tested for their appeal, or the performance of the project - under a variety of hardware platforms - can be tested.

In many cases, the work done for the pilot project can be very well utilized for the actual project also, and thus, prototyping cost can be justified.

22.15 Project design and development

We had already seen all phases of project design and development - in an earlier chapter. This phase has been purposely included in project planning to emphasise that - after all, the design and developmental activities are, but a part of the overall project planning activities.

22.16 Alpha and beta testing

Once the project is over, it has to undergo rigorous testing. Testing identities bugs; check whether the performance of the application is good across heterogeneous systems etc. Testing is undertaken in two stages.

22.16.1 Alpha testing

Alpha testing is the first phase of project testing. The alpha-testing group usually consists of colleagues (from other departments / projects), friends and those who are known to the organisation.

The tests are conducted under all possible conditions that can be expected in the client's workplace. The bugs generated are called 'alpha bugs' and are generally of more serious nature - if any.

The output of alpha testing is generated as a report, and the identified bugs / modifications are fixed by the programmers and fed to beta testing.

22.16.2 Beta testing

A wider and more heterogeneous circle of people does the beta testing. You can usually find many programs in their beta testing stage - in the Internet. A typical beta testing group should be a true representation of the expected user community. The test report of beta test should be given equal importance - as that of alpha test.

22.17 Delivery planning

Depending upon the size of the project and the user community, the delivery mode of the project has to be planned. The most preferred choice is a CD-ROM.

The finally distributed material should contain the following material, apart from the main project program:

- A friendly installation program - that'll install the project modules, on the user's computer.
- A printed user guide /manual
- The product registration card
- Certificate of authenticity, if any.

22.18 Summary

Project planning and costing are mainly concerned with the managerial and financial implications of multimedia project. The processes involved are: Idea generation, Market definition and segmentation, Planning skills and resources, Building the team, Project planning, Time and cost estimates, Pilot projects and prototyping, Production - design and development, Alpha and beta testing and Delivery planning.

Market segment refers to the well-defined group of people, who may be interested in the product. Identification of Market segment helps the producer, to develop the title, accordingly.

Operation research theories such as Pert and CPM can be used to plan the project time and activities. Project crashing method can be used to strike the optimum balance between time and money.

22.19 Keywords

- **Critical path:** The path of the Project - wherein, any delay in execution of activities will result in overall delay of the Project.
- **Critical activities:** Activities that are lined along the critical path.
- **Optimum project time:** The time duration for which the sum of direct and indirect costs will be minimum.

Chapter 23

Multimedia Skill Sets and Career Opportunities

CHAPTER OVERVIEW

This chapter is also relatively non-technical in nature.

It provides a preview of multimedia as an industry and talks about various careers that have sprung up around multimedia technology. It talks about careers in each and every discipline, tools that need to be learnt, attitudes and talents required and so on.

The later part of the chapter is about the multimedia team that is at work. Each team member is introduced and the responsibilities they handle are detailed. The last part contains approaches a student should take, in order to launch a successful career into the world of multimedia.

23.1 Introduction

The skill sets required in the multimedia industry are widespread and heterogeneous. When I say multimedia industry, I'm talking about an industry spread across the globe and not restricting myself to specific regions or countries. There are tremendous career opportunities available and the industry is growing at reasonable phase.

Having laid such a broad scope, let us see what are all the different skill sets required and who are providing them. Every other media involved with multimedia demands specific kind of expertise to handle. And that makes multimedia a truly heterogeneous industry, providing opportunities to a wide variety of people. On the other hand, not all companies can recruit and maintain all these different classes of people; hence, outsourcing is most common. This provides opportunities for entrepreneurs, who can concentrate on specific kind of service and make them available to multimedia production houses.

23.2 Multimedia companies

Before we start discussing on the skill set requirements, let us try to understand something about those companies, which are involved in multimedia business.

Multimedia has affected and continues to affect a wide variety of businesses. Multimedia technologies have revolutionized the way these industries were functioning and have created deep impact on a global scale. Some of the industries that make extensive use of multimedia include:

- ❑ Magazine and newspaper publishers
- ❑ Book publishers
- ❑ Web publishers
- ❑ Television stations

- Audio companies and studios
- Video and cinema production houses
- Advertising companies
- Training & development companies

Apart from these, there are numerous multimedia consultancy firms, which dedicate themselves to core multimedia development. One thing to note here is that not all of the above businesses involve themselves in exploiting all kinds of media. For example, publishing companies will be interested mostly in graphics and layout design software. Similarly television stations will be interested in video editing and three-dimensional software.

If so, then who are all the people, who involve themselves in true multimedia development? What sorts of companies are involved in the development of multimedia CD-ROMs, websites and games?

- Many publishing houses have started involving themselves in producing multimedia contents, through their multimedia division.
- Few international television stations like BBC are also involved in multimedia development
- Traditional software development firms have spun off multimedia division
- Few of the advertising firms have started doing multimedia presentations for their clients
- Quite a number of consultancy firms are also involved in the development of multimedia

All of the above-mentioned businesses provide opportunity for a budding multimedia professional to shape up a career in this exciting and creative world of information technology.

23.3 Multimedia skill sets and careers

A professional involved in multimedia development can specialise in any of the multiple media offered by multimedia. Depending upon the skill set, several titles and careers have sprung up over these years. These include:

- Graphics developer or Digital imaging specialist
- Graphic artist
- Digital audio specialists
- Animators – two dimensional and three dimensional
- Animators – Modelling and texturing specialists
- Character animators
- Video post production specialists
- Multimedia authoring / programming specialists
- Multimedia web content developers or Web designers

This is not really an exhaustive list, but it is enough to show that multimedia has been creating opportunities for countless individuals with creative talents and exposure in information technology. Down the line, as multimedia hits mainstream and becomes a part of everyday life like video and audio, more and more opportunities will spring up for professionals as well as entrepreneurs.

In the following paragraphs, we will look at the skills in which one should specialize – in order to become a professional in the selected area. I've also provided a glimpse of software that need to be mastered, in order to get decent career opportunities.

23.4 Careers in digital imaging

Digital imaging is expanding at a rapid phase. From publishing industry to advertising its impact is widespread and deep. Hence career opportunities are naturally in abundance in this field.

Graphics specialists are usually expected to work with digital imaging software like Adobe Photoshop and Corel Draw / Photo paint to create the desired effects and layout. Depending upon the industry, the nature of work might vary. For example, if you are working for a publishing house, the nature of work might be to produce decent layouts for the articles, create compelling graphics for the features and covers etc. if you are in an advertising field, you will be asked to create visuals that convey the message with strength.

Graphic artists are also required for many other industries like multimedia consultancy firms, architectural firms, engineering consultancies etc.

In order to specialize in digital imaging, a student must be highly proficient with the following tools:

- Adobe Photoshop
- Corel Draw / Corel Photo paint
- Any publishing and layout software
- Scanning and digital photographic software / process

Apart from the above-mentioned tools, specialization in any of the following tools / areas is most desirable:

- Vector illustration tools like Adobe Illustrator and Macromedia Freehand
- Three dimensional software like Maya and 3D studio max

Very strong senses of colours, a taste for artworks and preferably a conventional artistic background are the desirable qualities of a good graphic designer.

23.5 Careers in digital audio

Most recording studios have started adopting digital audio because of quality, flexibility and adoptability. These studios make use of state of the art hardware and software to do professional recordings. Career opportunities are available here for professionals who specialize in digital audio.

Since many of these studios are related to entertainment industry like cinema or television, it is good to have some background or contacts with that industry, in order to make out a successful entry here. Recording facilities attached to cinema studios in particular, offer lot of opportunities for creative individuals. Many special audio effects are required for movies, which are increasingly adopting international theatre standards like DTS and Dolby digital.

Students aiming at a career in digital audio need to specialize in the following software:

- Cakewalk Professional
- MIDI synthesizer pro
- Digital Orchestrator
- Voyetra Music Write

A formal knowledge of classical music – western or otherwise – is highly desirable.

23.6 Careers in animation

Two dimensional animation and more importantly, three-dimensional animations are evolving into a multi billion dollar industry across the globe. The need for creating imaginary characters and environments is on the increase at a feverish phase due to the exploding number of television channels and cinemas that are packed with digital special effects.

You will be surprised to know that this industry is very seriously in shortage of skilled professionals. True that we see hundreds of students taking up a course in three-dimensional animations – but their skill sets unfortunately fall behind the industry expectations.

Several specialised careers have evolved over these years, around three-dimensional software. Companies are prepared to hire dedicated professionals who are highly specialised in modelling or even texturing. Opportunities are widespread

– from Bollywood to Hollywood. The only thing is that you should really be a master in the field you specialize. The following carriers are offshoots of 3D:

- Digital animators
- Three-dimensional / Character modellers
- Three-dimensional texturing / painting specialists
- Character animators
- Three-dimensional Environment specialists

Since this field is becoming increasingly popular among the professionals, I've dedicated a few paragraphs later in this chapter – as to how one can approach professional companies for careers in three-dimensional software.

Let us discuss the skill set requirements for this field. Total expertise is required in any one or preferably more than one of the following software:

- Alias / Wave front Maya
- SoftImage
- 3D Studio max

Along with them, it will be great if you could get exposure to one or more of the following tools:

- Rhinoceros 3D (Modelling software)
- Pixar Render man (Rendering software)
- Painter 3D / Deep paint 3D

Apart from this set of three-dimensional tools, if you can train yourself in video post-production techniques, then you could specialize in composing i.e. the art of mixing three-dimensional images over live video footages.

What are all the attitudes desirable for a successful animator? First and foremost requirement is that you should be an artist who can draw good pictures in paper or at least possess great interest in doing the same. Most professional animators can draw characters and objects extremely well on paper. The attitudes seem to go together. A sense of rhythm and movements, keen observation, an appreciation for colours and some knowledge of human and animal anatomy are all the desirable qualities.

23.7 Careers with video post-production

Many cinema studios have now installed video post-production facilities within their premises. Apart from them, there are also dedicated companies that specialize in the art of video post-production. These places offer opportunities for multimedia professionals who are sufficiently trained in the art.

As a post-production specialist, you will be mostly working on video footages, editing them, mixing them with audio and doing the necessary composing work. Apart from these regular works, opportunities may come up for composing special effect or three-dimensional simulations with live footages – which can be much more interesting to work with. While top-notch studios make use of dedicated hardware / software for the purpose, middle range studios do make use of personal computers and workstations.

To be able to launch a successful career in video post-production, you should have good knowledge of the following solutions:

- Avid range of non-linear video post-production suites
- Adobe Premiere
- Adobe After effects
- Any good software that can add special effects to videos like Flint and Flame

Apart from the above, good knowledge of three-dimensional animation and composing is desirable.

23.8 Careers in multimedia authoring

Multimedia authoring and programming is required for those companies involved in producing multimedia websites, presentations and multimedia CD-ROMs. As a multimedia author, you have to stitch different media contents into a sequential stream of multimedia and present it as an integrated project.

Expertise in the following software is compulsory:

- ❑ Macromedia Director
- ❑ Macromedia Flash
- ❑ Macromedia Author ware

Apart from that, good knowledge of media editing tools like Adobe Photoshop, Premiere or sound editors is desirable. Also, when it comes to multimedia programming, it is good to have knowledge of GUI tools like Visual Basic or Visual C++ and installation utilities.

23.9 Careers in multimedia web design

Hundreds of websites are being developed every day using multimedia and web design tools. Opportunities are available for part-time and full-time work.

As a web designer, one has to conceive compelling web designs for their clients. Depending upon the choice of the client and budget available, the media exposure in the website may be increased or decreased. When it comes to web-based multimedia, one has to rely heavily on tools like Macromedia flash – whose multimedia contents can be directly embedded into web pages.

Apart from that, knowledge of java script can help one to write small titbits of code that will control the events happening in a website like mouse move and mouse click.

23.10 The multimedia team and its responsibilities

A number of people with varying skill set come together to form a multimedia team.

The team usually reports to a project manager who is usually the team leader of the project. A number of people and agencies report to him. In the following paragraphs, we will look at the people involved in a project and the responsibilities they shoulder.

23.11 The project manager

The project manager takes the overall responsibility of developing the product. He is the top man, as far as the team is concerned and is responsible for the total quality as well as the timely delivery of the project. Thus, his role becomes critical - as far as the success of the project is concerned.

The project manager is expected to carry rich experience in handling similar projects. He must not only handle the main design specifications of the project, but should also shoulder managerial responsibilities.

Responsibilities of the project manager include:

- ❑ Develop the multimedia concept of the chosen topic
- ❑ Co-ordinate and direct media content developers for developing the right contents
- ❑ Develop the storyboard, with inputs from the whole team
- ❑ Plan and schedule the project along a timeline and fix up the project network
- ❑ Allocate individual responsibilities for various team members
- ❑ Co-ordinate and direct the external agencies involved - if any
- ❑ Co-ordinate with the product manager or marketing manager for developing the product - as per the market segment's expectations

- ❑ Co-ordinate and direct multimedia authors or programmers - for developing the core program
- ❑ Monitoring the progress of the project - in all it's phases, on day- to- day basis

Because of these multiple responsibilities, a project manager is not expected to co-ordinate with more than one project - at any point of time.

23.12 Content experts

Content experts are hired to develop the basic material for the projects. For example, if you are doing a project on biology, you need to have all the basic material that need to be presented. You need a subject expert to do this.

It is better to hire the services of the expert for a specific period or for specific number of pages. Their responsibilities include:

- ❑ Delve deep into the chosen topic and coming out with the required pool of information
- ❑ Understand the concept of the project and gather information - accordingly
- ❑ Edit the raw information collected and organize it into a logical sequence of data
- ❑ Co-ordinate with the copywriter to produce the general contents booklet

23.13 Copywriters

Copywriters are usually engaged by advertising agencies for writing out advertisements.

Generally, they are good writers who enjoy a decent command over the language. In many cases, the content experts themselves may well handle copywriting job as well.

Responsibilities include:

- ❑ Develop the crude information pool provided by content experts into a material with good flow of thoughts
- ❑ Rewrite the entire information - adding notes, deleting unnecessary details and editing data - in co-ordination with content experts and evolve the master contents booklet.

As in the case of content experts, their services are mostly hired on project basis.

23.14 Media content designers

Media content designers take up the responsibility of evolving media contents for the original material provided by content experts. This is a very important responsibility and mostly, the project managers themselves take up this job, instead of entrusting the same to somebody.

Media content designers should understand every implications of the multimedia concept of the Project. They should have a very high degree of creativity and imagination - to identify the multimedia project that hides itself in the otherwise 'collected' form of data and information... it really demands a lot of experience!

The responsibilities shouldered by media content designers include:

- ❑ Co-ordinating with the project manager and content experts to develop the multimedia concept
- ❑ Decide which media is best suited to present specific piece of information
- ❑ Design the media contents and sequences
- ❑ Co-ordinate with designers and animators for possible modifications and revisions
- ❑ Co-ordinate with the project manager in evolving the storyboard

23.15 Graphic designers and artists

Graphic designers develop all the still graphics required for the project - including content design graphics and interface design graphics. They should be a master of at least one photo editing tool and one digital drawing tool. They have to perceive the graphics contents from the media designer's point of view and develop them accordingly.

Their responsibilities are:

- ❑ Develop all the required the graphics contents of the project - in co-ordination with the team
- ❑ Develop the interface designs and backgrounds
- ❑ Develop all auxiliary graphic material - like 3D Buttons, tool bars etc.

They are mostly employed full time by the company and handle more than one project at any point of time.

23.16 Audio developers and artists

Audio developers develop all digital audio and synthesised audio (MIDI) files required for the project. They usually possess very good knowledge of either classical or western music...and in many cases - they are players of one or more music Instruments.

Responsibilities of audio developers are:

- ❑ Developing the digital audio clippings, including voice-overs - as directed by the media designer
- ❑ Develop the music pieces for the project - including the background audios, either compiling from royalty free files available or by actual recordings
- ❑ Edit the raw audio data and convert them suitably, so that they can be embedded in the project

Their services may be full time or part time - depending upon the organisational strategies and the volume of work involved.

23.17 Animators

Animators develop the two-dimensional and three-dimensional animations for the project.

Animators should possess a very good sense of visualisation and artistic abilities. They should also be conveniently good at mathematics - particularly if complicated work is involved on three-dimensional platforms.

Responsibilities of the animators are:

- ❑ Develop the animation sequences involved in the project, in coordination with the media content designers
- ❑ Decide which type of animation – two dimensional or three dimensional - must be adopted for the specific sequences and develop them accordingly

23.18 Video professionals

Video professionals develop the necessary digital video sequences required for the project.

Their responsibilities include:

- ❑ Digitise the video sequences shot by cameramen for the project
- ❑ Edit the raw digital data and provide all necessary effects and transitions
- ❑ Deliver the video files in the prescribed format

23.19 Launching a career in multimedia

Like all other graduates, people who want to start-up a career in multimedia face the uphill task of getting an entry into the industry. The major problem is that the supply of professionals seems to be much more than the demand. I've used the term 'seems to be' because, in reality, companies are still hunting for talented people and are faced with the challenge of picking the best from hundreds and thousands of applications they receive.

While there are no quick or ready made solutions to this, let me share some of my thoughts in this respect– based on my experience in interviewing students as well as being interviewed by other professionals.

Launching a career in multimedia consists of at least a few steps, in my opinion. They are:

- ❑ Training yourself in the general concepts of multimedia
- ❑ Specializing in the discipline which inspires you most
- ❑ Presenting yourself to prospective employers
- ❑ Beginning your career
- ❑ Career growth path

The initial problems start with proper training. Many students develop a wrong notion that joining a multimedia training school is more than sufficient to launch them into the professional world. Unfortunately this is not true. While training schools can teach you some of the concepts, the overall knowledge provided by them falls short of what is required in the industry.

This is one of the main reasons why industry people hesitate to employ new bees and prefer experienced people – because they think new bees need to be trained for at least a few months before they can be productive. Unfortunately this is true in most cases.

So, what is the solution?

First, be very clear that the training provided by training schools is but a starting point. You may have to work above and beyond what is being taught – because things are changing so fast. Gaining an overall knowledge on all aspects of multimedia is a major step. Books like this one are just meant to do that. Try to read different books on multimedia and gain an overall understanding of the field.

See whether this is the field you really want to spend the rest of your life or not; there is no more danger than attempting to enter multimedia without proper interest or real aspiration – you are bound to fail sooner or later. Take as much time as you want to make this important decision – but once decided, do not be wavered by opportunities that may come up in other fields.

Once you have decided that you are going to make out a career in multimedia, you need to select specific discipline in which you can specialize. Paragraphs in the earlier sections of this chapter should give you some idea about the various choices available. There is no point in trying to be jack-of-all-trades – it is not only counter-productive but also dangerous in the eyes of a prospective employer. Hence, select a specific career in multimedia that will best suit your talents and attitude. It is also beneficial to look at your contacts and backgrounds in the given industry and see where you have brighter chances of success. For example, if you have good contacts in the film industry, try exploring three-dimensional animation or video post-production and special effects. If your circle includes publishing industry friends, try becoming a graphics designer or layout artist.

Once you have selected your discipline in which you are going to specialize, try to gather as much material as possible on the topic – books, magazines, product manuals, web pages – all of them. Select the tool or set of tools in which you need to specialize and get comfortable with it – working day and night. Take care not to become too dependent on a specific tool – concentrate on the concepts, rather than what menu has which effect and so on. This very book is a good example for learning concepts, which are independent of specific tools, as much as possible. The reason why I'm stressing this point is that a prospective employer may ask you whether you have exposure to certain tool which you may not have heard of. You must be confident enough to answer him that most of your knowledge is concept oriented and not product oriented – and hence you will be flexible enough to pick up any tool in which you have no exposure. This increases your chance of being employed.

After getting comfortable with the tools, it is time to think about a project or projects that will show case your talents. Unfortunately, most students attach little or no importance to this very critical step, which results in very weak demonstration of capabilities in the eyes of a prospective employer. It is sad to note that many training schools and even regular colleges do not provide enough guidance to complete a good project that will look professional and is of industry standard. Projects continue to remain as a mere academic formality whereas they can potentially become your gateway to successful entry into multimedia companies.

Whether it is a group project or an individual project, it is important to assign yourself a specific role and try to do justification to your work. The project should showcase all the potential talents you have gathered – it can probably speak more about you rather than your ten-page resume. It is a concrete proof of your capability.

Project concepts should be very unique and should stand out in the crowd as much as possible. Many professional studios around the globe are receiving hundreds of videotapes every day that show case the specific talents of the individual. Prepare one for your own, preferably in a CD-ROM and keep it ready before you start applying for jobs. If you are ever called for an interview, go with a laptop and ask for some time (not more than three to five minutes) to showcase what you have done. Rather than looking at your papers, a prospective employer will be much happier to see a live work in front of them.

Within these few minutes, you must demonstrate all you know – your creativity, unique way of looking at things, an impressive project concept as well as your command over the tool. Hence you can see very well how important the project concept is. This project to be demonstrated could well be a flash web page, a three-dimensional rendering or a video post-production work. If possible, do host a portion of your project on the web and give the URL reference on your resume.

Once your project is ready, it is time to score a few points above the rest so that you stand out from hundreds and thousand others who have applied for jobs. One good means of scoring is to participate in international competitions. Many magazines across the globe, which specialize in multimedia subjects, conduct periodic competitions and showcase the best entries. For example, there are at least a dozen magazines on three-dimensional computing and these magazines conduct monthly and annual competitions for the best three-dimensional images / animation entries. There are also national and international fairs in which you can showcase your work. Whether you win a prize or not, it is important to show that you had participated in these events. That adds lot of weight to your potentials.

Please do not wait for an application to be posted in papers. Paper advertisements are seen by thousands of people and there is a heavy rush always. Hence, be pro- active and collect all the addresses of your prospective employers or those companies in which you want to work – and start sending resumes and your works.

Phrase a decent covering letter and do not draft the usual "sir I am a student who graduated in so and so institution and I will be grateful if you can give me any job in your company" etc. Be specific on your talents and the job you would like to undertake. Sound confidant and let neither pleading nor arrogant tone come into your letter. List out what are all the talents and capabilities you possess and detail how useful you will be for the said company. If you have hosted your projects on the web, do reference it in the covering letter itself – apart from bio data.

Please do not draft a generic "all-purpose" covering letter, Xerox it and send it to all companies. Your resume can be the same – but not the covering letter. Be very specific about the company and try to substantiate why they should employ you. A good covering letter cannot be written if you do not have a decent knowledge of the different activities of the company – this is no difficulty, since most of them have a web presence. Get the URL of the company you are going to apply and learn all their different business activities before sending the application.

Whether you are a student or a professional, whether you have industry experience or not, your bio data should necessarily contain the details of at least a few projects. Detailing a single project done at the fag end of the semesters – as a part of academic curriculum, is unlikely to impress the employers. Instead, involve yourselves in solid projects as and when you find time and try to tell what you did in your bio data. Project should involve reasonable work – any work that spans below one month of man-days is not a serious project at all. Hence try to think of unique concepts and work to complete it.

Remember that your skill sets and creativity are the greatest assets. It may take a while before it catches the eyes of the right person – hence be patient till you get the right opportunity. If you have already got quite a few opportunities but were not recruited in, then you need to do a serious analysis of how things can be improved for better prospects. If you can implement even 50% what I have detailed in these paragraphs, your opportunities of success are pretty bright!

23.20 Summary

The growth of multimedia technology has resulted in a number of careers in different sectors. These include careers in digital imaging, animation, video postproduction and authoring. A number of existing businesses like publishing and broadcast, advertising, entertainment and movie studios offer opportunities to creative professionals.

A multimedia team is a heterogeneous mix of people with varied talents - it includes graphic designers, media content developers, copywriters, animators, video professionals, multimedia authors and programmers - all reporting to the project manager.

Launching a career in multimedia depends on proper training, attitude, presentation and project experience.

PART IX

DELIVERY MEDIUMS

PART OVERVIEW

This last part in our exiting exploration of multimedia technology will focus on two famous delivery mediums meant for distributing multimedia contents to end consumers: Compact Discs and Digital Video Discs (DVD). The total discussions will span over three chapters.

Chapter 24 starts with a brief history of the evolution of CD ROMs in the multimedia scenario and proceeds with details on what constitutes the physical structure of a CD-ROM disc and how data is being reproduced with the help of a CD-Drive. We will also be looking at other varieties of compact discs like CD-RW.

Chapter 25 will deal with CD-ROM replication process and packaging issues. This chapter is important for those who want to take their multimedia works to end consumers via distribution channels.

The last chapter is on Digital versatile discs or DVDs that are replacing compact discs in many fronts – including computer multimedia data storage and feature film distribution.

Chapter 24
Compact Discs

CHAPTER OVERVIEW

CD-ROMs have been the most popular mediums for distributing multimedia contents. From PC games to presentations, entertainment to edutainment – CD-ROMs literally stand as a symbol for representing multimedia.

In this chapter, we learn all about the secrets of compact discs – available in various flavours like CD-ROM, CD-R, CD-RW and DVD. We will look at the physical construction of each type of disc and understand the principle behind their working.

24.1 Introduction

The need for storing and distributing large chunks of data came into being, in the last ten years. With the explosive growth of information technology and the data associated with it, it is not surprising that this need very much exists even today – inspiring the next generation storage mediums like DVD-Rewritables and Blu-ray disks.

The CD-ROM technology sprang up from the audio compact disc technology invented by Sony and Philips. While audio CDs could store only audio data, CD-ROMs were able to store all forms of computer data – including audio files, graphic images and video data formats. The 1990s saw explosive growth of CD-ROMs as the preferred medium for distributing - not just multimedia, but even all other kinds of application software. Though the Internet is now considered as a cheaper and easier alternative to CD-ROMs, the latter still holds its position tight in those areas where the volume of data distributed is reasonably large – such as multimedia.

With the introduction of CD-R (CD Recordable) and CD-RW (CD Rewritable) standards, CD-ROMs have also become one of the most popular forms of storage media.

Let us begin our discussions by understanding the physical constitution of a CD-ROM disc.

24.2 CD-ROM discs

Okay, let us hold this little round polycarbonate disc (with attractive rainbow tints on it's surface) for a moment and try to understand its construction. It's mind boggling to note that this innocent looking cute silver platter can hold around 680 to 700 MB of data. If we were to distribute the same data in floppy disks, we will need roughly 475 floppy disks!

The enlarged side view appearance of a CD-ROM is shown in figure.

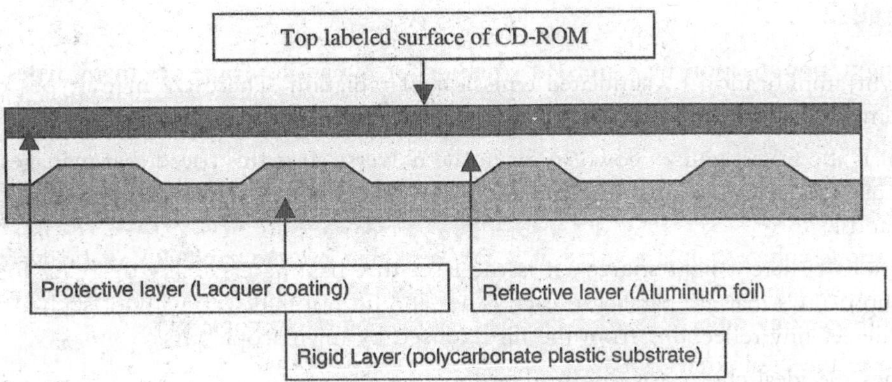

Figure 208: Composition of a CD-ROM

It is around 12 cm in diameter, 1 mm in thickness and around 16 grams by weight.

It has thee different layers, made up of three different substances, plastered in-between:

- The rigid layer: The first layer from the bottom surface of a CD ROM, also called the rigid layer, is made of a polycarbonate substrate. It's this layer that gives the otherwise flexible CD ROMs, the required strength and rigidity for handling and hence the name - rigid layer.
- The reflective layer: The second layer from the top surface, also called the reflective layer, is made up of Aluminium. This layer is the one that holds the actual computer data in the form of microscopic pits and lands. Since it reflects the laser beam that's cast over the CD-ROM during the data retrieval process, it's called reflective layer.

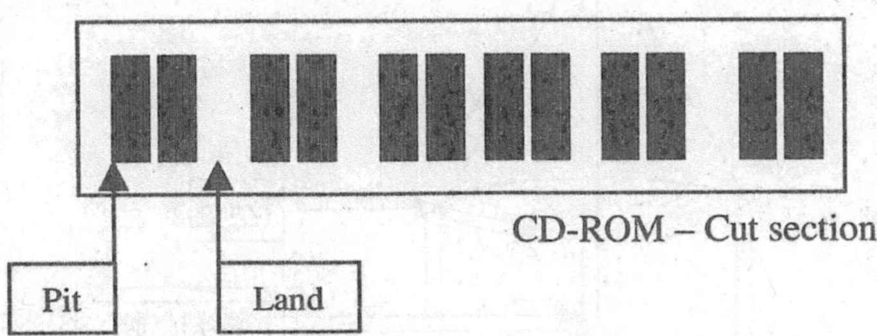

Figure 209: Microscopic pits and lands that save data

- The protective layer: The third layer, also called the protective layer, is a thin film of lacquer coating that safeguards the reflective layer, against scratches and other physical damages. The lacquer c coated side is more often called the label side as it usually contains a label printed on its face.

Only one side of the disc i.e. the side adjacent to rigid layer contains data; the label side is left blank. Data is stored in the form of microscopic pits (which are 1 to 3 micron* long, about 1/2 micron wide and 1/10 micron deep) that run as a single spiral track from the inner diameter to the outer of a CD-ROM - the total length of the track being...hold your breath...around five kilometres!

A single CD-ROM can contain more than five billion pits! The pits and lands (absence of pits) represent ones and zeros respectively. To read back the stored data, a laser beam is focused on the surface of the disc and the reflected beam is read and understood.

At this point of time, let us understand why we are using lasers to read data from CD-ROMs.

** 1 micron is one thousandth of a millimetre!*

24.3 Why laser?

Laser stands for light amplification by simulated emission of radiation. There are many types of lasers; the one being used in multimedia CD-ROM drives are called solid-state lasers.

By very nature, light is the fastest entity known so far in the universe. It is this speed that manages and retrieves the rapid on and off sequences associated with the computer-encoded data that spirals past the drive's read head, in the form of pits and lands.

And among the various coherent light sources, it is the laser that has the capability of being focused very tightly because it is made up of rays that are parallel to each other and do not intersect; without such a tight focus, it may not be possible to detect tiny reflections from the disc, caused by microscopic pits.

Hence, laser becomes the ideal choice for disc reading.

So, how data is read from the CD-ROM, using laser?

24.4 The CD reading technique

As soon as a CD-ROM disc is inserted into the CD drive and the data contained is being read, a laser beam is first produced from a laser source such as laser diode. The beam then passes through a prism (which is arranged in a particular position as shown in the figure, so that the source beam passes through the prism, unaffected), gets a very tight focus as it passes through the two lenses and is ultimately cast over the surface of the CD-ROM, which contains the recorded data. Remember that the label side, which is the top position as you keep a CD-ROM disc on the drive, doesn't contain any data and the laser beam actually falls only on the other side of the disc.

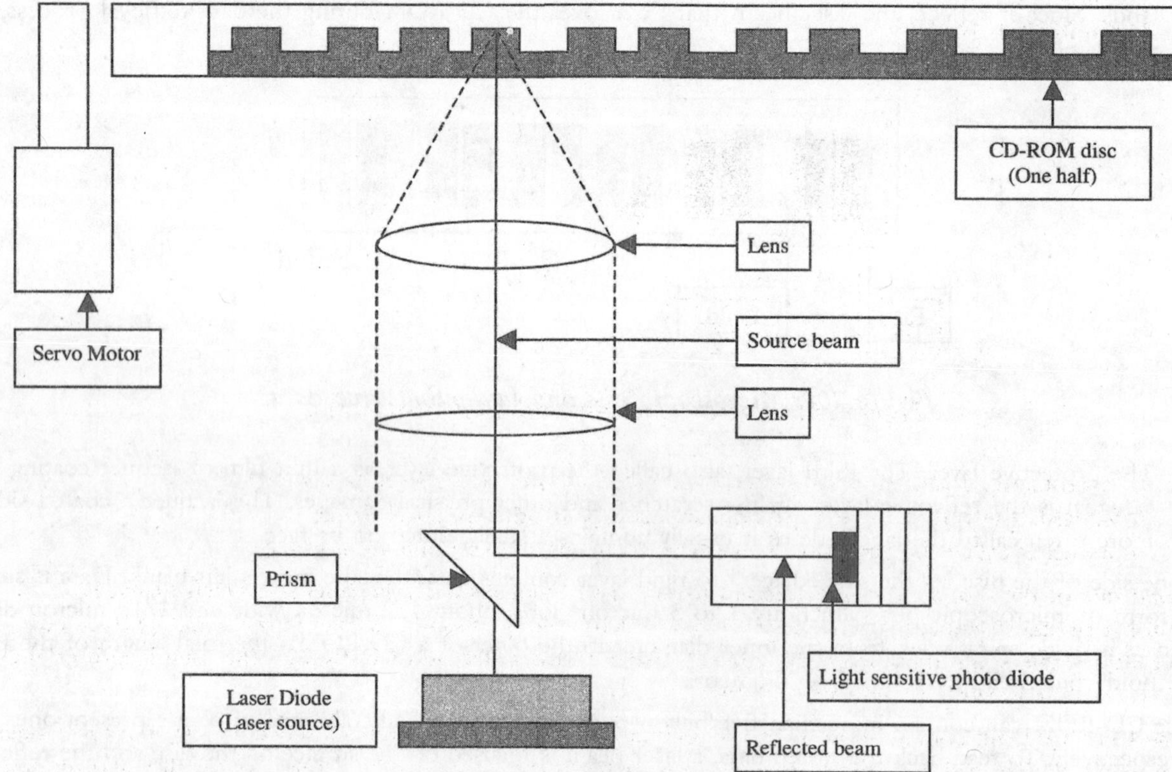

Figure 210: Laser beam reads the data reflected from pits and lands

Because of the microscopic pits and lands on the aluminium layer of the CD-ROM, this falling laser beam is promptly reflected back. Without the tight focus as that of the laser's, it will be almost impossible to detect every reflection from the pits and lands, which are only microns away from each other.

When the source beam encounters a land - which is the flat surface and denotes just the absence of a pit, it essentially follows the same path after reflection, without getting deflected; and when it meets a pit, the reflected beam branches out at a small angle of incidence.

These two reflected beams are diverted over a light sensitive photo detector diode, by the prism. Note that the position of the prism plays an important role in diverting the reflected beam, exactly perpendicular to the source beam. The beam reflected from a land is read as a binary one, and that from a pit as binary zero.

The story is still not over...as all of these ones and zeros themselves do not represent the final form of data! Because, if multimedia or other types programs are directly stored in the computer data format on a CD, the total amount of data that could be stored could be much lesser. Hence, the producers adopt various compression and encoding techniques to compress the computer data, before storing them in a CD-ROM. A series of ISO colour book standards, which will be introduced in the following section, define these compressed data formats.

Hence, a micro controller that's inside the CD-ROM drive is used to decode the compressed data, before the data is fed into the computer for processing.

24.5 The colour book standards

A series of compact disc standards like 'The red book standard ', 'The yellow book standard' and 'The green book standard', were evolved by the International Standards Organisation (ISO), to bring in some degree of standardisation into the new range of data storage mediums.

For example, ISO 9660 is the widely accepted format for storing digital data as files on a CD ROM. The table given below provides a snapshot of standards and the nature of media they control.

Table 35: CD Standards

Specification	Media
Red Book(System description CD Digital Audio)	Audio CD
Yellow Book(System description CD Read Only Memory)	CD-ROMs
White Book(System description Video CD)	VCD
Orange Book Part III(System description CD Rewritable)	CD-RW
Orange Book Part II(System description CD Write once) CD-R)	CD-WO (also known as
Green Book(CD-i Full functional specification)	CD-interactive

It is interesting to note that CD media formats like DVD do not come under this umbrella – because DVD is controlled by another standards body called ECMA. Having to cope up with too many standard bodies is one of the problems faced by the information technology community today.

24.6 CD-ROM drives

The data inside a CD-ROM disc is read using a CD-ROM drive.

CD-ROM drives could be internal or external. Internal drives fit into the system cabinet. External drives are separate devices that sit outside the system and connect using USB or any other interface.

We usually notice letters like 24X or 48X in front of the CD tray. These numbers denote the speeds at which the CD discs rotate inside the drive and the corresponding data transfer rate (The rate at which information recorded inside the CD-ROM is transferred to the computer). The earliest drives transferred data at 150 KB per second –

also called as 1X speed; the present day drive speeds are at least 24X to 48X – which is around 3.51 MB to 7.03 MB per second.

24.7 The interface cards

A CD Controller card maintains the interface between computer and the CD-ROM drive. These controller cards are interface devices that provide two-way communication between the computer and the equipment; they convert signals from the computer to a form that's understandable by the CD drive and vice versa.

CD controllers come in two flavours:

- ❑ An IDE card (Interface device electronics card) and
- ❑ A SCSI card (Small computer system interface card)

SCSI cards are better than IDE in many respects – but are also very expensive. Hence most home users prefer IDE to SCSI.

24.8 Data tracking

As with other forms of computer storage, the data recorded on a CD-ROM disc is not contiguous. In other words, even a single program may be scattered in different sectors throughout the disc. To perform this complicated search, a detailed data layout of contents inside the CD-ROM is stored in the first track of the disc. It is by referring to this layout track - every now and then, that the CD-ROM drive is able to read a given file in the disc.

Thinking about 680 to 700 MB of data that is contained in a single CD-ROM disc, we can very well understand the difficulty in retrieving specific files for a particular task. This process is what is called as data tracking.

Data tracking is usually handled by four different mechanisms – powered by four independent servomotors.

- ❑ One that governs the speed at which the disc rotates
- ❑ One to position the laser read head in the specific location
- ❑ One to calibrate the focusing apparatus accurately and
- ❑ One more to retrieve the data patterns contained on the disc.

24.9 Data transfer rate

The rate at which a CD-ROM drive transfers data to the computer is usually referred to as the data transfer rate and is perhaps the most important parameter that governs the performance of a drive. In handling text-based information, this may not matter much - but with typical multimedia applications involving intensive audio or video data, the data transfer rate is of utmost importance. Higher data transfer rate results in better performance.

You can see the effect of data transfer rates, when you try to play complex multimedia CD-ROMs in some old CD drives – the application will take a long time to respond and there will be noticeable delay in playing video files.

The unit for measuring the data transfer rate is KB / sec. The earliest CD drives transferred data at the rate of 150 KB /Sec whereas the modern drives offer 3 to 6 MB transfer rate per second.

24.10 Seek-time

Seek-time or the data access time is the time taken by the CD drive to seek and retrieve specific piece of data associated with an application. It can also be defined as the average time taken by the laser's reading head to move from one part of the compact disc to another.

The unit for measuring seek-time is milliseconds.

Shorter seek times results in better performance because it takes lesser time to retrieve required data. Any drive with a seek time of 200 milliseconds or less can give a decent performance.

24.11 CD Recordable discs (CD-R)

The standard CD-ROM discs can be read – but no data can be recorded over it. As the name implies, CD-ROM represents a read only memory that cannot be erased. In order to record our own data in compact discs, we should make use of another breed of discs called CD Recordable or simply CD-Rs. The specification that dictates the grammar for CD-R discs is the orange book part II.

The CD -R disc has a dye-recording layer in between the protective layer (lacquer coating) and the reflective layers of the usual CD-ROM discs. In place of aluminium, gold or silver alloy is used as the reflective layer.

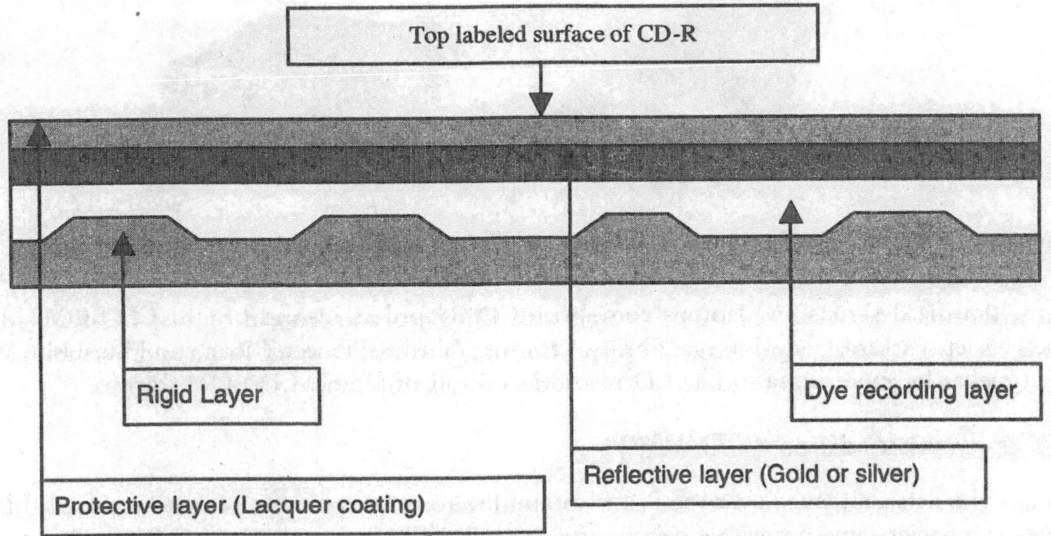

Figure 211: Cross section of CD-Recordable (CD-R) disc

To record data, a laser beam that is of higher intensity than that used for reading data, is sharply focused using the condenser lenses over the surface of the CD-R disc. The focusing is done whenever a pit is required on the disc. The dye-recording layer reacts to this intense laser assault, undergoing slight chemical fusion with the gold or silver layer near its surface and creates a pit. As we saw earlier, these pits and lands can together represent data.

Once the data is recorded on to the CD-R disc, it can be read back using any standard CD-ROM drive or any other CD Recorders. Note that data can be written only once over the total memory available – in case of CD-R discs. In order to erase and re-record data on the disc over and over again, you have to make use of another breed of discs called CD-Rewritable or CD-RW.

24.12 CD Recorders

The equipment, which is used for writing data over the CD-Rs, is called a CD writer or a CD Recorder. CD recorders can record data on disks in a variety of formats, apart from serving as standard CD-ROM drives. Apart from the recording equipment, we also need the necessary software for burning the data on the disc. Usually, this software is bundled with the equipment you buy.

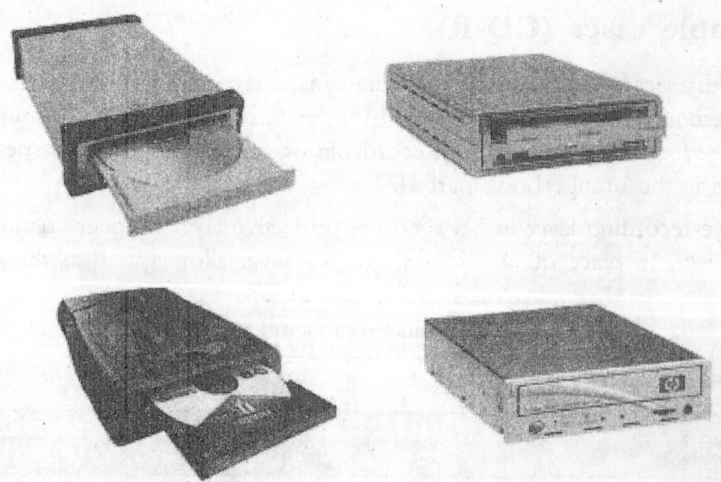

Figure 212: CD Recorders are available in different flavours from premium vendors

Today, most multimedia desktops and laptops come with CD Recorders instead of just CD-ROM drives. The brands include Hewlett Packard, Sony, Iomega, Philips, Creative, Yamaha, Pioneer, Ricoh and Mitsubishi. With their falling prices, it makes lot more sense to buy CD recorders instead of simple CD-ROM drives.

24.13 CD Rewritable discs (CD-RW)

CD-R discs can write data only once over the disc area and the recorded portions cannot be erased. In order to enable rewriting, companies came out with a new technology called CD-Rewritables or CD-RWs. The specification that governs this type of disc is orange book part III.

CD-R discs use a dye-based layer for recording data. Data recorded on this dye layer is permanent. In order to give the flexibility of erasing and rewriting on this layer, the CD-RW discs use a special crystalline compound sandwiched between two dielectric layers. This compound becomes crystalline or amorphous, based on the degree to which it is heated and subsequently cooled. The required degree of heat is achieved by controlling the power of laser beam that falls on the disc.

The CD-RW recorder equipment makes use of three different types of laser power, to achieve the desired effects:

- **Write power:** Creates a non-crystalline state on the recording layer. The power of laser beam employed is the highest in this case.
- **Erase power:** This melts down the recording layer and prepares the disc for rewriting. The recording layer regains its reflective crystalline state. The power of laser beam is less than that used for writing.
- **Read power:** This does not alter the state of the recording layer, since the data is just read back and not recorded or erased. The required power of the laser is obviously very low.

Have a look at the diagram, which schematically represents the cross section of a typical CD-RW disc.

The recording layer is a crystalline compound made of silver, indium, antimony and tellurium. This is sandwiched between two dielectric layers meant for drawing excess heat from the recording layer, during the writing process. The other layers like the reflective layer and the polycarbonate substrate (rigid layer) stay as usual.

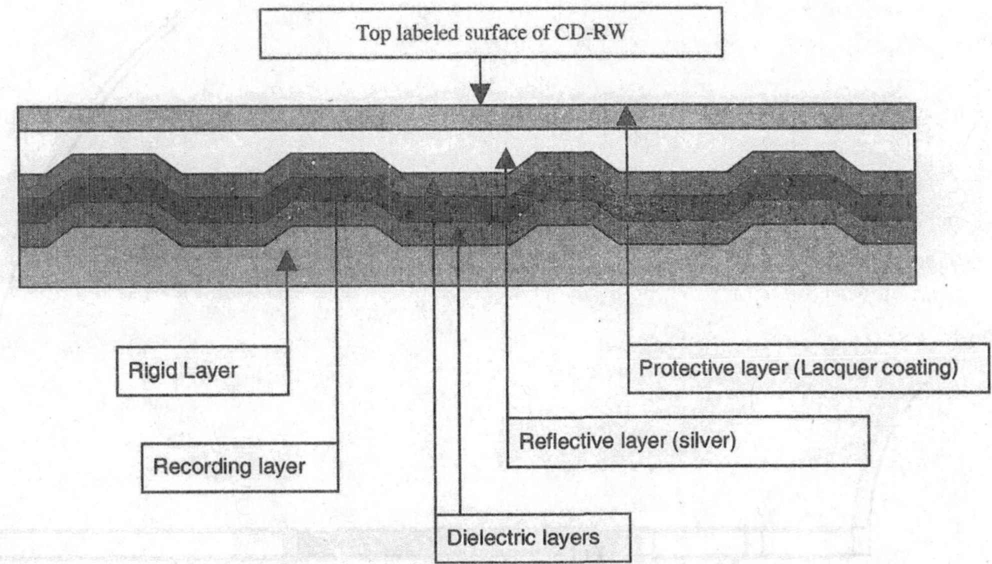

Figure 213: Cross section of CD-Rewritable (CD-RW) disc

During recording process, the laser beam at the write power heats up selective areas of the phase change material above the melting temperature. If it is then cooled, the amorphous state of the compound is obtained. This amorphous material shrinks, leaving pits in those places touched by laser beam. When a read power laser beam passes through these areas, the amorphous areas reflect less light, thus enabling the identification of pits and lands.

During erasing process, the laser beam at erase power heats the phase change layer below the melting temperature and above the crystalline temperature for a specific period of time. The atoms are rearranged in an orderly state – thus making the layer crystalline once again.

24.14 Data organization

When data is recorded on a compact disc, not all portions of the disc are available for storage. Apart from the user's data, the disc also has to store some system information and topic of contents file.

The following areas can be distinguished in all standard compact discs:

24.14.1 System use area

This can be called as the boot sector of a compact disc and it is 4 mm wide. It tells the reader device what kind of information to expect and what format the data will be in the disc. It is divided into 2 parts: PCA and PMA

- Power calibration area: This is meant as a testing ground for CD Recorder's laser beam. Every time a disc is inserted into a CD-R drive the laser is fired at the surface of the PCA to judge the optimum power setting for burning the CD.
- Program memory area: This is meant for storing sector addresses for the start of data files on the CDROM. If the compact disc is an audio CD, the PMA records the track numbers and their start and stop times.

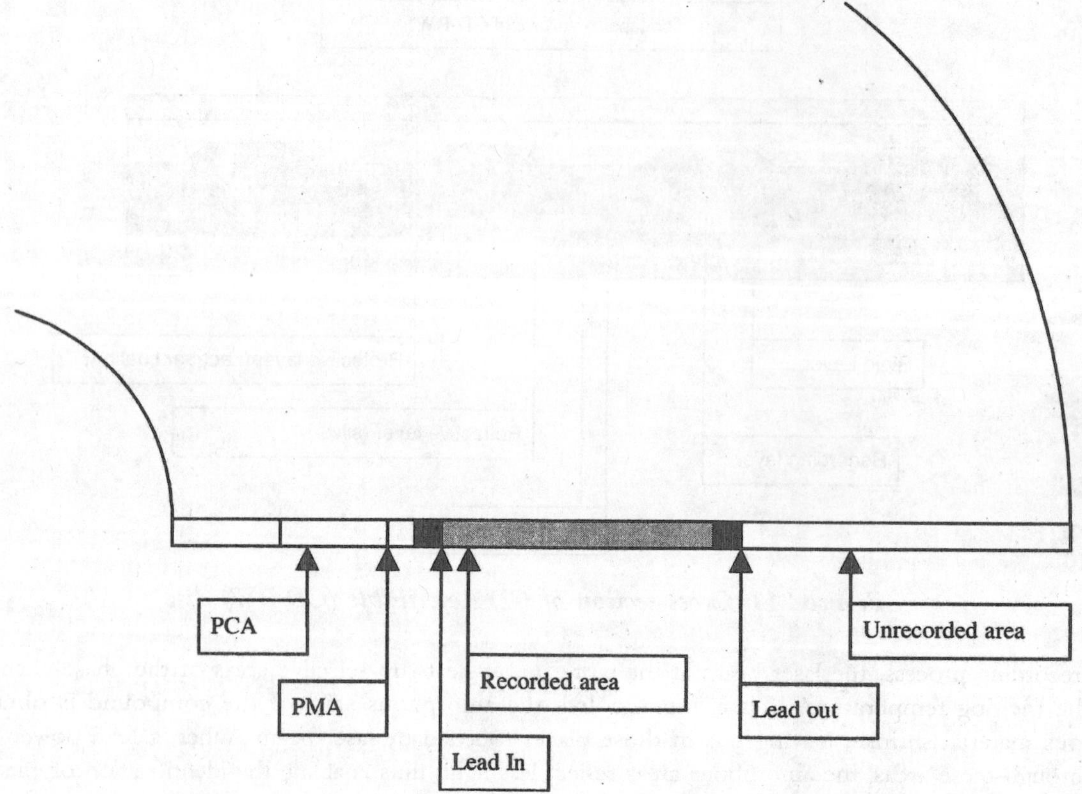

Figure 214: Data organization in a standard compact disc. Drawing not to scale.

24.14.2 Information area

Information area is divided into three portions.

- Lead in area: This area stores the latest table of contents. It allows the laser head to follow the pits and synchronize to audio or data before the start of program area.
- Program area: The program area contains the user's data – audio information or computer data. The storage of bytes of data is not a traditional eight bit – one byte formula. A complex algorithm called eight to fourteen modulations is employed to encode each of the 8 bit symbols to 14 bits plus three merging bits.
- Lead out area: The lead out defines the end of program area.

24.15 Summary

CD-ROMs evolved as a result of a dire need to store voluminous data – be it multimedia or otherwise. There are different kinds of compact discs – apart from CD-ROMs. These include CD-Recordable and CD-Rewritable.

A typical CD-ROM is made up of three different layers, the middle one being used to record the data. Laser beams are used to write and read back the data contained in a CD ROM.

A series of colour standards were introduced by the ISO, to standardise the recording and reproduction of data on compact discs.

The CD drive, used for reading CD-ROMs, can be external or internal drive, and can have either an IDE or SCSI interface. The two main parameters that ultimately govern the performance of CD drives are data transfer rate and seek time.

24.16 Keywords

- **LASER:** Light Amplification by Simulated Emission of Radiation.
- **Data transfer Rate:** The rate at which the CD ROM Drive transfers data to the computer, measured in KB/Sec.
- **Seek Time:** The time taken by the CD Drive to seek and retrieve a specific piece of Data associated with an application, measured in Milliseconds.

Chapter 25

CD Replication Process

CHAPTER OVERVIEW

When multimedia projects need to be distributed to a sizable number of clients, it is best to replicate the CD-ROM discs. This replication process involves strategic decisions as well as a number of steps. This small chapter is meant to detail this process.

It also covers some of the packaging issues and how to design a good CD cover etc.

25.1 Introduction

Multimedia projects that need to be distributed to end consumers have to be replicated. Replication is advisable only when the numbers of clients are substantially large. For a lesser group of people – say ten or twenty, it is economical to take individual copies of the CD-ROM using a CD burner. But as the number of copies increases, this kind of copying becomes impossible and one is forced to think of alternatives.

CD replication is quite a complex process and here we are not going to discuss the whole process cycle in detail. We will lay more emphasis on the roles and responsibilities of the project developer and much less emphasis on the replication process itself.

The main responsibility of the project producer is to produce a master CD of the project and deliver it to the replication vendor – who takes over the replication process from then onwards. Auxiliary responsibilities of the producer include jewel case cover design, CD face design and box design – if any.

25.2 CD production and replication process

The steps involved in CD replication process are:

- Preparing the application for distribution
- Pre mastering
- Deciding upon the minimum system requirements
- Testing
- Mastering
- Locating the right replication vendor
- Signing the agreement for replication
- CD Replication
- Testing

Let us get into the details of these steps.

25.2.1 Preparing the application for distribution

Once the application under production is complete, it has to be prepared for distribution.

This may, in turn, involve the following steps:

- ❑ Developing and testing an installation utility for the application
- ❑ Deciding upon the program modules and executables to be installed on the user machine and those that are going to be retrieved from CD at runtime
- ❑ Compression schemes that are going to be adopted for various media files
- ❑ Creating application auto run and
- ❑ Other steps required if any.

When an application has to run on a machine different from that in which it was developed, it has to be installed on that machine. This installation is nothing but the process of copying the required executables and runtime libraries required for the application, making the required changes in the windows registry, creating program short cuts etc. Complexity arises when there are variations in client machines – for example, if you want your application to run on Windows 95, Windows 98, Windows 2000 and XP – you have to take care of quite a number of variables and settings before you can go ahead with the installation process. If you are trying to support multiple operating systems – for example, Windows and Mac or Windows and Linux – then the task is even more complex.

Depending upon the authoring program you have used to develop the project, you may either generate an installation utility automatically or depend on third party programs to generate the required installation utility for you. Third party utilities like Install shield (http://www.installshield.com) are quite famous among the application developers as it makes the complex process of installation relatively simple. These utilities come with easy to use installation wizards, which ask you a number of questions about the application you are trying to distribute and generate an installation utility automatically for you.

Though the utilities make the task of creating installation utility simple, they do demand quite a bit of knowledge about windows or other operating systems and application know how – in order to use them successfully. For example, there might be questions about changing certain settings in the windows registry, installing a particular active X or COM components etc. Technical persons with appropriate skill set are required to evaluate what choice is best suited for your application.

The second task is to evaluate and decide which are all the program modules that should be copied into the user's hard disk and what are all the files that are to be retrieved from the CD at run time. Usually, the practice is to copy the main executable file and all the required runtime libraries (dlls) on to the user's machine and keep all the multimedia files like audio, video and animations on the CD itself and retrieve them as and when necessary. The purpose behind copying the executable in the hard disk is to enable faster access to the program. Anyway, whether to copy the main program to the hard disk or not, it will be loaded into the memory of the system – as long as it is running.

One think to make note of here – is the minimum system requirements required by the user. For example, the user may not have sufficient space in the hard disk in order to copy all the required files. In this case you may have to decide whether you have to give alternative options to the user or just fail to load. We are going to discuss such issues in the next section.

If the total size of media files is very big – bigger that that which can be packaged in a single CDROM, then problem arises. We can go for two CD-ROMs instead of one – like Microsoft Encarta CDROM, but this may mean the user has to alternatively load the first CD and the second CD. Depending upon the nature of application, this may well become a nuisance from the user's perspective.

One alternative to this issue is to compress all the media files using certain compression algorithms and decompress the required files as and when necessary. However, this decompression process during runtime may take some time – depending upon the size of the media file and this delay will be passed on to the user as well. It also means that user should have sufficient space in the hard disk for temporary decompression files. If you can tolerate these compromises, go ahead with this approach. One good parameter to see whether you can adopt this approach or not - is to look at the nature of your application.

Another alternative is to look and revisit the encoding methodologies you have used in your media files. The major memory consumers are the video and animation files. Probably you may decide to compromise on the quality of the video a bit, in order to achieve substantial savings in memory requirements. Remember: smaller video files load faster and run smoother than big chunks.

The last step in this exercise is to add relevant files, so that the application can run automatically, as soon as the user loads the CD in the CD-ROM drive. In windows, this can be easily achieved by adding a file called *autorun.inf* in the root directory of the CD-ROM. This file contains information about the program that should start up upon successful loading of the CD-ROM.

25.2.2 Pre-mastering

After preparation and conversion, the application software has to be transferred to a clean/virus-free hard disk with consolidated disk space.

By consolidated space, I mean 660 MB (or the size required for your application) of contiguous disk space, without any partitions or disk compression algorithms. It is a very good practice to scan the disk and defragment the same – before transferring the application data.

It is also important to write protect all the files that constitute the application, so that no files are modified accidentally.

Once all these things are done, we have to burn an image of the application onto a CD-R disc. This CD will be called the pre-master and will be used for testing the application on various machines and deciding upon the minimum system requirements.

25.2.3 Deciding upon the minimum system requirements

When you have completed preparing the application for distribution, you should get a fairly good idea about the minimum system requirements that might be needed at the user's end in order to run the application at fair speeds.

The system requirements that need to be thought of, include the following parameters:

- Supported operating systems
- Processor speeds
- Minimum RAM required
- Minimum hard disk space required
- Accessories required (Sound card, graphics accelerator card etc.)

Care must be taken to find out what are all the versions of the operating systems that support your application. If it is windows platform, find out what versions support your application: Windows 95, 98, 2000 or Windows XP. Forward compatibility is generally built in with the operating system – but backward compatibility must be tested. For example, if you have developed an application in Windows 2000, chances are high that it might run without issues in Windows XP – but you have to test if it works in Windows 98 and do suitable modifications if necessary.

Hard disk space requirement might become a constraint, if you are trying to install too many files in the hard disk. This is particularly valid, if you are distributing the application via the Internet and not using CD-ROM media. As far as accessories are concerned, most multimedia applications require sound card and colour monitor. If your application is built to take advantage of graphic accelerator cards (like multimedia games) please say so.

25.2.4 Testing

The pre-master has to be tested on multiple systems to ensure that the application runs well on all types of systems that satisfy the minimum system requirements. Chances are very high that you may have to revise a parameter or two in the minimum requirements you predicted earlier. For example, you may feel that the RAM actually required by your application is slightly more than what you have recommended or that the application does not run under Windows 95 as expected earlier.

The purpose of testing is to identify all such gaps and make sufficient changes by going back to step 1 or step 2 as necessary. It is imperative that the application is thoroughly tested on all possible platforms and combinations in order to avoid any nasty little problems that go unnoticed and are irreparable after replication. Hence, thorough and comprehensive testing is necessary under all supported operating systems.

25.2.5 Mastering

After rigorous testing and fixing up all possible gaps, the data has to be transferred once again to a CD-R. As usual, one should take care of disk scanning, defragmentation and virus protection. The CD thus prepared is the final copy that will be delivered to the replicator for replication. This time, the disc is called 'the master'.

When the master is handed over to the replicator, the replicator does his own rounds of testing before proceeding with the replication. This double round testing ensures that the disc is free from all bugs and viruses.

It's always preferable to burn more than one copy of the master and keep it as a backup.

25.2.6 Locating the right replicator

CD replicators are available in all major cities. One can go through yellow pages or other commercial directories to find out their location. It is best to get quotations from all of them and do a comparative study of their offers before taking the final decision.

Price per disk may vary with quantity – with the increase in number of disks, the price per disk obviously goes down. But price alone cannot be the deciding factor – there are many other things like the quality of discs, delivery etc. that need to be taken care of.

25.2.7 Signing the agreement

Before agreeing to replicate the discs, the replicator may ask you to sign an agreement with them just to ensure that you are the rightful copyright owner of the material you are trying to replicate. Hence it is important to ensure this, before commencing the replication process. For your reference, there is my paper on copyrighting your work in the appendix of this book.

The agreement will detail that you are the rightful copyright owner of the said work and that you are liable for any copyright issues that may arise in the future and that the replicator is not responsible for this etc.

25.2.8 Replication

The replicator prepares an optical glass master and stamper from the master disc and goes ahead with the replication. Each master can replicate up to certain number of discs – say 5000 for example, after which the master disc has to be replaced. This increases the overall cost of replication, as the preparation of master is the most expensive price component in replication.

25.3 Packaging

Packaging the product is considered, sometimes – more important than the product itself! Though this statement looks a bit exaggerative, good packaging goes a long way in selling your multimedia CD-ROMs.

Packaging consist of the following tasks:

- ❑ Designing and printing the CD face
- ❑ Designing and printing CD Inner lay and outer lay covers
- ❑ Designing and printing box or covers if any

25.3.1 CD face - design and printing

CD face is the design that appears on the top of CD-ROM itself.

In the early days, the designs that were printed over CD-ROMs were pretty simple in nature – with one or two coloured screens. But now, multi-colour printing is possible and this cost is usually bundled by the replicators with the replication charge itself. Of course, you may choose not to print anything on the CD-ROM itself or just limit yourself to simple prints – it all depends on how you want to present the product.

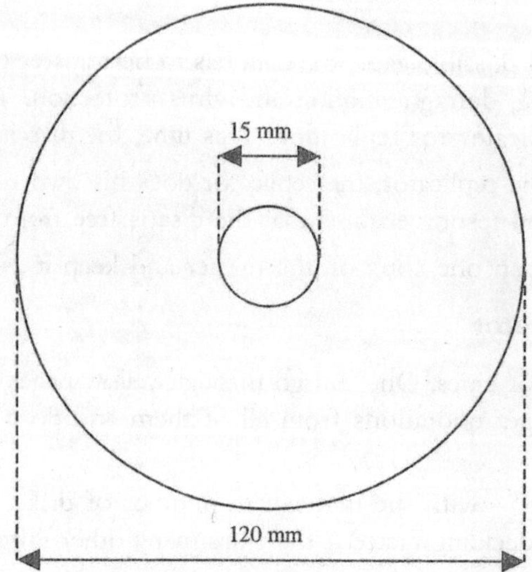

Figure 215: CD face dimensions

Figure 216: A simple CD face design

The figure shows the approximate dimensions of a standard compact disc. The area in between the outer rim and the inner rim is available for your design. It is always safer to leave a gap of one mm or two in the outer rim as well as the inner rim – to give room for alignments. Thus the effective outer diameter should be taken as 118 mm and inner diameter as 17 mm.

The CD face design should include vital information like the name of the product, producers, web address if any and copyright information.

An example for multi colour complex design is also provided for your reference.

Figure 217: A complex multi-colour CD face design

25.3.2 CD Inner lay and outer lay covers - design and printing

Many CD-ROM products are sold on the jewel case boxes. For such products, the inner lay and outer lay covers that are laid beneath the glossy surface of the jewel box become the advertising medium that communicates with potential consumers. Hence it is important to do proper design of the same.

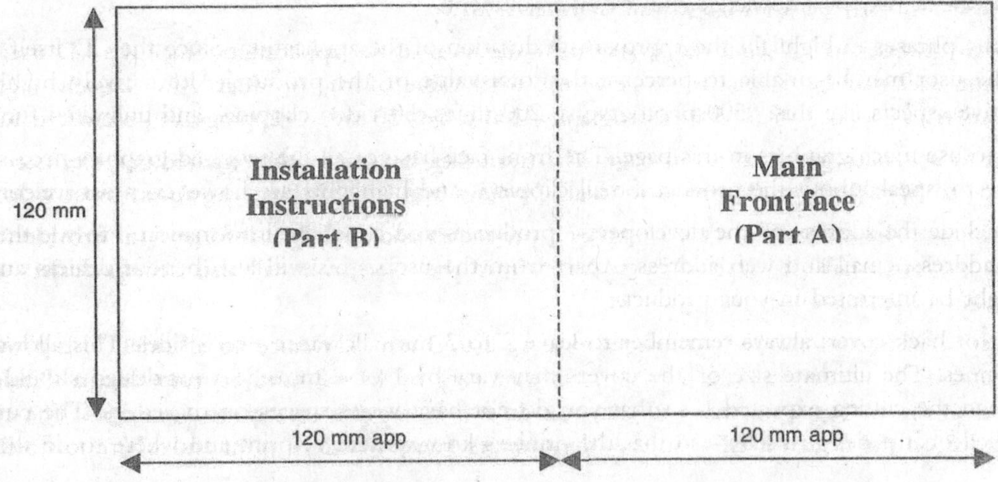

Figure 218: CD Jewel box - front cover

The front cover can be a single square (Part A) or can be a rectangle – folded to square (Part A and B). Part A contains the main design of the product and is the portion visible from the jewel box. It is almost the 'face' of your product – so give your best shot at it.

Here are some tips for good front face design:

- ❑ The area of this sheet is not very big – so don't fill it with lot of information.
- ❑ Just have the main title of the product and tell what it is very clearly. Something like "PC CD-ROM" or "Multimedia CD for PC and Mac" would be clear enough.
- ❑ Do not have extensive graphics either – leave considerable empty space and have one solid graphic that will covey the central idea of the product to the user.
- ❑ Try to distinguish yourself in design. Remember that the product might be sitting with many other products in the end retailer shop – all of them craving for attention. A difference in design or title attracts a casual observer.
- ❑ The idea that this is meant for multimedia computers must be clearly conveyed. Otherwise users will think that this is an audio CD etc.

Having Part B in your design will not alter the printing cost that much – hence it is always preferable to have both parts. This portion will be folded inside the jewel case and will be visible to the user only after he opens the jewel case. Hence it is best to contain information pertaining to the CD-ROM like minimum system requirements, installation instructions etc on this portion.

If there are too many things to convey, most producers produce a small square booklet of size 120 mm by 120 mm – and insert it in the place of front cover.

The back cover contains information about the product and is visible to the user from the backside of jewel case. Only when the user is interested in a particular title, will he take the CD out and read the backside contents – to find out more information about the product. Hence, this portion should contain vital information about the product in short and crisp phrases.

Here are some tips coming out of my own experience:

- ❑ Do not try to speak much. Cut sentences short. Small phrases with clarity and legibility have more chances of being read by most observers, than paragraphs that tell stories.
- ❑ Do not use very small or very large fonts. Small fonts will not be legible and large fonts will consume lot of space. A casual reader should be able to read the texts without pain.
- ❑ Try to highlight what the product is and what is contained in it. Speak about the benefits the product brings to the user – it may be knowledge, fun or entertainment.
- ❑ Use catchy phrases to highlight the approximate duration of the application. Since the CD itself looks very small, the user may be unable to perceive the total value of the product. Alternatively, highlight some quantitative aspects like this: "500 photographs, 200 tunes, 50 video clippings and unlimited fun!"
- ❑ Try not to use much graphics in this page. The front face has got all the required graphics necessary – here it is time to 'speak' about the product. Small clippings and highlights are however, most welcome.
- ❑ Try to include the address of the developers / producers and copyright information. Provide the complete mailing address, email and web address. Apart from the users, this will also benefit dealers and retailers who might be interested in your product.

Be it front cover or back cover; always remember to leave 2 to 3 mm allowance on all sides. This allowance is for the cutting machines. The ultimate size of the covers may vary by 1 or 2 mm. So your design should always be slightly higher than the cutting expected – so that you do not have white spaces on the edges. The cutting point should be specified on the design itself – so that the printers know where to print and where to do the cutting.

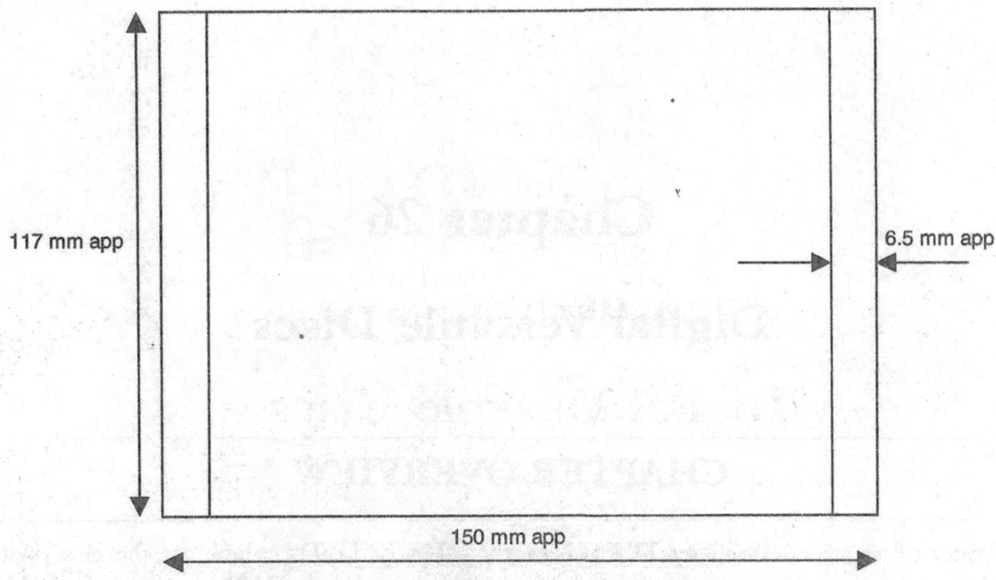

Figure 219: CD Jewel box - front cover

A typical example of a design with cutting edges is provided below.

Figure 220: A typical design with cutting edges marked

25.4 Summary

For distributing CD-ROMs in the consumer market, the disc needs to be replicated using specialised equipments. The decision to go for replication is dictated by the quantity of CDs that need to be distributed. It is worthwhile to consider replication if the number of discs required cross 100 to 150.

CD-ROM replication involves a number of steps like pre-mastering, mastering, replicating and packaging. While third-party vendors execute many of these processes, thc application developers still need to provide sufficient inputs for the vendors to execute their tasks.

Packaging the CD-ROM is a different ballgame altogether and is a mandatory exercise for all end consumer multimedia products.

25.5 Keywords

- **Pre-mastering:** The process of transferring the application software to a CD-ROM for testing
- **Mastering:** The process of producing a final master CD that has been thoroughly tested – to be given to the replicator for mass replication

Chapter 26

Digital Versatile Discs

CHAPTER OVERVIEW

This final chapter of our book discusses Digital Versatile Discs or DVDs, which are the new digital storage, and distribution mediums that are capable of voluminous storage of data. DVDs have taken quite some time to hit the mainstream market, but they look very promising and are set to dominate the digital disc landscape for quite some time to come.

We will first discuss the physical structure of DVDs and try to understand how they are able to store higher volume of data. Then we will focus on some of the physical variations that are allowable in DVDs, extending the total volume of data stored.

We will conclude with high-level discussions on DVD standards and Universal disc format (UTF).

26.1 Introduction

There were two major motivating factors or business requirements behind the evolution of disc mediums above and beyond CD-ROMs:

- The increasing need in the computer industry to store voluminous gigabytes of data
- The need for distributing digital movies in a single disc instead of multiple discs

This led to the evolution of Digital versatile disc or DVDs as we call them today.

Unlike the evolution of CDs whose specifications were cooked primarily in the kitchen of two companies – Philips and Sony, the evolution of DVD specification is a painful and long drawn one, which companies want to forget today.

It all started when two different groups of people started working on two different specifications for addressing the business requirements we saw earlier. Matsushita electric, Toshiba and Time Warner were the first group working on a format called Super Disc technology while the earlier pioneers Sony and Philips were going forward with another different format called Multimedia CD technology. Worried about having to cope up with two completely different hybrid disc formats, the computer industry majors forced the competing sides to form a consortium for evolving a single standard. This consortium, called the DVD Forum (http://www.dvdforum.org) evolved as a membership organization devoted to defining DVD standards for all kinds of DVD.

Though the first DVD specification was released in 1996 – but it took quite a while for the industry to work out the details and hit the mainstream. Today, DVD is being touted as the ultimate distributable disc storage technology available in the market, boasting a capacity of 4.7 GB, which can grow, to even 17 GB!

26.2 Digital versatile discs (DVD)

DVD technology was developed on top of CD technology. They share a striking physical resemblance: A DVD is also 12 cm in diameter, with slightly higher thickness (1.2 mm) and weight. But the similarity ends there. A DVD can hold around 4.7 GB of data or roughly the data contained in 7 CD-ROMs!

The enlarged dissected view of a single-sided single layer DVD is shown in figure.

The higher capacity of a DVD is achieved primarily with two significant improvements in storing data:

- In digital discs, data is stored in circular tracks. The distance between these tracks is called the track pitch. The track pitch of a DVD is 0.74 micron* whereas the track pitch of a CD is 1.6 micron. This naturally increases the number of tracks that can be recorded onto a DVD, providing room for storing higher volume of data.
- In digital discs, pits and lands represent the data stored in each track. The size of these pits is reduced to 0.4 microns in DVDs as compared to 0.84 microns in a CD. Thus, more pits can be stored in a single track, again increasing the volume of data that can be stored.

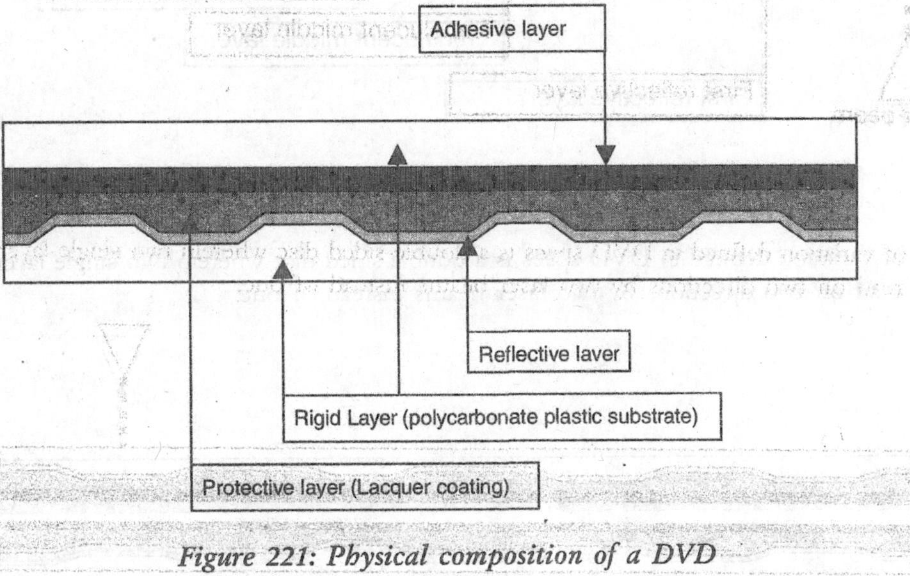

Figure 221: Physical composition of a DVD

On the flip side, decreasing the track pitch and the size of the pits has a direct impact on the equipment that is handling the digital discs. This is because of the variation required in the laser beam spots to read smaller sized pits and lands stored in DVD tracks. Thus, CD drives cannot read DVDs and hence one has to purchase a new set of equipment to decipher DVDs. However, these new equipments called the DVD drives are backward compatible and hence can read all earlier CDs like CD-Audio discs. That is the only solace.

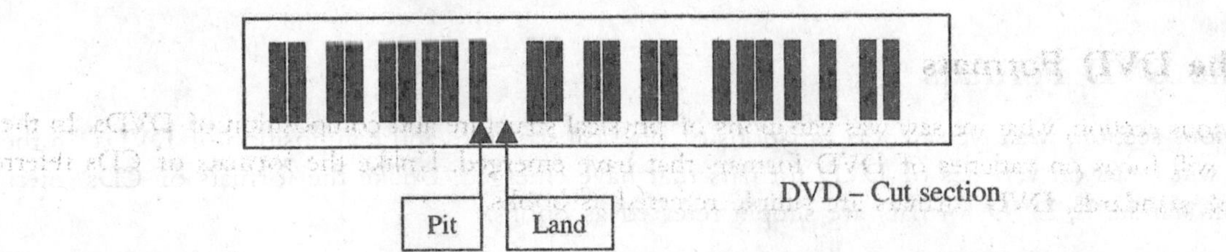

Figure 222: Microscopic pits and lands in a DVD are smaller than CDs

* *1 micron is one thousandth of a millimetre*

There are interesting variations of the above composition allowed in DVDs that enable significant improvements in the volume of data stored in DVDs.

The first variation is the double-layered DVDs. Instead of having only one layer to store data and reflect the laser beam, it is possible to sandwich two such reflective layers, one above the other and let the laser beam to change its focus to read data in the second layer. There is however, a need for introducing a translucent layer in-between. Thus, a double-layered DVD stores more data than a single layered DVD– around 8.5 GB.

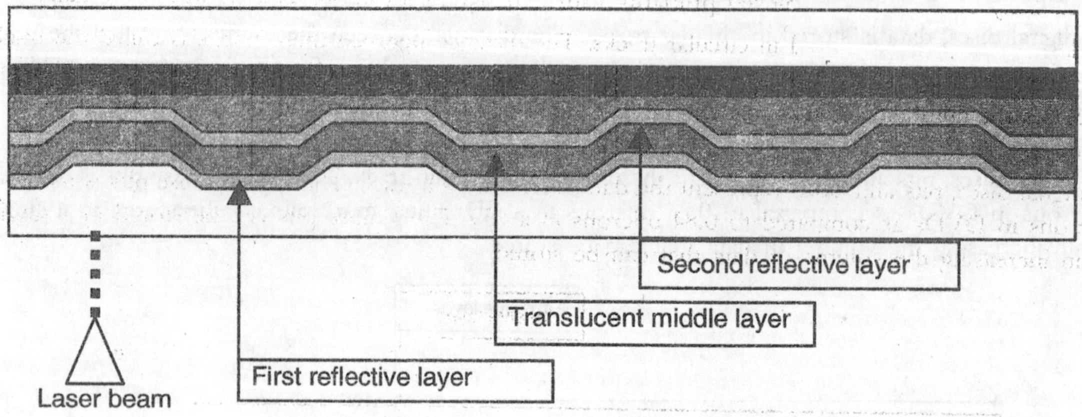

Figure 223: Physical composition of a double layered DVD

The second type of variation defined in DVD specs is a double-sided disc wherein two single layered discs are stick together and are read on two directions by two laser beams instead of one.

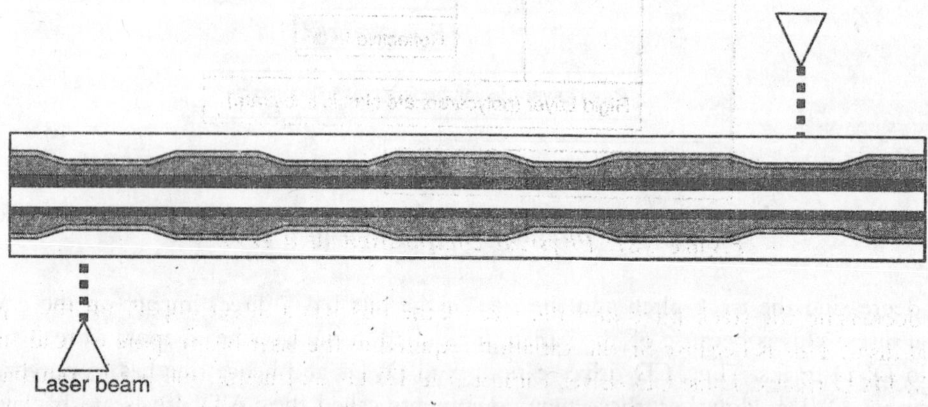

Figure 224: Double sided / Single layered DVD

26.3 The DVD Formats

In the previous section, what we saw was variations of physical structure and composition of DVDs. In the present section we will focus on varieties of DVD formats that have emerged. Unlike the formats of CDs referred to as colour book standards, DVD formats are simple referred as books.

Table 36: DVD Formats

Format name	Purpose
DVD-ROM	High capacity read only data storage medium. Capacity ranges between 4.7 to 17 GB
DVD-Video	A format for storing full length feature films with copy protection, using content scrambling system (CSS)
DVD-Audio	DVD counterpart of CD Audio
DVD-R	DVD counterpart of CD Recordable
DVD-RAM	First Rewritable form of DVD
DVD-RW	Another form of DVD Rewritable
DVD+RW	Another form of DVD Rewritable

26.4 Universal Disc Format (UDF)

One of the major problems of all these variations in DVD and CDs is the drive-disc compatibility. The industry has been plagued by problems like certain digital disc drives not able to understand specific file structure formats used in certain discs etc for quite some time.

The optical storage technology association or OSTA thought that with the emerging standards in DVD, it is probably time to standardize on the physical file structure of the digital discs as well. One of the pre-requirements was that all the different kinds of audio, video, data or a mix of all should be recorded using a single file structure definition. The result of this initiative was the Universal disc format or UDF.

UDF file structure ensures that any file can be accessed by any drive, computer or consumer video and is compatible with the ISO 9660 standards, which we saw, in an earlier chapter. DVDs implement a subset of UDF Revision 1.02, known as MicroUDF (M-UDF).

26.5 Summary

DVDs are hybrid varieties of compact discs that are slowly replacing the latter in all fronts – from computer data storage to feature film distribution.

There are several physical variations permissible in the composition of DVDs like single sided - single layered discs, single sided - double layered discs, double sided – single layered discs and double sided – double layered discs.

DVD books advocated by the DVD Forum, guide the DVD format specifications.

Universal disc format promoted by OSTA enables single file structure to store multiple forms of data.

26.6 Keywords

- ❑ **DVD:** Digital versatile disc
- ❑ **Track pitch:** Distance between two data tracks in a DVD
- ❑ **Single layered disc:** A DVD with one reflective layer containing data
- ❑ **Double-sided disc:** A DVD, which has to be read from both directions – top and bottom
- ❑ **UDF:** Universal disc format

Appendix A
Multimedia File Formats

AUDIO

- **.WAV** - Wave File. Windows Digital Audio File Format. The Most famous Audio File format for all Windows Multimedia Applications
- **.MID** - MIDI File. Windows MIDI Music File Format. This is also equally famous, in Windows Multimedia Applications
- **.AIF** - Audio Interchange File. Mostly used on Apple Macintosh Platforms.
- **.CMF** - Creative Music File. Some Creative Audio cards save songs in this format.
- **.VOC** - Creative Voice File. Records Digital Audio; compatible with all Creative's Sound Blaster Cards.
- **.MIF** - MIDI File Format. A standard MIDI file compatible with many of the Sequencer Software.
- **.MOD** - Module File. A MIDI File Format, whose design is based on Wave Synthesis Technology

GRAPHICS

- **.BMP** - Bitmapped File. Windows Raster Graphic file format. Very famous among the current day Multimedia Applications.
- **.DIB** - Device Independent Bitmapped File. Similar to .BMP Files - But with more compatibility.
- **.RLE** - Run Length Encoded File. Bitmap File format with higher compressions.
- **.WMF** - Windows Meta File. Used with many Windows applications.
- **.ICO** - Icon File. All Icons are stored in this format, in Windows environment.
- **.CUR** - Mouse Curser File Format. Changing the default Mouse cursers appropriately, will increase the excitement in Multimedia Applications - mainly games.
- **.CGM** - Computer Graphics Metafile. Evolved for transferring Graphics between a variety of platforms.
- **.GIF** - Graphics Interchange File. CompuServe's Graphics Format with best compression scheme and compatibility between wide varieties of Platforms. The most famous format for Internet Graphics applications; can also be embedded in HTML Documents.
- **.JPG** - Joint Photographic Expert Group. Very Good quality photographs can be saved with good size reduction. Famous among the Internet applications also.
- **.CMP** - Another Version of JPEG File format.
- **.PCX** - Windows Paintbrush File Format. Compatible with many Software
- **.WPG** - Word Perfect Graphics File. A very efficient vector file format famous among the Corel's Clip Arts

- **.CPT** - Corel Photo Paint File Format
- **.CDR** - Corel Draw File Format. Very efficient Vector File Format
- **.TIF** - Tagged Image File. Graphics file promoted by Aldus and preferred on many Printing Machines and Scanners
- **.TGA** - Targa Image File Format. Stores very good quality 24 - Million Colour files. Promoted by Targa, this is famous for Video applications too!
- **.PCD** - Photo CD File. Kodak's Digital Photo storage File Format

ANIMATION

- **.FLC** - Flic File. Autodesk's Animation File Format. Famous among the DOS based Animation Software like Animator Pro and 3D Studio
- **.FLI** - Similar to Flic File - promoted by Autodesk
- **.DXF** - Drawing Exchange File Format. Can store 2D as well as 3D data
- **.3DS** - 3-D Studio Modelling File. Stores 3D Model data - including Texture maps and environment variables
- **.MAX** - 3-D Studio Max File. Stores 3D Model data - including Texture maps, Atmosphere and environment variables
- **.OBJ** - Object File. Stores 3D Model data.

VIDEO

- **.AVI** - Audio Video Interleaved File. Stores Audio as well as Video - by making use of a number of Compression Schemes available. Windows preferred Video File Format and most famous among the Windows based Multimedia Applications
- **.MOV** - Movie File. Apple's QuickTime Video File Format; Can be played even in Windows - with the relevant Media drivers. Famous among the current Day Internet applications also
- **.MPG** - Motion Picture Expert Group File. The emerging Video File Format, capable of best File compressions and Full Screen - Full Motion Videos

TEXT

- **.TXT** - Text File Format for DOS / Windows . Windows Notepad File Format
- **.WRI** - Write File Format. Windows Write pad File Format
- **.DOC** - (1) Document File. Microsoft Word File Format
- **.RTF** - Rich Text File Format
- **.WPT** - Word Perfect Text File Format.

Appendix B

IPR Laws in the Indian Context

Introduction

One of the biggest problems faced by the Computer Software Industry, worldwide is the Software Piracy. Since almost all kinds of software can be easily copied from their originals, piracy has almost become a way of life, particularly in developing economies .The piracy rate was around sixty percent during the year 1997 in India - resulting in losses of millions of dollars, mainly to International Companies and a good proportion to the domestic players. In US, it's around 35 percent or even lesser.

As in most of the countries, , in InIPR Laws in the Indian Contextdia , Computer Software are generally treated as Intellectual Properties and are protected from illegal copying / reselling and other forms of copyright infringements by the laws that govern the Intellectual Property rights . The **Indian Copyright Act of 1957** and the subsequent **Amendments** to it in **1994** offer legal protection to the interests of copyright owners over their original works.

The initial copyright law of 1957 was meant for all forms of literary works - like books and scripts and did not clearly indicate the place of Computer programs. So, it had to be modified to suit Computer software / programs and was finally passed on May 1994 in the parliament, and henceforth came to be known as The Indian Copyright (Amendment) Act of 1994.

The amendments introduced have made the Indian Copyright Law, one of the toughest and foolproof in the world. The amendments include clear-cut definition for a Computer Program, the rights and limitations of the Copyright holder, Software Licensing (including the rights of the Licensor and the Licensee), the Backup copies issue and a whole lot of punishments starting from a simple jail term for seven days to a fine of around Rs.2, 00,000 and imprisonment for around three years for Software Infringement suits.

What is a Copyright?

Copyright is the form of **Intellectual property Protection** granted under the Indian Law for the creators of original computer software, both individuals as well as the companies. *The copyright on a particular work entitles the copyright holder to reproduce the work in any material form (including electronic means as in the case of computer software) or as a product, for distribution purposes. It also allows the copyright holder, to sell the software for commercial purposes or to give it on hire, either a part or the whole of it.*

It also allows the right to restrict any adaptation of the original work, for any other purposes. The Copyright also confers a number of other rights on the Copyright Holder, all of which or portions of it can be granted to others, either exclusively or non exclusively.

Important note: An exception to unauthorised copying is awarded to possessors of original software, keeping the practical usage of software in mind. As a possessor of a original copy of the software, you can make copies of the software, either for the purposes for which it was originally supplied or purely as means of a safe Back up copy, as a protection against system crashes, Computer Viruses or any other possible forms of loss, damage or destruction of the software.

Making such back up copies, it should be stressed, for expected and possible data losses doesn't constitute infringement of Copyright, according to the Law, but distributing them by any means to any other individuals or organisations is undoubtedly a crime and is punishable under section 63 A, section 63 B, section 63 C and section 69 of the Indian Copyright (Amendments) act, 1994.It should also be noted that this exception to copy is allowed only in case of computer programs that are sold to the consumers as individual titles, and is not applicable to other forms of usages such as licensing. In case of licensed software, the license agreement comes into the picture and it's the agreement that decides whether a licensee can have back up copies or not.

Copyright is applicable to both published and unpublished works. The original creator of the work automatically becomes the copyright holder of the work, the moment his or her work is recorded in any tangible medium (say a Hard Disk or the Floppy Disk, in case of Software). It's interesting to note that his or her rights over the work are corroborated even without a formal registration. Registration comes into picture only in case of an infringement suit - when somebody claims that the work one is distributing is actually a replication of his original - and the whole matter ends up in the court. (In such cases, The Registrar of Copyrights can come out with a copy of the original registered Work and prove the authenticity of the original creator.)

The Copyright Law treats all computer programs as "Literary Works" and all protection extends to almost all kinds of software by means of this phrase. The 1994 amendments include necessary instructions that clearly recognise that computer programs are Literary Works. In the Court of Law, a Computer Program is defined as " a set of instructions expressed in words, codes, schemes or in any other form, including a machine readable Medium, capable of causing a computer to perform a particular task or achieve a particular result".

It's advisable to indicate that the Work is indeed a copyrighted material, in case you are distributing your work to the public or publishing it, in a prominent place that will not skip the viewer's attention. (Letter 'c' encircled with the year of creation and the name of the creator). By displaying this notification, you are informing without ambiguity that the literary work is a copyrighted material and cannot be reproduced without your permission.

If more than one author is involved in a creation, they enjoy joint authorship, and hence correspondingly, multiple copyright ownerships. If you are working for a firm, however, the software created by you belongs to the concern and there's no way to claim any authority over the work. In case a third party develops particular software, it's necessary for the client to insist on a written deed of agreement, transferring the copyright to the clients, from the sub-contractor.

Copyright Infringement

When the copyright of the software is considered infringed? The following words have exactly been reproduced from section 51 of The Copyright Amendment Act, 1994:

"Copyright in a work shall be deemed to be infringed -

(a) When any person without a license granted by the owner of the copyright or the Registrar of Copyrights under this act or in contravention of the conditions of a licence so granted or of any conditions imposed by a competent authority under this act -

   (i) Does anything, the exclusive right to do which is by this act conferred upon the owner of copyright, or

   (ii) Permits for profit any place to be used for the communication of the work to the public where such communications constitutes an infringement of the copyright in the work, unless he was not aware and had no reasonable ground for believing that such communication to the public would be an infringement of copyright; or

(b) When any person -

   (i) Makes for sale or hire or sells or let for hire, or by way of trade displays or offers for sale or hire, or

   (ii) Distributes either for the purpose of trade or to such an extent as to affect prejudicially the owner of the copyright, or

(iii) By way of trade exhibits in the public, or

(iv) Imports to India,

Any infringing copies of work:

Provided that nothing sub clause (iv) shall apply to the import of two copies of any work, other than a cinematographic film or record, for private and domestic use of the importer."

The Law clearly mentions the punishments in case of proven infringements:

A jail term of minimum six months but which may extend to three years and with a fine of minimum fifty thousand rupees, which may extend to two lakh rupees! In case the infringement happens inside an organisation, all of those who were in charge of the crime, as well as the organisation itself, is liable to be punished. (In case there are no other persons to take the responsibility, the General Manager or Managing Director or any highest authority is convicted)

Intellectual Property Rights, though applicable only on territorial basis, are extended to other parts of the world through two International Treaties:

1. **The Universal Copyright Convention**, adopted in 1952 and administered by UNESCO and
2. **The Berne Convention**, established in 1886 and being maintained by the World Intellectual Property Organisation (WIPO).

India is a member country of both these treaties, and thus, software created by an India Author or first published in India is automatically protected in a convention member country to the extent that the member's current copyright status protects software.

Courtesy: "Nasscom's Guide to IPR Laws in India" published by NASSCOM.